THE
*W*oman
*A*wake

THE
Woman
*A*wake

Feminine Wisdom for Spiritual Life

Regina Sara Ryan

Hohm Press
Prescott, Arizona

Hohm Press
P.O. Box 2501
Prescott, AZ 86302
1-800-381-2700
http://www.booknotes.com/hohm/

Cover Design: Kim Johansen
Book Design: Debora Hogeland

Cover Art: "Thirty-Three Little Girls Set Out to Hunt White Butterflies," 1958, Max Ernst. Private Collection, courtesy Galerie Beyler, Basel Switzerland.

Photo Credits: see page 466
Permission to reprint copyrighted material: see page 468

First edition. First Printing, USA, April 1998.

Library of Congress Cataloging-in -Publication Data

Ryan, Regina Sara.
    The woman awake: feminine wisdom for spiritual life / Regina Sara Ryan.
       p.   cm.
    Includes bibliographical references and index.
    ISBN 0-934252-79-3 (alk. paper)
      1. Women--Religious life. 2.Spiritual life. 3.Ryan, Regina Sara.   I. Title.
BL625.7.R83 1998   97-51495
200' . 82--dc21   CIP

The only woman awake is the woman who has heard the flute!

— Kabir, poet-saint, 1440-1518

*To my Mothers
and sisters*

ACKNOWLEDGEMENTS

Brenda Ueland, the writer, inspired me. "Write a true, careless, slovenly, impulsive, honest diary everyday of your life," she advised in her book *If You Want To Write* (St. Paul: Greywolf Press, 1987). Those words gave me the permission I needed to dare this project, allowing me to violate, everyday, those rules that still echoed in my head about what makes a proper book. *The Woman Awake* is part and parcel of my process of liberation.

Merlin Stone inspired me. In her book, *Ancient Mirrors of Womanhood* (Boston: Beacon Press, 1979), I found a form of expression that thrilled me. It was a feminine writing form. Instead of an historical, linear treatment of her subject, Merlin wrote poetry or rambling reflections of the way history and myth touched her. She seemed to be having conversations with the characters she wrote about. She dared to break the rules, and her reading public appreciated her for it. This was something I desperately needed to witness.

Tessa Bielecki inspired me. Mother Tessa is a Carmelite nun who embodies the spirit of Teresa of Avila, the great mystic and saint of the 16th Century. Tessa's book, about St. Teresa of Avila, *Holy Daring* (Rockport, Mass.: Element Books, 1994), is, like the author's own life, an unashamed expression of passion, heartfulness, and deep commitment to her spiritual tradition. Tessa's is a life without apology. I learn that from her.

My treasured friend, housemate, and spiritual mother, Lalitha, inspires me. In her no-nonsense way of service and ruthless compassion she witnesses, daily, to the power of a life annihilated in love. This book is possible because she did the laundry and cooked the meals and grew fresh food in the garden and vacuumed the living room and screened my phone calls, but most of all because she held me in her magnanimous heart.

Elyse April, my first editor and courageous friend, demanded that I tell the truth. I have endeavored to be worthy of her trust. Paula Carfrae and Karuna Fedorschak read the manuscript and offered invaluable support and suggestions. Rabia Tredeau's encouragement and copyediting are deeply appreciated. Sylvan Incao proved to be an assistant *extraordinaire*.

I thank Jere, my husband and friend, who lived these stories with me and kept me focused on the "bottom-line" throughout.

Finally, and consummately, beyond inspiration, I acknowledge Khépa Lee Lozowick, my beloved teacher.

CONTENTS

INTRODUCTION—xiii

CHAPTER ONE—*1*
THE AWAKENING / A PATH OF ANNIHILATION
The Ras Lila—Krishna and the Gopis
Inanna—The Path of Annihilation

CHAPTER TWO—*25*
THE DESERT PATH: SILENCE, SOLITUDE AND PRAYER
Catherine de Hueck Doherty / Poustinia Movement / Everyday Women
of Prayer: Tessa Bielecki / Eileen Caddy / Evelyn Underhill

CHAPTER THREE—*59*
THE PATH OF WAITING / THE WAY OF SURRENDER
Irina Tweedie / Miryam of Nazareth /
Waiting in the Tavern of Ruin / Rabi'a—Her Life and Work

CHAPTER FOUR—*93*
THE PATH OF MOTHER
Everyday Mothers Who Found Divine Mother God /
Dina Rees

CHAPTER FIVE—*137*
THE PATH OF COMPASSION
Avalokitesvara / Tara /
Kuan Yin / Dalai Lama's teaching on compassion

CHAPTER SIX—*175*
THE PATH OF DARKNESS
Divine Mother Kali /
Ma Jaya Bhagavati—On Death and Dying /
Mother Mayee of Kanyakumari

CHAPTER SEVEN—215
THE PATH OF THE WARRIOR / THE WAY OF POWER
Simone Weil—Internal Power / Irina Ratushinskya and the Babushki /
Joan Halifax—Contemporary Woman of Power

CHAPTER EIGHT—255
THE PATH OF SERVICE
Mother Teresa of Calcutta /
Etty Hillesum—Service Through Writing /
Elisabeth Kubler-Ross

CHAPTER NINE—291
THE PATH OF ART AND INSPIRATION
Meinrad Craighead / Hildegard of Bingen /
Mirabai

CHAPTER TEN—331
THE PATH OF THE BODY / THE PATH OF SEX
The Path of Divine Pride / Lalitha Ma—Tantric practice /
Tessa Bielecki—Celibacy

CHAPTER ELEVEN—371
THE PATH OF DEVOTION
Ma Devaki and Yogi Ramsuratkumar /
Mother Krishnabai and Swami Ramdas

CHAPTER TWELVE—401
THE PATH OF COMMUNITY
The Rasa of Women in Love / The Beguine Spirituality /
Hadewijch of Brabant / Kathryn Hulme—With Gurdjieff /
Women's Culture

Endnotes—445
Select Bibliography—456
Photo and Image Credits—465
Text Credits—468
Index—472

INTRODUCTION

"Just hold her in your arms, without saying a word," he told me. "Don't assign any fancy esoteric significance to it, either. Just hold her." My spiritual teacher's directions couldn't have been clearer. I was to sit with my friend Eva for twenty minutes at a time, once or twice a week, letting her nestle in my lap, embracing her. I was to be "mother," she was to be "child." Nothing more.

I had known Eva for about eight years, as a friend, a coworker, a member of the same spiritual community. She was one of the brightest and most creative women I knew—an accomplished musician, a caring mother and a respected teacher. Yet, daily, she suffered on a cross of her own making; a cross of self-doubt and fear. Despite her serious intention to do spiritual work—she *wanted* to love and to care, for herself and others—Eva often felt lost and stuck. The habits of a lifetime of skewed perceptions (in her case fed by the pain of a childhood of neglect and abuse) were rising up to meet her. Eva found herself up against a wall. I did too. And for many of the same reasons.

So we started meeting for our "holdings." My size (I am six feet, three inches in bare feet) made me an ideal "holder." My long arms easily enveloped Eva and my ample lap gave her a generous couch to rest on. After a few minutes of initial embarrassment, Eva and I would start to relax. As she let go, for the moment, of her need to be strong and her habit of taking care of everybody else, Eva would often start to cry, quietly. Most of the time, however, she was just silent, resting in her own thoughts, absorbing the warmth and nurturance that my body provided.

Except for my physical build, I was probably the least-suited woman for such a task as holding. Certainly I had an idea and an ideal of what "mother" meant, yet, unlike Eva or any of the other women I held, I had never borne children of my own. My strong perfectionist qualities, moreover, made "mothering" a challenge. My typical way of dealing with a problem had always been to buckle down and try harder—a decidedly masculine approach. While I rarely admitted it, these sessions of playing mother proved, at times, to be threatening. But, they were also immensely compelling. In the paradoxical way that my spiritual teacher's recommendations often work, I began receiving something that I never expected, yet something that I desperately needed.

Holding Eva, a subtle transformation was being effected for me. I was *being opened*, in much the same invisible way that buds open into flowers—slowly, over time. For many years I had studied the writings of great women—mystics, contemplatives, saints—of all the great spiritual and religious traditions of the world. My seminars about this subject were well received in both the U.S. and Europe, and I had even begun, in times of prayer or under stress, to call upon the Feminine expression of the Absolute—Divine Mother in one of her many forms (as Mary, the Mother of Jesus; as Kuan Yin, the beloved female deity of Chinese origin; as Tara, the female Buddha of Tibetan Buddhism). In my bedroom I had set up a small shrine to Shri Anandamayi Ma, a contemporary Indian holy woman renowned throughout the world for her blissful and radiant presence. Yet, the more I held Eva, and the more this new fragrance of closeness began to intoxicate me, the more I began to realize how motherless I generally felt. My own longing for the arms of a mother who would never let me go became a dull ache that greeted me in unguarded moments. I began to miss children, and the experience of having birthed one. I felt more deeply the heartbreak of human suffering that I read about in the newspapers and saw reflected all around me. Despite my many acquaintances, I yearned more passionately for one special sister/friend with whom I could confide all my deepest secrets.

These were not new longings, although this time they were exceptionally poignant. My years of spiritual work had taught me to recognize in such experiences a more abiding longing—my hunger for God. And I knew that this flower of fulfillment that I searched for, not unlike the thousand-petalled lotus that is planted in the mud, was growing in my ordinary life and activities.

Though this longing has been called by innumerable names, both esoteric and homely, the only one that suited me, at that time, was the Sanskrit syllable applied to the feminine power in creation: I sought the heart of "Ma."

The cries of her children never fail to draw the Mother, sometimes against unspeakable odds. And my cry was no exception. Not knowing how this mysterious power of prayer worked, I nonetheless witnessed to its effectiveness. Divine Mother drew nearer to me, not in visions or great revelations, but quietly, simply, almost invisibly. Children started showing up in my life—my sister's children, children of friends, kids from a local home-school—children with needs, children with questions, and children with irrepressible energy which stirred my own. In their eyes and smiles, and in the timeless moments of silliness we spent together, I was being instructed in the ways of Ma.

She appeared in other ways too—in the torturous pain of a dying friend whom I was gifted to serve for six months, in the tentative words of students who told me about the horrific events of their childhood, as well as in the tender labors of my friend, mentor and housemate, Lalitha, whose pampered garden filled our salad bowls with such constant nourishment and delight. From every corner of my life, it seemed, I was meeting "Her." Even my

guru, the powerful and uncompromising man to whom I had dedicated my life and with whom I had worked for more than thirteen
years, began to change. . .to take on soft curves in my presence.
Qualities of motherly affection, which I had always appreciated in
him, were now keenly accentuated in all our exchanges. A few of
my friends even remarked about the noticeable softening of my
usually hard-driving, matter-of-fact nature. There was no denying
it; I was holding Eva, but I was being held by Woman.

This book was begun as my intellectual knowledge of great
women was interrupted by my bodily relaxation into the power of
Ma. I had wanted to write it for years, but the distractions of other
projects continued to take precedence. Then, one day, out of the
blue, my teacher called me to his office. "I think it's time for that
book about great women," he said, his eyes twinkling. I was thrilled.
With his blessing, I now had the motivation I needed to bring the
dream to reality.

I write in the hopes that these reflections about prayer and
practice, and the lives of the great women who are remembered
here will be useful to Eva and many others. But, to be honest, I
write them most of all for myself. My teacher's suggestion for a
book was an invitation for me to take the next step in my spiritual
process. I write to bring Ma more alive so that, once again, She
can birth me.

A DISTINCTION

My religious roots lie in monastic and mystical Christianity—I was a Roman Catholic nun. However, my spiritual education and practice over the past thirteen years has been most closely
aligned with the Bauls of Bengal, India, an ecstatic sect of singers
and dancers whose poetry exalts the Divine Beloved who dwells
in each heart. The Bauls are followers of the *bhakti* path to God or
Realization. *Bhakti* is Sanskrit for devotion, so this path is the way
of the heart, the path of love and surrender. The erotic and worshipful play of the Hindu god, Krishna, and his first disciples, the
gopis, epitomizes the *Bhakti* path. The *gopis*, or young cow-herder

girls, were irresistibly drawn by the sound of Krishna's flute, and once drawn, were entirely transformed by the personal love they experienced from the boy-god Krishna. God, or the Divine, in *Bhakti* worship is always revered as a transcendent being, but paradoxically related to as passionately and intimately as one relates to one's closest friend. In fact, depending upon the *gopi's* "type" (interestingly there are nine types, according to the *Bhagavata Purana*, and other *bhakti* scriptures), he or she will empathize with Krishna as lover, friend, child, sister or brother, or parent. To the *bhakta*, the devotee, God does not live in the sky. God lives embodied, in the form of one's teacher or guru, in one's own heart, and in the muscle and bone of other human beings. God lives in everything.

The Christian mystic is often a *bhakta* too. The Divine Beloved is Jesus, and the path is one of mystical marriage. Both men and women, like the *gopis* and *gopas* of Hinduism, must become feminine (open, receptive, surrendered, nurturing) in order to be betrothed to the Divine spouse, Christ. And the same is essentially true for the Sufi mystic, who sings of her relationship with The Host, The Guest, The Beloved, The Friend.

Not every path is a theistic one, however. Some readers, while enlivened (or fascinated even) by the stories of great women of passion, will find that the language of devotion in which I am steeped is simply not their cup of tea. Moreover, even as I write about Buddhist women, or the female *dakinis* and buddhas of Buddhism, my understanding of their significance is undoubtedly colored by my affinity with the path of the *bhakta*. Hence, a warning or distinction may be in order. This book was not meant to be a scholarly treatise encompassing all traditions in depth. Rather, it is an offering to any woman on the path who enjoys stories of other women on the path. This book is also a prayer of gratitude to my teacher and the lineage which blesses me.

Another distinction may also be in order. This is not a book for the timid. The genuine spiritual path, as I am being instructed in it, is one that consumes the life we think is ours—this work chews us up, digests "us," transforms "us" into useable food for a body larger than our own, and then shits "us" out, so that new plants can grow out of "us." And while that may sound poetic, it isn't. In my own case, I am more likely to enter kicking and clawing, fighting to keep my territory intact. And what is this territory that I so passionately guard? Usually it is a castle of self-importance, or some limited belief system that I hide inside, hoping that I don't have to take the risk and the responsibility for really being "great." To walk out of such a fortress is to commit to a path that may take us into dark and unfamiliar country, not knowing if we will ever find our way through. Yet, that is exactly what every woman must do who is convinced that a life of half-measures and good feelings is not enough.

This book may actually be more for the desperate and the hopeless. Self-satisfaction, peace and contentment may be by-products of this journey, but we can't be assured of such rewards at the moment we place a foot firmly on the path. All we may know then is a consuming hunger, or a question that won't go away, like a belligerent dog that won't stop barking. Or we may feel a terrible sense of dissatisfaction—we may know that *this* (whatever our life is focused on) *is not all there is*, but we may not know where to go to find what we can't name.

Many of us don't yet have the all-consuming hunger. If we did, we would be well along the path, carried in the arms of the Guest, as the poet Kabir says: "When the Guest is being searched for, it is the intensity of the longing for the Guest that does all the work. Look at me and you will see a slave of that intensity."[1] But, I think we all have the *intuition* of this all-consuming hunger or the intention for it. That is enough. That merest thread of desire to know absolute love, or genuine service, or truth, can (if we follow it) guide us on to the point where our heart's desire is within sight. Julian of Norwich, a great mystic of the fourteenth century, advised that the worst hindrance to spiritual growth was the failure to trust that what God had begun in us, with that spark of intuition, would be brought to completion by God as well.

Admittedly, such trust doesn't come easily for many of us. Perhaps this book will make some small contribution in reminding us of that intuition. If it fans the spark of an internal fire in even one reader it will have well surpassed my hopes.

How To Use This Book

When I was a young nun I was privileged to participate in a yearly retreat—an intensive eight-to-ten day period of silence and prayer in which normal work tasks were suspended. Retreat days were spent in devotional practices, meditation, reading from spiritual books, taking slow, leisurely walks in the garden, saying the rosary as I walked. And, interspersed in these activities we had the lectures of the retreat master (in those days it was always a man, but that too has changed, fortunately, in many places). The talks were usually thematic, deriving from the life of Christ, or a commentary upon a passage of scripture. And they were usually inspiring—something to write about, pray about, think about as you did the dishes or hung out the laundry.

These retreats were always a high point of the year, and something that I missed sorely when I left the convent to pursue my life of service elsewhere. In later years I created a retreat for myself, going to a cabin in the mountains, or to a friend's house by the seashore, to enjoy this necessary re-creation. Always I took along a favorite book or two—not for diversionary reading, but to serve the same purpose as the retreat director's lectures.

I thought of this process as I put together this book, and encourage you to consider using it in this way. Rather than reading it cover to cover, you may prefer to use one chapter at a time as a source of inspiration for meditation, or writing, or your art or your service. Each of the chapters is whole in itself. Each chapter will present one or more stories of great women of the spirit grouped according to my totally subjective decision to label them as representatives of the path of prayer, the path of compassion, the path of darkness, the path of art, the path of women's culture. Let these women speak to you. Walk with them through your day. Call upon them, as you might call upon a friend for advice. Remember them as you interact with others. Acknowledge their presence.

Long ago, when I first began to write about great women, my friend and editor Kate advised me to make contact with the women I was writing about. "Ask them what *they* want you to say," she commented, urging me to involve myself in their lives rather than remain on the surface talking *about* them. It was good advice. Many of these women have come alive in me. What I mean is that the courage, the devotion, the sense of humor, the compassion and the passion that characterized their lives is more accessible to me now than it was before I met them and started "using" them. Use them for yourself. They are large. They have ample laps.

And, if you can create the opportunity to get away to a place of solitude and silence for a few days, take this book along.

An Invitation

I have learned that great women are tremendously accessible. The less great are sometimes too busy or important to take time for me, but the truly wise are more than happy to meet me for tea when I pass through their town. I have spent some wonderful afternoons just listening to these women talk.

The women I write about here are great women. "Taking tea" with them, even the ones who lived centuries ago, I learned that these women faced the same questions, the same fears, the same challenges that we all face. (I must keep that in mind or I will relegate them to the position of ineffective icons.) They fumbled through their lives as we do. Years after going through a very messy process they were able to look back on the steps and say, "Ah, yes, this is the way it progresses. . ." They stumbled, they were confused. They looked for help. They cried out for a guide. Many of them didn't get serious about their spiritual awakening until late in life. It wasn't until forty that Teresa of Avila was shocked at the way in which her life was unfolding. Irina Tweedie, the wise Sufi teacher, was over fifty when she began her spiritual search.

One thing these great women have in common is that each one had to make a break with convention. Each one broke the rules—some in large ways, others in small ways. Not arbitrarily, however. These breaks were the result of their intuitions, of inner listening that grew so strong that even the dictates of the largest patriarchy in creation (the Holy Church, in some cases) was not strong enough to silence it. These are women who played life as a game, as "wily as serpents" while remaining as "innocent as doves." They have something to say to each of us in our lives today.

Put on the tea-kettle.

Friend, wake up! Why do you go on sleeping?
The night is over—do you want to lose the day
            the same way?
Other women who managed to get up early have
            already found an elephant or a jewel ....
So much was lost already while you slept ...
and that was so unnecessary!

The one who loves you understood, but you did not.
You forgot to make a place in your bed next to you.
Instead you spent your life playing.
In your twenties you did not grow
because you did not know who your Lord was.
Wake up! Wake up! There's no one in your bed —
He left you during the long night.

Kabir says: The only woman awake is the woman
            who has heard the flute![1]
                                        —Kabir, 13th century

1

THE AWAKENING

A Path of Annihilation

"*Wake up! Wake up!*" cries the poet Kabir, echoing an urgency that many of us feel about our spiritual lives. In Kabir's celebrated poem, the long-desired lover or Beloved is forced to wait while the woman (every woman, or every man) sleeps on, wasting precious hours, forgetful of her purpose and unimpressed with the critical nature of the situation that surrounds her.

"What will wake this woman up?"

Every spiritual tradition offers one or more answers, but admitting the condition of sleep is commonly the first step. After that, some answers rely almost exclusively on the forces of the upperworld, or the heaven realms, for this wake-up call; with grace or inspiration serving to roll us out of bed, to get us moving and then to carry us along (although our attention and effort are almost always required). Other paths demand a trip into hell—the underworld—and back. Without suffering a symbolic yet painful death, they assert, we will never have the guts to open our eyes, to wake up and face things as they are.

Using feminine wisdom to explore the many paths of the spiritual life will take us into both worlds. Mary of Nazareth or the all-compassionate Tibetan Buddha, Tara, may essentially comfort us in our struggles, mercifully intercede on our behalf, and offer us role models of exquisite tenderness. Yet, this same Divine Mother will flash a shining dark face. In her manifestation as the fierce Hindu goddess, Kali, she may show up with sword in hand, dripping with the blood of her recent victims, demanding that we awaken from the sleep of ages. Illusion is thick, and it is her eternal task to dispel it.

The women whose stories unfold in the pages that follow have a bit of both Mary and Kali in them, and lots more. While they may be mystics, or servants of the poor, or caring mothers to their children, they can be ruthlessly demanding and radical in their commitment to God, or to their practice, or to their work for others.

Mother Teresa certainly showed us many faces of the Divine Mother. One of my favorite stories happened when she traveled to New York City to find a location for a hospice which her nuns could operate for the destitute and dying. When she was taken into the basement of a renovated convent and shown the new furnace, the elderly nun exclaimed, "Oh, we don't need that. Take it out."

Now that is radical! That someone would choose to take on the discomfort and downright pain of living without hot water or heat in a New York apartment building, in the dead of winter, is unbelievable. Such a decision is only made by a madwoman or a masochist. But, the radiant happiness and selfless service which characterized Mother Teresa's life belie such easy judgements. She simply decided that "staying awake" required radical moves—that a body dulled by comfort and convenience (the hallmarks of contemporary culture) could encourage the spirit to nod off. She was willing to do anything necessary to keep the edge of aliveness in herself and those entrusted to her care. Mother Teresa was a woman awake.

Not all the women in these stories are eminent role models of either unbounded compassion or fierce detachment, nor are they all acknowledged as "fully enlightened" beings or archetypes of feminine power. Some are actually quite unremarkable, in the sense that they are invisible in their love and service. They used the ordinary challenges of daily life, like mothering their children, or building relationship, or cultivating their gardens as a means of waking up. They can inspire and challenge. They may also insult rational sensibilities, as the ways of ultimate transformation are not necessarily polite. Like Mother Teresa, each of these women in her own way has witnessed to a type of madness, or foolishness at least, which "the world" will probably always judge as naive, insane or dangerous. Yet, love does such things. The words of E.E. Cummings, which describe what it takes to be a poet, apply as well to any woman (or man) who chooses to walk the path of liberation or awakening.

> If you wish to follow, even at a distance, the poet's calling ...you've got to come out of the measurable doing universe into the immeasurable house of being ...Nobody else can be alive for you; nor can you be alive for anybody else ...If you can take it, take it—and be. If you can't, cheer up and go about other people's business and do or undo till you drop.[2]

This book is written for those who want to "take it."

Two famous stories illuminate what it means to leave the "known universe" to enter into the "eternal house of Being." One story is about heaven, or in this case Vaikuntha, the eternal realm of the Hindu god, Krishna. The great women of this story are simple cow-herders (actually ten thousand female cow-herders, to be precise). The other is about the Queen of Heaven and Earth, Inanna, who journeyed to hell, the Great Below, according to Sumerian legend. Each story demonstrates something vital about how woman awakens, and what she needs to do, day in and day out, to keep from falling back to sleep again. Both stories reveal aspects of the one divine feminine, different viewpoints or faces of Ma.

THE RAS LILA

From Hindu mythology comes the compelling tale of the *Ras Lila* or Love Play, in which the god Krishna attracted ten thousand women, on one night, with the irresistible sound of his flute. Grannies and maidens alike, he danced with them all. These love-struck *gopis* (cow-herd girls and women) were taken to heaven in the arms of their beloved, and their lives were never the same again.

The story has been a favorite of mine since I first heard it. As fantastic as it sounds, it is highly instructive as an archetype of the spiritual journey, and deserves to be more widely told. Perhaps it was the story of the *Ras Lila* that inspired Kabir to write: "The only woman awake is the woman who has heard the flute."

"Once upon a time," the story begins. "Long, long ago," it begins. In the hills outside of the village of Vrindavan, and along the banks of the Yamuna River in northern India, the eternal, limitless and formless Divine took the body of a startlingly beautiful boy—a boy painted dark blue in the art that celebrates him. Enter Krishna, the playful one who loves nothing better than to wander through the countryside playing his flute to the delight of the cowherd girls and boys—the *gopis* and *gopas*. Krishna, a mischievous boy who tantalizes his companions, and even embarrasses them, especially when he steals and hides their clothing as they bathe in the Yamuna, cooling themselves from the scorching heat of the tropical day.

The *Ras Lila*, or Love Play of Krishna and the *gopis* happened on a magnificent night, the night of the full moon of autumn; September, perhaps, in our calendar; the time of the blooming of the jasmine flowers, when the sweet air is thick with their fragrance. On this auspicious night, Krishna, overtaken with the mood of love for the bodies, the hearts, and the souls of humanity, began to play his flute. The alluring, hypnotic sound of this flute—the sound of longing, and the promise of fulfillment—wafted out over the hills. Like a soft breeze, the notes drifted into the huts and hovels of the *gopis*, some of whom were eating alone, while others were in the midst of preparing dinner for their husbands. Some *gopis* nursed their children, others languorously looked at the night sky, dreaming of the lover who would one day take them away.

And then, that sound; and suddenly their reveries, together with their lives, were interrupted. This call of the Beloved, singing through the trees, touched them and like a well-aimed dart, wounded and aroused their hearts. This sound and the sentiments it called forth was so captivating that everything else paled in comparison. And as the scriptures report, they "...heard the music that made the love-god, Ananga, grow stronger within them," (Chapter 1, Stanza 4).[3]

Turning in the direction of this rare but hauntingly familiar music, the *gopis* rose up, left whatever they were doing, and hurried towards the source of that sound, "their earrings swinging back and forth in their haste," (Chapter 1, Stanza 4). Literally, the food they were bringing to their mouths dropped back onto the plate; they put down the ladle and stepped away from the pot on the fire, leaving the milk to boil away, and leaving their husbands with wrinkled brows and shouting for supper. Taking their nursing children from their breasts, the *gopis* were now deaf to all except the sound of that flute. They departed their homes, their hair uncombed, some still half-dressed, nervous and excited, to hurry after the source of the music.

One by one they go; to a grove on the banks of the Yamuna River, at the edge of the forest, they go. Here to meet the one who has been calling to them throughout lifetimes. Krishna, sparkling with light, ". . .like the moon surrounded by stars," (Chapter 1, Stanza 43). This mysterious one, this dark one, who calls each one by name. And the love games begin.

Krishna questions them haughtily about why they have come, commanding them to go back to their husbands, as if to say that nice little girls shouldn't be out on a night like this. Go back to your homes, he reiterates, "...to the cowpens. Your children and the calves are bawling. Give the children your milk and milk the cows," (Chapter 1, Stanza 22). He teases, yet with a serious face, until they become irate, growing more passionate with each moment, and protesting their love with tears. Surely Krishna knows that he is the cause of their being there, that he himself has called them, and they object. Their fury and frustration brings the sweat to their foreheads and hands. He is testing them, teasing them, until they hit the depth of their desolation. Then, the Lover succumbs. "Or, if you have come here because your hearts are compelled by intense love for me, that is only right. For all beings love me," (Chapter 1, Stanza 23).

Thus the great dance begins. "Stretching out his arms and embracing them . . ." (Chapter 1, Stanza 46), Krishna takes each of the *gopis* to himself. Each one is totally enthralled. They dance, the symbol of their growing attunement, and as a prelude to their lovemaking. Krishna playfully caresses his partner's hair, "pleasurably stroking their thighs, loosening their waist-cloths and fondling their breasts. . ." In this manner, "the Lord aroused the lovely women of Vraja to the peak of passion, and made love to them," (Chapter 1, Stanza 46). Miraculously, each *gopi* knew herself as the sole lover of Krishna. Alone with her beloved for a night of ecstasy and bliss, she found complete fulfillment.

In the morning, as the first rays of the sun appeared over the horizon beyond the river, and as the cool night fled on the warm breath of the day, Krishna and his lover straighten their clothing, brushing the leaves and twigs from their tousled hair, and slowly emerge from their trysting place. Coming to the river bank, they refresh themselves. But there, as the *gopi* bends down, scoops some water into her hand and splashes it onto her face, she looks up to discover that Krishna has disappeared. Instead of her solitary lover, there is now a crowd of women—her friends, her sisters—each pointing to another in astonishment. One can almost imagine them saying: "What are *you* doing here?" And as they begin to share their tale, it is revealed, to their amazement, that Krishna has been with each one—mystery and outrage! What shock, wonderment and embarrassment must have rippled through the crowd.

But now Krishna is gone. "Where did he go?" "Did one of us drive him away?" "Was it you?" "Was it I?"

The scriptures answer the question for us. The great Lord disappeared in order to awaken in these women the most precious of gifts, the gift of longing—of "love in separation." What this required of them, then, after the first wave of their jealousy and anger had receded, was to realize that, ". . . He was, after all, their very Self," (Chapter 2, Stanza 2) and so they must find Him in their own bodies and hearts, in their own breath, in their every word and movement and in one another.

So must we.

LOVED ALIVE

Krishna's flute plays a strain of music that not only wakes a woman up and reminds her of her true home, but actually carries her there, if only for a moment, often despite her best intentions to resist the call. Certainly any woman who seriously engages spiritual life can relate to having heard this flute in one form or another. Possibly the music came as one or more numinous events or "peak experiences" in which she was temporarily drawn out of herself, in which she immediately knew or was shown the unitive nature of things, or was simply immersed in a silence permeated with compassion. Maybe she looked into the eyes of a newborn child, and felt love that surpassed all understanding. Maybe she was drawn into deep meditation. Maybe, in her own great pain and confusion, she witnessed a person who lived so magnanimously towards others, and so genuinely without pretense, that she knew such life was actually possible. And in that moment she glimpsed the possibility of awakening. In fact, in that moment she *was* awake.

For many, this awakening—whether it feels consoling or terrifying—heralds the beginning of a search, goading the seeker on

Ras Lila

to discover the nature of reality, or truth, or God. Others will try to bury it, file it away or run from it, afraid of the immediate implications, uncovering it only years or even decades later. Regardless of when the flute's call is acknowledged, however, each hearer will then be faced with the challenge of "living" the music of awakening—making her next decision, speaking her next sentence, applying her hand to the next act of service or art, taking her next breath on the basis of what she has seen, heard and known. Awakening, then, becomes the job of a lifetime. This tale of Krishna and the *gopis* offers some help and encouragement in this task.

The notion that each soul is deeply good, expansively beautiful, or uniquely and personally "beloved," is found in many of the world's great spiritual paths, and this story of the love play of Krishna and the *gopis* gives a tangible personality to that concept. Just as Krishna could dance with ten thousand women, the *Ras Lila* reminds us that there is no scarcity of love (or anything else) in the domain of the Absolute, and that the personal relationship of lover to beloved is the perfect metaphor for the relationship of the one Eternal Heart with the individual human heart.

In this domain of paradox, mystery and miracle in which Krishna dances, we can dare to say that each woman alive is the one and only object of the Lover's attention. To deeply contemplate this mystery could, I think, transform our lives. To rest in and embody the knowledge of who or what that Lover is, and where that Lover resides, would be a further awakening. Beyond knowing this for ourselves, such recognition would create a tremendous opening for relationship with others—as I awaken to the reality of my unique goodness and the unique Love which embraces me, so I come to find you, washing your clothes in the same river. It is awesome to imagine the implications of such awakening. Imagine living and working with a family of people—men and women— each one knowing himself, herself, to be good, to be the lover of the Divine! And each one knowing that every other one was also that lover, beyond competitiveness, envy or jealousy.

Another wondrous part of the *Ras Lila* story is that after it was over Krishna had to leave. Christ left too. The Buddha died, urging his followers to be "a light unto yourself." In the Christian gospels, Jesus appeared after his death in the disguise of a gardener and spoke with Mary Magdalen who was inquiring about where her Lord had disappeared to. When he spoke her name, "Mary," she recognized him and reached to embrace him. But he stopped her saying, "Don't touch me...I have not yet ascended to my Father..." (John 20:17). And later, "If I don't go away then the Holy Spirit can't come," (John 16:7). That holy spirit that Jesus promised was Love in creation: your love for me and my love for you, and our love for all of us.

As much as the *gopis* may have wanted to have Krishna's bodily form around forever, unless Krishna "goes," in some way, these women may be tempted to doze off again, satisfied and dreaming in his arms. They may never create the necessity to progress from the external to the internal lovemaking of the heart—a lovemaking not restricted by time or space or even the presence of the lover. The mystics throughout the ages have told us that this "love in separation," the love created by longing, is in fact the sweetest love.

Unless the form of the lover, the guru, the God, the teacher or the mother eventually goes, or demands that we disengage our dependency or attachment to itself, we may tend to keep our attention on that form as the sole object of worship and celebration, foregoing the necessity of establishing relationship with others. We may miss the truth that Krishna, Christ, the Buddha or the Divine Mother lives everywhere. And only with that realization will we awaken.

As sweet and alluring as the story of Krishna and the *gopis* appears, it hides a terrible but ultimately liberating truth—that the individual *gopi* must leave her former life behind her in order to enter fully and completely into Krishna-*loka*, that dimension of creation in which Love reigns supreme. And while she will most likely return to her same hungry husband and child, or her wandering cows, or her unweeded garden, she will be entering a new life, because her context for living will be different. Knowing the reality of infinite and personal love, *everything* will be different.

Inanna: Winged Goddess with her foot on the back of a lion, and a worshiper. Cylinder seal. Iraq, c. 2300 B.C.E. Courtesy of The Oriental Institute, University of Chicago.

What the *Ras Lila* heralds is nothing short of a path of annihilation—a context which characterizes the lives and teachings of the women whose stories are told in this book.

INNANA'S PATH OF ANNIHILATION

Annihilation was the path of Inanna, the Mother Goddess from ancient Sumer—Inanna, the queen of heaven, life and fertility. Inanna, goddess of war, was also the goddess of sexual love. The story of her descent into the underworld gives new meaning to this notion of waking up. Terrifying meaning, perhaps, yet necessary—she who embodies the life force will descend, deliberately; she will be stripped of her power and die, only to be transformed.

Inanna had a "sister," a part of herself, who lived in the underworld. Not only was Ereshkigal an inhabitant of the domain of death and terror, she was the absolute queen of it. She was horrifying, although beautiful; she was cruel (by our standards) although powerful. She was jealous and possessive and deceitful. With all her heavenly inspiration and knowledge, and for all her status, Inanna herself could not be saved from encountering Ereshkigal. She had to go into the underworld, as every woman must who wishes to be made whole. She had to confront these elemental forces of death and destruction, surrender to them, and be resurrected, sadder but wiser. There was no way around it—Inanna had to descend, otherwise she would remain forever an icon, rather than a living embodiment, the true Mother of all Creation.

Different renderings of the myth explain the reason for Inanna's visit. In one of the oldest accounts, she goes because Ereshkigal's husband has died, and she wishes to attend his funeral. Rather than being pleased at such generosity, however, Ereshkigal's jealousy gets the better of her, and she decides to destroy Inanna.

Inanna's descent is not a pretty one. Rather it is a series of the most profound humiliations and tortures. Seven gates have to be passed through, and at each gate a sacrifice is demanded. One by one she is disinherited of her powers, and her entire journey becomes an initiation into darkness, pain and loss. Not only does she relinquish her powers, but she must strip herself naked, and bow low in order to enter the dark kingdom's door. Finally, she is slaughtered, her body impaled on a stake and displayed for public mockery. Here her dead body swells, the skin turns green, she rots. Completely helpless and abandoned, Inanna has no choice but to wait.

The queen's salvation comes about through the intercession of her trusted woman attendant, Ninshubur, whom the goddess had instructed before her descent. If she was unheard of for more than three days, Ninshubur was to plead for help among the gods, and create a plan to rescue her. The dead queen lives on, therefore, with her spiritual self embodied in Ninshubur, who turns out to be a loyal and powerful agent.

The woman servant gains the ear of Enki, the God of Wisdom, and the father of Inanna's mother. While others in the heavenly realm refuse to understand the nature of Inanna's fated journey, Enki knows better. He has admired her, and knows how vital her life is to the life of the whole kingdom.

From the dirt of his fingernails, Enki enlivens two creatures that will enter the underworld on his behalf. They will enter to console the screaming Ereshkigal, who now moans like a woman in labor, inconsolably mourning the loss of her other part, her lightness, Inanna. Some say the neglected Ereshkigal had mourned this loss even before the demise of her sister, and that these same cries actually drew Inanna to the underworld in the first place. Ereshkigal herself also needed to be reborn.

Moved by the empathy of the messenger creatures, Ereshkigal offers them great gifts, which they deliberately refuse. The only recompense they will take is the resurrection and release of their Queen of Love. Actually, what the creatures skillfully ask is that the Dark Queen let go of her own pain, anger and despair by releasing her former nemesis, Inanna. Thus, Ereshkigal herself is offered spiritual transformation. The Dark Mother says yes, to herself and her sister, and Inanna is reborn, itching to leave.

There is one big problem, however. Even Ereshkigal cannot fully undermine the laws of her own kingdom; namely, that no one, once initiated, can depart from the underworld. While she cannot change the rules, however, she will write a few new ones. After all, Inanna has been something of an exception all along. She has been reborn! So the gods of the nether lands agree to a mitigating clause. She can return, but she must send someone in her place. And with this interesting twist, for which Inanna will forever be responsible, she will never fully be able to turn her back on the dark kingdom. "A passageway has been created from the Great Above, the conscious, to the Great Below, the unconscious, and it must be kept open. Inanna must not forget her neglected, abandoned older 'sister'—that part of herself that is Ereshkigal."[4]

And whom does Inanna send in her place? Her beloved husband, of course; the one whom she has passionately desired, the object of her sexual longing; the shepherd boy whom she has enthroned as her king, Dumuzi. And why? Because he has grown cold and casual, more interested in the affairs of state than in his adoration of her. She will show him once and for all how unwise it is to neglect the worship of the goddess, especially when she is the Mother of Fertility. Naive, indulgent, unconscious Dumuzi must also suffer dismemberment and abandonment in the underworld.

The king's sister, Geshtinanna, is so grieved by the departure of her brother, that she offers her own life to save his. She appeals to Inanna to be allowed to share his fate, and the once irate Queen relents. She indeed misses her husband and lover. She wants her king! So, the bargain is finally sealed: Geshtinanna will reside in the underworld for half the year, while Dumuzi reigns gloriously with Inanna. At the end of six months, he will again journey to the Great Below, where he will reside with Ereshkigal, replacing both his sister and his wife, eternally.

And so it is that man is spiritually awakened, at the goddess's word; for he will live with both queens—the Love goddess and the Mother of death. He too will suffer, and he too will rejoice. And thus, he will be made whole.

The Descent of the Goddess

Inanna's story compliments the *Ras Lila*—she also has heard the flute. Though instead of sensuous music leading her to heaven, Inanna is irresistibly drawn to hell, called there by the cries of her sister, Ereshkigal. Like the *gopis*, Inanna wants a broadened perspective, of life and of herself. She too wants to wake up.

This descent of the goddess is a story that every woman must take to heart if she is serious about her spiritual life. As much as we might wish to keep our focus in the upperworld, we must face the raw truth that we each have a sister who lives in the Great Below; a sister who can and probably has hurt us, yet who herself is in great pain, longing for our compassionate embrace. It will take great courage to enter into her domain of pain and death with eyes open, to endure the suffering which is in her, and everywhere in the world, without anesthetizing ourselves to it; it will take guts to die well ourselves, or to wait patiently for *who knows what*, abandoned and helpless, perhaps for a long, long time. It may take even more courage to be healed, to rise up, to start again, to assume more responsibility than ever.

Annihilation is unequivocal. It literally means to reduce to nothing. In terms of atomic physics, however, to annihilate is to convert rest-mass into energy, in the form of one or more photons (a quantum of electromagnetic radiation). What this tells us is that, far from leaving only a smattering of ash, this process is actually an alchemical one—converting matter into energy and light. A perfect way to speak about the spiritual path! Annihilation in this regard may be thought of as utterly destroying the dead mass of illusions—that beauty, power and possessions will some-how protect us from pain and death; that self-importance to the exclusion of others will achieve some worthwhile prize; that small-mindedness, aggression and grasping will not have their sorry con-sequences in our own hearts. These are among the sacrifices that Inanna was called to make at each of the seven gates. At the same time, however, annihilation destroys by converting dead things into energy—useable energy. Light energy. Energy for knowledge, for prayer, for service, for love. Which is why Inanna was different after her descent, or why, in a German detention camp awaiting her transference to Auschwitz, twenty-six-year-old Etty Hillesum (whose story will be told in Chapter Seven), could write:

> The misery here is quite terrible; and yet, late at night. . .I often walk with a spring in my step along the barbed wire. And then time and again, it soars straight from my heart—I can't help it, that's just the way it is, like some elementary force—that feel-ing that life is glorious and magnificent, and that one day we shall be building a whole new world.[5]

Inanna's descent instructs us that no fluffy initiations or weekend meditations will make the grade in the type of awaken-ing to wholeness that she sought. So called "new age" principles—as demonstrated in a recent runaway bestseller that found the main character pursuing the spiritual journey through a series of ten revelations—are often founded on a lie. In this book, for instance, the protagonist moved along his path in a matter of weeks, or months. While he felt fear and even had to run for his life at times, his pain was superficial and short-lived. The lie of that book is that it leads the reader to believe in this kind of instant enlight-enment. It is no different from the seminars that promise to turn you into an *avatar* (the Sanskrit word for the ultimate savior of an age) in a three-day weekend retreat.

Poet William Stafford described the times when he wrote: "The darkness around us is deep." As much as we might hope for heaven on earth, and try to interpret the signs of the times as some

Inanna: Winged Goddess. (Detail) Cylinder seal. Iraq, c. 2300 B.C.E. Courtesy of The Oriental Institute, University of Chicago.

indication of an advancement in human consciousness, we need only examine our own minds, observing our easy susceptibility to the cultural malaise—the disease of false security based on comfort, fascination and accumulation—to recognize just how thick the illusions are.

The darkness around us is particularly deep because it is lit by halogen lamps which convince us that it is not the night. Under such light, like chickens in a factory farm who are conditioned to lay as many as eight eggs a day, we are duped into thinking that the number of our experiences is the measure of our progress along the path. Under such light we are convinced that the night can be magically vanquished. We are led to believe that it is possible to walk this path without having to be left alone in the dark, without having to feel confused and doubtful, without having to join the human race and face the fact that life is suffering.

As both Inanna's story and the *Ras Lila* reveal, the path of spiritual practice and serious spiritual work is a path of disruption and regeneration, death and resurrection. Separated from our old familiar ways, we will encounter experiences of both intense suffering and deep satisfaction, even bliss. One sees this in work with the dying—in the midst of their pain, they are often opened to loving their families and caregivers in profound ways. My friend Inge, whom I nursed for over a year and a half before her death, moved frequently from the darkness into the light and back again. She had days of near despair, followed by days of great joy, in which she experienced the light again. Once she told me, "This pain is terrible, but what I have learned about love would have me choose it all over again."

In 1988, I visited a great woman named Dina Rees, who lived outside of Freiburg, Germany. (I write about Dina in Chapter Four.) Dina, who had been a medical doctor and had served the starving of Bangladesh in the 1960s was, in 1988, a spiritual guide and healer for hundreds of students. She left enormous impressions upon me, especially that moment in which I literally saw the Divine Mother in her. Dina's words are as clear to me today as when she first uttered them. "Ours is a desperate time,"

Dina said. She explained that when people feel desperate, as if they are drowning, they will grasp at anything, even straw, to try to keep themselves afloat. She noted that many unscrupulous or ego-based "spiritual" teachers will throw out the straw of a "quick-fix" to their naive disciples, and will thereby increase the illusion that some progress is being made, when in reality the opposite may be true.

Inanna's example demands that we cease our grasping and drown, or descend. Only by dying or surrendering (in the language of the spiritual life), do we have any possibility of being transformed into light.

DOES IT HAVE TO BE SO HARD?

Paradoxical though it may seem, the passage through consciousness or self moves contrary to self, rubs it the wrong way—and, in the end, rubs it out. Because this passage goes against the grain of self, it is therefore a path of suffering....

So, the storms and sufferings of life are a way of finding the eye [the center of calm, or the "Spirit within"]. When everything is going our way, we do not see the eye, and we feel no need to find it....So the avoidance of suffering and the desire to have everything go our own way runs contrary to the whole movement of our journey...[6]

—Bernadette Roberts

Irina Tweedie, another wise woman and spiritual teacher, author of the amazing chronicles, *Daughter of Fire* and *Chasm of Fire*,[7] spoke in San Francisco a number of years ago. A friend reported to me that at the conclusion of Irina's talk, a young man in the audience, in all sincerity, questioned her: "Is it possible to come to know what you know, to realize what you have realized, without the intense suffering and pain that you describe as being part of the journey?" The audience was hushed in expectation of her reply. He had spoken everyone's question.

"My dear young man," she replied softly, compassionately, her smile smoothing the wrinkles in her eighty-three-year-old face, "I'm afraid there isn't." Silence. The audience was stunned at the candor of her answer.

Irina Tweedie's eyes, even as she spoke that grave sentence, sparkled with a secret joy. Here was another woman who knew something about being awake. Here was a radiant witness of what is left when annihilation is complete. Yet, this tender-hearted women refused to grant her audience an easy way out. To emphasize the celebratory aspects of the spiritual path would create only a partial picture. And such a half-truth would be as damaging as a full lie.

Like Dina Rees, Irina Tweedie knew that mediocrity is deadly, and that spiritual mediocrity is endemic of our times. While we gave Mother Teresa the Nobel Prize and an internationally broadcast funeral, and lots of us cried at the loss, when all was said and done we settled back into life as it was within a few days, or hours even, perhaps with some tears or a bit of discomfort at our own guarded generosity. A woman awake—a woman with a fierce and awesome commitment—is a fearsome confrontation to our mediocrity and casualness. Most of us, myself included, would rather defend ourselves *against* our own potential greatness, because we know the sacrifices that living such greatness would require. Instead, we content ourselves to use the lives of others for inspiration, and thus keep the hard questions they raise at a safe distance. But, unfortunately, inspiration is a cheap substitute for life. If we want the goods, in our own unique way, as these are demonstrated by our heroines and role models, we're going to have to pay a price —some price. That's why the path is hard.

Another reason this path is so hard is that our mind, the source of our thoughts, can become a tyrant. Without our awareness, mind can build iron-clad strategies for coping with the painful, the unknown or the fearsome qualities or experiences of life. Whether that strategy is one of naivete, optimism, belligerence or pessimism, all strategies are designed to protect us from "losing," that is, from feeling the pain that is part of human existence.

Of course, self-protection is necessary at times—the survival instinct is basic! What happens, however, is that mind's interpretation of what "survival" means in any particular situation can become an obsessive preoccupation—*everything* gets cast in the light of being a threat to survival. It is as if we declare: "I can't be bothered with the immediate needs of the situation as a whole, or with the next step in the task towards a goal, because all my energy is focused on protecting myself right now." As a result, we may hold on desperately to patterns of behavior that have only led us to dead-ends in the past—we are stuck, afraid to move, afraid to step, afraid to follow the call of the flute.

Changing old mind-patterns is not a swift process. It will require time and careful attention. We will need to observe the mind under myriad circumstances, to softly illuminate its dark chambers and small passages, to make our peace with its preoccupation with self-criticism and judgement of others. It has been immensely painful for me to see my selfishness and to admit how all-pervasive it is. I need support, internal discrimination and grace to begin to tell the truth about that selfishness, without being swept into a wormhole of self-denigration because of it. To face the truth of my pettiness, while at the same time continuing to build appreciation for my basic goodness, is no easy task.

The path has been hard for me because to see and live the truth requires a wearing down of all that has kept me buffered from reality. There is tremendous pain and suffering in the world. The innocents are slaughtered day after day, not simply those "out there" who are at the effect of political turmoil or famine or disease, but children very close to home who are fed the values of a media-machine, or children who are ignored because adults (myself included) are too busy to listen to them. Facing the Noble Truths, as the Buddha spoke them, that "all life is suffering," and that "desire is the root of all suffering," is one thing. Living with these truths in continual awareness, and making decisions from this state of awareness, takes great courage, energy and dedication.

The path is hard because to build an "interior castle" (as Saint Teresa of Avila would describe it) takes work. A deep, rich inner life is bought dearly, especially in this day and age when glittering distractions are too numerous to list. From all directions we are urged to settle for prefabricated, plastic substitutes. An interior castle contains a temple, a sanctuary, a love chamber, and a laboratory in which all life experiences are transformed into prayer or energy for the service of humanity; such mansions are designed and then built with conscious intention, coupled with a fierce commitment to their upkeep and beautification rendered over a lifetime.

Finally, the path is hard because we make it harder than it is, in countless ways. I do this by my inability to hold the paradox that spiritual life is simply ordinary, simply "what is"—full of moments of light, inspiration and self-discovery, as well as full of hardship, messy edges and death. My mistaken notions of spirituality have created enormous confusion and suffering for me, to say nothing of a lot of wasted time. For years, I have pushed and pulled to be holy and good and special. I have not wanted to be ordinary. Instead of relaxing into the context of Love, I have more often chosen to struggle to be perfect! I think another reason we descend is to find that we are not much different from the other suffering humans—that we are not special; not "saved" from anything because of our association with spiritual life. If we are lucky, we eventually learn that perfection, or specialness is not the goal—but we generally learn this only after a lot of hard knocks.

A Renewed Sense of Urgency

In the summer of 1994 comets began hitting the planet Jupiter. One day during this interesting time, a friend called me to say that he had heard there was a slim chance that the "whole universe" might explode—something about a chain reaction set off by the gases. I asked him what time this might occur and he playfully noted that it would be anytime between 6 P.M. and 10

P.M. that evening. Since I was on my way to the movies, the mind flashed a quick image of being instantly incinerated while sitting in the theatre, the last image before my eyes as I entered oblivion (or the hereafter, or the *bardo* realm) was that of Arnold Schwarzenegger with a grin. I admit it was a sobering thought.

For days after this, I thought of that moment when I had contemplated instantaneous death, not only for myself, but for the entire universe. Death has always been a great teacher—the kind of teacher who shocks me into awakening, demanding that I quit the realm of denial, if only for a few minutes. Despite my solid conviction that this Great Process (which I call God) is always evolving, and that I will never be separate from that, nonetheless, since I am in a physical body right now, I must admit that I shudder at the thought of annihilation. I don't want to die.

Reflections about death can be humbling. They tend to fill me with a great sense of urgency that has something to do with accomplishing the things I dream about, and with getting myself healthier so that I don't have to die prematurely due to gross neglect. But, beneath all that, the urgency has to do with waking up to the immense privilege of life and how readily that privilege is squandered in my moment to moment activity.

The ever-present possibility of death can be a great friend and teacher urging our spiritual life forward. Women awake were generally women of enormous urgency. They were not frantic or self-condemnatory in this urgency, but they were often obsessed—passionate and generally tireless in their efforts toward the purification and enrichment of their own lives, as well as in their service to others. Their writing, particularly their poetry, reflects the urgent longing of those who have been captured by the Beloved's glance. The ecstatic Hindu poetess, Mirabai, whose adoration for Krishna caused her to be annihilated in love, wrote:

> ...life disappears second by second
> and never comes back,
> a leaf torn from its branch
> goes twirling away.

Look at this raging ocean of life forms,
swift, unappeasable
everything caught in its tide.
O beloved, take this raft quickly
and lead it to shore.[8]

The time to follow the flute is now—this day, this moment. Not with grand gestures or impossible promises, but with getting quiet, with slowing down, with opening our eyes, with telling whatever hard truth we may be turning away from in the immediate situation in front of us, with asking for help, if necessary. These are the qualities that attracted and inspired me in the women, and men, whose stories follow. May their witness benefit all.

Krishna Dancing with the Gopis. Painting, Indian, Punjab, 17th century.

2

THE DESERT PATH

Silence, Solitude and Prayer

I will espouse you,
lead you into the desert,
and there I will speak to your heart.
　　　　　　　—*Hosea 2:14*

ny woman today who desires a deepened spiritual life would do well to start out in the desert. Yet "the desert" does not necessarily mean some barren expanse of sand, or the scrub and cactus-filled land which so blesses me in Arizona. The desert experience essential for today is an experience of temporary sanctuary in which we can stand still long enough to gain some perspective about our lives and intentions. The desert's call is for a bit of silence, a moment of solitude in which one may "listen" for guidance, for encouragement or for clarification, with fewer external distractions.

We need the desert desperately, probably much more than our ancestors did. Despite the immense technological advances of our times, women are dissatisfied, fear-driven, compulsive, and obsessed with material security. It was exactly this mood in the culture that drove hundreds of spiritually-minded men and women to the desert during the time of the Roman Empire. To these rebels—known to us today as the Desert Fathers and Desert Mothers (who outnumbered the men two-to one, according to Palladius)—the newly-arising civilization was a misguided attempt to control life, and thus a sure way to destroy the soul. Rather than succumb to such death of the spirit, they chose instead the life of the hermit or monk (some of them lived communally)—a life of immense hardship and deprivation, but a life of liberation focused on the Absolute.

In our times, the growing popular interest in solitary vision quests and personal retreats, and the fascination with the practices of monastic life (witness the success of Kathleen Norris's wonderful book, *Cloister Walk*; or the fact that a recording of cloistered monks singing Gregorian chant actually makes it to the top of the pop music charts!) seems an urgent cry for relief from the pain of the rat-race, a pull to re-establish some basic sanity by entering the desert.

Is such hunger really a desire for the raw Divine, for Absolute Truth? Well, that depends; but it is, potentially, a first step—one that must be taken if that deeper longing of the heart is ever to be realized—that longing for the strength and courage to wake up; that hunger to fully live the enlightenment which is our birthright.

The woman who will lead us into the desert may initially seem like an unlikely candidate. Her name is Catherine de Hueck Doherty, but she was more generally referred to as "The Baroness." As a child in Russia, Catherine was immersed in a religious culture. Among her strongest memories, she recalled accompanying her mother into the forest that surrounded their village to find the simple hut and patch of garden which indicated the world of the *poustinik*, a renunciate hermit who had entered the forest as the seekers in times past had entered the desert—to find God and to pray for

26

humanity. In fact, this tiny domain in the forest was called the *poustinia*, the desert.

Catherine remembered how she and her mother would enter the hermitage, bow as a sign of respect, and be served tea and bread, or whatever else the *poustinik* had in his meager larder. (Hospitality was the hermit's trademark.) Only then would her mother ask for the spiritual guidance of the man of prayer.

In her mid-sixties, after a lifetime spent in active service to the poor, Catherine Doherty began to teach the people who had gathered around her about the notion of *poustinia*. Far from being a message reserved for members of a religious community, Catherine's teaching about the desert of silence and solitude is one that can be integrated into anyone's life, since the desert to which she calls us is the desert found in the heart, and it is here that every true seeker can, and in fact must, build her own *poustinia*. To more formally experience the *poustinia* simply involved taking an occasional day, or more, to leave behind normal activities and to allow silence and solitude to bring rest and sanity to a tired and distracted soul. The Poustinia Movement is another means of establishing a few more tiny sanctuaries of peace in a troubled world.

MEETING THE BARONESS

In 1997, at eleven on a late August morning in Winslow, Arizona, it was over ninety degrees in the shade. There was no breeze, which was fortunate, as one of the locals told me, because the wind there can leave you with dust in your mouth. (There is little in Winslow to slow its relentless progression across the pancake-flat expanse of desert.) Driving down the main street of town, the signs of poverty are immediately evident—a conglomeration of weathered shops, now boarded up, and small groups of ramshackle adobe dwellings are interspersed among the usual tourist stores, the cafes, the large retail chain stores.

The Madonna House of Winslow, founded by Catherine Doherty in 1957, the place I am searching for, is lost in a tiny neighborhood behind the sawmill on the south end of town. I have come here to learn more about Catherine de Heuck Doherty. I have come to meet Mariann Dunsmore, the current director of this Roman Catholic lay missionary community, who knew Catherine for seven years prior to The Baroness's death. (They call her affectionately, "The B.")

The men and women who staff any of the twenty or so Madonna Houses around the world are enjoined to live and work among the poor, but not as social workers. (Mariann said this many times to make the point for me.) Rather, they are a contemplative presence in the marketplace—that means they are there to pray, and to listen intensely for what the Holy Spirit dictates as being wanted and needed. In Winslow, for instance, they have served as a food and clothing bank, provided shelter for the homeless, hosted AA groups and built a library for the neighborhood. Currently they run a Montessori school and catechetics program for dozens of preschool children. As Janet, one of the staff members explained the need: "Some of them have moms in prison, or dads in prison or strung out on drugs. For many, grandparents are raising them. Yet children of this age are so close to God. They *know* that God loves them."

Besides praying parts of the Divine Office, the Mass, and one hour of silent prayer each day, Madonna House missionaries spend one twenty-four-hour period of each week alone in the Poustinia, where they are enjoined to listen, to rest, to wait. In Winslow they have two Poustinia sites, where guests of any faith are always welcome to stay for solitary retreat. The B's missionary spirit, together with her total immersion in prayer as a way of life, was evident everywhere.

Over lunch, most of which had been donated by caring neighbors, Mariann and Janet spoke to me with devotion and enthusiasm about Catherine's life and work.

Catherine was born to a wealthy Russian family in 1896, and impetuously married her first cousin (Boris de Hueck) at the age of fifteen. When war with Germany broke out, and the Revolution seized Russia, Catherine was on the front lines as a nurse, bathing her aristocratic hands in the blood of hundreds of dying soldiers, and having her heart repeatedly broken at the horrors she witnessed. After one particularly gruesome battle, for instance, she spent hours carrying amputated limbs from the operating room to a pit dug outside the building.

In 1918, she and Boris fled Communist Russia and in 1921 emigrated to Toronto, where, penniless, in poor health, having just birthed her son, Catherine took a job as a sales clerk, while her husband worked as an architect until the Depression left him among the ranks of the unemployed. As the sole support of the

Catherine de Hueck Doherty— The Baroness

family, Catherine labored at the most menial tasks, both in Toronto and later in New York City, where she joined the faceless, working poor as a laundress, a maid and a waitress.

Catherine had a feisty and dramatic nature, and this, coupled with her forceful voice and passionate anti-Communist sentiments, earned her a job with a lecture bureau, as part of the Chautauque circuit—a traveling company that presented programs of interest in rural areas throughout the northern U.S. and across Canada. Dressed like Russian royalty, Catherine would fascinate audiences with exotic stories of her early years, followed by her narration of the bleak life under the totalitarian regime. Within a few years, Catherine had gained a reputation for herself, as a speaker as well as a woman of action. Financially, she was also well rewarded for her efforts.

Catherine paid a grave price for her small measure of success, however. In order to travel she had to leave her child, George, in the care of others for long periods of time, and this became a lifelong source of anger and resentment for him. Her extended separations from her husband encouraged Boris's self-indulgent tendencies—he profligately used the funds that Catherine sent back from her work to support his mistresses and his facade of nobility. Again and again, after tedious weeks on the road, Catherine returned to an unhappy home, and suffered the indignities of an emotionally domineering and abusive husband, coupled with the scandalous whisperings of polite Toronto society.

Despite the pain of her married life, Catherine's worldly sophistication and wealth grew until she was not only able to support her family, but supply them with a fine apartment, a car and influential friends. And here is where the story of an immigrant's rise to success may have ended, added to the archives of a thousand similar accounts of hardworking and lucky people who realize their dream of success. Instead, at the height of her career, Catherine began to be bothered by God, or at least by some insistent internal voice which questioned: "Has God saved me from death in Russia so that I should return to bourgeois society...?"[1] In 1929, when Catherine was thirty-three, a gospel passage in which Christ advised the rich young man to, "Go, sell what you have and give it to the poor and come follow me," began haunting her waking hours. Slowly over the course of that year and the next, the insistent voice laid out for Catherine a way of life—in later years this became known as the "Little Mandate." She was hearing a call to a life of radical trust in God through selfless service to the poor. And by 1932 she was *living* that trust among the poor in the slums of Toronto. In 1934, with a small following of like-minded others, she established Friendship House, a place that provided food, clothing, shelter and educational programs to the poor of Toronto.

The Toronto place was followed in 1938 with another house in Harlem, New York where she literally became a forerunner of the Civil Rights movement in the U.S. Besides the charitable efforts of this center, Catherine worked tirelessly to get young "negroes" accepted in Catholic colleges, and struggled to help change the consciousness of American Catholicism. One day, in speaking to a group of church women about this "negro issue," she said that any poor black man or woman was Christ himself in need. Despite the shocked expressions of her listeners, Catherine went on to beg them to examine their prejudices. The implications of her words were too much for these polite ladies. A group of them rushed the stage platform and began to beat Catherine and tear her clothes.

The stories of these years in the 1930s and 40s read like a *Who's Who* in American Catholic history—her friendship with Dorothy Day the founder of the Catholic Worker movement, her marriage to Eddie Doherty, a fiery and respected reporter for the *Chicago Tribune*, her relationship with a young English literature professor named Thomas Merton...the list goes on. This period was also filled with more of the suffering, the misunderstanding and the humiliation which was to characterize all her great ventures.

Her biography and the reports of her friends and followers honestly assess the dilemmas which Catherine faced for long years of her adult life. With a strong personality that often neglected the niceties of communication, Catherine's style of leadership challenged nearly everyone in her sphere of influence, at one time or another. She was simply in a hurry to lead people to God. Often she missed the obvious—her violations of the rules of protocol, her failures to take into account the fragile egos of others, the denial of her own stubborn attachments, trusting people who had not yet proven trustworthy, not trusting people who could have been her strongest supporters in times of need. When, in the early 1950s, as Catherine's mystical life grew and she admitted to being overwhelmed by the "sins" of a lifetime, she was admitting her own helplessness. She suffered through dark days and nights of despair and loneliness that left her in doubt about whether she was on the right track.

Even her staunchest critics were constantly amazed, however, at the way in which Catherine would admit her failings, her gross neglect, her blatant exaggerations. Yet, despite her honest confessions, Catherine was not to be tamed. She was genuine in her remorse, but just as likely to take a bigger risk, or make an even bigger blunder (in her critics' minds), a few weeks later. Often, the misunderstandings resulted because her critics lacked the wide and prophetic vision that impelled Catherine. In the mid-1940s, for instance, she foresaw disaster in the attempts at democracy and a limited apostolate of service within the Friendship House movement, which she had founded and infused with her intense commitment and spirit. Catherine felt that such an evolution would undermine the spirit of sacrifice and surrender she had worked so hard to achieve. Her relationships with the directors (whom she herself had trained) were fast deteriorating. "If I were to do what you suggest," she wrote finally to her Friendship House directors, "it would last a year and then another question would pop up and we would be at it again. If you are ready to trust your spiritual mother to do what she taught you how to do, then OK, if not, then the question is on the floor ...."[2] The question was answered. The directors chose a democratic model, and in 1947, Catherine and her husband Eddie moved to a rural area of Ontario.

In Combermere, between Toronto and Ottawa in the Ottawa valley, Catherine began the third chapter in her life story. Still dedicated to the poor, the Dohertys' lives became a magnetic center that drew a small but dedicated following. Over the next fifteen years, Madonna House, as the community came to be called, served as a beacon for a life of simplicity and charity soundly based on Christian gospel principles.

A fourth chapter in Catherine's life began in the 1961. At the vibrant age of sixty-five, Catherine wrote that she, "...started thinking again about *poustinia*,"[3] the old-world model which had always fascinated her. Mariann had told me that The B was fond of saying that those in the West needed to drop out of their heads and into the body and heart, and that she had carried this embodied spirituality with her from Russia and was dedicated to passing it along. "Could such a form be transplanted to the West?" Catherine had pondered that question for thirty years. Her wondering led to waiting, and to prayer. At last, after months of self-reflection she brought the subject of *poustinia* to her Madonna House family, who enthusiastically embraced her lead.

At the time of Catherine's death in 1985, Madonna House had grown to a staff of over two hundred women and men (including many priests) who wished to live communally and practice the prayer and service that characterized her Little Mandate. "The main aim of Madonna House," Catherine wrote, "is to form a community of love. The success of a mission is never in its works. It rests first and foremost and last in the love that its members have for one another."[4] In 1998 there were twenty-three Madonna Houses throughout the world—from Paris, France to Magadan, Siberia, to Volta Region, Ghana to Winslow, Arizona.

My visit to Winslow, together with reading her biography, *They Called Her Baroness,* turned Catherine into a living, breathing presence for me. The B was fleshed out into a remarkable, controversial and daring yet tender and compassionate woman whose risks and failures were evidently as big as her heart. Far from being the quiet mystic, the fact that she *was* so big, in many ways, and so outrageous at times, convinced me that I had to put her story in this book.

We like saints to be perfect, and always according to *our* definitions of perfection. When saints don't measure up, we doubt them, the power of their work and the validity of their message. The "B" challenged these standards.

She decried false holiness. She did this, Mariann told me, by her outspoken directness, which was a source of humor as well as a great challenge to those who were blessed to meet her. One day at the Training center in Combermere, a visiting priest was waxing eloquently about some issue when Catherine interrupted him in mid-sentence: "Father, that's a load of horseshit..." Mariann drawled out the words with mock expressiveness in imitation of Catherine's speech. While describing the seemingly unlimited tenderness and the expansive heart of the great woman, Mariann also reflected the paradox of associating with one whose life was completely dedicated to God's work. "There was no chitchat at The B's table," Mariann remarked, communicating a bit of the discomfort she had felt around Catherine. Mariann recalled the fearsome, yet compassionate candor with which The B had first addressed her, a few minutes after sitting down to lunch during her initial visit to Combermere. Looking Mariann straight in the eye, The B had asked: "So, what are *you* going to do for God? Why did you come here anyway?"

Catherine Doherty's great value to me is that she lived passionately, and moved forward, regardless of criticism or consequences. She bore the pain of her own mistakes and she didn't crumble. She allowed herself to be slowly roasted throughout her life, until she was cooked enough to become the sort of mystic and champion of prayer which her Poustinia Movement and her writings reflect.

I think Catherine is worthy of following. She'll "tell it like it is," to the best of her ability. Let's use her to guide us into the desert, and listen as she instructs us about silence, solitude, prayer and sanity.

THE DESERT OF THE HEART

Catherine Doherty taught that the entrance into the desert begins with *kenosis*, a Greek word meaning emptying. Such a notion is perfectly described in a famous Zen story: A verbose scholar comes to the Master asking for instruction and the Master offers him a cup of tea. As he pours tea into the visitor's cup, however, the Master lets the tea fill the cup and spill over into the saucer. The visitor, aghast, watches in amazement. The Master continues pouring tea, which is now leaking over the saucer and onto the table. At last the visitor cannot contain himself. "What are you doing?" he shouts, leaping up from his seat, afraid that the tea will soon be dripping onto his lap. "Oh," says the Master, nonplussed, placing the teapot back on the brazier, "such is the condition of your mind." He continues, "How can I proceed to give you any teaching when your head is already so over-filled with its own notions. My words would simply spill over and be wasted, just like this tea."

Kenosis, then, implies a state of innocence and simplicity, of spaciousness gained by the willing surrender of our sureness based on position, book learning, financial security, and especially our theological assumptions. The *poustinia* is the place where the heart is instructed in a new way of seeing and being.

The *poustinik* of the Russian tradition achieved this *kenosis* literally by leaving everything behind—his or her home and family, job, possessions—taking only a loaf of bread, a gourd of water, a bible, and the clothes on his back. But such outward signs were only indications of the greater emptying which the pilgrim sought. His or her desire was to be annihilated in the love of God such that only God remained, and that often entailed a path of rigorous prayer, fasting, and selfless availability to the needs of the nearby community.

So, *kenosis* was not a "done deal" prior to entering upon the path. Rather, it was an intention, wrestled with daily, by the constant wearing away of ego's demands, and the constant remembrance of prayer. *Kenosis* demanded patience and persistence; namely, an attitude of "waiting upon God."

Years ago, reading the contemporary monk and scholar, Thomas Merton, I was struck with a phrase which he used about his life in the hermitage. He spoke of refusing to "impose his will upon the day." Rather, he tried to hold himself in readiness, waiting to see how "God's plan" for the day would unfold in and through him.

This waiting, and awaiting, as Merton described it, permeated the *poustinik's* prayer life as well. Prayer was not something he or she "did," but was something she received. Prayer was an entrance into the great mystery, or the "void which is God," as Catherine would refer to it. It was a relationship between the Divine and the human. Only one who was willing to stand at the door in humility, waiting for the host's good pleasure (or waiting for one glimpse of the cloak of the Beloved, as the mystic Sufis describe in their poetry and prayer), would find admittance to this sacred chamber. One entered *poustinia* to wait for the Spirit to descend upon the soul.

As the *poustinik* waited, he listened to requests for service. Hospitality and immediacy of service—that is, a complete offering of self—marked the hermit's life. As Catherine described it:

Hospitality has to be total. It is not enough to share
your bread or your tea or your coffee with whomever comes to visit, though this is the first kind of
hospitality offered. Thus, when a person comes
in, the first thing you offer is food. We live by
food. God comes to us as food...The ideal to strive
for, however, is hospitality of the heart...Christ said
that man cannot live by bread alone. The *poustinik*
should practice this by also offering himself.[5]

Whether it was spiritual guidance to be offered, or a barn to
be raised, the man or woman of the desert had no hesitation in
leaving the retreat to work among the people of God. And here,
Catherine Doherty pointed out, is where we learn the most profound mystery of the *poustinia*. The hermit had no hesitation in
leaving her hut because she knew that the real *poustinia* was a mood
carried in the heart. Whether she was attending to the sick or
weeding her garden, or helping with the harvest at a nearby farm,
the *poustinik* was in silence, at prayer within the chapel of the
heart, the same as if she was on her knees alone before the icon of
the Virgin Mary. Silence, for the *poustinik*, was not the mere absence of speech. Silence was a condition of absorption in the Beloved; a one-pointedness, a peacefulness, an attitude of emptiness
which was always ready to be filled by the Spirit, and ready to
move upon that wind.

True silence is a key to the immense and flam-
ing heart of God. It is the beginning of a divine
courtship that will end only in the immense,
creative, fruitful, loving silence of final union
with the Beloved. This silence then, will break
forth in a charity that overflows in the service
of the neighbor without counting the cost.[6]

Always this marriage of contemplation and action. Always
this injunction to pray and to serve.

Catherine de Hueck Doherty

LEARNING SILENCE / LEARNING PRAYER

In all her outreach centers of Madonna House, Catherine encouraged the creation of *poustinia*—a room or two, or a small hut, set aside for the solitary retreatant. Like many great teachers of prayer, Catherine was realistic in advising us about what to expect when we first entered into the *poustinia*, or any other retreat setting. She knew the modern mind well; she appreciated the difficulty a woman would face in silence when her ordinary life was filled with noise and busyness.

"Relax," she advised. First of all, the entry into the *poustinia* is no big deal. "Be simple," she said. Be honest about what happens. Don't be expecting great mystical revelations or instant enlightenment.

> Sometimes we are so exhausted mentally, morally and physically that we just can't do much of anything. Going into the *poustinia* we just flop down....It may be that you will only sleep for the first few hours, in which case remind yourself that you are sleeping in the arms of God. Don't put on some fancy spiritual face. Just let yourself be, exactly as you are, exactly as God has always known you to be.[7]

Anyone who has ever tried to meditate knows that the wild mind rises up at every turn to distract her and thus convince her that she can't do it or isn't "doing it right." Here again, relaxation is the recommendation. The Tibetan Buddhist teacher, Chögyam Trungpa Rinpoche, expressed this beautifully when he said: "Take a friendly attitude towards your thoughts." Catherine reiterated that such distraction was natural. It takes time to learn silence, to relax enough to fall into silence. In the meantime, she suggested an exquisite image to help in the process:

For those of you who go into the *poustinia* for a day or two, this is the essence of it: to fold the wings of your intellect. In this civilization of the West everything is sifted through your heads. You are so intellectual, so full of knowledge of all kinds. The *poustinia* brings you into contact first and foremost with solitude. Secondly, it brings you in contact with God. Even if you don't feel anything at all, the fact remains that you have come to have a date with God, a very special rendezvous. You have just said. . . "Lord, I want to take this 24, 36, 48 hours out of my busy life and I want to come to you because I am very tired. The world is not the way I want it, and neither am I. I want to come and rest on your breast as St. John the Beloved. That's why I have come to this place." Or you might say, "Lord, I don't believe in you. I don't think you exist. I think you are dead. But they tell me that in this strange little cabin in the midst in the woods you might be alive. I want to come in and see. May I?" There are a thousand reasons why a person might come to a retreat like this, but the essence is the folding of that intellect that makes so many towers of Babel and is still doing it—and opening the heart that alone can receive the word of God.[8]

"It takes a long time to become young," Picasso said. And the same can be said of learning silence.

In the spirit of waiting that should characterize all prayer, Catherine advised that we put ourselves in readiness to receive the Word of God. In *poustinia*, one is often graced with an actual word or two that describe a theme for consideration—like *faith*, or *liberation*, or *relaxation*, or *service*. Such words are the gift of the Spirit. Some may light up a person's heart or life, other words may provoke a difficult wrestling with an issue that the soul needs to face. At times there are no words; at others, the word or words will come as a surprise, and only after many hours. Then again, a theme for one's solitude and prayer may be available the moment one enters the *poustinia*.

Sitting with the word that has been given, if any, one simply entertains it, like a friend, allowing insight to arise naturally, if it does, without trying to force anything. Writing about the word is also encouraged, as is accepting all that is given (or not given) in a spirit of tremendous gratitude, even though the rational mind might not approve of what enters in.

When the *poustinik* left her place of refuge, Catherine encouraged her to share what she had been given with the community or friends who had supported her. The idea was made clear: what is given in *poustinia* is for the world.

ALL FOR OTHERS

The *poustinik* was a man or woman who had sacrificed his or her life for others. In striking contrast, spirituality in our times has a tendency to degenerate into self-obsession. Many of us will admit that a preoccupation with understanding the psychological motivation of everything has infected our relationship with God, drawing us into an intellectual or analytical mode which closes off the domain of the heart. We can become so obsessed with our own growth and self-development that we lose sight of the pain and suffering of the world around us. Precisely here the *poustinik* of old can be a tremendous teacher for us.

I know that words like *sacrifice, penance, mortification, surrender, atonement* are far from popular these days. We may have thrown them out with the bath water of a childhood religious experience based on fear and guilt. (And perhaps rightly so). Yet, I'm convinced that such concepts bear reassessment.

In one of the most memorable stories in her book, *Poustinia*, Catherine recalls an incident that her father told her, about his meeting with an old friend who had become a *Urodivi*. Somewhat like the *poustiniki*, the *Urodivi* had embraced voluntary poverty to live among the poor. This man, well-educated, wealthy and accomplished, had one day just left it all behind. Years later, in the midst of a crowd outside a church in Kiev, Catherine's father recognized the familiar face of his old friend—one, in a group of many blank-eyed retarded persons. The once-wealthy man looked sick and worn. When her father approached the old friend, the man's eyes again sparkled, and he returned an embrace full of warmth. As they talked and shared a meal together the *Urodivi* explained his life's vocation: "I am atoning for the men who have called Christ a fool during his lifetime and during all the centuries thereafter."[9] Is this any different than the dedication of Mother Teresa who served the wounded Christ by caring for the poorest of the poor in Calcutta and around the globe? Or the missionaries of Madonna House who witness to a life of prayer and work-service in their marketplaces at the dead-ends of the world?

Many *will* call such actions foolish—a kind of psychological illness, even. But, for the man or woman who intuits the need for waking up, such stories are instructive. These stories remind us that we do not enter upon this path alone. We enter as a part of a larger body of humanity knowing (or at least wanting to know better) that whatever we do, individually, in the *poustinia* or in the marketplace, will have its effect upon the whole.

Contemporary biologists and physical scientists attest that we are all part of one energetic matrix (a morphogenetic field, Rupert Sheldrake calls it). Larry Dossey, M.D., author of *Prayer is Good Medicine* (New York: HarperSanFrancisco, 1995) has surveyed the literature on controlled experiences in the efficacy of prayer. Important studies by Timothy Wirth and R. Byrd show that people who are prayed for, whether they know they are being prayed for or not, recover more quickly and more completely than those who are not prayed for.[10] My actions, my thoughts, and my prayers *do* affect you, and yours affect me. In the domain of the heart, time and space are irrelevant. Is it then so hard to believe that one could actually participate in relieving the sufferings of humanity in war-torn parts of the Earth by raising our hearts from the center of our quiet sanctuary?

BUILDING THE *POUSTINIA* OF THE HEART

For one who has never had the experience of "walking on holy ground" which a retreat in a monastery or a visit to an ashram can afford, for one who has never felt the immense silence and emptiness created by a weekend of sitting *zazen*, for one who has never done any outdoor backpacking, sleeping under the star-studded sky, such an opportunity can be an incalculable blessing, granting a taste of the sweetness of infinity.

On the other hand, we may easily create unrealistic expectations about such retreats. Those who have undertaken a lifestyle of contemplation, or participated in an extended meditation session, will attest to the searing boredom, the excruciating loneliness, the temptations to run away, to say nothing of the doubt, the fear, and the insanity of the mind stripped naked. To jump into such a battleground, even for a day or two, one is best prepared by putting time in the boot-camp of daily reflection and simple self-observation. Monica Furlong, author of the book *Contemplating Now*, writes:

> The difficulty about solitude is that it heightens experience. It may therefore either speed the movement towards wholeness (if taken at the right stage in a person's human development), or encourage regression into pathological attitudes. That is why a lot of "inner work" may be necessary before it is right, or safe, to explore the inner territory too far.[11]

A greater challenge for women today may be first to acquaint ourselves with the possibilities for silence, solitude and sanctuary that are around us everywhere, and secondly, to build an inner desert, a *poustinia* of the heart, where we can retreat many times a day to nourish and strengthen ourselves and to pray.

Like a bird's nest, the *poustinia* of the heart is built straw by straw. The persistent bird plucks one weed, flies a distance, carefully places it, and sets wing again to find the next straw. In the case of building a matrix for inner silence and inner prayer, the straws are our daily practices. For years I have told the women in my workshops that doing five minutes of silent sitting once or twice a day, every day, was infinitely more efficacious than planning for or hoping to do one or two hours of prayer or meditation a day, and then feeling guilty when they couldn't manage it.

There are hundreds of ways to remember to pray, or to remember to "listen" to the silence. As a young nun I lived in a four-story novitiate building. All day long, as I worked and went from one assignment to the next, climbing stairs was a constant interlude. A wise novice-mistress taught me that I could use those hundreds of stairs as a means to pray. "Practice recalling the Presence of God on every step," Mother Genevieve counseled. A practice like that can literally change a life. Just think of how many opportunities there are in the course of a day to remember the *poustinia*? Eighteen stairs to climb? Remember. Twenty-three dishes to be washed? Remember. How many times a day do I look in the mirror? (Ever ask yourself what you are *really* looking for?) What about using that magic mirror as a reminder to take a deep breath and attend to the silence?

The constant use of a short repetitive prayer is another way of building the *poustinia* of the heart. In fact, the Prayer of the Heart, originally the domain of a select group of initiates within Russian Orthodox Christianity, is now commonly used by many people who have read and studied it. "Lord Jesus Christ, Son of God, have mercy on me a poor sinner." These words, spoken to and "from" the heart, tend to focus the practitioner at the place within the body where psyche and soul are wedded. In many different religious and esoteric systems the heart center or heart *chakra* is the jumping off point for movement into higher domains of consciousness.

Teachers of both Hindu and Buddhist practice give *mantras*, or empowered words or sounds, to their students. More than just a means of remembrance, repeating a *mantra* is used for the vibrational resonance which these select sounds and syllables ef-

43

fect in the physical body, as well as for the cumulative effect such sound creates in the larger vibrational field of the environment. On a more personal level, continuous *mantra* (singing and chanting does the same) builds up a "charge" (not unlike an electric charge) which can change the energy field of the practitioner, putting him or her into greater resonance with the teacher or guru who has empowered the *mantra*.

The *poustinia* of the heart is built by bringing conscious attention to the activities of every moment. Such attention tends to slow us down. Catherine Doherty spoke of it as the necessity for standing still.

It is easy to get taken up in the whirlwind of daily activities, forgetting a larger purpose. Slowing down, consciously, allows one to see the small things, to savor the beautiful things that are missed when rushing overtakes the day. Years ago, as a new student of the ancient art of Tai Chi, I stood still and moved deliberately in what can best be described as "slow motion." I remember the first time that, in the midst of my practice, I looked at the trees being blown by the wind and actually saw the branches enacting the same dance that I was doing in my exercise routine. Nobody had to tell me, in that moment, that life was all one piece. Faith in such concepts as "all is one" was replaced by bodily experience. And so it is with other deliberate forms of slowing down.

The meditative walking of zazen, the conscious deep-breathing of Yogic *pranayama* practice, the movements of Tai Chi, the focused attention on the ritual movements and words of the Consecration of the Mass, these are the means by which we may sacramentalize every moment of our lives. Then, the *poustinia* of the heart, formerly confined to the inner world, a place where one retreats for silence and sanctuary, actually reverses itself, turning the practitioner inside-out in the process. The whole world (or the marketplace, as Catherine Doherty liked to say) becomes the *poustinia*. One lives in the silence, the solitude, and the sanctuary of the *poustinia* whether she is formally "practising" or not. Such was the life and work of this great woman.

SELECTIONS FROM CATHERINE DOHERTY'S WRITINGS

About Prayer

Thousands of books have been written on prayer. I don't suppose God minds the books, but I think he wants you and me to *be* the book. He wants us to *be* the word. He wants us to reflect his face. It's as simple as that. How do we do it? We pray....

If you want to know what prayer is like, listen to a child of two or three. When we address God in a childlike way, that's a prayer. When we fall in love with someone and begin slowly, shyly, reticently, to explore each other's lives as lovers do, that's prayer. When we are husband and wife, having entered into the fullness of our love in the great sacrament of matrimony, and experience the tremendous silence of a unity that is both physical and spiritual, that silence is prayer.

Loneliness can be prayer, for every man and woman, married or single, in every vocation, at some time, is lonely. When that terrible loneliness comes upon us, a cry wells up deep in our hearts like the cry of a mute person, and rises to God. That cry is prayer.

How can you define prayer, except by saying that it is love? It is love expressed in speech, and love expressed in silence. To put it another way, prayer is the meeting of two loves: the love of God and our love. That's all there is to prayer.[12]

Prayer is the passionate desire of a human being to become one with God. It is the slow discovery

that in order to reach this union, one must be dis-
possessed of one's very self. There is a deep mystery in all this, and I am not good at probing mysteries. I wait for God to explain them, if he so
wishes, or else I accept them without explanation.
Patience is the key word here.[13]

About Service

The real answer to our modern problems, whatever they may be, is to turn toward God with lifted
hands, moved by love, trusting in God's promises
and mercy. There is no other answer. If one stands
in intercession with uplifted hands, as Moses did,
then the miracle of God's action will take place. It
seems strange, but the prostration of prayer, the
dance of prayer, the rock-stillness of prayer, or whatever form prayer may take, floods the whole world
with action. He who turns his face to God in prayer
is in the eye of the hurricane, the eye of action.[14]

About Silence

A pure heart is a silent heart. It is a heart that
watches carefully over its words. This doesn't mean
that one doesn't speak. The silence is the silence
of love. My heart is silent, and thus there is created an inner space where I weigh my words. The
words that come at me from without also enter
into silence and are evaluated there, not in accordance with my emotions, but in accordance with
my love. Into this great pool of silence can be
thrown all sorts of hurtful words, words that make
me feel rejected and abandoned. The silence of
love, coming from a pure heart, will examine with
wisdom all that is said to me, and this love will
determine my response.

It is like a laundry. The words that are thrown
at me go through the cleansing process of love,
faith, silence and hope.[15]

EVERYDAY WOMEN OF PRAYER

While I know that prayer can happen in the midst of chaotic
activity, like many busy women I often struggle with finding quiet
time to pray, in a more leisurely way. Prayer is a lot like lovemaking,
our waiting in a mood of relaxation and receptivity is the foreplay.
One can't just sit down and expect that the Beloved or the infinite
silence will descend immediately, according to our time schedules.
So, the issue of when to find this "leisure" for prayer is significant.

Mother Tessa Bielecki, a radiant-looking and enthusiastic
contemplative monk and the spiritual director of three Catholic
monastic foundations, is unapologetic in her answer to the question of time for prayer. "We must steal it," she says with a characteristically playful smile, echoing the words of her great spiritual
mother, Teresa of Avila. We "steal" time for prayer, Mother Tessa
elaborates, in the same way we would steal time away from our
business ventures if we needed to attend an important seminar; or
the way we steal time from household tasks when we need to plan
for a special party. We simply make it a priority, and somehow we
work it out. What if a long-awaited lover were coming to town?
Where would we steal time for that? Most likely from our sleep.
The silent hours of the late night or early morning are the times
for lovers.

This lesson, of using the night hours for prayer, was impressed
upon me as a young adult. The Mother Superior of the Ursuline
Sisters (the order of Catholic nuns to which I belonged for many
years) was a woman with huge responsibilities. Her nuns staffed
houses in several countries so her job required that she be a tireless correspondent and financial planner, as well as the spiritual
counselor for hundreds of her "sisters." In one lecture, which I will
never forget, she told us that no matter how busy or critical her

work became she always put business away to attend to the *Grand Silence*, the period from evening prayers (about 8:30 p.m.) until after morning prayers the following day. "The time of the *Grand Silence*," she said, "is my time with my Beloved."

Eileen Caddy, the co-founder of Findhorn, was another women who learned that she must steal time from sleep in order to pray. Her daytime hours were filled with business and the enormous demands of establishing a flourishing farm, spiritual community and education center on a rocky and formerly barren coast in Northern Scotland. Consequently she used the nights for prayer and contemplation.

In her enticing book, *Holy Daring*, Mother Tessa Bielecki goes on to say that besides stealing time we can also reclaim time that normally would be spent on less productive activities. The time we spend looking at ourselves in the mirror might be a perfect place to start, as would be the time we spend worrying, or watching TV, or doing things for people as a way to win their approval. Her third recommendation for creating time for prayer is to celebrate a Sabbath—whether that is the traditional Saturday or Sunday, or a Sabbath of our own design, like a few hours on a Tuesday morning when we block out our appointment books and steal away to the local church or to a favorite nature setting, to do nothing but appreciate the silence.

A woman in one of my seminars, the mother of three children, stole her time early in the morning before the children were awake. "I would go into the bathroom, fill the tub with water, and climb in for one hour before anybody in the house was up. And even if they were, who would begrudge mother her morning bath? Little did they know that was my time of prayer. I wouldn't miss it for the world." Depending upon our life circumstances, we will have to be creative in setting up a time for daily prayer.

We will also have to resist the fear that such diminished sleep will de-energize us. Quite the contrary, prayer time can be revitalizing in a way that makes an extra hour of sleep irrelevant. A balanced approach is always suggested, and is essential for beginners. A half-hour or hour of silent time is usually all that is necessary. Beyond that, the Spirit will be the guide. While some may be led to extraordinary practice, most of us will do well to establish simplicity and consistency as the guidelines in our daily approach to prayer.

Women who feel a stronger call to prayer can establish a physical place of sanctuary within their homes. Catherine Doherty suggested that one could convert a closet into a chapel, or hang a cloth to separate off a prayer chamber from the rest of one's bedroom or office. It continually amazes me how secular our homes have become, even for those of us who claim to be living a spiritual life. Who dares to create a shrine or altar in the midst of her living room? What would visitors think? Instead, it is most common to see a living room designed around a television set. Interesting furniture and art prints have replaced the icons and altars of the *poustinia*. No wonder we have difficulty in remembering our purpose.

In my bedroom I have devoted a corner of the room to my *puja* table. *Puja*, a Sanskrit word, is a ceremony of ritual purification, usually done with incense and light. On the table, which I have decorated with blue silk, the picture of my spiritual teacher has the center place of honor. Fresh flowers, incense and a candle adorn the picture. Every night, before bed, I light the candle, and sit down to enjoy the silence in remembrance of my teacher's enormous benediction in my life. In the morning, particularly on those mornings when I am not joining my friends for a group meditation, I sit in front of this shrine for an hour or more. I light the candles and use the incense for any special occasion. Hearing of the death of a friend or family member, I go to the *puja* table. Feeling the sting of ego following a disagreement with my husband, I go to the *puja*. Overjoyed at the good news of some project I am working on, I go to the *puja*. As a nun I did a similar ritual in approaching the altar. Over time, then, my attention to this humble shrine actually serves to empower it. Almost as if it becomes "soaked" with the impressions of many hours of prayer. Going back to the *puja* each day, like going to my writing desk, the Spirit knows where to find me. Whereas it might ordinarily take time to relax into silence, praying in an empowered spot facilitates the relaxation. Somehow the mind and body have gotten the message, loud and clear, that this posture, in this location, are the posture and location of prayer.

When I travel I take along a "traveling *puja*"—a small picture, a silk scarf to adorn the night table of the Motel 6, plus a stick of incense to chase away the aromas and the distracting energy vibrations of the people who have worried there before I entered. These accoutrements are often enough to re-establish the mood of sacred remembrance that I have in my home. I also bring along a thin cotton prayer shawl—indistinguishable from a large head scarf. Like the veils worn by nuns or Islamic women, I use this shawl to cover my head and to create a natural means of sheltering my eyes from wandering. Instead, this shawl serves like my cotton chapel. I envelop myself in it, like those wings of silence that Catherine Doherty spoke about. With these simple props I have established a means of remembrance for myself no matter where I go.

A New Way of Seeing

I do not require of you to form great and curious considerations in your understanding: I require of you no more than to *look*.

—St. Teresa of Avila

There are many benefits to prayer. For some, prayer is a much needed rest from the insanity of over-stuffed lives. For others, prayer opens the heart in a way that inspires generosity and service. For Catherine Doherty and other mystics, prayer is the communion of lovers.

Evelyn Underhill (1875-1940), one of the foremost authorities on mysticism, described the man or woman of prayer or mystical understanding, of any spiritual tradition, as one who had attained a union with Reality. The mystic longs to see things as they *really are*, without the screen of separation which distorts everything; a striking contrast to the vision of the "plain man" whose universe is full of ". . .conventional waves, first seen in pictures and then imagined upon the sea; of psychological situations taken from books and applied to human life; of racial peculiarities generalized from insufficient data, and then 'discovered' in actuality; of theological diagrams and scientific 'laws,' flung upon the background of eternity as the magic lantern's image is reflected on the screen, ..."[16]

I think we all have a capacity for (albeit in different degrees), such a new way of seeing. Most of us have had "peak experiences" in our lives that have granted us a view of the big picture, if only for a moment. We have known those timeless glimpses in which there was no separation between ourselves and the life around us. But, like the fantastic insight afforded by a drug-induced high, such experiences fade. To hold to them, moreover, trying to reproduce them, can become a serious distraction. To think that the enlightened life will be a series of one such blissed-out moment after another for all eternity is to seriously limit Reality. Rather, we need to de-sensationalize such moments, and bring this kind of seeing that Underhill describes into our simple, everyday experience.

Courage will be needed for such a task, however. We might imagine that we would be much safer and happier living in such a domain of bliss, yet the mystic instructs us to give up any and all fantasies on this path. Persistence is needed; the mind trained to wander and obsess in dreams will not easily be focused on what is immediately at hand. Humility is needed, when day after day, hour after hour, we have to keep starting over, a rank beginner.

Underhill instructs us in her simple, yet highly confrontive and compelling book, *Practical Mysticism*, in a method for enhancing this entry into Reality. Her recommendations, drawing heavily upon the writing of Teresa of Avila (1515), rest upon a three-stage/ three-element practice: first, a training of attention, second, a purification of the will by the cultivation of discipline towards non-attachment, and third, by the development of an attitude of passive alertness to the flow of life around us.

About the first step in the training of attention, the idea here is to "re-collect" the many scattered threads of attention which keep us anywhere but here and now. Underhill writes:

> Turn your consciousness inward...Retreat to that point whence all the various lines of your activities flow, and to which at last they must return. Since this alone of all that you call your "selfhood" is possessed of eternal reality, it is surely a counsel of prudence to acquaint yourself with its peculiarities and its powers.[17]

The next step, the purification of the will, provides an even greater challenge to the man or woman who wants to see, clearly. Evelyn wastes no protocol in asserting the point here:

> The very mainspring of your activity is a demand, either for a continued possession of that which you have, or for something which as yet you have not: wealth, honor, success, social position, love, friendship, comfort, amusement. You feel that you have a right to some of these things ...
>
> These dispositions, so ordinary that they almost pass unnoticed, were named by our blunt forefathers the Seven Deadly Sins of Pride, Anger, Envy, Avarice, Sloth, Gluttony, and Lust. Perhaps you would rather call them—as indeed they are—the seven common forms of egotism. They represent the natural reactions to life of the self-centered human consciousness, enslaved by the "world of multiplicity"; and constitute absolute barriers to its attainment of Reality. So long as these dispositions govern character we can never see or feel things as they are; but only as they affect ourselves, our family, our party, our business, our church, our empire—the I, the Me, the Mine, in its narrower

or wider manifestations. Only the detached and
purified heart can view all things—the irrational
cruelty of circumstance, the tortures of war, the
apparent injustice of life, the acts and beliefs of
enemy and friend—in true proportion; and reckon
with calm mind the sum of evil and good. Therefore the mystics tell us perpetually that "selfhood
must be killed" before Reality can be attained.[18]

It is certainly beyond the scope of this book to provide in-
depth training or guidance in this vast arena of prayer, meditation
and contemplation. Many fine books are available along these lines,
and I strongly recommend finding a spiritual teacher or guide, or a
meditation teacher; someone who witnesses to this type of seeing.
For our purposes here, I suggest that if we seriously desire what
Underhill is recommending that we be prepared for the long haul.
It is completely unrealistic to expect that the habits of a lifetime,
reinforced by the cultural conditioning of millennia, will unloose
their grasp in a weekend workshop or a fifteen-minute, eyes-closed,
deep-breathing session.

A Prayer of One's Own

Beth and I sat before the fireplace one night to talk about
prayer—a rare and pleasant opportunity for us to share insights
and encouragement about a subject of interest to both of us. I have
always thought of Beth as a natural mystic, one whose inner vision
shows up in her appreciation of nature, her blazing involvement
with life, and her tremendous generosity of spirit.

Her questions were intriguing, starting with, "What kinds of
environments are more conducive to prayer?" and "How do you
keep going to prayer even when you are feeling dry and discouraged?" Soon, however, she was asking about particular methods of
prayer, and then moving on to ask me about my experiences in
prayer. That's when my inner warning bell sounded. My hunger
for Reality has led me to study the writings of the great mystics,

which have instructed and inspired me. But frequently, that inspiration has bled into imitation of their form of prayer or practice in a way that has been detrimental to me over the years. I have often tended to compare myself with others, and then to denigrate my own experience when it didn't match up to theirs.

I have met remarkable women—women whose lives reflected a simple and joyous apprehension of Reality—who have never read a single treatise on prayer or the mystical life. I have met others who could talk with authority about the stages of the spiritual journey, yet lacked the kind of spontaneous appreciation of life that characterized their less educated sisters. I told Beth that. I urged her to trust the way in which prayer was currently unfolding in her heart, rather than to try to understand how I prayed. I recommended that since she had a spiritual teacher whom she trusted, she could call upon her teacher's guidance (both interiorly and externally, as necessary) to show her what the next step was in her prayer life.

There are common elements that seem to characterize prayer and meditation across cultures, but, as far as I'm concerned, the most important recommendation to prayer and meditation is to "just do it." Align with one approach, one spiritual tradition, one respected teacher and then follow that approach, diligently. As the teacher's instructions become deeply absorbed and integrated, the inner teacher is awakened. At this point, it is anybody's guess where or how one will be led. The Spirit moves where and however it will. If we maintain close contact with a trusted spiritual advisor or spiritual teacher within our tradition, we will know when it is time to let go of the preliminaries and when and how to take that next step which our soul seems to be yearning for. In most cases, we will not even have to ask. It will be given to us.

Brother David Stendl-Rast, a contemplative monk and respected writer on the spiritual life, suggests that to irrigate the land on the other side of the desert we would dig one deep channel so that the source-water would flow in a directed path. To dig numerous shallow trenches is to risk having the water dry up before it gets much beyond the source. If we wanted to be an Olympic ice-skater (to use a more mundane example) we probably couldn't be an Olympic diver at the same time. Each of these disciplines requires full-time dedication and concentration. To try to balance the two would be to invite mediocrity in both.

To try out too many approaches to prayer before one is firmly grounded in one approach is to dissipate the energy of transformation that could be generated by consistent practice. Staying a beginner in each of twelve daily disciplines from a variety of traditions may not be a bad way to spend one's life, but, it may also prove ultimately dissatisfying. The idea of being an apprentice in any art or trade is that someday we graduate to being a master. When prayer forms are many, one can seriously undermine the possibility of plumbing the depths that one path, intensely pursued, can afford.

The distractible mind will often suggest that we hesitate when things get difficult: "Stop and try a different approach." And while it is also true that "giving up," in the sense of surrendering, is assuredly part of the journey, in prayer (as in the field of sports) it is often simply a matter of getting through the wall of resistance or fatigue before the second wind, that new, more expanded view of the horizon.

Our paths of prayer and meditation will differ in the degree of our social involvement. For some of us, our prayer will be developed within the world of our home and family. For others, the vocation to prayer will call us into places of high visibility within the community and even the world at large. There should be no comparison here too. The precious New Testament story of Martha and Mary will serve to guide us in this respect.

MARTHA AND MARY FOR OUR TIMES

Martha and Mary were the sisters of Lazarus, a much-loved friend of Jesus. In one of two stories in the New Testament in which Jesus is reported to have wept, one story relates his sorrow upon learning of the death of Lazarus. It was this love that apparently inspired a great miracle—Jesus called the dead man from his tomb, and Lazarus came back to life. Such was Jesus' love for this family.

Throughout his public life (and who knows for how many years before that), Jesus was a frequent guest at the home of Martha, Mary and Lazarus. And it was on these occasions that the two sisters each performed her tasks of love. Mary would sit at the feet of her beloved teacher, listening to his stories, asking him questions, or perhaps only silently gazing at him with love, while Martha would bustle around the house, cleaning, cooking, preparing the space in all the ways she knew; loving him in her own way.

One day Martha must have been feeling a bit overwhelmed by her sense of duty. She was undoubtedly the perfectionistic type who flourished with doing the jobs of four people, loved busyness and creativity, but sometimes resented the interior demand that these inner drives placed upon her. When that happened, instead of simply lowering her expectations of perfection, or asking for the help she might need, Martha would look at her sister, lazing gracefully at the Master's feet, and feel deprived or abandoned. Then she might release her frustrations upon Mary. "Master," she cried out that day, "Tell my sister to help me. There is so much work to be done."

Jesus's reply to Martha has come down through history as a gentle rebuke. "Martha, Martha," he said, and one can almost hear the sweet pleading in his tone as he spoke her name twice, "You are worried and troubled about so many things, but one thing only is needed. Mary has chosen it, and it will not be taken away from her."

Often I have heard this story told as a call to contemplation at the expense of the path of active service. But that seems unlikely. This same Jesus would urge his followers to go forth and teach all nations—to feed the hungry, to clothe the naked, to visit the sick and dying. Surely he was not suggesting that only those privileged to live in a cloistered monastery are doing the right thing.

I believe that the injunction to Martha is rather an injunction to a different kind of service. Martha is being invited to animate her every activity with an interior focus of Divine communion, similar to what Mary is reveling in as she sits quietly at the feet of her Beloved. Martha is not being told to stop working, even though that may be helpful when her neurotic need for cleanliness, or order, or "fair is fair"-ness has temporarily obscured her deeper knowing that she is loved for *who she is*—which includes her desires for service, order, cleanliness, but is not limited to her accomplishments in these areas.

Further reflection on this story expands the individual personalities of Martha and Mary into archetypal forces in creation. The one—the force of passive receptivity. The other—the pull to active service. Aren't these two archetypes, Mary and Martha, present in most of us? Aren't they often in conflict with one another? Don't we often fall into a mood of self-judgement and even self-hatred at one or the other of these women, whom *we are*? Are we ever judgemental of our sisters who do less than we do, or jealous of the vocation of those who seem called to do more?

The mystic and social reformer, Simone Weil, who spent years of her life working anonymously among the poor in Paris factories, wrote that our times are calling for a new type of contemplative— one who can combine both contemplation and action. It is time to appreciate that both are called for, and that different degrees of either will be appropriate at differing times of our lives, and for different needs. We need to love Martha as she shows up in our lives. We need to encourage and nourish her with the recognition that she is as dearly the bride of the Beloved as is her sister Mary who sits in silence. And vice versa. We need to love Mary as she shows up in our lives, daring to give ourselves the creative leisure for prayer and contemplation that alone will satisfy her. Acknowledging that her contribution is as vital and dynamic as that of her laboring sister.

3

THE PATH OF WAITING:

The Way of Surrender

*We have only as much being
in accordance with what we can bear.*
— Madame Ouspensky

I don't like to wait. I've been ill prepared for it.
Instead, I've been encouraged and rewarded for
taking the hard and fast route—for making things
happen, for pushing against deadlines, for demanding results.

Instant gratification, certainly one of the characteristics of
our times, has infected me. I buy my clothes and my new washing
machine with a credit card, feeding the fanaticism of material acquisition and undermining the value that waiting and saving gives
to things. When I'm hungry, I want to be able to satisfy that hunger immediately. I get frustrated when a movie doesn't start on
time in the theatre, or when the meeting doesn't open when the
schedule says it should. I've got such a busy life that I can't afford
to waste time, and I resent it (actually I take it personally) when
other people don't recognize that I AM HERE and get on with
things so that I CAN MOVE ON!

I've come to expect and appreciate fast service—in overnight mail, in my computer's operation, and most of all, in myself. Yet, in other domains of my life—particularly in the cultivation of my friendships, in my growing intimacy with my husband of over twenty-five years, and in the enriching of my inner life of prayer and remembrance—here I am constantly thwarted. Pushing doesn't work to bring me into greater communion with my friends. Neither is there an overnight train to transformation, despite the myriad claims of workshops and programs being offered today for hungry seekers of the spiritual path.

I am discovering more each day, as I grow in age and my teacher's benediction, that the path to union with God and humanity is essentially a path of surrender. One of the primary "things" I am being called to surrender is my illusion of control in this process of unfoldment. Granted, there are many ways I can willfully orient myself so that I am more likely to fall into the path of the Holy Spirit; yet, here is the paradox again. Spiritual awakening is so closely akin to the process whereby a seed becomes a flower, that it is almost frightening when I realize how little is actually in my own hands. Since when does the seed stand up in the gardener's palm and demand its rightful place in the furrows? Can the seed direct the rain? Like an embryo awaiting birth (another perfect analogy to the surrender necessary in the spiritual process), the flower seed will erupt, out of control, pushing its way through the soil in a paroxysm of agony and ecstasy, when the timing and the environment say so, and not a moment sooner. The way of surrender is a way of waiting.

WOMAN'S WAY

Waiting is woman's way. Her body is built for it. She must wait for the egg to gestate into the child, and this nine months of pregnancy is a flawless parallel to the patience and carefulness, the creativity and fruitfulness, the interiority and depth which will characterize her spiritual life, if she is attuned to it.

When a woman knows how to wait, and is at peace in her waiting, I find it immensely compelling to be with her. When Susan is nursing her child, she rests in a way that I long for. When Lalitha works in the garden, her mood is one of overwhelming abundance and silence. When Tina sits at the bedside of her dying friend, holding her hand and stroking her head, I want to be there too.

There is nothing weak about woman's ability to wait. Her surrender is not resignation, but rather a whole-hearted "Yes" to life as it shows up in both the joyous and excruciating details of everyday existence. When woman is attuned to her own body, she is resonant with and willing to serve the concrete reality of other human needs. And such service usually demands courageous waiting. Take, for example, the image of the women standing at the foot of the cross of Christ (and it was a group of women who stayed 'til the bitter end while the men-folk fled in fear of their lives). These courageous women endured the stripping away of all their hopes and expectations for what Christ was to be for the world. Ann Belford Ulanov, in her article "The God You Touch," describes the fallout of such patient and tangible love:

> All that [their hopes and expectations] is stripped away, annihilated, made into nothing. Yet still the women remain, near the concrete person, wanting to tend the concrete body. They stay through the death of their projections, through the suffering of their disidentifications, stay on through a painful, ignorant, frightened waiting, wanting to receive the utterly new, even if afraid, waiting and wanting even unto the dark coming of his death. They stay on in the dark and through and beyond the dark. And so it is to women that the resurrection is first announced. To the emptied, waiting, disidentified ego, keenly aware of its poverty and its dependence, something special happens. Someone comes.[1]

A woman of the spirit is a woman who waits with both passion and equanimity. Such a woman has felt the hand of God upon her—she has known the sweetness of prayer or intuited the possibilities of what surrender and union can be. And she wants that, fervently.

A waiting woman is a wise woman. She has learned that by struggling, by demanding, or solely by assuming the attitude of rigorous practice (I am going to "go for it." I am going to pray more, and work harder.) she actually rigidifies herself, becoming more judgemental of others and more out of balance with herself. Her body, moreover, may not be able to stand such a masculine "do or die" attitude of commitment. Her headaches, backaches and emotional breakdowns will evidence that. Unless she connects to her own feminine rhythm, until she has access to the company of other women who will model such connectedness and receptivity for her, she may mistakenly come to believe that her suffering is a sign of her spiritual warriorship rather than what it more likely is, the result of her neurotic and egoic attachments to doing things her way!

One of the most excruciating things about waiting is that we don't necessarily know *what* we are waiting for. We don't know the form that our transformation will take. We may give it a name, based on the intuition of the heart; we may even cry out for relief or fulfillment based on the suffering we feel; but, ultimately, we never know if things will be accomplished in the way we imagine they should. Only at the end of the path, it seems, will we realize what it was we awaited. A lifetime of waiting, however, can be a lifetime of love. As the story of Krishna and the *gopis* demonstrated, it is "love in separation" that kindles the greatest passion.

Regrettably, many of us are stuck in a vicious circle of our own creation. We have lost the feminine pole of spiritual practice—the pole of waiting and watching, celebrating and receiving. We have misinterpreted what it means to "take the kingdom of heaven by storm," thinking that the storm was necessarily some kind of battle, rather than a fire within one's breast created by a heart smoldering with love.

IRINA TWEEDIE—A WOMAN WHO LEARNED TO WAIT

The spiritual life of Irina Tweedie has been an immense source of strength and encouragement to hundreds of men and women throughout the world since the publication in 1979 of her book, *Chasm of Fire*, the edited version of the journal she kept while she was in training with her spiritual teacher, a Sufi guru whom she refers to simply as Bhai Sahib (elder brother). Irina Tweedie's story is that of a woman in waiting. The heat, and literal fire, created in her by that waiting, caused her to be slowly and inexorably undone to her past, and transformed into a woman of immense wisdom and compassion. Having surrendered her life at the feet of her guru, Irina Tweedie became, after his death, a spiritual teacher in her own right. For the past thirty years she has worked with hundreds of students from her apartment in North London.

Unlike many young and enthusiastic spiritual seekers who travel to India to sample the wisdom of the east, Mrs. Tweedie was fifty-two years old at the time of her journey. A woman of worldly means, she had been married twice, had studied in Vienna and Paris, played the classical guitar, and loved fashion. In 1954, the untimely death of her much loved second husband, an officer in the British navy, had left her with no financial worries, but absolutely bereft of hope. This vibrant and accomplished woman was cast into the depths of darkness, no longer feeling any reason to live. Her husband had been the focus of her life; she had no children. Without him, what was there to survive for?

Consolation came when a friend took her to the library of the Theosophical Society of London. Here, in one of the first books she read, was a treatise about life after death. Reading that there was no death, as we usually think of it, but only a change of consciousness, Mrs. Tweedie was immensely comforted and intrigued. And thus began her spiritual search.

In 1961, Irina Tweedie traveled to India where she continued her studies at the center of the Theosophical Society in Adyar, near Madras. But, after a time, this study alone was not satisfying her heart. Whatever it was that guided her life had begun to call

63

her in earnest—she desired now to see more of India. With a friend, she set out for the Himalayas, wishing to learn the methods of yoga, and to receive the teachings of great masters (her training in Theosophical work had convinced her of the presence, on earth, of a great brotherhood of ascended masters who were secretly guiding the course of history). When she finally arrived in the city of Kanpur, the destination of one of her friends, she was agreeable and even excited to meet her friend's guru, a great yogi, but nothing had prepared her for the impact this meeting was to have on the rest of her life.

Feeling lighthearted and happy, with a sense that she had "come home" at last to the India she had hungered for, Irina was ushered into the presence of her friend's teacher before she had time to think twice. As she described her first impression, the teacher's presence was so powerful that she immediately felt herself to be in the company of a great man. Her heart stood still, and her breath came in a gasp. Here was something she had not reckoned before; something so outside of her ordinary experience as to leave her without words.

A moment later, the man was gone, after having exchanged a few pleasantries with Irina. But he had invited her to come back to see him the next day. This she did, and thus began her initiation into the workings of a spiritual teacher. For this great man was imminently to become the most significant person in her world; leaving her to report, years later, that prior to meeting Bhai Sahib she had led a completely worthless life. This teacher was to be the catalyst for her transformation, and finally her annihilation into the heart of God.

The story of Bhai Sahib's work with Mrs. Tweedie is the story of a great seduction. The teacher made use of the powerful infatuation of new love to draw her closer to the flame. He wooed her in the sense that he made himself available to her, asking and answering her questions. He invited her daily into his presence to sit with his other students. He dominated her dreams, and insinuated himself into every activity and thought. He occasionally pointed out her stubbornness or prejudices, but essentially these early

Irina Tweedie

months were characterized by a blossoming of love and attachment. This is often the way with spiritual teachers. Without this initial "romance" there would be no ability to bear the pain that will inevitably follow—the pain caused by the burning away of everything that separates one from complete union with the Absolute.

Within three months of her initial meeting, while traveling in a distant city, Irina Tweedie was already aware that her bond to the teacher was extraordinary. Not only did she think constantly of him, she "saw" his face in everything—in flowers, in the waves breaking on the beach, in the faces of people around her. She felt his presence around her all the time. The notion that "the guru is everywhere" was experienced as her moment-to-moment reality, bringing with it untold bliss and rapture.

Since meeting Bhai Sahib, Mrs. Tweedie had felt the intensity of longing for God, which she often described as a burning in the heart. But, with this experience of union with the guru, her longing magnified. My own teacher has said that the guru's job is to break your heart, totally, in such a way that only God can heal you. And certainly this applies to the process Irina went through. For her, the guru was the doorway into a chamber of the heart. But, once inside that chamber, she found an immense labyrinth that had to be traversed. She discovered that although the guru was everywhere, her own attachments, doubts and fears were keeping her from surrendering to that—she was still holding herself as separate from God. Thus began the next phase of her work with her teacher. Returning from her "honeymoon" away, the purification commenced.

The way Bhai Sahib worked with this longing, hungering woman was to keep her at a distance. It was clear by December of 1961 (she had met him in October) that he was treating her differently from everyone else. Most visitors and any students were permitted to sit with him daily, and many quickly entered a state of meditation, *dyanna*, in his presence. Irina, however, was made to wait. And the more he worked with her, the more he would leave her alone, outside of his house, or away from him altogether, for longer periods of time. On some days he did not invite her in at all. Her agony of separation was made all the more acute when she knew that everyone else was inside with him, receiving instruction, enjoying his company, entering these bliss states, while she was feeling abandoned and alone, full of anguish and confusion. Often, he'd send her home, where she had nothing to do but lie in the heat and experience the pain of waiting until she could return to him again.

Imagine the pain of this older, cultured woman being made to wait outside in the rain, being asked to endure the extreme heat of a summer in India, fighting the flies, appalled by the "filth." Imagine the further humiliation of having her teacher seem to spurn her longing looks, neglect to speak to her, accuse her of things that she did not do, or publicly make some disparaging remark to her or about her.

As if these public tortures were not exquisite enough, the pains she suffered alone were even more horrific. Under her teacher's potent influence, she was being purified—forced to face the darkness within herself. In her own words: "I was beaten down in every sense till I had come to terms with that in me which I had been rejecting all my life. . ."[2]

Because her teacher stopped treating her with "love" according to any conventional understanding of the word, she was forced to access Love within herself, at a deeper and more profound level. Bhai Sahib had told her many times that suffering was necessary. If bliss states were all that was given, the disciple would become complacent; he or she would cease to make efforts. Because of the pain, efforts were maintained. So longing, hunger and separation were all ways in which she was kept awake.

Her teacher was relentless. He *had* to be. He was fulfilling a spiritual law that calls forth from a teacher whatever is necessary to meet and satisfy the longing and hunger of the student who approaches with sincerity. Irina Tweedie had, in fact, asked him for nothing less than this relentlessness. "Then help me," Irina had pleaded, "give me longing, intense longing, and sorrow, and fear and love. The other name for longing is love."

"Yes," Bhai Sahib had responded slowly. "Love and longing are one and the same thing. They are synonymous."[3]

Early on in her time with her teacher, Irina had declared that what she wanted was the Absolute. Unlike many seekers who were content to simply ride on a current of bliss, being carried by the master's grace, her questions to her teacher convinced her that so much more was possible. The ultimate surrender, the ultimate annihilation into God, which her teacher pointed to, was the only thing that would satisfy her. And, while this is all well and good in theory, and sounds poetic and holy when spoken, Irina's process instructs us all that we rarely have an idea of what will be involved in achieving the ends to which we ascribe. Early in her diary, before the great purification work even began, she wrote:

> To reach the goal you have to be turned inside out, burned with the fire of love so that nothing shall remain but ashes and from the ashes will resurrect the new being, very unlike the previous one. Only then can there be real creation. For this process is destruction, creation, and love. Another name for love is Pain and Effort.[4]

She longed for God, and she stayed firm in that resolution, despite the immense suffering involved. Her spunkiness, her courage, her outspokenness, her passion for life, the tremendous love which she had for her husband, her attachments to things—all these qualities were turned to good as she engaged her work with her teacher.

Over and over, in interviews, she has been asked what it was that kept her there. Many others would have left long before, convinced that such "abuse" was unjustified. Many more today use the stories of such testing as sorry examples of patriarchal male teachers exerting their power over naive females. And such an interpretation might have gone down in history if Irina's immense resolve had not kept her in place long enough for the effects of this work to flower in her. She was ground down, her personality attacked on every front, and she did not retreat. Instead, she struggled, she questioned, she worked, and most of all she waited and endured. "I could not even put a finger on it, but I knew I could not leave. There was some quality there that would give me a kind of fulfillment, a kind of destiny."[5]

Her teacher taught her about surrender, about how she would have to give up everything to have what she said she wanted. One day as they walked together, she admired the sunset, speaking of how much she loved the Indian sky. When he asked her how many things she loved, Irina replied exultedly, listing the things in nature to which she was attached, all the people she loved. " 'Your heart is like a hotel,' he interrupted darkly. 'One can love only One, you cannot love two masters; either you love the world or you love its Creator.' "

"Oh, Bhai Sahib," Irina sighed.[6] Her sigh, undoubtedly, was her recognition of the degree of surrender and detachment that was being asked of her, and her acknowledgment of the price that was going to exact. She knew in theory, that everything was going to have to go, such that only God would remain. But when that call to detachment took tangible form it required a degree of courage, persistence and faith far greater than she imagined possible.

More tangible than her attachment to birdsong or other wonders of nature, her teacher asked for control of her money so that finally she had nothing to depend on but him. He even requested that she turn over her guitar, the last remnant of her love of classical music. When the money wasn't forthcoming, she fasted, waiting upon his recognition. "I live on potato soup," she wrote in her diary during one period. "The little bit of rice I had was finished a few days ago, as well as a little flour. Have still some sugar left and a little tea."[7]

She took these occurrences as tests of her resolve, and refused to ask for anything beyond what was given. After one grueling ten-day period towards the end of which she was forced to fast on lime juice and water, her teacher finally inquired about her food situation. Learning that she had no money, he passed it off as being an oversight on his part. But Irina would not accept this superficial explanation. She had come to learn, over time, that her teacher knew everything that was going on for her—her dreams, her physical states, her distracted thoughts. "I cannot believe it; and I don't believe it," Irina countered. "If you are the man I know you to be, you must have known. . . ."[8]

Her words are a testimony to the kind of iron-clad faith that Irina was cultivating and relying upon, and a further reflection of a sort of divine madness that was seeping into her life. The fire of longing was causing her to lose her mind—not in the sense that she became dysfunctional or raving, but rather that she was allowing herself to be slowly separated from the conventional world and its reasonable demands. A new way of seeing was being refined in her; her mental understandings were taking a back seat to the movements of her heart.

"Mind is nothing," Bhai Sahib had told her on numerous occasions. The only attitude that would further her work with him would be "the right attitude of the heart."[9] Later he explained:

> To surrender all possessions is relatively easy but to surrender the mind is very difficult. It means one has no mind of one's own. One is like a dead body in the hands of the Master. How is the dead body? It cannot protest.[10]

Having endured the preliminary training, toward the end of her two years in her teacher's company, Irina's growing mindlessness and surrender reflect itself:

> I sat in the doorway. It was cold and draughty. My feet were wet. I began to think whether it was right to let an elderly woman [she was 55 at the time] sit in a cold doorway on a rainy day. But I stilled the mind. A dead body, if it is put in the rain, gets wet. If it is put in the sun it gets scorched. Can it protest? It cannot. Can I protest? I cannot.[11]

Irina Tweedie lived the *sadhana* (spiritual practice) of separation and longing while she was with her teacher, but perhaps her greatest test came when, two years after their first encounter, he sent her back to London, penniless, and with the directive that she was to teach and write. Purportedly he sent her away to hasten her progress along the path and told her:

> Here you cannot work and you must work. We are
> not given for ourselves—never. We are given for
> others. And the more you give, the more you will
> receive. This is how the Essence works.[12]

In London, once again, she would be called upon to wait upon God, completely dependent upon the benediction of her teacher, in the graciousness of friends, in all the events of her life. For another two and a half years she waited. While she wrote to him every week as he had recommended, she received no word from him. Then, just prior to December 1965, as he had predicted before she left, he sent for her.

She returned to spend seven final months with him. Even though her spiritual work was flowering, and she was experiencing more profound revelations of the teaching, together with a firmer and more complete knowledge of her irreplaceable union with her teacher (which was the goal of all her work), she was subjected to ongoing humiliation, trial and testing.

Bhai Sahib had said that the testing would never end as long as the teacher was alive. This was the way it had been with him and his guru. The same remained true for Irina.

Bhai Sahib died in July 1965.

Irina reported, "I felt he had betrayed me. I was desperate, and I felt I needed to be absolutely alone." So, this time she left on her own and traveled to an ashram in the Himalayas. Here, in a sense, she waited to die. For three months she waited, alone and disconsolate.

There one day, in deep meditation, I discovered I could contact my teacher. . . . My teacher was there. I can't explain how . . .He had no physical form; he was just pure power. . . there was total communication, total guidance. . . .At that moment my real spiritual training began. From that moment, I had to lead a double life: a normal life in this world and a kind of constant listening within.[13]

Everything else, all the years of work and struggle and bliss, was just preparation for this.

Concluding her journal in December of 1966, she was able to write without apology or equivocation, that the presence of her Beloved was constant with her, that all was One—the "infinite endless Him"—and that she rested at last in the deep peace of his heart. But she also knew that her work required that she move out again to teach and write. There was no staying on the mountain top. The work of waiting and longing would continue, more exquisitely and more painfully.

I know that I go back to a life of fire. For you, dear Guruji, told me what to expect. I know that sometimes my health will fail, and I shall be burned. But I know also that I can never be alone any more, for you are with me always. . . . You did not deceive me, Guruji. You pointed out the Way, and now the way has taken hold of me . . .fully . . . irrevocably.[14]

THE SADHANA OF WAITING

The desire for God, or Absolute truth, that eventually turns to longing and consumes the human heart in love, is a seed that blossoms slowly over years. We grow in the capacity to yearn, to long, to hunger. Irina Tweedie's journey teaches us that the cultivation and flowering of that longing are the results of our long-term fidelity. It is as if the pain and the longing burn away what is not true, finally emptying us out. Our trials create a deeper and more expanded chasm within the heart, a grander space in which the Lover can dance.

If, however, we defend ourselves against the risk of surrendering, trying to keep our options open at all times; if we tenaciously cling to logical reasoning to determine all our life choices; if we guard our possessions, our opinions, our beliefs and all other personal territories to the point of shutting out any potentially contradictory influences, we literally shrink the soul. One needs to become very big to even approximate a hold on the Infinite. Waiting, done consciously, allows one to grow bigger in emptiness. As hollowness grows, over time, the things we thought we were yearning for will fall away— "Ah, not that, not this..." If one is gratifying every whim, however, there is no momentum for the cultivation of this emptiness.

If we are trained in an appropriate context of waiting for simple things, we build the matrix that allows us to hunger for higher things, since divine grace builds on nature. The discipline, attention and purification that such waiting-practice can generate will form a solid foundation for our spiritual life.

Life gives us so many opportunities to practice the *sadhana* of waiting. The thousands of tiny daily invitations to wait with patience and elegance—like at traffic lights, on lines in the supermarket, being put on hold on the telephone—can be refused, or they can be accepted as moments in which to remember ourselves, to pray, to sing in celebration or gratitude.

Then there are the big waits—like the terrible waiting in darkness when it seems that all hope is gone. Whether this is a bout of depression, the aftermath of a devastating loss, or a genuine dark night of the soul, such periods of waiting test us and refine us as powerfully as any alchemist's fire, teaching us the ways of surrender.

Consider the painful waiting of "not-knowing"—as we await medical test results, or wait to learn if the long-desired pregnancy is

73

viable or not, or wait to find out if our loved one is going to live. In times like these we feel our utter helplessness and vulnerability, since in most cases we can do nothing to change the menu of circumstances that life is serving up to us. It is equally excruciating to wait for the inevitable, for instance, as we take up vigil at the bedside of a friend or family member who is undergoing a slow and lingering death.

For those who have committed to a spiritual path, a similarly painful waiting takes place as, month after month or year after year, one sees one's failures to love, to serve, or to trust, despite all good intentions. It is agonizing to keep crashing into the veils of illusion which keep one separated from God. In times such as these—when we feel that all is lost, when our normal means of dealing with the world and keeping all things under control no longer work—the opportunity for spiritual transformation presents itself. Like Irina Tweedie did, we will probably fumble our way through these trials. But if we keep ourselves in place as she did, if only by the merest thread of intention; if we can voice our desire that this situation be used to draw us closer to the heart of God, or the gateway to the Absolute, or that it be used to fuel the fire that will find us annihilated in love, our suffering will not be wasted.

WAITING FOR MEANING

During many periods in my own spiritual life I have felt tremendous discontent caused by thinking that I should be somewhere else, or doing something else. Reading the stories of great women, moreover, I often had the notion that perhaps I needed to go off to India to work with Mother Teresa's community for a few years, or start some social action program in the inner city. And all of these fantasies reflected a mistaken belief that my life was devoid of purpose or value if I was not doing something grand and dramatic, or something for which the world at large would give recognition and approval.

Serious examination of these thoughts and discontented feelings over many years has revealed their paradoxical nature—such discontent can actually be a very good sign. Rather than being interpreted as some weakness in my *sadhana*, these thoughts may simply be the mind's way of trying to interpret and give form to a wordless longing of my heart which is always hungry for God. "Our hearts were made for thee, O God," wrote St. Augustine in the third century, "and are ever restless until they rest in thee."

My friend Barbara told me a story that perfectly casts Augustine's point in the contemporary metaphor. Late one afternoon, after several hours of running around town doing errands, she and her two young daughters found themselves in a large department store in a shopping mall near their home. Pausing to catch her breath and look around to get her bearings, Barbara reflected aloud, "I don't know what I'm doing here." To which her five-year-old daughter, Amelia, immediately replied: "Yes you do, Mom. You're looking for God."

The sign on my friend Anita's refrigerator door says the same thing in different words: "What you're really looking for is not in here." When we realize that our desperate searching for things to fill up the void left by waiting is really the sign of our spiritual hunger, such a remembrance can be life altering, leading us to ask the question again, "What is it that I *really* want?"

"Fiction is the art form of human yearning," said author Robert Olen Butler, to the audience at a large writer's conference I attended. "A character," he went on to explain, "may be besieged by problems, but that is not yearning. It is our yearning that defines us as human beings."

Think about it: there is no story in union. Merged into the "Light of the One," who is there to speak and who is there to listen? And what are words? The story that inspires and moves us, both in great fiction and in the lives of those around us, is the story of a great yearning.

Ultimately, human beings hunger for many of the same things, although they may call their longings by different names. We all yearn for meaning, for truth, for love, for relationship, for God. Yet, the degree to which we recognize our deepest desires varies greatly. Many live out their whole lives, only recognizing what it was they sought when it is too late to go after it. Others die in self-imposed ignorance, their lives unexamined. The myriad ways in which we choose to work out the fulfillment of our yearnings, these are the substance of human history.

The core questions asked of the spiritual aspirant in any tradition are always the same: "What do you want?" "Why did you come here?" "What are you looking for?" "What do you long for?"

"There is only one question," my teacher has said, "and once the question can be sharpened to a razor's edge of precision, then the answer will be there simultaneously." To sharpen one's question is not something that the mind can do, however. Like the directive Bhai Sahib gave to Irina Tweedie, the ultimate question only arises from the right attitude of the heart. And the heart is not transformed by force of will. Rather, it is slowly melted, the way pure gold is extracted from the ore. It is burned.

Spiritual work then, might be defined as a process of waiting with one's question, until the refining fire has reached the right temperature. Then, into the fire it all goes—question and questioner, answer and answerer alike.

Discontent and restlessness can engender valuable considerations of destiny or vocation. A few years ago I felt the concern of the audience in Boulder, Colorado when Mother Tessa Bielecki, the fiery contemplative monk, expressed her view that many people miss their spiritual destiny because they too quickly buy into the societal program of success, or the conventional form of lifestyle—college, marriage, children, nice house in the country—before they have allowed themselves to question more seriously what it is they really want.

I too have come to appreciate that we each have a "calling," and that this calling will express itself uniquely in each of us. As individual cells in one huge body we are all connected, but we are also specialized as well. One of us is a finger cell, so to speak. Another is a liver cell. A third is a heart cell.

One of the most important aspects of spiritual development and a sign of great maturity in the process, is the ability to wait, to listen, and then to respond to what our particular role in the "Body" is. Instead of thinking of destiny as something outside of ourselves waiting to be discovered, however, it may be more beneficial to think of it as something for which we are internally and externally prepared by life's circumstances, and therefore something that we have only to attune to, by listening within.

One can speak of a calling to a particular occupation, like the work of a doctor or teacher, or to a particular structure or form of life, like the married life, the single life, communal life within a religious organization. Generally, however, one's vocation is usually much more subtle than a choice of occupation. Rather, vocation may refer to a living of the qualities and more refined gifts of the Spirit (like kindness, generosity and compassion) in any lifestyle or occupation. Some of us, I think, are "called" to be enlightened witnesses for children (something that may be done whether one's job is that of an accountant or a nurse). Others are invited to a life of healing through forgiveness and compassion, or to a vocation of prayer or gratitude regardless of the form. I have found, in speaking to hundreds of women over the years of my teaching and workshop presentation, that while we are busy thinking or fantasizing about our calling, we may well be missing the obviousness of our vocation. It is easy to overlook the "calling within the calling." That is, to miss the opportunities for greatness that are being offered to us in small ways every day.

Mother Teresa's vocation didn't start out in the slums of Calcutta. She taught in a school for wealthy girls for over twenty years before she literally heard the call to a different form of service. Because she recognized that her truer vocation, beyond her job, was her intimate love of Jesus, her Beloved, she was able to have the flexibility to drop the external form and substitute another, when that was asked of her. She paid her dues—she earned her calling. She waited.

DIVINE MOTHER WAITS: REMEMBERING MIRYAM OF NAZARETH

The vocation to waiting which characterized the life of the Divine Mother of Jesus provides another opportunity for meditation about this essential aspect of the woman's way of spiritual life. But further, it offers us a chance to reflect upon almost any mother's willingness to wait for her children to come home, no matter how long as it takes. As we come to recognize the presence of the Great Mother in creation, with all her many faces, we will grow in our appreciation of how much she wants us near her.

In Hebrew, the name of the mother of Jesus is Miryam, a word that translates surprisingly as "rebellion." I have long thought, as have many other women (whether theologians or simply lovers of the divine and Blessed Mother), that the picture of Mary I was given in my childhood was a very distorted one. Her purity was so aggrandized and so misunderstood that, by the time we were teenagers, many of us raised in Catholicism knew her as the cool icon of chastity, designed to keep in line those who were feeling the wonder and warmth of emerging sexual energy. For lack of the passionate, voluptuous, raw and compelling Divine Mother Kali or Lakshmi of the East, whom we desperately needed in our Western culture, we were given a mother who more closely resembled a celibate medieval nun.

Nonetheless, as children we loved Mary. To be picked to play the role of the Madonna in the Christmas pageant held in our elementary school each December, was tantamount to canonization. (I was never quite sure why the nuns picked whom they did for this honor. But they never picked me, probably since I would have towered over any grade-school-aged Joseph.) The month of May every year found my sisters and I setting up shrines in our home, decorating them with pink and white facial tissues crunched up to resemble flowers, and crowning the plaster statues of Mary with a floral wreath to celebrate her eminent status as Queen of the May. In a culture devoid of meaningful religious ritual, I consider myself blessed to have found resonance with Mary so early in my life.

In my adolescence I was taught that Mary was the entryway into the Kingdom of God—that in the arms of this Divine Mother, even the most hardened sinner could be shielded and carried into heaven. Running to the feet of this Mother, placing everything in her hands, was a way to circumvent the justice or the wrath of the Father God. Mary was the Mother of Mercy, "our life, our sweetness, and our hope." Being in trouble of any kind, one could count on her.

But if I were called to answer where I really met Mary (as Elyse, my friend and editor asked me one day), I would have to say that it was through meditation upon the mysteries of her life, which are imaginatively commemorated as one "says her beads." I loved to pray the Rosary. (I still do. The parallels of this practice to the *japa* of Buddhist or Hindu practice are astounding.) Since I commuted by train to high school, the rosary was a consoling companion on the daily mile-and-a-half walk home from the station each evening. The recitation of each "decade" (ten) of "Hail Mary's" was supposed to be accompanied by thoughtful consideration of an incident in her life. Besides the five joyful and five glorious events, known as the Mysteries, which I contemplated with all the passion of a budding devotee, the Five Sorrowful Mysteries gave substance, or roundness, to her as an object of love and reverence. Here was no detached idol. Here was a woman who knew pain, far greater than I had yet experienced. Here was a woman who must have cried, a woman who certainly questioned, and a woman who waited, longing, in her pain and silence, faithful to her destiny to the end.

In 1988 I climbed the steep stone steps to the monastery complex of Andechs, in the glorious hills of Bavaria in southern Germany. This popular tourist stop was, as usual, thronged with people drawn there by the promise of the outstanding beer that is made by the resident monks. The Andechs brewery has sustained this religious community for generations.

Making my way to the church that overlooked the beer garden, I sat for a brief time before the high altar, relaxing into the coolness of the ancient stone, and enjoying the silence that many

European churches hold—this one a welcome respite from the shouting festivities below. My attention was eventually drawn to a closed wooden door near the back of the church. A sign on the door requested entry in silence, and I observed a few tourists entering and leaving with a sober air.

Making my way to this door, I opened it gently and stepped inside a tiny chapel that contained only a few chairs. Dominating the space and filling the room with its terrifying and compassionate presence was a statue of the Sorrowful Mother holding the crucified Christ in her arms. Life-size, the figures seemed to breathe. Although painted in gold leaf, nothing detracted from the overriding communication of passion and pain which the Mother's face emanated. This Mary was literally speaking to the tourists (temporarily transformed into pilgrims) who knelt or sat or stood in stunned silence at her feet. There was no gossiping in this chamber. There was no rustling around. Her message was too loud for that. Of those who found their way to this room, most stayed for longer than the usual cursory visit. I sat for nearly an hour, held by her eyes.

The Pieta of Andechs shows Mary's heart pierced by seven swords. I had not thought of this particular mythology about Mary for many years. Sitting there, however, the seven sorrows of her life came easily to mind.

Because Mary had said "Yes" or "Fiat" ("Be it done unto me according to your word") to the invitation of an angel asking her to be the mother of Jesus, her destiny was inextricably tied to his. Not only would her heart be broken again and again on the hill of Calvary (four of the swords: meeting her son as he carries the cross, his crucifixion, the taking of his body from the cross, and his burial), but throughout the life of her child there would arise inexplicable, awesome and fearsome events which she would be called upon to bear: a journey into Egypt to avoid an extermination of first-born Jewish sons; an early prophecy that her child was set for both a glorious and an ignominious end and that she would be called upon to suffer it all with him; and the terror of loss when, at the age of twelve, he disappeared into the crowds of Jerusalem for three days.

The Pieta at Andechs, Germany

This mother's incomprehensible grief has bonded her to the hearts of the poor and suffering throughout the world, for ages. In our own day, the artist Robert Lentz has created an image of the Madonna for El Salvador called: *Madre de los Desaparecidos*, the Mother of the Disappeared. Mary in this painting is dark-skinned. She holds a crown of thorns in her hands, as if presenting it as a reminder. The jungle plants of El Salvador form the background of the picture, which is done in the traditional style of the Byzantine icon. In the lower left-hand corner of the painting, a stark white handprint desecrates the sacred image—the white hand is the symbol of one of the El Salvadorian death squads.

China Galland, an author whose quest for an understanding of the Green Tara of Tibet brought her full circle to the feet of the Black Madonna in her own hemisphere and around the world, wrote of her impression of Lentz's painting:

> This is a Mary we have not seen in the West. This is a Mary that we need now, a fierce Mary, a terrific Mary, a fearsome Mary, a protectress who does not allow her children to be hunted, tortured, murdered, and devoured.[15]

Looking at Mary's surrender to her destiny and her fierce courage in fulfilling that destiny through the depths of sorrow as well as the heights of ecstasy, brings her close to all of us who suffer in any way.

This Woman inspires my own courage, and devotion. Her story is the story of every woman who seeks union with God. After all, aren't we each invited to conceive the Sacred One within our own bodies? Aren't we each called upon to wait for the overshadowing of the Holy Spirit in a spirit of openness such that the seed of Divinity will find a receptive vessel in which to grow? Is it not our job to nurture the God Within over nine months (nine years, ninety-nine years) by our healthy and devotional and attentive practice, honoring the body, celebrating the mystery of life that is taking place within us, using the company of other women to teach us and inspire us in the ways of being mother? Is it not our task to give birth to that Son of God—in the myriad forms of our family life, our work and our art, our kindness, generosity and compassion? Are we not called upon daily to trust the unfolding of the Divine plan regardless of apparently contradictory circumstances? Are we not compelled, because of our love for our families and friends, and even for all human beings, to walk the path of sorrow, illness, dissolution, and death with them? Are we not asked, like Mary was asked after Christ's Ascension back to heaven, to wait, helplessly and hopelessly at times, for the fiery infusion of the Holy Spirit to empower our work?

"There are many paths to God, but the way of Mary is the sweetest and most gentle," spoke the Sufi, Hamid, to his wide-eyed pupil, Reshad Field. Making their pilgrimage to Ephesus, the site of Mary's house after the death of Christ, Hamid instructed Reshad in the role of Mary in one's life:

> If you can melt into Mary, the matrix, the blueprint of life, the Divine Mother, you will be formed and shaped in Christ and Christ in you and thus through the breath of God's Mercy you will come into being and know Him.[16]

I first read this startling passage in 1977, shortly after Field's book, *The Last Barrier*, was published. This esoteric understanding of Mary's archetypal position in the Middle-Eastern spiritual hierarchy was intriguing. This passage brought me full circle to a rediscovery of Mary's value in my adult life, and reminded me of the devotion of St. Louis Marie de Montfort, a seventeenth century French priest who advised that one be always in relationship with Jesus as he was "*in sinu Mariae*," in the womb of Mary.

I remember vividly the night I read this passage to my husband, and how we both cried at the recollection of our relationship with Divine Mother, which had fallen by the wayside in the years of our spiritual search outside Catholicism. Mary had found her children once again, seeking them out from where they were

Our Lady of Guadalupe. Folk art, on canned-ham lid.

hiding, welcoming them back into her arms with a new and enlivened understanding of her role as a model in their spiritual lives.
The morning after this revelation, rising early, I walked through
our living room en route to the kitchen. There, on a shelf among
my houseplants, two orange day lilies bloomed. I was totally unprepared for the sight—I thought the plant from which they blos-
somed was a variety of spider plant, and had no recollection of
having seen buds. I could not have been more surprised if the lilies

had fallen from the ceiling onto my head. Here was the flower that represented the Virgin Mary, a fitting affirmation that my tears had been answered.

Mary was back in my life again. Not in the simplistic, devotional way of my childhood, but in the way of being my introduction to the Divine Mother as she manifests in many cultures, at many periods of history. Without knowing it, I was yearning for the feminine face of the Divine, and Mary was there to point the way—the first step on the journey that continues to Ma.

Author Ann Johnson beautifully expresses the relationship that is possible with the Blessed Miryam if we allow ourselves to meet her in a new place in our hearts, rather than confine her to the images that have been given to us.

> Miryam, my kinswoman,
> I have called your name
>   and you have answered me.
> Across time and space we have journeyed
>   groping through the mist of legend and fantasy
>   squinting between the cracks in the dogma stone
>   sensing delicately the palpitations of your life
>   beneath blue plaster mantles
>   and benign stare-fixed smiles.
> Woman of witness.
> Woman of prayer.
> Woman named the Hebrew name Rebellion.
> Share yourself with me, with us,
>   this day, this time, forever.
>
> Share yourself with those of us who seek
> companionship of this salvific
>   journey of self-knowledge and renewal,
> remembering you are a woman by whose hand
> we were saved,
> ...according to the book of truth and promise,
> the gospel words we read from day to day ...

remembering you are a woman by whose hand
we were saved,
walk with us, our enabling sister,
through the confounding mazes of our time.
We in this moment are the saving hands
joined across the ages of travel in the fertile
wilderness,
a people with dusty feet and hearts that listen
to hidden words,
dancing together around a tent pitched in our midst
in which resides the Shatterer of War and Death.
We are the desert people of winding and colorful design
    weaving and woven
        in the mandala center which is God
           which is our Source and our Shalom.[17]

WAITING IN THE TAVERN OF RUIN

The Sufis write extensively about the power of waiting. The prolific poetry of Mevlana Jalaluddin Rumi, the Islamic mystic of the thirteenth century, celebrates the sublime longing for the Divine Beloved in thousands of verses written to his teacher, Shams-i Tabrizi, in whom Rumi first glimpsed the face of God. After Shams' mysterious death or disappearance, the disconsolate Rumi is said to have whirled endlessly in his grief (the origin of the traditional whirling dervishes) crying out the poetry for which he is remembered.

Who is more miserable
Than the Lover without patience?
This Love is a disease
Without remedy or fantasy.
The cure of Love
Is neither hypocrisy nor moderation.[18]

Rumi's poetry, like other Sufi poetry, is filled with references to wine, to a wine-pourer (Saqi) who constantly fills the waiting cups of his guests, to intoxication or drunkenness, to a Tavern— the Tavern of Ruin—in which the lovers of God wait, endlessly and patiently, for another glimpse of the same Divine Beloved who has destroyed their lives to all conventional values and wisdom, leaving them like fools, drunkards and madwomen.

Reading this poetry, one feels the mood of the Tavern of Ruin to be one of overflowing femininity. Male or female, the lover of God must be soft and humble and receptive. And while "she" waits, she sings of her longing, thereby increasing her passion, sharpening the edge of her desperation, calling down upon her head the fire of annihilation which will ultimately destroy her to herself.

The Sufi saint Rabi'a whose poetry of longing has endured for centuries (she lived from 717 C.E.-801 C.E.) is perhaps one of the greatest exemplars of a woman "ruined" by the power of love. I close this chapter with a few reflections and poems from Rabi'a's work, not because I think the logical mind can appreciate the path she walked, but rather to warm and awaken our similarly yearning hearts.

RABI'A, LOVER OF TRUTH

"Where are you going?"
And she said, "To that world."

"And where have you come from?"
And she answered, "From that world."

"And what are you doing in this world?"
And she said, "I am sorrowing."

"In what way?" They asked of her.

And Rabi'a replied:
"I am eating the bread of this world,
and doing the work of That world…"

In the summer of 1997, at a retreat for women, I met a remarkable dancer and songwriter named Zuleikha. Each day, as the
twenty-four women in our group gathered in a circle, Zuleikha
would open and close the sessions with songs and chants, playing
her harmonium (a traditional Indian instrument) with great fervor. We sang chants to the Great Mother, and songs about the
Native American Spider Woman, all with tremendous warmth
and enthusiasm. But by far the most popular of our invocations,
and the song that became the standard of our group, used at every
opportunity, was Zuleikha's rendition of a poem by the eighth century Sufi holy woman, Rabi'a.[19]

Sung as a dialogue between a questioner and the woman of
God, the song's haunting lines capture the strength, the passion,
the sorrow and the longing that characterized Rabi'a's life. Over
and over our little group would sing the poem's refrain: "I am eating the bread of this world, and doing the work of That world…,"
each woman feeling her own longing. Each in her own way relating to "That world," within her own heart. Each of us, in her own
way, "sorrowing."

Rabi'a lived in Mesopotamia, what is now Iraq. The name
Rabi'a literally means "the fourth" and tradition has it that she
was the fourth child of a wretchedly poor family in the town of
Basra. Supposedly her parents both died in a widespread famine
when Rabi'a was quite young. She and her sisters were separated,
and she was sold as a slave.

Legend recounts that early in her life Rabi'a was freed by the
master who owned her. One night, awakened from sleep by a light
streaming into his bedroom window, the slave-master walked to
the window and looked out into the courtyard below. There, kneeling in prayer, was the young slave girl. Above her head, suspended
in mid-air, was an oil lamp with a flame so bright that it illumined
the whole area like a newly risen moon.

Released from bondage, Rabi'a began wandering. Expecting nothing, she lived completely dependent upon God to supply all her needs. When there was no food, she fasted, praying in gratitude for the opportunity to praise God in that way. Everything that happened to her was interpreted as God's hand in her life, and she desired that her full attention be upon contemplation and worship of the Holy Names.

She lived alone, despite the scandal of such a situation in her times, and usually in the poorest of dwellings—what she called "a ruin," an apt word to describe her house as well as her life in the opinion of the world. As one of her short poem-stories tells, she was given a beautiful home in which to live—the generous gift of one of her devotees. But no sooner had she set foot in the house than she turned and walked out, returning to her ruin. "I was mortally afraid I might fall in love with that house," Rabi'a said.[20]

In terms of the distraction of a normal, married relationship, let alone a marriage of political or social expediency (which was the usual case in her times), she was adamant. To one would-be suitor who had offered a huge dowry she admonished: "As for you: Remember the day of your death. As for me: Whatever bride price you come up with, Understand that the Lord I worship can double it. So goodby."[21]

With regard to the seduction of wealth itself, she made a curious and wise suggestion. To a rich man she counseled: "Better share your inheritance with them [other people], And suffer like they do, the common suffering of the time."[22] Rabi'a saw wealth and comfort as buffers against the suffering that was all around, a vain attempt at best, but one that could feed self-deception for a lifetime.

As Rabi'a matured, her wisdom deepened. Moved by her inspiration, many received her instruction, and her stories and poetry were preserved in the oral tradition. Still today, after many translations and probable alterations, her words still pulsate with life. Rabi'a was a mystic of the highest order, an iconoclast who lived what she preached, a woman of courage who was unafraid to speak out to those who were considered the authorities of the time—whether temporal or religious.

One famous story tells of an ardent devotee of Mohammed who took fourteen years to make his pilgrimage to Mecca, to see the Kaaba, the sacred black stone which stands as the central icon of worship in the great holy city. All along the route this male devotee stopped to pray at shrines, to perform ritual ablutions and to fast in humble and joyful preparation for his journey's end. But when he finally arrived at the entrance to the holy city and made his way to the place where the Kaaba stood, he was stricken with the most profound grief. The Kaaba was nowhere to be found. Crying out to heaven, "Have I gone blind...what is this?" A voice from within informed him that the Kaaba was not there, it had traveled out to meet a woman who had been unable to make her way to Mecca.

Aghast, and filled with jealous rage, the worshipper got up and ran toward the city gates where he met Rabi'a, who was just arriving. Knowing her to be the woman in question, and noticing also that now the Kaaba was back in its rightful place, in harsh and demanding tones he remonstrated to her. "You are the one who is crazy," Rabi'a replied. "While you have spent your life in ritual prayers and fourteen years in pilgrimage, I, with only my inner prayer, have attracted the Kaaba as my companion."

Rabi'a surrendered herself to the object of her longing by placing everything in the hands, or arms, or eyes of her Beloved. In every decision, in every question, in every hardship, in every joy—she put herself within the fire of the Beloved's heart, in thanksgiving.

One poem reads:

"Rabi'a—Rabi'a—how did you climb so high?"

"I did it by saying:
    'Let me hide in You
    From everything that distracts me from You,
    From everything that comes in my way
    When I want to run to You.'"[23]

One of her biographers referred to Rabi'a as "a woman on fire with love." Her passion and longing are expressed exquisitely in this prayer of praise to her Beloved:

My Joy—
My Hunger—
My Shelter—
My Friend—
My Food for the Journey—
My Journey's End—
You are my breath,
My hope,
My companion,
My craving,
My abundant wealth,
Without You—my Life, my Love—
I would never have wandered across these endless
countries.
You have poured out so much grace for me,
done me so many favors, given me so many gifts—
I look everywhere for Your love—
Then suddenly I am filled with it.
O Captain of my Heart,
Radiant Eye of Yearning in my breast,
I will never be free from You
As long as I live.
Be satisfied with me, Love
And I am satisfied.[24]

Rabi'a held no illusory boundaries keeping herself separate from the rest of life. What she sought after and longed for as the highest good for herself, therefore, she also sought for others:

I carry a torch in one hand
And a bucket of water in the other:

With these things I am going to set fire to Heaven
and put out the flames of Hell
so that voyagers to God can rip the veils
And see the real goal.[25]

Her desire to worship Truth, without the overlays of fear of punishment or hope of reward, are exquisitely captured in one of her most renowned prayers:

O my Lord, if I worship Thee from fear of Hell,
burn me in Hell,
And if I worship Thee from hope of Paradise,
exclude me from thence,
But if I worship Thee for Thine own sake then
withhold not from me
Thine Eternal Beauty.[26]

There is a way to view Rabi'a that can serve us beyond the trite applications of "her great longing versus our small longing." Rabi'a can be appreciated as an un-owned voice, an unacknowledged part of our own soul which craves expression. Rabi'a is us—what she witnesses to, is what we have craved. While we may feel her longing and her love and say, "How far is mine from such love?", the fact that we have the fleeting recognition that a love such as hers exists is to know the seed of that love within ourselves. There is no difference between Rabi'a's voice and our own voice except that she refused to deny the power of hers.

Just listen.

4

THE PATH OF MOTHER

*At the present time God should be worshipped
as "mother," the Infinite Energy. This will
lead to purity and tremendous energy will
come here in America....*
— Swami Vivekananda, 1893

*God is not only fatherly,
God is also mother
who lifts her loved child
from the ground to her knee.*[1]
— Mechtild of Magdeberg (1210-1280)

For many women the idea that the Divine might
have a feminine face—that God is as much
Mother as God is Father—is completely foreign,
if not downright heretical. Raised with the images of God as Father, directing their worship to Master or Savior Jesus, reciting
prayers which called upon "Him" to intervene in our world, and
being excluded from any priestly functions, women have also been
excluded (or have excluded themselves) from the precious gift of
receiving the consoling touch of the feminine to their hungry souls.

Knowing that the ultimate principle in creation is neither male nor female in the way in which we define these terms, we can still consider the Motherhood of God, since this ultimate principle would be all-encompassing—both male and female, fully and completely. It is beneficial, I think, for women to both imagine and relate to the Ultimate in female form and female energetic terms, and then to see what happens within their souls as a result.

For ages, long before any of the organized religions of today, humans worshipped the goddess, the Great Mother. Woman's body perfectly spoke the miracle and mystery of creation. What else but the milk from woman's breasts could sustain the life of the young, the promise of the continuation of the species? Her monthly shedding of blood, her swelled belly, her full breasts, her abundant soft flesh, her lap which held both infant and mate, these became the symbols of life, and the foundations for the development of sacred rituals.

Sadly, in the evolution of humanity, this primal connection was divorced and distorted. "Woman in the train of history," writes Judith Duerk in Circle of Stones: Woman's Journey To Herself, "has been orphaned by the death of this Great Mother, has suffered loss of connection to her own beingness, lack of sense of legitimacy and belonging in the universe and in her own individual life."[2]

This chapter will consider the power of woman, not through protest or aggression, but as Mother, based on the sacredness of her feminine body, with all her creative, generative and nurturative possibility. If women can re-own and take responsibility for this power of Mother, if they can hear the voices of their muscles and blood, if they can express the milk of their breasts in some act of creation—whether that is the bearing of a child, or within the form of art, service, healing or act of loving, then women are healthy, happy, fulfilled, radiant, powerful. If they are unable to express the innate wisdom of their cells, either because they have drowned out the voice of the Great Mother, or had her voice drowned out of them, then women are sick, depressed, anxious, competitive, worried, codependent, abusive and abused. Many of us vacillate somewhere between these two extremes.

By looking toward the Divine as Mother, we may draw closer to the True Mother within ourselves (whether or not we have borne or ever will bear children). The women whose stories are shared here have discovered, or are discovering, that. They can guide us.

> Woman is the creator of the universe
> the universe is her form....
> In woman is the form of all things,
> of all that lives and moves in the world....
> there is no kingdom, no wealth,
> to be compared with a woman;
> there is not, nor has been, nor will be
> any holy place like unto a woman.
> There is no prayer to equal a woman....
> no mystical formula nor asceticism
> to match a woman.
> There are not, nor have been, nor will be
> any riches more valuable than woman.
> —Shaktisangama Tantra

MEETING MOTHER

Locating our Mother again—the Divine Mother, the Great Mother—is an individual affair. But, for many, the tears we shed and pain we bear are often the keys that open the door of Her chamber. That was true in Amber's case. As a woman in her early forties, Amber gave birth to her first child. For years she had diligently pursued a path of spiritual practice, choosing a celibate lifestyle, almost that of a cloistered nun, in order to devote herself fully to her exploration into God. She speaks with candor here, nearly four years after her son's birth, describing the crisis that drew her to the embrace of Divine Mother.

Amber's Story

> I turned to Divine Mother when I felt poverty-stricken in my ability to "mother," especially when I felt myself withholding my attention from my child. That was the way my own mother related to *me*. With the pain of that, and bereft of any other model, I turned to Divine Mother. I prayed to her: "I *know* there is true mothering in the Universe. I know that You, Divine Mother, exist." Sometimes I would actually feel her holding me, teaching me how to hold my child. The way the Divine Mother loved me is that She received me *as I was*. In being totally held and received *as I was* at that moment, I was freed, released to *become*. . . to be "made new."

As she spoke these words, Amber began to weep softly. I was weeping too. Then she drew a deep breath and began again.

> Because my mother was not there for me, I had not believed that Divine Mother existed. I had buried Her presence. But, from the depth of my need and my remorse in seeing how strong the impulse was to push my own child away, I began to identify Divine Mother's reality. Even if I did not know how to approach her, even if I didn't know how to *feel* her presence, She was there regardless. And I realized that because Divine Mother does exist (and it is *because* of her existence), it *is* possible to mother, to really become a mother, no matter what one's own childhood was.
>
> Children call forth a decision to love, whether they are our own or others' children. They call forth the place in the heart that may have been wounded, shut, twisted. . . and they demand that we open the wounded living heart. They draw it out of us. To me, that is why being with children is a profound path of spiritual practice and a

profound path to God.

In the process of giving birth I felt that the veils separating life and death, and human and Divine, were pulled away, so that the unity, the bondedness, the relationship and the reality of all things was tangibly present. And that seems a central part of spiritual life. Certainly there is a place for celibacy, but there is an important place for the vitality and the total, raw aliveness of physical, as well as spiritual birth.

Amber sat back in her chair and picked up her teacup. In speaking with me she had chosen her words carefully, and her reflection had taken her deeply within herself. I silently acknowledged my gratitude for her willingness to share her need for Divine Mother. That was my need too.

MEETING DINA

I met Divine Mother, alive, in a woman named Dina, during a tour of Europe with my spiritual teacher in the spring of 1988. Dina Rees's story is a grand one, full of amazing travels and adventures and accomplishments, and full of many unanswered questions. From the little I have been able to piece together from what Dina revealed about herself, and from the reflections of her friends and students, a tale of enormous love, devotion and service has emerged. I know, for instance, that she lived in Tibet, India, China, the Philippines and Indonesia after the Second World War. According to a sketchy biography contained in the book of her prayers, *Nimm Mein Herz*, compiler Johannes Galli writes:

> For many years she wandered through Tibet and India, as a researcher, studying alchemy and physics. In Peru, Bolivia and Mexico she studied Indian medicine.
>
> She was initiated by many spiritual teachers but found healing with Sathya Sai Baba, of whom it has been said, "He is love."[3]

Dina was a woman who had long listened to the voice of God within herself and had lived her birthright (which is the birthright of all of us). Dina's lifetime of personal vigilance, service to others, devotion to her teacher and prayer had allowed the objective Presence of the Divine Mother to show itself, relatively undiminished, in her being.

As I write this chapter, Dina's picture sits on the bookshelf next to me. I remember my first impression of her: A woman in her sixties, Dina had no frailty about her, despite the fact that she had suffered from cancer for over ten years. Her large frame (she was probably close to five foot ten) created the impression of power and immense nurturance. Seated, it was clear that many could rest in Dina's lap. All her features were large—hands, feet, face, mouth, teeth. Wide and open and welcoming. Her long silver-gray hair fell softly around the unwrinkled skin of her face, framing her in beauty. In my photo she wears a simple gown, one piece, like the robe of a nun, but light blue, the color of the sky. Around her neck hangs a medallion on a white ribbon, obviously a treasured object of worship or protection.

I clearly remember the room in which she hosted our small party—it was an oasis of devotion. Here, in this middle-class neighborhood outside of Freiburg, Germany, behind the facade of this lovely house, who would have suspected the existence of a power station of prayer and love? Incense, candles and flowers everywhere, the room was filled with religious objects and artifacts from around the world. Conventional statues of the Blessed Virgin Mary shared the same altar with elegant depictions of the *Bodhisattva* of Compassion and the Chinese Kuan Yin. A larger-than-life-size portrait of her guru, Sathya Sai Baba, a painting of Jesus, a crucifix, the face of Krishna, and more. Sarah, another friend, wrote:

> There was always room for more in that space. Dina's room, like herself, was very much like the archetypal mother with the infinite skirt, or the Goddess with infinite breasts...Hindu pujas, cluttered and overflowing with respect, filled every corner. The array of relics, amulets, prayer beads and such would lead one to surmise that every pilgrim

who had sat at her feet had left something of themselves for her to pray upon....[4]

And pilgrims there were. People came to visit Dina as the faithful visit the gurus of India, bringing her their concerns, their illnesses, their disturbed lives. It was natural and easy to sit at her feet. Dina was transparent—her wisdom and compassion communicated itself in a look, a touch, a smile or an offer of ice cream, which she claimed was "...like a benediction on the earth." (Who but a mother, delighted at feeding her children, would dare speak such a creed?) My friend Greg Campbell, a Zen monk, who had met Dina several years before I did, had written to me of *Unsere Lieben Frau* (Our Lady Love) explaining:

> In India, there is a tradition whereby women who are profoundly compassionate and wise are publicly acknowledged by the title "Holy Mother." Unfortunately, no such social tradition exists in the West. Still there are profoundly compassionate and wise women of the West: Mother Teresa being one example. And, there is a French woman who has lived many years in Germany. She is a pediatrician now widely acknowledged to be a Holy Mother.

Dina Rees and Greg Campbell

I watched Dina closely during the four hours I spent in her company. What impressed me the most was the single-focused attention that she paid to my teacher. A woman of immense spiritual maturity and evident saintliness (her phone never ceased ringing, with requests from around the world for her healing attention or prayer), Dina's aura was that of an innocent child at her own mother's knee as she looked reverently at Lee, my teacher, asked him questions and warmly invited us, his students, to celebrate our good fortune at having such a one as he in our midst. Her eyes riveted upon him whenever he spoke. "Lee and I have no need of words," she gently informed us. "But we speak anyway because it is good for creation." Seeing such an exchange was like watching two long-separated lovers kiss and embrace. Even though they had met only briefly, once before, Lee and Dina were lovers of the same Beloved, and in that great love they loved each other, intimately.

The longer I sat in Dina's presence the more I was touched with awe and tenderness. Were it not for the fact that I had the job of transcribing the notes of her conversation, I might have swooned on the spot. While many of my friends had casually spoken for years about their relationship to God as Woman, about the feminine aspect of Divinity, and had used the term "Divine Mother" quite regularly, I was less inclined to do so. I didn't yet have a bodily reference point for "Ma." But, the compelling energy of what I saw in front of me as I watched Dina move, watched her serve Lee and the rest of us, listened to her laugh, listened to her speak, was undeniable. Here was one in whom the Divine found a clear outlet for expression. And the form of that expression was Mother, pure and simple.

But the most extraordinary part of seeing Dina was that it was obvious to me that I was looking at myself. This Woman was Divine Mother, and in those moments of relaxing in her presence I knew that I was not separate or different from her. I was her. She was me. Certainly the paths of our lives were different, and the forms of our expression of God were also varied, but nonetheless, I saw that Dina was so much more than an individual woman with a personality, a family and a history. What I saw before me was Woman, the Feminine principle, the Mother, and I recognized myself.

Greg Campbell wrote in a similar vein of his meetings with Dina:

> In 1986...I was given the opportunity of meeting Dina Rees. I had never heard of her and she was explained to me as an unusual spiritual teacher and healer.
>
> As a man I have a strong interest in women in general and I also have had a long-standing interest in those women who in India are called "Holy Mothers." I had read about Sarada Devi, the Consort of Ramakrishna, and I knew something about the amazing Anandamayi-Ma as well. But I had, to my knowledge, never met a "Holy Mother" face to face. Dina was the first.
>
> I met Dina on only two occasions. It's very strange—our "conversations" remain among the most intimate I have ever experienced and yet I recall very little of what was said and I know almost nothing about her personally...The main thing that Dina did was to enchant you. Dina was an Enchanter.
>
> About twenty minutes into my first visit, half of my mind was saying, "My God, Greg, no one can be this loving!" and the other half of my mind was saying, "My God, Greg, get out!" I think I made some excuse about having to use the toilet although when I got into the toilet all I did was sit and breathe.
>
> Two years later I was again in Freiburg and asked to see Dina. This time I was more prepared—although I doubt if anyone could ever "prepare" for Dina! She seemed to remember me clearly which, given the fact that she met an endless stream of people, quite surprised me.
>
> Throughout both my visits, Dina's phone was regularly ringing in another part of the house. Oc-

casionally her assistant would come in to tell Dina of some crisis that demanded her attention or some "telephone healing" that had to be done now. I felt I was in the nerve center of the real United Nations. I don't think Dina got any rest from requests and I don't think she ever wanted any.

During my second visit Dina went on about how beautiful my ears are! Now it seems that women in general do not find me unattractive but no one had ever praised the beauty of my ears! She even ran the tip of her index finger around the edge of both of my ears! I was so embarrassed I didn't know what to do.... I suspect a lot of people felt that way when they were with Dina. She was very embarrassing in her love.

But I am happy to report that at the end of this second visit (which turned out to be the last time I saw her alive) I did have the courage to ask her if she would allow me to kiss her feet as is the custom in India. She kindly agreed and in a standing position slipped out of her shoes. As I bowed and kissed her feet it seems to me she was chattering on about how the Divine Mother is so totally joyous to be able to serve the Father; but then Dina was always saying things like that.

Not long after she died I was again in Freiburg and I asked to be taken to her grave. It is in the little village where she lived. In the cemetery there I found a mound of fresh earth with some flowers on it. There was a small wooden cross with just her name and dates. I thought: "This is a small tribute for such a great Saint." But then Dina lived for Love. Love is its own tribute.

Like Greg, the effect of my own meeting with Dina is with me today as strongly as it was on that June day in 1988. Since then, my work with my teacher, Lee, has been to uncover and live out what it was that I saw in Dina and in myself in that exchange. Lee's invitation for me to write this book has been a part of that process.

When Dina died of cancer, in July of 1990, I did not mourn her. In fact, I felt that her spirit came closer to me than ever. Yet, in other ways, I hungered to know more about this remarkable woman who had touched my life so profoundly. When I had the chance to travel back to Freiburg in January of 1992, I knew I had to find something more of Dina.

On a cold, wet Monday afternoon I criss-crossed the city of Freiburg by the electric trolley, arriving at a lovely suburban flat belonging to a couple who were the custodians of Dina's papers. They seemed guarded to me, at first, the outspoken American that I am. But, with tea and a bit of explanation, we all soon relaxed. Their guardedness, I realized, was that they wished only to assure that Dina's work would be treated with the respect it deserved. They gave me a photo of Dina, and her two books—one of prayers, the other a series of lectures about the love of man and woman.

The greatest gift came the following day when, by telephone, I spoke to another of Dina's disciples. "Could you sum up for me what you think is the essence of Dina's teaching?" I asked this stranger, wanting to get straight to the point. I expected him to speak about her great compassion, about prayer, about surrender to God, about her service to humanity. The man did not hesitate. "That is simple," he said. "Dina said that everyone, male or female, must become Mother."

I filed this bit of information away for future contemplation, carrying it home as a prize of that trip. After all, I had never borne a child myself. So, this teaching that everyone should become Mother was a challenging, even a threatening injunction. In 1993, when I wrote a book about loss, I told my own story of childlessness and I shared Dina's directive as a guiding principle to all mothers.

Clearly, I know that whether we have ever borne a child ourselves, whether we have ever had a significant relationship with a child or not, the challenge remains that we must become Mother—to ourselves, to one another, and to life in all its forms. To be Mother, however, is different from simply being "mother."

Just because someone has carried a child in her body doesn't necessarily earn her the title "Mother," just as every woman has not necessarily realized herself as Woman.

Mothers don't destroy life—they can't. Their job is to nurture it. Reading back over my notes from the 1988 trip I found that Dina herself had said this to me then: "Your heart is a mother. I think it's about time we all became Mother. For too long we're just women and not Mothers. The earth needs Mothers. It's very important."

The depth of Dina's Divine Motherhood took form in her twenty-two children, most of them adopted. She was trained as a medical doctor, a pediatrician, and during the terrible famines that raged through Bangladesh in the 1960s she had literally worked miracles among the poor. She told us that there were no supplies with which to relieve pain or bandage wounds, so all she could rely upon were the resources of the earth—literally, the leaves and the dirt. As she described the helplessness of the situation her hand gestured. She reached down towards the floor as if to gather a handful of sand and gravel, bless it and offer this dirt-made-medicine. This was the medicine that Dina administered within the context of her absolute faith in the power and love of God.

Someone remarked to Lee, after our visit, that Dina was unwrinkled despite her years. "It's because she faces life as though there were no problems," he said. "She *lives* her life."

As Dina spoke about her own full schedule of work and prayer she gave away this same secret herself.

> In the East they called me "Lady-No Problem." You have to know that all your thoughts are becoming manifest. If people "see" problems they will create problems. Be careful not to create problems. Practice hard to learn this. Problems only delay [the work]. These are all mental games. Your work now is to get rid of all the trash [in your minds]. Love and healing will become manifest if you learn to think that way.

Dina Rees

Two or three hours of sleep are enough if you eliminate the mind or the worry. The soul leaves the body during sleep and works "out there." [You can only do that] if you don't have a monkey-mind screaming for bananas. But to work with little sleep, your nerves must be in order and your emotions must be under control (but not re-pressed), because emotions eat up power and time. I'm just not interested in feeding my time to my emotions. I'm not interested in that mon-key any more. He's starving as far as I'm con-cerned. If emotions are going wild you have to sleep a lot, otherwise you have emotional break-down and a mentally difficult life. The more you can love deeply, however, the less you are both-ered by your emotional superficialities.

The beauty of Dina's approach was that she seemed to be speaking our unasked questions. Certainly almost every woman alive knows how her emotional storms can easily drain her of much needed energy.

If you are always emotionally overwhelmed, like: "Does everybody love me?" "Is this man going to love me? etc." That's very difficult, and very crazy. But if I know in my soul that I love many people ... if you know that you can trust your heart and your soul ... then you can be spared a lot of difficulties.

About Death and Life

Dina's work as a healer demanded that she be present to death, and it was her joy to serve as a midwife in this process. In fact, the first time she heard of Lee, my teacher, was through a phone call from a student of hers who lived in the U.S. This young man was dying and had called Dina for help. In the course of their conversation the young man told Dina that he was reading some extraordinary writing from a young American spiritual teacher. He read to Dina some of Lee's words, from his book *In the Fire*.[5] "This guy is great," Dina remembered saying at the time. "He speaks the truth. We need more people in the world who speak the truth."

Dina used the simple, earthy language of a mother talking to her children when she spoke to us about the great and awesome cycle of life and death. Her teaching emphasized the naturalness of letting go into death, because death was simply an entryway into another dimension, another time, another "game" as it were. With objectivity and compassion she told us that her own grandchild was dying, and that she was the child's doctor. A clear-sighted appreciation of non-duality animated her words, yet I could feel her underlying heartbreak, part of her job, as Mother.

> What has to happen will happen. I have neither hope that he will stay nor hope that he will die. As a doctor, what I can see is that it's over. But, I'm just a doctor, and then there's the Lord, and He will deal with it through the child's soul. Definitely it is much harder for the child's mother than it is for me, his grandmother. But she will learn to accept that this child she was given was a gift.
>
> Life comes and goes. We have to learn to give back the presents we've been given. Everything we've been given is a present, no matter what it looks like. And I find it perfect that life is as it is. We must all learn about the presents we've been given, but also realize that the gift can't stay forever. My life was full of gifts, and full of releasing these gifts, full of giving things away. We don't own our children, they're just a big gift. And the gift always leaves—whether the child grows up and leaves, or whether he moves into another plane of existence. That's very important for parents to know. One of these days the child will leave its life.

I help people to die, through my love. And people can only take with them what they have really lived, and what they realized in this life, particularly that their soul is like a guest in this body. The soul can leave! With people who are holding onto things in this life—to husbands and wives, their children, their religion, their job, whatever it is—we have to be very patient and caring. We have to hold them a lot, hold their hands a lot, hold them in our arms so they can learn how to let go. And then it's good and it's easy for them. Then they beam like the children. I've always been happy when I see them beam and when I see myself beam when the time comes for them to pass on. It's like a feast.

The more I help people to die, the stricter I am about the necessity that people learn about these things, and especially that the children learn. Because then, whenever their time comes—whether they are fourteen, forty, or eighty—they are ready to move onto that new dimension. And the more reality the better!

I was with an eight-year-old child who had leukemia. I asked him, "What do you like the best right now? I'll bring it to you." And he said, "My red ball."

I brought him the ball and asked: "What does this mean to you now?" And the child gave me a big lesson. He said, "Mama Dina, when I was playing with that ball I was in another time—I was so wrapped up in playing that I didn't know what else was going on. So if you give me the ball now, I know that I am going to another time."

What a big teacher! He has experienced, through playing, that there is another time. I taught all my children—we have twenty-two

adopted children, and the child from my daughter now—that there is "another time," and that is
Reality, and not something painful. It's like a big
game, but a holy game.

And about her own death which had been so close on many
occasions, Dina again betrayed her absolute trust in the ways of
God as she reflected on the many diseases that she treated in India,
including cholera—diseases that could easily kill the healthiest
social worker. "The last time I was in China there was a special
epidemic of A and B hepatitis. Left and right of me even doctors
died, but I didn't get sick because death doesn't want me. So I
didn't get ill."

Like so many mystics who speak simultaneously on more
than one level, Dina consistently gave us several messages at once.

A lot of people told me I was going to die when I
had cancer for ten years. And I really was dying,
but I realized that dying is not important. You have
to become resurrected. That's what's important.
Everybody can die, but not to die...that's what you
have to learn—not to die in spirit. Because I didn't
die in spirit, my body had no choice but to go
along. What can the body do alone? Nothing. It's
just a vehicle. Every once in a while it's beautiful,
but you have to take care of it quite a bit. It's nothing but a vehicle.

The death and resurrection that Dina spoke about, far from
being some event at the end of this experience called life, was
rather an ongoing, moment-to-moment realization. Death and resurrection are happening in each instant, for those who have the
eyes to see and the awareness to appreciate. In other words, humans are always being offered the choice of resurrecting their lives,
dying to whom they think they are so that *who they really are* can
be present.

About the Spiritual Crises of Our Times

In Hindu Scripture it is written that the highest virtue of the
Kali Yuga is discrimination. (*Kali Yuga* is the Age of Iron, the Sanskrit term for the dark ages in which we live. These ages are dark
because humankind has allowed its illusions to overpower reality.)
Despite her wide-ranging ecumenism, which embraced many spiritual cultures, Dina's was not a watered-down teaching. In fact, she
was adamant that the temptations of the times required a kind of
radical annihilation, which few were willing to accept. She de-
plored "the hobby of our times" which she described as a type of
"esoteric craziness" of those who denied their own humanity while
masquerading as saints. "I always meet these crazy people who think
they fell from heaven. But they're not clear."

Dina lamented that many teachers today, together with their
illusion-bound students, were merely multiplying the means, having lost sight of the true end.

> People always want to grasp at straws, and that
> would not be good of us as teachers to do. It is a
> crime to pass out straws. People have to be able to
> help themselves. If they trust a straw they'll sink.
> People can read a hundred books, and every book
> has something different in it. But the only thing
> that holds true is what we experience in our hearts.
> Many people want help, yet they will only accept
> help from the outside—they're not willing to do
> something for it. Often my patients and my cli-
> ents are unwilling to come up with any effort.
> I'm supposed to supply a miracle! This phenom-
> enon is present on the whole earth because people
> have been given straws, over and over again. It
> has happened too often.

Speaking specifically to our small entourage, in the company of Lee, she affirmed:

> Fortunately, now there are teachers showing up who are telling people to drop the straws. It's their only chance! You have to be very grateful that there's some sort of straight path—a clear path that you can follow.

About Marriage and Relationships

Because she was a mother of our times, Dina knew the heartbreak of unhappy relationships which were (and still are) more often the norm than the exception. She told us that men and women are constantly coming to her for advice about what to do about their "unions" of three years, four years, seven years, nine years. Her "advice" was not moralistic at all, although it could be interpreted as such. Rather, she was speaking from an extremely refined metaphysical viewpoint when she recommended:

> Many young people think, "Well, we can live together. It's like being married. It has only to do with the laws anyway." But that's not true. That's a very limited way of thinking. If you are married, that closes the karmic connection and you receive a lot of blessing and support. The angels are supporting you. Marriage is giving love to Evolution, to God; a love that you enliven by being together.

Dina went on to explain that when people live together without a closed karmic connection, this serves to discourage the souls of children who would rightfully "belong to us" from reaching us. A true marriage provides the safe nest that children need, Dina affirmed. I understood her to be speaking of much more than a legal marriage ceremony. The type of marriage she was referring to would be characterized by a deep commitment, and "love communion" (to use her words).

Nature has a nest for everything; even the smallest seed is being carried by something else. A short
time ago I took pictures of trees that grew around
each other. They had communion—love communion. They were married, so to speak, and they
make a very clear example for stupid people.

"A marriage is a process—a destruction of ego; and that is
very important for us," Dina explained. Although such words sound
discouraging for anyone looking for a conventional relationship,
for those who seriously wish to pursue spiritual life, the recognition that marriage and family life can be a source of profound transformation should come as no surprise. Dina clarified: "On purpose
I don't say it is "painful," because by "pain" most people think of
drama. But, the work we do as a couple on ego is like a benediction, not just for us but for the whole universe."

You will have a warm nest when your children
have a warm nest. This understanding is very important in our time when most people tend to
handle their relationships from such a viewpoint
of individualism. That's why there are so many
lost birds...let's say people. Hopefully such people
will come across you [speaking to Lee] or me, and
will find a way again to deal with this.
     What nature is we are. Just take a look at the
nest the birds prepare. What all is in there? The
birds even pick colorful things to decorate their
nests with. That's selfless love. Nature is our
teacher. And if the birds have a nest like that, our
children need it even more. And if we are married, and even if the process is very difficult, we
should be very grateful for it.

Dina expressed to us, quite personally, that her husband was
her teacher in many ways.

112

He didn't know it. He really drove me crazy a lot of times. But he taught me a lot at the same time— patience, understanding, giving myself, dedication and happiness. This romantic, wonderful notion of what marriage is supposed to be is just something we make up. We think that everything has to be all right, when it's not we're helpless. But life is ups *and* downs...not just a linear plane. We may think that every day he has to tell me he loves me and everything has to be always rosy and bright. But that's all mind! Life is *lived life*. It is full of teaching gifts. We can accept that everything is fine *and* accept that it's very hard on our emotions too. Great!

About Feeding Body and Soul

"I've met seventeen saints in my life and they all loved cakes, and licked their plates clean of whipped cream. And their eyes would light up at the very mention of ice cream," Dina said as she served us another round of tea and cookies.

Another of my traveling companions summed up her impressions of Dina exquisitely:

Two things I remember about her, like the memory of a woman's perfume—I only have to think of the nightingale in her home, and remember the exquisite song which I heard for the first time and I am transported back to her. And secondly, I recall how Dina fed us. As long as we were with her she kept bringing food—the most bizarre combinations of food. Watermelon, then pickles thirty minutes later, then ice cream, then crackers spread with mayonnaise. So peculiar; totally spontaneous. And the food would end up being great.

As it got towards evening, the nightingale started singing. That sound was so haunting, so enchanting. I had never heard a nightingale sing before. And we kept being fed.

Like a baby always knows the smell of its own mother, there was something about the aroma of Dina, the perfume of her, that has stayed with me, that has identified her as "my mother" is a certain way. Her smell was very rich and more than nurturing. It communicated that she could never be used up; there was so much of her. Dina was always there beyond forever. Her food, her love, was there to be taken, and it was our duty to take it. It is the child's duty to drink the Mother's milk.

In taking her leave of us Dina remarked, like any good mother: "I hope you go to bed full in the stomach and happy in the heart."

About Surrender to God; Letting God Direct One's Life

Dina described an experience of riding in an airplane, thinking of a patient of hers who was in a "...very dangerous situation with cancer and mental sickness. And I prayed: "Please help me, my God. And I closed my eyes, and when I opened them, Shirdi Sai Baba came to me and said: 'Not your work, this is my work. You pray.' "

Speaking to all of us who work in the helping professions, as well as to all mothers, she advised: "It's not your work to heal the sick and worry so much. It's *His* work to do that. As long as you are praying, that is all you need to do that everything will be all right."

The surrender Dina spoke about was not different from the surrender through waiting that Irina Tweedie demonstrated.

Waiting means patience. Without patience, nothing works. Even if you become too euphoric out of happiness, you can overlook something. Patience

114

is an unlimited way of healing a lot of problems. If you wouldn't make decisions so rashly you would have a lot less problems. It is very rare in a lifetime that you have to do something *immediately*.

What powerful motherly wisdom! Ah, the impatience of children! Isn't it mother's job, again and again, to keep calling us back to the sweetness of resting in her arms before jumping off the cliff. "Something happens while you wait! Yes, it's hard, but in waiting you learn what the situation means in other dimensions, and spiritually."

Dina's words are based on a lifetime of suffering and experience. She was not offering her children these words without having embodied them herself. "I waited a long time to become healed or whole. Ten years of cancer are an eternity, but I waited and it happened. I got healed. The spiritual waiting—*that* you have to take into your heart."

About Woman

The truly evolved woman is smart, wise, open, intelligent, and not codependent, but experienced. She knows her body and her mind, her pains and her loneliness, but she is spiritual. She doesn't take second place behind man, but she is not a man. She has been born to preserve the world. She has a great mission.[6]

About Prayer

Many people have asked me how to pray correctly. There is no right or wrong praying, there is only prayer. If in your prayers you are saying, "I, I, I" God will even hear that, but it takes longer than when you say, "You, my God." God always hears, so you can't pray wrongly, you can only pray. Even when I say, "I want this, I want that," God will give it to me, but it takes longer than if I say, "Lord, Thy will be done." Then I get it straight away.

Above all we must learn that prayer is a natural law and that prayer belongs to evolution, not to religion...prayer is a matter for every tree, every grain of sand, every blade of grass, every drop of dew, and also for us, because we *are* evolution. That is, we are physically in the process of evolution.

So let us become what we really are, souls which are united with God, so that we may receive help. We are always in need of help....

Prayer is selfless surrender, love, *dolce amore*: only Italians can say that, "sweet love".... Saint Francis of Assisi is the perfect example of "sweet love." When he prayed everything around him, the whole of creation, was one with him in selfless love...When he opened his eyes his whole body was covered with birds, everything that could run lay at his feet...Animals know better than anyone else....

Prayer is an act of love. It is an experience of everything. That is why prayer is so important. I have prayed with so many people on this earth, with so many religions, with so many beings, and it was always such a tremendous experience to know the other people, the other beings, in the depths of their surrender—such a gift to become one in heart and spirit. We were one and yet we didn't know each other...

I knew a great Tantra teacher when I was still studying Tantra, and when she prayed the whole of nature was still. All the people who were there experienced this stillness without her saying a word. The whole of nature prayed ... because her surrender to all things living was so great ... The energy of her prayer was so strong that the laws of nature bent before it.

Prayer means to be aware, to be aware of everything. Someone who is praying is always aware, always prepared; he hears and sees and feels everything. He becomes more and more finely tuned, even for things that are not in his consciousness or his understanding. He may not see and hear those things but he knows them all the same....

When the Holy Books say, "Go to your chamber and pray for yourself," it means go into your heart, and not that you should lock yourself in your room and shut everything out so that no-one can see you; that has nothing to do with consciousness. You should pray in your heart. The quiet chamber is your heart.[7]

About Unconditional Mother-Love

My friend, Sharon, meeting Dina for the first time, described how she landed in this lap of compassion. Sharon spoke to Dina about the insecurity and lack of self-appreciation that had plagued her all her life. Calling my friend to herself, Dina embraced Sharon like a long-lost child. "O my dear, dear child," she said over and over again, as she stroked my friend's hair. "My dear, dear child. . . ." Dina taught Divine Mother's love by embodying it.

> Dina was so easy to be with. She did not evoke from me the same self-consciousness that any other male teachers have. And she was like this big ball of appreciation, so full of a childlike wonder and love for life. And her "being" appeared so open, it was like she embraced the universe. She really exemplified organic innocence, and yet her innocence was not naive, because she had seen and been instrumental in caring for many adults and children who experienced profound suffering, and never did she appear to veer away from what she

117

stood for—which was that life was worth living
and basically good, and that all difficulties could
be overcome with love. And we all felt like children at her feet, including our own teacher,
whom she loved so dearly and treated as one of
her close children.

Dina was healing us all, she just had so much
to give, and she kept giving. She was a great example of giving everything and keeping nothing
for herself, not even her love for God. It seemed
the more she gave away, the more she had. She
feeds the teachers and the students, she feeds the
mother and she feeds the child. She feeds the lover
so that new children are born. She just feeds a
continuous birthing—of God. She is God and she
feeds the continuous birthing of God.

In her curriculum vita, Dina wrote:
"My life was only a path of learning; for thirty-five years I
tried to find the essence of life, and I found it—serving mankind."[8]
In one of her poems she sings a lullaby:

Beloved
Great is my yearning
For You
You have opened my heart so,
Through everything
I can see and feel,
Through You
Let me become one
With You.
Let me be quite Yours.
Nothing shall belong to me

Until I am eternally one with You,
Beloved.
My yearning is so great,
Free me from all bonds
And let my heart sob,
Let me be surrendered to You
For ever, eternally,
Let me be with You,
One with You,
You, my Beloved.
Hear my yearning,
Take my heart,
Hold it in Your Hands.
Take my all.
Let the perfume
Of all roses
Rise up to You
And let the perfume
Of my heart
Rise up to You.
Let it be
United with You
For all time, Amen.[9]

MOTHERING AS SPIRITUAL PRACTICE

If I had the opportunity to interview Dina again today, I would
have asked her about how to integrate the responsibilities as mother
to a family with the desire for a deeper and more tangible relationship with God. Since I have lived in and around communities of
spiritual seekers for many years, and given workshops for hundreds
of women in both the U.S. and Europe, this question is almost
always an issue. Buddhist teacher and Zen monk Yvonne Rand is a
woman of celebrated wisdom who in her early years of training made
a difficult decision to put her children first. Her vocation as priest
at the time took a back seat to her vocation as mother. Speaking

about this period of her life in an interview with Sandy Boucher, author of *Turning the Wheel: American Women Creating the New Buddhism*, Yvonne said: "I made a clear decision to make my life as a householder, as a parent, as somebody who lived if not entirely in the world, with a real appreciation for people in the world, and that I would want to find some way to express my understanding of Buddhism, given all of that."[10] Another Buddhist, Zen Master Maurine Stuart, when faced with a similar conflict, found wise counsel in her teacher who told her to make her children her "practice."

Since I have never been a mother myself I am sensitive to watching the ways in which my women friends change during pregnancy, and how the demands of their lives, after childbirth, affect them—for better or worse. In preparing this book, therefore, I wanted to gain greater insight into the possibility of childbearing and childraising as a form of spiritual practice. I wanted to learn more about Divine Mother and I guessed that the mothers around me might have more insight into her than I did. So, I asked them. And they told me their stories.

We need inspiring role models of "great" women with family responsibilities. So many times the great Mothers who are written about are celibate women—nuns and single mystics who lived a detached life from the things of this world. But I wanted the example of mothers like Dina, especially those even less visible than Dina was. I wanted stories of how one can be annihilated in love in the monastery of daily life. I wanted to share these stories with the vast majority who would never have the benefit of a cloister, or a life of contemplation lived apart from the world, or even a life of great healing ministry.

The women I interviewed for this section *are* great women, as far as I'm concerned. They live ordinary, almost invisible lives. Meeting them at the supermarket on a good day you might be struck with the serenity of their smiles, or you might simply be impressed with the gentle way in which they speak to their children. On a difficult day, they might look exhausted, or be caught biting their lips to keep their frustration, at anything, from spilling out around them. But, these women are unique in that they have each dedicated themselves to a tremendous spiritual intention, and sometimes great asceticism, for as much as twenty-five years. I chose them because they have been much needed mothers and sisters and friends to me, and most especially because I see them as women who have a deep commitment to using the stuff of their lives as their spiritual practice. I have given them names here, but each one asked, characteristically, to remain anonymous.

Agnes Speaks of Divine Grandmother

Agnes is the mother of a twenty-three-year-old son. She is a brilliant writer and the editor for a small religious publication. Much of Agnes' time, however, is spent in quiet service to the members of her spiritual community, often to the new mothers and their small children. Like a grandmother, whom Agnes identifies as the model of spiritual wisdom, Agnes speaks with gentleness and authority about the transformation which the job of "mothering" or "grandmothering" can provide for any woman.

Like the response that I received from Amber, whose story is told early on in this chapter, Agnes too spoke of her great remorse in regard to her childraising practice—"for all the ways in which I don't love..." she said. This theme was echoed by other women, and seems to be a particularly important catalyst in the process of spiritual transformation. Certainly, when our sisters and friends are feeling that their mothering was less than perfect we want to console them, reminding them that they have "done the best job they could, under the circumstances." Nonetheless, such consolation is not what these women are looking for. Rather, they are grateful that the pain of their inability to love fully is creating a burning fire within them. They know they will never love enough, until they are transformed into Love itself. This is what they seek. Their children, husbands, friends and family are the reminding factors that keep them awake.

When asked about how mothering is a form of spiritual practice my first response was waves of

sadness, of remorse for all the ways in which I don't
love, and don't do what I know is possible in becoming what Woman really is. *Mother* is inseparable from what *Woman* is, in the most human
sense and the most cosmic sense.

I was so young when my son was born, but still
I had a strong spiritual foundation for my life because I was raised with values for the soul. I had a
lot of longing for spirit—at twenty I was already
reading spiritual literature, and searching for spiritual community. It was a few years after my son's
birth that I hit on the idea of the goddess...of Divine Mother. And this understanding was very immature for a long time.

A turning point came, at a nonverbal level,
when I realized how I was failing my son. I think
that was "the" turning point in my life, and the
critical opening in my relationship to Divine
Mother and the spiritual path. The shocking realization that I was *totally* self-referenced, rather
than referenced to sacrifice and service to others,
came from such an archaic space of the soul, from
the very cells of the body. And, this recognition
was incredibly painful—sorrow, longing and grief,
all mixed up in it.

When you realize that you are failing someone
you love so deeply, the pain is so piercing that it
connects you to the suffering of all humanity,
because that is what *Mother* feels; She feels all the
sorrow of the world, intimately.

I still have that wound—of bearing a child and
failing that child, and being unable to prevent that
child from suffering. Even when your child is
grown, in some ways you still bear the child's suffering. And it is a wonderful wound to have. You
don't only get it from having children, but from

experiencing the suffering of the world in a way that shakes your foundation. You can't stop from feeling the suffering of the world, the *anima mundi* (the world soul)—all the human beings, the animals, the fishes that have cancer because they swim in polluted water. Whenever any animals dies, a part of our Being dies. If we are killing off the rainforest we are killing our own souls. Having a child is a fast road into the heart of the world.

The total sacrifice, the self-effacement in love that is required in raising a child is no different from the self-effacement that goes on between lover and Beloved, between devotee and God, between Radha and Krishna in the Hindu cosmology. To mother a child is a huge task. To be present to a child and to sacrifice our own needs, wants and desires for the well being of the child is immense work. Through that kind of selfless sacrifice we tap into the most profound necessities of sacrifice and surrender to the Divine.

When mothering is done in the context of a spiritual practice, that practice puts you up against yourself. In some expressions of spiritual life you can fool yourself that you are holy and pure because you are in the chapel or chanting all day, and that's all you do. When the forum of your life is the ordinary, everyday activities—with friends, with the work you have to do, with cooking and cleaning—then you are up against whether or not your life is *really* sanctified. There it is in front of you—your inner state—and that is obvious.

I had a lot of guilt as a child—guilt and sin. But, this real conscience (this remorse I felt at having failed my son) was born out of a different place: that of tapping into the world's suffering. When this realization of my failure to love hit me,

I just got blasted wide open, and I was never the same after that. Thank God.

Like Agnes, women throughout time have dived deeply into their own river of sadness, and there have found a heart of sadness that was an entryway into, as she put it, "the heart of the world."

I took a long time in silence to absorb the words Agnes gave me. She was silent too, although her face was flushed and I could tell that she had much more to say. When I asked her to explain her understanding of God as Mother she was happy to reply.

Many of us aggrandize the egos of our children, projecting our own ego needs, wishes and desires onto them, full of sentimentality and nostalgia. Thinking your child is "the most darling thing in the world" is totally selfish! It does not provide the child with a sound spiritual basis. It's not *that* kind of attention that a child needs. What a child needs is a steady, benevolent presence from a mother; that is what Divine Mother is. She is pervasive, all embracing, accepting; She affirms you, witnesses, understands and knows you, and sees you most deeply at your essence. Real Mothering, at its core, is *presence* to what is deepest in the child—that is what brings forth the being of the child.

We need to take the mother-child relationship beyond the physical relationship of a woman and her child. At its best, it should be the model for relationship among all human beings. It would be more accurate to say that we must be like grandmothers to each other, all the time. Grandmother is able to genuinely love because she is so detached.

My own grandmother raised me for ten years. She brought to my teenage and young adult life that quality of total self-acceptance. She had seen it all; she had been through it all. . .having raised

124

four children, having been through two wars, and the Depression. I once asked her how she had so much peace, and she said that the only way to have peace is through acceptance.

"Grandmother" is Divine Mother. She has peace and simplicity and a deep bodily steadiness, and calmness and joy in the face of adversity—because she has acceptance. From that place she can look out at "the other" without any jealousy, without competition. Grandmother has a vast capacity for love. Because she is old and wise, she is not struggling within the arena of the world anymore. She has found her place in the universe and she is centered and steady in that place. She can "witness and bless" as Rabbi Zalman Schachter says. She blesses us with her acknowledgment of our essence.

Blessing children with our unspoken, heartful blessing—that is the essence of Mother, and that is what we must do with each other. There is a core principle in spiritual life that we can and must bless each other. . .but to do that we have to believe in our own essential goodness and saintliness as part of the Divine Being. It is not the ego that blesses, not the personality, but something mysterious and unknown within us. Blessing is an act of faith that we are whole. If we can move "ourselves" out of the way a bit, that Being will bless all that is around it.

Miranda Speaks About Loving and Serving

Miranda is a new mother in her mid-thirties. She met her spiritual teacher when she was eighteen, and since then has devoted her life to spiritual practice in his service. Over the years, Miranda's compelling radiance has continued to speak volumes about the authenticity of her inner life. Yet, she has never hesitated to share with others the weaknesses, struggles and failures she encounters daily in her attempt to live with the kindness, generosity and compassion which her teacher demands.

Miranda candidly admits that being a mother has been the greatest "purifying fire" she has yet endured. What Miranda has taken on is no ordinary relationship to mothering. She has willingly engaged this aspect of her life as a means of surrendering her ego completely. The reason she sounds so uncompromising in relationship to her own weaknesses is because she knows, intuitively, a larger possibility for love, and she will be satisfied with nothing less than that fulfillment.

> Before I had a child I was under the illusion that I had come to some degree of patience. But, having a child has pushed me to anger and impatience that I had never touched on before. So, today, when I was trying to get my daughter dressed, I realized that my tone of voice and my manner had become harsh, and my body had become rigid, and that I was no longer in communion with her. Often my anger and frustration are a failure to "feel into" what she is working with in her development. At other times it is simply my habitual refusal to put her first. After all, I unconsciously reason, "I have *my* schedule and she is interfering with *my* schedule; and if only she would come to some reason. . ." Remembering that I was going to speak to you about mothering as a spiritual practice helped me go the extra mile of coming back into relationship with her.
>
> To love is to serve, and I can always detect in my child's face, especially in her eyes, when I have unconsciously withdrawn love out of my desire for self-preservation, that is, my desire to preserve "the self" I have presumed to be.

126

There is the tendency to approach spiritual practice the way one approaches almost everything—with selfish motives. It is a fantasy that doing "practices" will bring one closer to God or awaken one to a state of enlightenment, unless the matrix is that one's *life* becomes practice. Whenever one is required to suspend some formal spiritual practices (as happens when you have a child, or because of the demands of a job, or because of an illness or accident), that can be a revelatory experience. Then you can begin to get a taste for how much maturity you have gained during your previous years of formal practice. As my teacher said to me, in regards to having a child, "Now it's time to put your money where your mouth is...it's time to put into action what you've been considering for many years."

True mothering is nothing less than a life of surrender, as all the great spiritual teachers and masters have embodied it. And to fall short of that demand for surrender in relationship to my child is a very painful and humbling experience. On the other hand, there is ecstasy and joy when there is natural surrender. And that is a tremendous impetus for me as a parent.

Mothering [parenting] is a twenty-four-hour-a-day affair. In the middle of the night when I need to be with my child, I have often recalled the stories of great saints who would spend little time sleeping, but much time praying. In those graceful moments I was very happy to let go of my attachment to sleep. But that did not come without a lot of painful grappling and soul-searching first.

In practical terms, the attachment we have to being able to sit and eat our meals, undisturbed,

uninterrupted; our attachment to our sleep schedules; whether we get our laundry hung out or not...all
the minute details of daily life become a glaring example of whether we are practicing or not.

I asked Miranda to comment upon her understanding and
experience of God as Mother.

Divine Mother is uncompromising, powerful yet
soft, full of integrity, compassion, generosity, kindness and unending patience. Divine Mother is the
embodiment of the understanding that the only
true joy is in service.

Perhaps I am naive, but I sense that even the
"worst," most abusive, most selfish mother, still
has moments of being *Mother*. And so, any sin-
cere desire to be free of self-centeredness, greed or
crippling neurosis *can* override ego and reconnect
a woman to the organic imprint of what a true
Mother is.

Nothing is so important that it can't wait five
minutes to allow you to answer a child's question. I
found that if I am willing to drop everything to
serve my child (or my spiritual master, or my
friend)—if I'm willing and ready and happy to drop
everything at a moment's notice, very often it becomes unnecessary. If a child can't feel Mommy's
attention she'll do anything to get it, including behavior that would attract negative attention. But,
if Mom, like Divine Mother, is willing to drop everything, the child relaxes, sensing that flexibility.

I think almost every woman knows, in her
heart, the essence of Divine Mother. While she
may not admit it, woman knows when she is being true to herself; she knows that joy arises from
doing what is integral with her intuitive sense of

how to live. That is true self-respect! And, even though she may be putting her own needs aside to serve another, she is never diminished at all.

Becky Speaks About Telling the Truth

The oldest of the women I interviewed, Becky, at fifty-five, could reflect upon her lifetime as the mother of four girls. What I have always appreciated about Becky is the simplicity of her view of spiritual life. For her, there was no mystical experience more vital than the awe she shared with children. Now, as a "grandmother" to many children, including the women in her spiritual community, she continues to turn serious spiritual seekers on their heads, inviting them to find God in the obvious details of their daily lives. Her view of mothering as spiritual practice was expressed joyfully, directly, and with an interesting twist that afforded a new perspective on the topic.

> With children you get to experience the wonder of it all. We are so busy doing what we have to do all day that we don't take much time to stop and appreciate how amazing life is. And it's all amazing to children. Half a child's life is meditation. They can do the same things three hundred times, and with such constant delight. That is a form of meditation. I love to go on a walk with a three or four-year-old. In twenty minutes we may only get ten feet, but we will have inspected everything in our path in this wondrous way; or we may go up and down every step twenty times, and never get bored. If you can get into that space with children, you can see all of life differently too.
>
> Going to India with my children was like that. I had been there twice before, and seen the poverty, the dirt, the "pitiful beggars." So, I tried to prepare the kids for this; I was ready to protect

them from all the "horrible things." But when we got there, the children weren't seeing horrible things. They were seeing animals; they were seeing other kids to play with; they were seeing magic, everywhere.

This whole question of mothering as spiritual practice is somehow backwards for me. If you're being a mother so that you can have a relationship to God, I think you are doing it wrong. You are still serving your children for some selfish reason—even though a spiritual reason. Sort of like having a perfectly clean house so your neighbors will think you're a good housekeeper.

I believe we all have a relationship to God, but we aren't aware of it. Of course, having children can remind you of your relationship to God, but it's not about your relationship to children *bringing you to* relationship with God. You already have that relationship with God, regardless.

We are all going to fall down sometimes. Everybody makes mistakes. As a mother you are going to make mistakes. How you handle your mistakes can be one of your greatest lessons as a parent, and in spiritual work, too. Letting your mistakes be okay, and then trying again is what is necessary.

Just tell the truth about things. It's good to acknowledge mistakes with kids. It's good for them to see how you handle it when you make mistakes. . .that you don't deride yourself too much. What more can you teach a child to better prepare him or her for life?

Katie Speaks About Unknown Saints

As a prolific writer of children's books, Katie's commitment to the needs of children is evident in her writing as well as in the model of mothering she presents. For years, prior to meeting her teacher and immersing herself in the education of the children in her spiritual community, Katie taught severely handicapped kids in a rural school in the south. Her experiences in this crucible broke her heart, but simultaneously awakened a wisdom and dedication to service which has remained undiminished in her. Now, in her mid-forties, Katie is passionate about what it means to be Mother.

If a mother is really doing her job, there is nothing else. That's why you don't hear of mothers as saints—because they are busy being mothers.

On the wall of my room I have a quote from the great Divine Mother, Anandamayi Ma, which I try to read every day. It says: "The mother wishes to give everything to her children. It is the mother's sole desire that whatever she possesses should belong to her children."[11] For me, that quote is not about giving material things, rather it is about who God is.

With that kind of dedication to raising a child, there is no longer the luxury of placing attention wherever our egoic whim wants—whether it is on the evening news, or what's in fashion, or who's gossiping about whom. And that is a tremendous gift. Sure, I still think about those things, but in another sense I'm acutely aware that there is no "free" attention. The Bible talks about God like this—as the Good Shepherd. The shepherd's attention is always about the flock. He may be sleeping, eating his bread and cheese, or daydreaming, but his primary attention is always on the flock. It is the same for a mother.

There seems to be this bottomless well of God's energy that is available to mothers. It's infinite. When I find myself completely exhausted, so exhausted that if somebody asked me to take down a telephone number I couldn't do it; still, if I need to show up for my daughter, the energy is there. God gives you that—the second wind. And truthfully, I am not always kind, compassionate and loving with her; sometimes I have impatient attention, but nonetheless the energy is there. For me, that is another proof of the omnipotent or absolute wisdom and intelligence of God that is built into this whole system of creation. In the divine plan, what God has set up for mothers to have available to children, is not random.

It is an awesome responsibility to be a mother. To a child, mother is God! I had a little kid in school, an eight-year-old boy, Allen, who was severely physically abused by his mother. He'd come to school with belt marks across his face, or on his back. The social workers all knew about it; his mother had been through lots of social help programs.

One day he was in a pretty bad way, and I reported it to the school nurse. Of course he didn't want me to report it. The next day he came into school so angry that he wouldn't look at me. He just hid in the corner. Finally, he spoke, the last words he would ever say to me: "I hate you. Because of you they came and took my mom to jail."

It didn't matter what this woman was like, or what she did to him, Allen loved his mother. And, no matter what, as long as the child's innocence was somewhat intact, he would rather be with his mother. You have to live with those children to understand something of what I'm talking about. Of course, all the social reformers have their take on codependency, and the cycle of abuse; but I'm talking about what goes deeper than all of that. This little boy just looked at me like, "Don't you get it? She's my *mother*. They are taking my mother to jail."

It has taken me twenty years to get it. To see through the eyes of the child is really hard.

Katie paused and drank a glass of water, reflectively. The power of her words was devastating in one sense, yet the truth they communicated provided a type of raw food that I craved. When Katie speaks her truth it is not so easy to defend myself with superficial explanations or "spiritual" notions. I wanted to hear more from her.

Just as she was about to speak again she warned me that she might start to cry. Then she continued with the subject of mothers as saints.

If I ever saw this infinite wisdom and compassion of God anywhere, it was with the mothers of the kids I used to teach. These kids were profoundly impaired; and their mothers were saints! Nobody is going to hear about them, but the kind of work they did everyday of their lives was the stuff of real sainthood. I see what it takes in simply caring for a normal child. Then I imagine having a four-teen-year-old child who is still in diapers, who can't walk, who can't feed himself. For these women, these mothers, their mystical experience was their life. To see the reality of their lives and the infinite compassion that these mothers had was awe-inspiring.

Lisa was a beautiful girl, with long black hair ... the sweetest child. She was eleven when I taught her. Born normal, but when she was a few years old, riding in the car with her father, they had an accident. The child's head went into the gearshift. After that, she couldn't walk, she couldn't talk, she couldn't move her arms. She was totally disabled for the rest of her life. But, her parents showed up for her in a way that wasn't guilt-ridden or condescending. They treated her as God. From that point on, their lives were consumed with "doing" for another human being. Every moment was about picking her up, putting her in her chair, dressing her, feeding her, inspiring her when she got depressed. And she was basically very happy. The way her parents were with her—that is the work of a saint to me.

This child's parents were performing miracles every day. Why does nobody ever hear about them? Because these people are too busy taking care of their children, too busy serving. Most of us, and the people who write the books about the saints, are too interested in "nice-nice" miracles; in situations where the pain gets healed or goes away. For Lisa's mother, the pain doesn't go away.

I know all the times I've hurt my child, all the time I've been unconscious with her. The pain of that unconsciousness and impatience and invulnerability doesn't go away. And I think that what we look for in saints, in the "miracles," is the absence of the suffering. "Oh, isn't this great—they were healed." Or, "Isn't this marvelous, they overcame all their trials." But the mothers we don't hear about are the ones who don't get healed. Lisa didn't get healed. Her mother's ego was annihilated! People want to hear about the death and the martyrdom. But the martyrdom we are attracted to in the saints so often has a romantic quality to it—"Ah, what courage in Joan of Arc!" But isn't it even more miraculous that Lisa's mother had the courage to not put her daughter in an institution? That she chose to serve her daughter with no glamour and no thanks? That kind of work is totally selfless. In one sense, Lisa's mother's life is irrevocably ruined. For her, there are no other options...like, "Oh, after the kids are grown..." or "After we retire...." There is just, "This is it."

My life with my child is full and rich and filled with the regular series of ups and downs of learning and growing and evolving—a divinely-given relationship. But what I am talking about with Lisa's mom is the stuff saints are made of.

Wise Innocence. Contemporary rendering of the Divine Mother, by sculptor Kelsey Bogart

Becoming Mother is about creating—bearing life in the body, nurturing that life, and then delivering that life whenever and however it is needed. Mother's creation may be a child, a garden, a meal, a sacred idea, a room full of warmth, or any other act of service or beauty. Creating is Mother's job.

In our day, as throughout history, that creativity has often devolved into an obsession with appearances—with clothing, with cosmetics, with home furnishings. Woman's inherent desire to create beauty on the earth has been co-opted in the marketplace, to the detriment of her soul. Mother has been denied, abused, seduced and offered the flimsiest substitutes for the proud, strong force of creation that drives her.

If we are to become Mother, which is to become Woman, we are going to have to wrest that primal creativity back. We are going to have to wake up, to face the insidious ways in which we contribute to our own denial, abuse, seduction and superficiality, day in and day out.

One way to do that is to ask another mother to tell us the truth about what she sees us denying. And then to listen, carefully, to what she has to say. If she feels confidant that she can speak freely, without the fear that she is going to hurt our feelings by what she says, she will be a great friend—a sister, a Mother! She will show herself to be capable of great love. We will be able to rest with her, even if we cry.

5

THE PATH OF COMPASSION

If we are to preserve our sanity amidst the mind-shattering horrors of the modern world, it is well to have an intimation of serenely abiding beauty underlying the grim facade visible to our senses. Could we but choose our own symbol of that beauty (and why indeed should we not?), it would be hard to find a form lovelier than Kuan Yin's; or, if the Chinese conception of the goddess seems just a trifle too sedate, we could opt for her Tibetan counterpart and twin, the compassionate and slyly playful Tara.[1]

— John Blofeld

As I write, a small icon of the Green Tara leans against my computer. She is ornately enshrined: lotus blossoms, bursts of flame, clouds, a gilded frame created by snake-like creatures entwines around her. A halo of orange light offsets the rich texture of her green skin. She smiles sedately. Her left hand is raised, palm exposed, in a gesture of blessing or welcome. The other hand is at her side, open too. She is reaching out to me, and to all her children. As she sits, one foot is draped over the edge of her lotus-throne. Iconographers agree that this means she is ever ready to step into the world to help suffering humanity.

Tara, the embodiment of compassion, is a female Buddha in Tibetan cosmology. Some say she has twenty-one different forms, other sources report 108, and she is represented in many different colors (red, black, white, green), depending upon her particular job. Green Tara is the dark or "swarthy" Mother, the more active Tara, while her sister the White Tara, who stands or sits in state upon a lotus, is the internal or passive form of this beloved deity.

As a Catholic girl, raised in a New York middle-class home, the art and the meditation practice of the Tara of Tibetan Buddhism, her counterpart Kuan Yin from China, or their predecessor, Avalokitesvara, the *Bodhisattva* of Compassion of India, were far removed from my experience. In the past years, however, as the subject of compassion has become a daily consideration, I have turned to these "Blessed Mothers" of the East to learn more of their secrets and their teaching.

In honoring Tara, the embodiment of compassion, we venture beyond the personal into the vast impersonal domain of existence, discovering the living principle of the Feminine as it exists in all time; discovering how we can access this energy for our own lives and work.

THE BODHISATTVA OF COMPASSION

Avalokitesvara, the Sanskrit name for the *Bodhisattva* of Compassion, entered my life before I could even pronounce the name. It was early 1986, and our tiny meditation hall on the grounds of my teacher's ashram in northern Arizona was being renovated to accommodate a gift he had recently been given. A big gift—the roof of the hall was being raised by four feet!

Our new guest, a thirteen-foot, oak, hand-carved statue of Avalokitesvara, had been a treasured artifact of the twentieth century spiritual teacher, Rudrananda (Rudi) who had kept the piece for years in his antique shop in New York City. Following Rudi's

Avalokitesvara, The Bodhisattva of Compassion

death, the statue ended up in Massachusetts at the home of some friends of my teacher's. Unable to house such an immense shrine in their suburban home, and wanting it to have an appropriate resting place, they donated it to our ashram. So it was that, in November of 1986, a couple of the men from our community drove a dilapidated green delivery truck from Arizona to Massachusetts and back, a journey of over 2400 miles. It was an odd sort of pilgrimage, a bit like bringing the mountain to Mohammed.

> Around 2000 years ago a most remarkable psychological event occurred in the consciousness of the peoples of northern India and near-by countries. An Archetype was constellated, or Empowered, and the quality this particular archetype represents had never before (and has never since) been excelled! This Archetype expresses the Energy of Infinite compassion and it has proved to be one of the most powerful and profound Archetypal Energies .... In Sanskrit this Energy was named Avalokitesvara, and in the early centuries of its constellation it was considered to be and worshipped as masculine. But as the worship of this Archetype passed into China and Japan it was re-polarized and became Female. ... Among the numerous abilities of Blessings which this *Bodhisattva* can confer upon His or Her devotees, the most important is "the Gift of fearlessness" in the midst of terror and trouble. An Archetype ideally suited to our Age.[2]
>
> — Greg Campbell

Once our honored guest arrived, women and children watched in amazement and anticipation as the parts, wrapped in packing quilts and tied with thick cords, were carefully unloaded and carried, like so many corpses, into the hall. For the next several hours the meditation space was off-limits while the re-assembly was underway. What greeted us that night, as we gathered in

140

the hall, was a thirteen-foot monolith, draped in sheets, filling the right front corner of the room, towering over everything else. The statue's communication was already being made—despite the shrouds, the sheer size of the figure was working its effect. We entered and left with a newfound sense of reverence, perhaps only out of fear that these curtains would suddenly part and some otherworldly terror would pounce upon us.

As the weeks went on, we began the preparation for the installation of the new presence. A Zen monk, Greg Campbell, one of my teacher's students, had been specifically invited for the ceremony. And as the days of anticipation stretched out, we learned more about Avalokitesvara, or Kuan Yin (as the Chinese refer to this being), or Kannon/ Kwannon/ or Kanzeon Bosatsu as the Japanese call it ... him ... or was it her? When we finally laid eyes on this serenely benevolent face, the soft lines of the body, the delicate hands—one extended in a gesture of welcoming or bestowing blessing, the other holding a jar of nectar from which a lotus bloomed—we understood that the male and the female were perfectly married in this one.

> Moonlike mother of buddhas,
> Whose form is that of a beautiful goddess ...
> Empty by nature, you [emerge] from emptiness
> In the form of a woman
> And tame living beings thereby.[3]

Avalokitesvara (or Avalokita) according to the *Saddharma Pundarika Sutra* was decidedly a male deity who had 337 earthly incarnations, 336 of which were human males (one was that of a horse). The name, Avalokitesvara, meant: "One who hears the cries of the world." As the earthly embodiment of the compassion of the Amitabha Buddha, Avalokitesvara's job, which is the job of every *Bodhisattva*, was to awaken all sentient beings from their illusionary sleep, and thus relieve them of their suffering. We also learned that the Dalai Lama was considered to be the most recent incarnation of Avalokita.

141

The scene is a small crowded room at the Free-
dom House in New York City. It is the Dalai
Lama's first press conference in the United States.
A voice somewhere in the back of the room asks,
"Your Holiness, do you have a message for the
United States?"

His Holiness the Dalai Lama XIV, emanating a happy and peaceful radiance, replies,
"Compassion."[4]

It was this same message of compassionate service which, in
his blunt and often confrontive manner, my teacher, Lee, stressed
to us in preparing us for the arrival of our great friend:

If we were to sit in front of the *Bodhisattva* and
meditate, that's fine, but if the *Bodhisattva* were
genuinely organic it would kick our ass out of the
Darshan Hall and say, "Somebody needs you, go
serve! I'll be here to remind you, so when you're
done serving, you can come and tell me how it
went!" So the *Bodhisattva* of Compassion is not
an idol to worship. It is a living presence demanding that we serve; that we practice.

On the great day of the statue's installation, a bright day in
late November, with over a hundred men, women and children
stretching the walls of the hall, the *Bodhisattva* was unveiled in a
cloud of incense smoke, and amid the slow and reverential chanting of the *Heart Sutra*. Together, we recited the *Bodhisattva* vows,
promising as did this Great One who had come for our benefit, to
be available to the needs of all, always and forever.

As Zen master Maezumi Roshi once described: "We shouldn't
think of Kanzeon as being someone else, who is somewhere else,
someone whom we contemplate or to whom we pray to do something for us. Each of us is the Kanzeon *Bodhisattva*."[5]

What a tremendous gift we had been given! And what a tremendous responsibility had come with this gift! I didn't know, in 1986, that I had only a short time to absorb the benediction of this Avalokitesvara's presence. (We humans constantly deny the nature of impermanence.) But, in the enigmatic way that circumstances unfold around a spiritual teacher, after seven years of constant vigilance towards us, the *Bodhisattva* was given to a place where "he/she" would be more highly regarded, and thus honored in a way more in keeping with its inherent grandeur. Lee gave Avalokitesvara into the keeping of Zen Buddhist Master Jokusho Kwong, Roshi, of the Sonoma Mountain Zen Center in northern California. There, among the followers of the tradition that "he" birthed, Kanzeon Botazu is revered by hundreds of blacked-robed monastics and retreatants every year.

MEETING TARA

Just prior to the departure of Avalokitesvara, while on a trip to France, my teacher was given another gift. This one a treasured *tanka*—a hand-painted cloth which details the gods or deities of the Tibetan pantheon. The French spiritual teacher, Arnaud Desjardins, had acquired this priceless treasure in one of his many journeys to the East, and as a token of his appreciation wanted Lee to have it. In response to my teacher's enigmatic comment that he was "afraid of women," Arnaud good-naturedly reported that he was giving Lee a *tanka* with the largest collection of *dakinis* (female enlighteners; women who are available for the benefit of humankind) in one place. This *tanka* featured a central female figure surrounded by twenty smaller figures, each with a slightly different dress, a slightly different pose. Some of the *dakinis* were seated among the clouds, others sat on lotuses poised on the mountain tops, and the lower row were surrounded by water. Within a few weeks of the departure of the *Bodhisattva* of Compassion, a new shrine was erected in our meditation hall, an encasement for the *tanka*, which was now to work its power on our assembly.

For several months I paid visits to the shrine, absorbing the gentle and elegant strength of the twenty-one *dakinis*. But, one aspect continually intrigued me. Why were there twenty-one women? That number was my biggest clue in searching out *who* these marvelous women were, since I had already read about the twenty-one forms of Tara. As I studied the piece I observed that every deity was seated on a lotus, and the right foot of each was extended, ready to step off into the world. The background color of the entire *tanka* was green, although the female figures were light-skinned, so that threw me off temporarily. But, the deity's crown, the tilt of her head, the blue lotus extending from under her arm, the hands poised in blessing ... everything about this shrine bespoke that this one and her entourage were all Tara.

My study also revealed some stories about Tara—that she was formed from a tear of the Avalokitesvara as he wept for the suffering of humankind. What a striking coincidence, I thought. Where once we hosted Avalokitesvara, now stood his female counterpart, The Buddha Tara, who is also considered a *Bodhisattva*. It was as if this great Mother of Compassion had come to take us the next step in our understanding of this all-embracing virtue. In replacing the "Father," we were actually coming closer to our community's roots within the Baul tradition, which has always worshipped the Feminine principle, and has always known that all must become Woman in relationship to the Divine.

WHO IS TARA?

The earliest depictions of Tara identifiable to us today come from the sixth century. These portrayals typically show her at the right hand of Avalokitesvara. In traditional scriptural texts, while Tara is almost exclusively spoken of as an archetypal *Bodhisattva*, some have reported that she started out as an ordinary woman, who, after lifetimes of dedicated spiritual practice of the *Bodhisattva* way, eventually achieved the status of a perfectly enlightened Buddha. Like all the *Bodhisattvas*, she had vowed to save all sentient beings, but despite the traditional Buddhist teaching that only male births had any possibility of gaining lasting merit and achieving the final goal of enlightenment, Tara vowed to live and work for others, eternally, in the form of a woman. About this revolutionary position, Martin Willson, in his warm and scholarly commentary, *In Praise of Tara*, writes: "This practical yet limitlessly inspiring resolution somehow makes Her seem very real and close to us of the late twentieth century, although it [Her decision] is supposed to have been made unimaginably long ago."[6]

From Willson's study we learn that the *Bodhisattva*, Tara, has three main titles: Compassion of Lord Avalokita, Mother of all Buddhas, and Savioress. As the Mother of all Buddhas, she is the perfection of wisdom, which is "the eternal and immutable source and ground of all that is,"[7] or the "womb...that has nurtured the embryo of Buddhahood...."[8]

This association of "mother" with wisdom is key to our appreciation of what Woman is. What that means, in essence, is that Woman perfected is not other than Wisdom perfected. Out of Woman's womb/Wisdom's womb all enlightened beings are born. Contemplation of such a mystery should afford endless encouragement and strength to the woman who seeks to find Herself as she walks this spiritual path.

Regarding her role as Savioress, the name Tara is thought to come from the Sanskrit *tarare*, meaning to carry across. In the text, *The Hundred and Eight Names*, Tara says of herself:

> I, O Lord, shall lead (beings) across
> the great flood of their diverse fears;
> Therefore the eminent seers sing
> of me in the world by the name of Tara.[9]

Universally, Tara is identified as the one who saves us from the eight great fears: lions, elephants, fire, snakes, robbers, imprisonment, water, and the man-eating demons. The First Dalai Lama, however, suggested that these were actually the great inner fears: pride, delusion, anger, envy, wrong views, avarice, attachment and doubt. Despite her gentle demeanor, then, our Mother Tara is no wimpy deity. With the power to vanquish such demons as pride and attachment, she is a Goddess not unlike her dark sister, Kali, Mother of the world. Tara is a Mother who knows the underworld as well as she knows the upperworld. Her familiarity with the darkness, with the sources of human terror, make her a Mother to turn to in the midst of our suffering, our doubt, our confusion, our despair.

A beautiful prayer, given to author China Galland (quoted in her book, *Longing for Darkness: Tara and the Black Madonna*) by a spiritual renunciate in Nepal, expresses a humble approach which any beginner can use as she proceeds to the feet of this all compassionate Mother, Tara:

> Alas, I do not know either the mystical word ...,
> nor do I know the songs of praise to thee, nor how
> to welcome thee, nor how to meditate on thee ...
> nor how to inform thee of my distress. But this
> much I know, O Mother, that to take refuge in
> thee is to destroy all my miseries.[10]

Green Tara is the *karma-devi*—The Goddess of Action, or Queen of the Action Family. A big factor in Tara's appeal to us common folk is that, as the benevolent and powerful Mother, she wastes no time in coming to the assistance of her children in need. Foregoing the red tape of formal invocation, or even the simple six-word *mantra* (sacred word or words) which is recited in her honor (*Om Tare Tutare Ture Soha—Om*) devotees in distress need only say her name to cause her to leap into action.

I know that to be true. At the Tara shrine in our meditation hall, a basket is placed. Here we drop off our urgent requests. I rarely ask for favors for myself, but when a friend was dying in great pain, and crying for help in her transition, I appealed to Tara. When another woman was battling fears in her own hell-realm, I entrusted her to Tara, by intention. In both cases, regardless of circumstantial evidence, I sensed the benediction of this celestial Being. During a time of great inner turmoil, when I felt I had no

Green Tara

more options of any human consequence, I broke down and wrote a simple request for assistance and carried it to Tara's feet. The result was quite dramatic. For the next few days the situation heightened in intensity, similar to the crisis that often occurs just before healing takes hold. Then, on the third morning, the cloud lifted and dissipated completely; peace settled in. I knew that Tara had heard and answered my plea, not in the dramatic external way in which the materially-minded demand a miracle, but in the subtle direction of my own energy and attention.

As for the White Tara, Erich Neumann, in his treatment of the archetypes and the depictions of the Great Mother throughout human history from the Paleolithic era up until the modern era, places her as the crowning glory of all Great Mother manifestations. He describes her as inseparable from the Ultimate manifestation of the Divine Feminine, the symbol of ultimate transformational energy—the embodiment of compassion. White Tara is supreme, sublime Womanhood. She is turned both outward and inward, simultaneously, since her eyes are often half closed as she sits in the posture of meditation.

If compassion is the ultimate expression of the Great Mother, then merging with ultimate compassion is where we are all headed in our spiritual journey. How much clearer (though not necessarily easier) our path becomes once we have the destination in mind. Instead of having to develop a myriad of forms, or undertake a myriad of practices, we can put our attention on the one ultimate practice, the practice of compassion, allowing Tara—our mother, our vehicle, our sister and our friend—to carry us home.

Meeting Kuan Yin

And the beautiful Kuan Yin, where does she figure? This lovely one who graces Oriental art? For some of us, Kuan Yin's image is much more familiar than Tara's. The next time you make a trip to a local Chinese restaurant you might look around for a depiction of her, or even a shrine in her honor, she is so beloved.

The name Kuan Shih Yin means precisely the same thing as Avalokitesvara: "She (or, the One) who hears the cries of the World." John Blofeld, author of *Bodhisattva of Compassion: The Mystical Tradition of Kuan Yin*, tells us that she is the Chinese manifestation of both Avalokitesvara and Tara—a beautiful amalgam of compassion, taking the stately power of the Hindu *Bodhisattva* and the playful and motherly attention of the Tibetan Buddha and merging them into one.

Kuan Yin is decidedly feminine, even though in the first centuries of her introduction *she* was a *he*. Vestiges of this integrated femininity and masculinity exist today in those pieces that show Kuan Yin with a moustache. Because she is a composite, she is sometimes seen with the implements of the one deity and sometimes with those of the other. Sometimes she is seated in the meditation posture, like Amitabha Buddha or the White Tara. At other times she appears with one foot extended, as does her sister Green Tara. Kuan Yin holds a nectar jar and lotus, as do her other manifestations. She too is the serene embodiment of the wisdom of the Divine Mother, at whose feet the people come to beg for assistance. She is always ready to hear the cries of her children! As one who grants children to those who desire them, Kuan Yin is worshiped extensively.

> Kuan-yin holds in her left hand a sprig of willow as a sign of healing ability (both physical and psychological) and in her right hand the vase of *Soma* —the nectar of *amrita*—the symbol of life committed to the practice of effective Compassion. She is always barefoot because nothing should interfere with her contact to the earth. This is the path of healing energy. She is always shown in long, flowing, graceful robes, appropriate for a woman, and also she can be shown with a moustache representing union with the masculine.[11]

Blofeld recounts a striking story told to him by a British-educated Chinese friend. This man, on one of his many travels for a mining company in China, accidentally took a wrong path and so unknowingly was separated from his staff and servants. When he realized his error it was too late in the evening, and the weather was becoming much too cold for the man to risk turning back. Thinking that he was sure to find some human habitation ahead of him, he kept walking forward. With icy winds buffeting him, and terrified by the sounds of the night and the thoughts of robbers along the way, the distraught man huddled by the side of the path and whispered a fervent prayer to the patron saint of his childhood—the Christian saint, Bernadette—begging her to save him.

Within moments of his earnest plea, a young Chinese girl dressed in a blue silk robe and white trousers, her hair piled up on her head in the style of a noble maiden, and wearing jewels at her neck, appeared before him, standing on a rock. Addressing him sweetly as "Elder Brother," the child led him to a cave only a short distance away. Here she instructed him to lay down and sleep. The floor of the cave, he remarked later, was as soft and warm to him as sleeping upon a silken quilt, although the next morning when he awoke, fully refreshed, he observed that he had been sleeping on cold, pebble-strewn rock. A few moments after leaving the cave he met up with a mule train that safely led him back to his companions.

Nearly a year after his miraculous deliverance by the marvelous "Chinese Bernadette," as he called her, the man found an image of the stately Kuan Yin accompanied by her two attendants, the male Shan Ts'ai, and the young girl, Lung Nü, each of whom are traditionally known and honored for their devoted service to Kuan Yin. Imagine this man's astonishment when, in the image of Lung Nü, he recognized the clothing, the posture, the face, everything about the young girl who had saved his life on that dreadful night. Despite his erudite understanding of the workings of the human mind, this educated man found no problem in accepting that the benevolent Kuan Yin in her constant mercy had heard his cries and had sent her servant to him in a form that he could welcome and revere.

Kuan Yin with attendants Lung Nü and Shan Ts'ai

To hear her name and see her form,
Delivers beings from every woe.

— Lotus Sutra

It was Blofeld's heartful treatment of Kuan Yin which first alerted me to the power and benevolence of this tender mother. Eschewing my Christian system of checks and balances wherein the good are rewarded and the bad are punished, Kuan Yin revealed herself as the Mother of Compassion free from all vengefulness. Even the most recalcitrant of children were welcomed to her feet. But this kind of "asking for favors religion," this running to the goddess for protection, while it may indicate a faith of profound depth, is often nothing more than a manifestation of our extreme human fear that we really are alone and abandoned in this world, and that we are doomed without the help of an otherworldly presence of immense proportions. Such an approach denies the real power of the Mother, however, which is to consume the devoted child in the fire of Her heart and thus to merge Divine and human nature. Or, put another way, to give Herself so completely to her child that the child so embodies the Mother's attributes as to be indistinguishable from Her.

For those who are willing to keep vigil at Her feet, either literally or by the active practices of compassion in daily life, protection is only the beginning. Like the Tara and Avalokitesvara, this Divine Mother Kuan Yin wants to give her children the most lasting of gifts—that which will allow them to serve others in complete surrender. The real gift of the *Bodhisattva* of Compassion is nothing less than complete and absolute liberation from the world of illusion.

PRACTICING AS A BODHISATTVA

The Ego is annihilated in the reality of the *Bodhisattva* of Compassion, until there is nothing left but the *bodhisattva* itself. Thus, a lifetime of intensive practice has reached its fruition in the

> merger of lover and beloved—in meditator and
> the object of meditation.
>
> —John Blofeld

Tara, like the other forms of the *Bodhisattva*, is a feminine model for practice. The aim of Tantric Buddhist practice is to actually *become* the deity—to so closely identify with her that she comes to possess one completely, and therefore to manifest herself through the devotee. Kuan Yin or Tara are not separate from the benevolent manifestation of one's own mind. And when mind is pure, calm, at rest, she is present. This is why meditation practice is so essential, since it brings one to this state of pure calm, thereby allowing the Goddess to emerge.

The acknowledgment of Tara's Buddhahood was only possible because of the revered status of women within certain sects of Tantric Buddhism, particularly Tibetan Buddhism. Within this cosmology, women, and indeed all female life forms, were considered the sources of wisdom and the embodiments of the Great Goddess. And indeed, Guru Padmasambhava, who carried Tantric practice to Tibet, even proclaimed that the woman's body was *better* for realizing enlightenment than was a man's body.

This tenet is especially prevalent in the scriptures written by the great female teacher, Laksminkara. In communicating the teaching of the Mother of All Buddhas (here given the name Vajrayogini), Laksminkara has her proclaim: "Wherever in the world a female body is seen, that should be recognized as my holy body."[12]

Learning to embody Tara, or another form of the great goddess, involves a bit more than dressing in flowing robes and speaking in gentle tones; more than what is communicated on the bumper sticker that reads: "Back-off, I'm the Goddess." Tara's practice—intense meditation under the guidance of a meditation teacher or master—involves a series of complex and exacting visualizations. Between these meditation sessions, one assuredly attempts to move and act as the deity, yet such embodied behavior requires a degree of sharpened attention that few are capable of without serious practice and probable assistance. As Willson reports:

...you should recognize all you see as Tara's body (made of green light), all you hear as Her divine speech, and all your thoughts as Her divine wisdom. Every particle of food you eat is Tara, every molecule of air you breathe is Her divine energy, the house you live in is Her, when you lie down your head rests in Her lap. Thus Tara is the Basis from which spiritual practice starts, the mud of samsara, with all it defilements and other obscurations, in which the lotus of spiritual awakening grows.[13]

In this day, when the secrets of the ages are cheaply available to anyone who reads the popular "spiritual" magazines which fill the stands in the local health food store or alternative bookstore, the idea that years of disciplined practice might be required for the realization of the truth of Tara is at best discouraging, at worst, abhorrent. Nonetheless, I believe that is true. The masses of seekers have always been satisfied with the crumbs from the table—a few experiences of a warm glow around the heart, or a blissful blast of light inside the head, and many are convinced that they are ready to start giving workshops in cosmic awakening.

For those who know how readily mind can co-opt the experiences of enlightenment and use them for the purpose of ego gratification, the path through visions and revelations is one that must be walked with extreme care, and then ideally with the guidance and ongoing benediction of a living teacher who has traversed this same path often and well.

In this spirit then, with the ultimate desire that each of my readers might find her or his way to the feet of the Great Liberator and there be stripped of all illusion (as hard-line as this approach might sound), I encourage those who have felt a resonance with these ideas and stories of the *Bodhisattva* to take the next step—to ask the deity for the assistance of a teacher, and to wait patiently, yet trustingly, upon her good pleasure. The section which follows will offer a few clues to the practices of the *Bodhisattva*. Our teacher and guide here will be the Dalai Lama, the living embodiment of Avalokitesvara.

The Dalai Lama's Message

"The Dalai Lama? What's *he* doing in your book about great women and Divine Mothers?" one of my friends asked. My response surprised me: "Why, he's one of the wisest mothers I can name," I said. We both laughed.

My friend's question also prompted an important distinction for me, namely that, although ninety percent of my stories are about women, this book is about feminine wisdom. And feminine wisdom is certainly not the exclusive privilege of human females. Both men and women have masculine and feminine energies within themselves. In fact, our wholeness as human beings depends upon our ability to access these polarities and live them in a balanced and integrated way. Man or woman, one who is unable to access his or her masculine wisdom is just as crippled emotionally and psychically as is one who cannot get in touch with their feminine wisdom. As far as I'm concerned, Tenzin Gyatso, the 14th Dalai Lama, is one of the greatest exemplars of the balance of masculine and feminine wisdom alive in our times.

In 1959, when Tibet was being overtaken by Communist China, the Dalai Lama, at the age of twenty-two, was forced to flee from his beloved homeland. Officially, he still remains both the political and spiritual head of the Tibetan people. With his government in exile located in Dharamsala, India, His Holiness (as he is reverently called) works tirelessly to keep alive a remnant of Tibetan education and culture, as he keeps his fingers on the pulse of the world, looking for every opportunity to make known the cause of Tibet's freedom.

Day after day, for thirty years, the Dalai Lama is heartbroken by the news of what is happening within Tibet, as he hears of and witnesses to the horrors perpetrated on his people by the Chinese Communists whose stated goal is to systematically subsume Tibetan culture. An estimated 1.2 million Tibetans have already been murdered in the process, and more than 6000 irreplaceable monasteries, temples and other historic landmarks have been destroyed.

Tenzin Gyatso, His Holiness The Fourteenth Dalai Lama

The Dalai Lama travels the globe, addressing political leaders everywhere. Without intervention from other world powers, he knows only too well that within a few years, the Chinese will have accomplished their purpose in the destruction of Tibet. Still, he continues to urge non-violence as the only way to lasting peace; in 1989, he was awarded the Nobel Peace Prize for his uncompromising stand. Yet, at the same time that he utilizes these masculine energies so emphatically, the Dalai Lama has become a living witness to compassion. The same man who fearlessly addresses the United Nations, is also unafraid to cry publicly, openly, when news of some new horror in Tibet is communicated to him. With all that he has seen and suffered in his own life, and for all he carries as the leader of his people, the Dalai Lama is unashamed to admit that he is completely without rancor—he bears no hatred for the Chinese. He remains the embodiment of compassion.

What is this mysterious compassion which has so transformed this man that, despite the most aching tragedy, he still lives with an open heart and a peaceful mind, completely dedicated to the service of others—all others, Tibetans or Chinese alike? What is this profound virtue which is such an enigma to the forces of retribution and "justice" which govern world politics? Perhaps by contemplating the Dalai Lama's explanations of the practices of the *Bodhisattva* we can gain some insight into these questions, and find for ourselves some useful platform on which to stand as we attempt to integrate compassion into our own lives.

THE PRACTICE OF COMPASSION

According to the Dalai Lama's instruction, the common element in our humanity is that we all desire the end of suffering.[14] Or to put it positively, we all desire happiness, in whatever way we define that. This is primary for the realization of inner freedom. This is where we start.

For instance, when tragedy strikes on a grand scale, as happened in the 1994 bombings in Oklahoma City, we are shocked into the recognition that those previously nameless, faceless others whom we pass on the street every day, have instantaneously become our brothers and sisters. We feel for them. We identify with their plight. We long to reach out to do something to help alleviate their pain. And granted, while much of this action may be motivated by our own fear that such a thing could happen to us, we can nonetheless see the commonality of humanity in such trials.

Our common link is that we all possess a body—a fragile, wound-prone body. In the hospital wards and at the grave sites we come to share the society of the wounded; we come to recognize how similar our fates, how similar our desires and hopes. We want to live. We want to be happy. Yet, all of life is suffering—within us, next to us. When we allow ourselves to feel the sorry state of human beings, and to acknowledge their suffering, we have begun the practice of the *Bodhisattva*.

Feeling a hit of compassion, however, is far from living compassion as a way of life. "You have to train in an aspiration toward bringing about others' welfare,"[15] His Holiness wrote. And indeed, this is perhaps one of the greatest contributions which the Tibetan Buddhist path has made to Western culture—a systematic training of the mind and heart, together with a program of practice of compassionate action. Listing some of these training "steps" here may be beneficial in the way a map is helpful in planning a trip. Yet, it is necessary to realize that what is being summarized is, in fact, the dedicated work of a lifetime, not some exuberant rush of heart energy which sends us out to "do-good," while our own internal war-like tendencies get glossed over.

It is also particularly important for us to realize that the practice of compassion applies to our relationship with self as much as it applies to our dealings with and attitudes toward others. In fact, for women, the tendency for self-hatred, and lack of self-forgiveness will often be the major obstacle encountered at the gateway to the path. As we proceed with this overview then, keep in mind that genuine compassion for ourselves is integral to this approach. (A section on self-forgiveness will follow our consideration of the Dalai Lama's instruction.)

Equanimity

As we allow ourselves to be penetrated with the truth of our common heritage and legacy of suffering and vulnerability (step one in the method of compassion), we can move into the consideration of equanimity—step two. Naturally, we feel close to our friends, and we feel angry or resentful of our enemies, and we feel neutral towards those we do not know. Yet, the compassion practice of the Tibetan Buddhist path testifies that it is possible to bring friend, enemy and stranger into a state of equal regard, holding all with internal equanimity. Sound difficult? Unreasonable? Probably so, to our Western minds. Yet the alternative, as we have seen, is one of growing alienation, war, slow death by hatred and resentment—all building the illusion of separation wider and wider.

It helps to contemplate the fleeting nature of existence, realizing that one's closest friends (one's children, one's mate, one's family) will die or will move away before we ourselves die; or will simply change. Nothing stays the same. Since everything is always in a state of flux, it is possible that even our worst enemy may become a friend. Is has happened before, hasn't it? Almost all of us have a story or two of this unlikely kind of transformation.

Specifically, the Dalai Lama suggests that we can enhance this practice by actually visualizing three people: a good friend, an enemy, a neutral person. Watch the arising of emotions and thoughts that accompany each mental picture. Without doing anything about these thoughts or feelings, or judging ourselves negatively (or positively) for them, we just let the usual feelings arise. Then we ask ourselves whether the cause of these feelings or thoughts is from something permanent, or from something that could change? This recognition that things can change is the basis for eventually—slowly and gradually—dropping this unequal attitude.

The Buddhist believes that one has lived many lives, and will continue to live an almost infinite number (remember, that's the job of the *Bodhisattva*—to keep coming back until all beings are enlightened). From this viewpoint, they assert that our enemy is connected to us in this life because he or she was connected to us in previous lifetimes. In fact, it is quite possible that a contemporary "enemy" was actually a friend many times, even our closest intimate relationship, perhaps. Maybe that person is here in this life as a blessing to help us come to the realization that all things are passing, and that only equanimity is lasting.

It is entirely possible that throughout lifetimes all beings have been in relationship to us as mother is to child. Radical? Well, consider the fact that we are one common family of humanity. The cells of our bodies are recycled from the stars, literally. We are all connected in the sense that we breathe the same air. We are all related in that we are born from woman. Allowing that everyone has been our dearest friend, or even our own mother, might just seem like a pleasant fantasy, but if undertaken seriously, it is a consideration that dramatically interferes with our usual rigid lines of definition of about who or what is "good" and who or what is "bad."

Remembering Kindness

The practice of compassion progresses into remembering the kindness that other beings have extended and continue to extend to us, day in and day out. Even if our parents were insensitive, they gave us life. Our dear friends and beloved family members have given us gifts that we cannot even begin to count. All beings— rocks, the earth, the water, fishes—are constantly offering kindness to us, whether they directly feed us, or simply serve to bring beauty, elegance or wildness into our lives. As we may well imagine, a long time could be spent in such contemplation.

Consider doing an inventory of a lifetime, attempting to recall, in as much detail as possible, all the ways in which beings throughout the universe have expressed kindness that has benefited us. How about doing that for yesterday alone? Anonymous others are feeding and clothing us by the labors of their hands, giving us the precious minutes and hours of their lives. We are doing the same for others, perhaps without ever knowing it. I remember the radical help I received from a nun who was a high school teacher of mine in sophomore English. Sister Caroline recognized that my obsession with being good had me caught in a loop of guilt and fear. I wasn't going to Holy Communion despite the fact that I was attending Mass almost every day. My active imagination, picking up on my body-negative attitudes, had me convinced that I was committing mortal sin every time the thought of sex passed through my mind. Caroline intervened in a way that literally transformed my life. She told me that I had to listen to *her* in this regard, rather than my own mind, which had become seriously imbalanced. She told me to receive Holy Communion every day, regardless of my fear that such an act would pile another mortal sin upon my already overburdened soul. She told me that she would take responsibility before God for my acts. She told me, unequivocally, that the God I was afraid of did not exist.

Her recommendation worked. Within two weeks, the debilitating scruples which had tormented me for almost three years were soothed. She had provided a living witness to the mercy and love of God. She had given me some breathing room, allowing me to relax enough for grace to intervene.

Who have been our witnesses to goodness? And to whom have we been witnesses? We may never know. When we let someone pass us on the highway, or get ahead of us in line; when we send a contribution to a charitable cause, or say a prayer, or offer our old clothes to a clothing bank; no matter how insignificant the act may seem, we are serving as "mother" to others, and all others are serving in this way to us, and have been over lifetimes. As we contemplate this with people close to us, we can then extend this recognition to include the whole creation. The Dalai Lama urges all of us to remember the interdependence of all beings.

Even our enemies have been kind to us. For instance, we would have no need to develop patience, one of the transcendent virtues, unless our enemy was challenging us in this regard. Whether our enemy is the person next door, or the weather, or the delays on our computer screen makes no difference. "Enemies are to be valued because they are useful to us, despite their motivation."[16] Ah, the pain that the Chinese have caused to the Tibetans, and yet the Tibetans have used this as a source of their own profound dedication to humanity. Unable to return to their homeland, they are taking over the world (in the spiritual sense)—their teachings are now being shared everywhere.

Repaying Kindness

An intention to repay the kindness of others is the natural overflow of *Bodhisattva* practice. We want to serve in some way, yet the question of what genuinely serves may haunt us. (See Chapter 8 for a more in-depth consideration of this subject.) While we realize that we can give food and clothing to others, we also realize that these resources will be quickly used up. We recall the famous saying about "teaching a man to fish so he can eat for a lifetime," and we recognize the wisdom of that. But, as our contemplation deepens and expands, we know that even though people may be taught the skills of survival, they are still suffering—attachments, anxiety, illness and the fear of death, these are still present for all. The ultimate form of service, therefore, would be to "be a light" in the darkness. That is, to be one who has boldly faced the very roots of suffering in themselves, and has found a calm inner center in which to live, regardless of circumstances. Living from that center would have the effect of inspiration and guidance to others, far beyond instruction for physical survival alone. It is for this reason that one practices compassion. This is the aspiration known as *Bodhichitta*—that is, realizing Buddhahood or enlightened mind for the sake of others.

Disadvantages and Advantages

Meditation on the disadvantages of self-centeredness is the next step. When, through rigorous but gentle self-observation, we get to see how all-pervasive our negative tendencies have grown—how our self-centeredness has blocked out the needs of others; how from morning 'til night we choose our own safety and comfort over the safety and comfort of others; how our petty selfishness has been a source of increased pain to others—to our own children in fact—a great sense of real remorse, or real conscience can develop. And here again, this process is not one that is accomplished quickly. We have taken twenty, thirty, forty years to reinforce these habits. They are not going to be undone in a few days. As the recognition of the suffering caused (to ourselves and others) by our self-centeredness penetrates into our cells, we naturally, even effortlessly change.

Concomitant with the disadvantages of self-interest, the Dalai Lama explains the need to meditate on the advantages of cherishing others. To give happiness and service to others benefits both them and us. It creates a sense of harmony and peace. It creates joy. It creates ease. If that can be done in a marriage, furthermore, it can also be done in the world community at large.

Roshi Jiyu Kennett, the abbess of the Mt. Shasta Monastery, herself a woman of tremendous resourcefulness who attempted throughout her life to bring Zen to the West in a way that it could be used, spoke about the other-centeredness and the detachment which genuine practice engenders:

A lot of the practice here [speaking of the monastery she directed]...is not only intended to help you get beyond self and be less opinionated and soften you, but also it is intended to constantly open you up and offer the merit of your practice wherever it's needed, so that you don't hold onto anything. The deeper you go in meditation the greater the reward, the spiritual fruits, are. All the offering of incense and the bowing is a way of always letting go and offering that up for the benefit of all beings. So a monastery is a little like a spiritual powerhouse, always sending out merit. [17]

The Great Exchange

"The exchange of self and other," becomes the next consideration. After all that has come before, we are at last motivated to regard others as ourselves, and to give them the same love, comfort and joy that we desire. But more—the *Bodhisattva* will actually sacrifice his or her own welfare so that others might be well.

Most mothers and fathers know what this exchange of self and other is about. At least in their better moments, and for short periods throughout their lives, parents are genuinely less concerned about their own survival than for the well-being of their children. If by causing themselves inconvenience or even pain they can effect an easement of the sufferings of their children, they are often ready to do this. They are willing to be diminished so that their children may be served. The point of this *Bodhisattva* practice is to cultivate that kind of attitude toward the whole world.

The Dalai Lama says that as one takes on the sufferings of others with an attitude of compassion, one finds that she wants to "...give up [her] own periods of relaxation in order to serve others at a hospital, to care for the aged, or to take care of defenseless children."[18] Here the *Bodhisattva* resolves that her life is no longer her own. Rather, it is her good pleasure to donate her life for a purpose in order that genuine love be shared.

At this point, there is no longer the issue of "getting my needs met," because truthfully, one doesn't have needs apart from the desire of serving others. This is a very high state, and it is extremely dangerous to assume that we have achieved such an altruistic position too early. It is all too easy for helpers to become persecutors, bringing an attitude of resentfulness to their service, as they wait for some acknowledgment of their "great sacrifice" for others. Therefore, tremendous self-honesty is called for as this practice deepens. However, knowing that such a pure condition is possible for a human being should give us courage and inspiration.

In taking on the sufferings of others it is also foolish to squander our energy and resources in ways that are ultimately ineffective. This is where great wisdom is needed for discrimination. "Idiot compassion," which doesn't hesitate to throw valuable seed on rocky slopes, must be foregone in favor of "skillful means"—a balanced, sane cultivation of the soil which makes it receptive for planting.

The Breath Practice

One form that this practice of "giving away happiness" takes is called the *Bodhisattva* breath. As the Dalai Lama briefly summarizes it: "When you inhale, you breathe in all the sufferings of beings and dissolve them into yourself, and when you exhale, you breathe out your own happiness and causes of happiness to others. This is just a visualization, but it builds great inner strength."[19]

The breath is synonymous with life. While we can go several days without water and several weeks without food, we cannot live but a few rare minutes without oxygen. The breath is therefore our constant companion. Like an alarm clock that rings several times a minute, the breath holds the power to wake us up from the sleep of illusion to the reality of the present moment. The acts of inhaling and exhaling literally fill us with the power of creation, energize and cleanse our systems, and release accumulated toxins to the environment. Because of this intimate and constant connection to the source of life, the breath is used by every religious culture to serve as a reminder to prayer, or as a literal act of dispensing "prayer" or compassion to others.

Tibetan Lama Chagdud Tulku Rinpoche described the meaning of the breath practice of the *Bodhisattva* precisely, suggesting that it is the exact opposite of the grasping that usually characterizes our activities in most domains of life. In the area of physical well being, for instance, the usual goal orientation is a grasping for health, yet this approach is antithetical to maintaining good health. With the *Bodhisattva* breath, however one gives away rather than grasps. On every exhalation, through visualization, the *Bodhisattva* makes a gift of all her health, wealth, understanding and realization—all virtue, and anything that might be beneficial to others. All is sent out on the breath for other beings to absorb and profit from. With each inhalation, the *Bodhisattva* breathes in every problem, predicament, illness or disease, all suffering and every cause of suffering, for the purpose of creating relief for others.

It is best to undertake such practice under the direction of a teacher or guru. Until such time as one has found a teacher, however, the profound recognition that it is possible to sacramentalize every moment by sacramentalizing every breath is an inestimable gift for the creation of both awareness and charity.

The Final Resolve

The last step in this preparatory process for *Bodhisattva* practice is called the development of special resolve. Akin to a marriage vow or other lifelong commitment, we promise to work to bring about "the removal of suffering and the acquisition of all happiness for all beings."[21] In the moment in which we make such a resolve, we are in effect experiencing the goal we have aimed for, since the resolve itself is an expression of enlightened mind. We also experience that we have arrived at the base of a new mountain; that for all the efforts that got us there, we are beginners once again. The last step has become the first step. We must now live on the basis of what we have promised!

The work of climbing this new mountain—of putting this attitude of the Buddha to use in everyday life—is known as the practice of the six *paramitas*, the six perfections. These are: giving (generosity), ethics (refraining from self-centeredness and from harming others), patience (both forbearance, as well as the willingness to undergo suffering yourself), effort (including the willingness to work on yourself without discouragement or inferiority), concentration and wisdom. Considering the magnitude of each of these virtues or perfections, we should probably consider that the journey will encompass not one, but actually six mountains, since each of the *paramitas* is a huge realm for both self-exploration and practice.

Buddhist teaching offers in-depth consideration of each *paramita*, together with specific and eminently usable practices associated with each one. For example, in practicing generosity one would not just think about giving, but would be enjoined to give in a variety of ways, all focused on the development of compassion.

Whether we are Tibetan Buddhists or not, those of us who long to bring our lives into alignment with such a preeminent virtue as compassion would do well to avail ourselves of the tremendous resources which are currently available from the Dalai Lama and other great teachers of this lineage. Theirs is a technology of compassion, refined and deepened over centuries, that men and women of every spiritual path can profit from.

FORGIVING OURSELVES

> You didn't come into this world. You came out of it, like a wave from the ocean. You are not a stranger here.
>
> — Alan Watts

Throughout my life I have been harder on myself than I would ever be on my friends or family. By the same token, my hard edge toward others has simply been a reflection of the intolerance and judgement I have toward myself. I know that other women suffer this same condition—a vicious cycle characterized by self-hatred, distrust and over-control.

Unlike the brilliant insight of Alan Watts, I have rarely had a sense that I belonged here on the Earth. Rather, all my training and upbringing convinced me of precisely the opposite—that Earth was my testing ground on which to prove my worth so that I could eventually merit something *else*—call it heaven, or enlightenment, or liberation. Life on Earth, the simple and ordinary engagement of the here and now of one's humanness was not enough. The reality of compassion as a "ground of being" out of which all things (myself included) arose, was not understood. Instead, I was convinced that I had to be good in some special way; that I had to be in a constant struggle against the forces of "sin," resisting temptations as these occurred both within myself and in the world at large. And while it is true that a woman of power does need to cultivate a type of discipline that enables her to stand firm when necessary, the ways in which this message was communicated to me as a child and a young adult caused it to become internalized as a type of self-doubt, at least, and self-hatred at worst. And this condition of self-alienation grew over the years, encouraged by the cultural voices and circumstances that denied basic goodness.

There is an old joke which a big hearted priest told me years ago that captured the mood of my lifelong struggle to be good: A diligent and hard-driving Catholic man died and found himself in front of St. Peter at the Pearly Gates. "Come on in, brother," said Peter enthusiastically, "glad to see you."

A bit confused by his own unfamiliar circumstances and by Peter's exuberant presence, the man stammered: "Uh, aren't you going to check the Books?"

"The books?" Peter asked. "What books?"

"The BOOKS, the BOOKS!," the man was clearly getting anxious. "The Books that record all the sins and all the good deeds of a lifetime?"

"Oh, *those* books," sighed St. Peter, smiling gently. "We don't keep any books."

The man was dumbstruck. His eyes widened and his breath came in short bursts. "No Books, No Books?" He was now even more disoriented than before.

"Tell you what," said St. Peter, "you come in and walk around for a few days, just enjoy yourself like you're on a little vacation, and I'll meet you back here on Wednesday morning. We can talk about books then."

The man, still flabbergasted, was beginning to feel like he'd better move ahead, as the line behind him was growing longer. While nobody in line was grumbling, he still wanted to be a good citizen. He stepped through the Gates and into the most wondrous realm that he had ever imagined, and for three days he wandered the gorgeous countryside in bliss.

Just as he was heading back to the Pearly Gates to meet with Peter, however, he saw an extraordinary vista, and jogged over a field to take a fuller view. There on a plateau of lush grass stood a circle of women—hundreds of them—moving methodically in a sort of ritualized dance. The man crept closer, fascinated by the strange sight.

As they moved, each woman stopped, turned towards the woman on her right, raised her knee and then gingerly swung her foot, kicking her neighbor in the buttocks. The dance continued unabated. Step, turn, swing, kick. On and on and on.

Hurrying to meet Peter, the man scratched his head, wondering about the odd sight. "Yes, everything's great here ... I love it," he admitted, with deep gratitude, in answer to St. Peter's question about how things had been for him. "But I have only one question. Over that hill," the man gestured in the direction from which he had come, "that enormous circle of women? Dancing? Kicking each other in the ass?"

"Oh that," said Peter chuckling, and shaking his head like a man who'd answered the same question innumerable times. He rolled his eyes and bent forward, as if to tell his new guest a secret. "Those are our nuns." Peter whispered. "They thought we kept Books too."

That story came back to me at a most unexpected moment in my life. In 1980, during my first trip to India, I sat in the presence of an Indian saint and felt myself being systematically disassembled. The room began to spin and I had to hold onto the floor. The next thing I knew I was lying face down with my cheek pressed against the cold stone slates. I was sobbing uncontrollably. And what was the thought that was going through my mind in this profound moment of ecstasy and bliss? "No Books." I gasped through my tears. "No Books." (My companions were at a loss to figure out the nature of this esoteric communication.) A lifetime of tension and fear over the accumulation of sin was suddenly dissipated. The saint's aura of enormous compassion had triggered the opening of the floodgate, and my fears with my tears came pouring out.

The same basic awareness came crashing through again in 1996. I had just returned from my second trip to India where for five weeks I had availed myself of the presence of another Indian saint—this one, Yogi Ramsuratkumar, the spiritual master of my own teacher. A few days after returning to the states, as I drove my car to town, the tears began again. The feeling-tone of that incident was another of enormous relief.

As I described later in my journal, I felt as if I had been to the highest court in the land—no, the highest court in the universe, and despite all my protests to the contrary I had been found "Not Guilty," completely innocent. There was no longer anywhere else to appeal. This was the final sentence, and in its own way it was terrifying.

A sentence of innocence is actually much harder for me to bear than its opposite would be. The quality of unconditioned love, of a sort of universal compassion, beyond judgement, which has occasionally embraced me, can be almost excruciating. It annihilates everything in me that wants to keep separation alive in all its myriad forms—separation of me from you, separation of me from the Divine, separation of humans from the earth, the list goes on and on.

It can be devastating, in the most liberating sense of the term, to recognize that "No Books" are being kept—at least not in the way in which I thought of "Books," as the lists of my sins, the record of my failings, the judgements of a punishing God. Yet, as times goes on I realize that such a recognition is only a first step in the appreciation of compassion. The second step is seeing that I am still keeping copies of my own Books, despite acquittal by the universe. How will I go about undermining the power of these neurotic lists, while at the same time encouraging a type of rigorous self-honesty that will ultimately serve my practice? Buddhist teachers, particularly some of the women teachers I have read or met, have an immediate answer for that—by developing an attitude of gentleness and forgiveness toward myself.

Meditation Is Key

Forgiveness begins with meditation—simply sitting, with no agenda, allowing ourselves to "be" just as we are, without the need to change anything about ourselves. Imagine that! What if we just accepted ourselves, the way flowers and animals and mountains live in the presence of "just this"-ness, without laboring over "better" or "bad" or "holy," or whatever?

The practice of meditation continues on a moment-to-moment basis (that's why the Buddhist teachers call it "training"), with systematically undermining the internal voices that speak the lie of separation. We do that by refusing to fight with ourselves, and by being willing to "hang out" in the discomfort between the extremes of justifying ourselves as right, or condemning ourselves as wrong. In this tender and undefended place, vulnerability lives. Vulnerable to ourselves, we see the uselessness of trying to appear good or holy. When we can approach another person with this attitude, genuine communication can take place.

"You're not enough..." the internal voice says, again and again.

"Interesting, there's voice of a judgement," we might observe, while noting how our emotions want to get embroiled in the skirmish.

"You've made a mistake, you're bad," the voice tries another tact.

"Hmm, that's the way mind works—it offers a sentence of either good or bad, with no alternatives," we can counter.

"Oh, you've really screwed up this time," the self-hater screams.

"Well, I can forgive myself for that. The human condition is one in which mistakes are made," we reply with gentleness and strength.

A big part of compassion is being honest with yourself, not shielding yourself from your mistakes as if nothing had happened. And the other

big component is being gentle. This is what meditation is about, but obviously it goes beyond sitting on a meditation cushion. You begin to see your
moods and your attitudes and your opinions. You
begin to hear this voice, your voice, and how it
can be so critical of self and others. There is growing clarity about all the different parts of yourself.

Meditation gives you the tools to look at all of
this clearly, with an unbiased attitude. A lot of
having compassion toward oneself in staying with
the initial thought or arising of emotion. This
means that when you see yourself being aggressive, or stuck in self-pity, or whatever it might be,
then you train again and again in not adding things
on top of that—guilt or self-justification or any
further negativities. You work on not spinning off
and on being kinder toward the human condition
as you see it in yourself."[22]

—Pema Chödrön

Such compassion for self is extremely necessary for women
today. It is virtually impossible to progress in spiritual life if one's
foundation is constantly crumbling in upon itself. The constant
feeding of self-doubt and self-hatred is the primary way in which a
foundation crumbles.

The vigilance that is required to work with self-hatred day in
and day out will not come from mere casual attention, however.
Rather, undermining the lie of separation is a serious undertaking
that a woman will need to commit to, especially if her roots are
deeply mired in this poisonous swamp. Moreover, self forgiveness
or gentle non-attachment may start out feeling phony to us (after
all, when the lie of separation from basic goodness has been the
predominant motivator for twenty, forty or sixty years, it is bound
to feel strange to start trying to counter it; we don't believe its
alternative, at least for a long while).

Since we abhor being phony, therefore, we may be tempted to drop the practice, sliding down into an even more sickening swamp of despair. But, that's where courage must enter. It takes great courage to keep moving ahead in an arena that feels uncomfortable; forging ahead simply on the basis of a truth glimpsed in a moment of revelation. Yet that it is what every woman has done who has successfully extricated herself from this swamp. She has pushed through self-denigration into self-honoring, not for the purpose of self indulgence, but rather because she has come to appreciate some connection between herself and all the rest of creation. She has come to appreciate that in learning to forgive and love the dis-owned and un-pretty parts of herself, she is learning to have compassion for the whole world.

It is by seeking to know oneself that the
Great Mother of all
may be found.[23]

—Anandamayi Ma

I have a feeling that forgiveness is more than its dictionary definition, that it bespeaks something about the nature of reality and is not dependent on someone acting badly but it is something creative in its own right.[24]

—Joanna Macy

Kali

6

THE PATH OF DARKNESS

I don't know what your condition would be
if you were to catch sight of Her.
You might even die of shock.
She is very tall, and Her skin is a beautiful
deep midnight blue color. Her eyes are beautiful ...
she has a long red tongue lolling from Her mouth.
Blood, the blood she is eternally drinking, drips slowly from the tip.
She is ... pot-breasted and ... full-bellied.
Around Her neck there is a garland of freshly-severed human heads
which are freshly bleeding. She wears wristlets and armlets of bones,
and anklets of snakes ... She wears a skirt of human arms,
and to me, She is one of the loveliest beings in the universe,
because She is my Mother.[1]

—Aghori Vimalananda

Over fourteen years ago, just prior to meeting my spiritual teacher, I went through an "undoing" that left me devastated, and actively contemplating suicide. Nothing in my previous life experience had prepared me for the sweeping depression that literally took away the light, and wiped out all meaning. All perceptions were skewed—I was convinced that everything I did was a source of pain to others, that everything I touched turned rotten, that everyone who tried to help me was only doing so out of obligation or pity, and that they resented the burden of reaching out to me.

At the time, I was a writer, a teacher, a workshop leader in holistic health and wellness (my first book was fast-becoming a classic in the field). I'd probably even spoken to other men or women in similar circumstances, offering them simple formulas such as, "Just look at all you have to be thankful for," or worse, "Just trust in God." Not that such recommendations aren't true—because actually they are, brilliantly true. The sorry thing is that when such "truths" are used as pat formulae by one who has no genuine appreciation of the pain of the other, these words come off as empty; "a clanging gong...a tinkling cymbal" as St. Paul described false charity. Since people in immense pain are exceedingly vulnerable to the nuances in the speech of others, what actually gets communicated to the listener in such moments is the speaker's real desire to be done with them. Without intending to, the speaker is most often implying, "Your pain is too threatening to me, and your suffering disturbs the illusion of peace in which I live. Please just cover up your suffering with a smile so that I can feel better and continue along my rosy path, unaffected."

Put another way, one who is in great pain can be said to be in the "underworld"—the domain of death; a place of passage or transition which the soul must navigate before reaching its final destination or rest. The place of death is not just for the transition from physical existence. A sojourn in the underworld is the necessary journey for a major transition of the spirit. Before one can emerge as a woman of compassion, able to legitimately bear the pain of the world without turning away, she must see and embrace this pain within herself, but not just as an intellectual concept. She must meet her pain and be annihilated in it, as Inanna was annihilated by the dark forces of her sister Ereskigal, in her passage to the nether realms. Before one can be a healer, one must know illness as an intimate lover—all the illness and disease of the entire humanity. To recognize this passage of devastation, the "dismemberment" as it is called and literally is, as being a necessary and even valued expression of the Divine Process whereby all things are born, all things die, and all things are once again made new, is not something that many of us are coached in, particularly in our traditional religious training. I certainly was not. More often, although the rhetoric may say otherwise, such periods are felt as a withdrawal of God's grace, a sense of abandonment, or even worse, as some presage of the punishment one deserves and which awaits on the "other side." People in pain, therefore, are often counseled to fight the whirlpool which is trying to suck them down; to wage war, albeit valiantly, against such forces. All of which creates the impression that this state is somehow aberrant, unnatural, or diabolical—something which we must fear and fight and flee from if possible.

It is here that Kali, the Dark Mother (or any of her sisters, like the Hindu Tara, or Chinnamasta, or the other fierce goddesses of the Hindu pantheon) steps forth for those fortunate enough to have met her, or fortunate enough to have been told about her; or sometimes, to those who have never even heard her name. She steps forth not to console, but rather to complete the devastation—to sever heads, to destroy all vestiges of hope. She steps forth because she knows that this annihilation which the individual, or the family/community, or even the whole world is undergoing is never a separation from the One. She is the Divine Mother. And just as she births all in her Eternal Womb, so she deaths all, consuming the corpses so that no drop of precious blood is wasted. All is recycled so that life may be restored again.

And so it was that I first "met" the Mother of Destruction, although at the time and even for years following this encounter I didn't really have a name for what I was going through. I called it depression, or a nervous breakdown, or the end of the world. Whatever it was that precipitated this plunge into the darkness is incidental now; the fact is I was in so deep that I couldn't get out. I was so lost that I didn't recognize anything or anyone as familiar enough to be a road sign, or a source of direction.

I'm sick of living, Mother, sick.
Life and money have run out

But I go on crying "Tara, Tara,"
Hoping. You are the mother of all
And our nurse. You carry the Three Worlds
In Your belly.

So am I some orphan fallen out
Of the sky? And if You think I'm bad,
Remember, You're the cord connecting
Every good and evil
And I'm a tool tied to illusion.

Your name can blot out the fear
Of Death—so Shiva said,
But, Terrible One, You forget all that,
Absorbed in Shiva, Death, and Time.

Prasad says: Your games, Mother,
Are mysteries. You make and break.
You've broken me in this life.[2]

—Ramprasad Sen

One morning I awoke drenched in sweat from a most terrifying dream. Actually, it was more of a journey than a dream. To this day I'm convinced that I was taken on a trip to the underworld. In the "dream," I stood on a small pier at the edge of the ocean. In my hand was a short-handled fishing rod, much like a child's toy. The line from my rod stretched out to sea where, like a tiny speck on the horizon, I saw the fish that was pulling on it. I began to slowly reel the thing in. But, the closer the fish got, the more terrified I became. I was unprepared for the catch. With this tiny fishing pole I had snagged a whale—a monstrous, black whale. A whale so huge that as it neared the pier it towered over me, blocking out the light of the sun. Paralyzed, I neither put down the fishing pole, nor turned to run. Something more powerful than I was, held me in place.

Horrified, I watched as the whale opened its enormous mouth: a gaping maw, razor sharp teeth; a tunnel that led only down and into darkness. Then "she" appeared, with the face of a demon— was this Kali, dancing on the tongue of the whale? Fiery eyes. Black limbs. Naked. Contorted figure, huge smile, wild hair, sharp teeth, and billows of smoke exuding from her repulsive mouth. Whom- ever she was beckoned me to come, to enter into this chamber of horror, to fall into her strangling arms, to be broken by her grind- ing jaws. She could not pull me in forcibly, that was clear. She could only reach out, offering me a fate worse than death, as I knew it then.

I did not know her. She seemed, at the time, to embody all that one should shrink from, all that one has ever feared, all that is evil, terrible, devastating. I could not enter into the annihilation that she offered, but I also couldn't turn back. As if the rest of the world had simply dropped away, there was no other place to go. There was a pier, there was the palace of the Dark Female, and there was endless and infinite space where previously the ocean had been. My choices in the moment were quite clear—either en- ter the whale or leap into the abyss. The pier was quickly vanishing.

I jumped into the void, leaving the whale and her dancing inhabit far above me as I plunged in chaotic free-fall into endless nothingness. Arms flailing. Legs flailing. Head over heels. Spread- eagled. I grasped for any figment of imagination to slow down the speed of the fall or steady my spinning body.

Like a trip through some cosmic fun house, the faces of ghouls would emerge from the absolute darkness, glowing with fluores- cent green or orange mist. Laughter, a fiendish laughter, sent me twisting and turning in another vain attempt to find a platform in space. The horror of this moment could not have been greater, until the realization dawned that I would be falling like this for all eternity. There was no end, and never would be a bottom to hit. This was the beginning and end of all.

And then her voice (I guess *now* that it was her voice, at the time it was like the truest voice I had ever heard)—a voice that served as a parachute; a soothing and yet completely authoritative voice. "Stay conscious through it all," the voice boomed. "Stay conscious through it all," it demanded of me while it held me in its force field.

Here was the platform in nothingness that I had grasped for. Suddenly, my flailing free fall became a gentle descent, as if I were merely sinking to the bottom of a familiar swimming hole, feet first, aware of my hands and arms. I slowly drifted down. The faces of the monsters and their accompanying freakish laughter continued to interrupt, but instead of fighting to free myself from them, I simply looked at them as so many curiosities. "Stay conscious through it all," I repeated now, over and over to myself. This was still the end of the world, and I was still doomed to fall forever, but the overwhelming fear was suddenly put in its place. I was still fearful, but I had a weapon, a strategy against it. To stay alert. To not run from it. To simply watch it. No more powerful weapon in the Universe than this.

I opened my eyes to find myself, sweat-drenched, in a quilt-covered bed. The Iowa winter landscape outside the window was gray, white, black. My friend, Anita, was bending over the bed, wishing me good morning.

This dream wasn't the magic act that ended my passage in hell, but it was a benchmark. From the mouth of the Benevolent Destroyer herself I had been gifted with a tool which potentially would grant me access to a whole new way of "being with" what had previously been unmanageable horror. She had not abandoned me even for an instant. Quite the contrary, She had thrown me a lifeline, a thread, the tiniest suggestion which had become like a halogen lamp in the unfathomable darkness. It would take many years before this tool would even start to become a regular practice, but the unquestionable power of it—the power of self-awareness in the midst of chaos, illness, stress, even death—impressed itself deeply within me.

By a conviction born of experience, I mark the definitive entrance into the Dark Night of the Spirit as the first phase of the unitive life. Here begins the cauterizing, the burning-through to the deepest center of being, which is painful and shattering to all aspects of the self. The deep, deterministic reins of self-control have been taken away and the will power that glued together this fragile unity has dissolved. From here on, the reins of our destiny are in the hands of a greater power, a higher Will, and though we may unconsciously kick against the goad in painful rebellion, it is all to no avail. The only way out is to be submissive, to accept our helplessness and to recognize that peace of soul—the day it can be found—is our greatest ally. With no place else to go, nowhere else to turn, we have no choice but to go down into the depths of our nothingness where, at rock bottom, God eventually reveals Himself and discloses to us the rootedness of our existence in Him. Thus having traveled through the bottomless void of our being, we eventually come to rest in a deep union with God—the abiding stillpoint at the center of being.[3]

—Bernadette Roberts

Over the years that followed this descent and dismemberment, I have met scores of women for whom this story has been like a port in a storm. I have held their hands. I have spoken slowly and authoritatively to them, in late night hours over long-distance telephone lines. I have held them in my arms as they trembled. This sojourn into the underworld of a pain which couldn't be "smiled away," or sung away, or meditated away, or exercised away, and certainly not counseled away, had helped me to be a silent witness to the inevitable that was taking place. I had been lost, and I had been found, and not of my control. The same Divine Mother who had birthed me had actually brought me to this. She herself had pushed me over the edge. Why? Because in my own weird way I had asked her to. I had begged her for Wisdom,

Divine Wisdom, throughout my life. I had prayed to be a servant of God. I had prayed to be able to heal the wounds of the children of the earth. I had asked for Truth. I had asked for nothing less than the raw Divine.

When one makes such genuinely inspired requests, it is often because she is carried along on a wave of devotional fervor, or touched by some altruistic dream. But, there is still a kernel of real love that motivates such prayers. At the time such requests are made we usually have no idea exactly what form their fulfillment will take. Especially if we were raised in Western, middle-class, Judeo-Christian homes; especially if we were shielded from the raw meanness of a slow death from cancer which many of our older relatives were going through; especially if we had the perverse notion that God "rewards" the good and "punishes" the wicked, we will have no context with which to approach Kali, the Dark Mother. I believed for years that my prayers would somehow carry me through the "vale of tears" in some enclosed palanquin. They did not, and can not.

When, in our youth, in our adolescence, or even not until our middle-age, we meet with a force of pain which cannot be idealized away because we are literally crushed by it, we often make no connection to the prayers or dreams of our youth. "Thy will be done," "Lord, make me an instrument of Thy Peace," or "Let my life make a difference"—these are not idle words. They are received, and they are remembered, and they are answered. Divine Mother Kali is the receiver of the cries of her children. She knows that without the descent there is no true compassion. She knows that without the hopelessness there is no genuine hope or faith. She knows that without death to the ego, and death to all the concepts of God, there can be no resurrection into selfless service, nor worship of the True Divine.

The fisherman has cast his net
And sits there waiting, waiting.

The Path of Darkness

What will become of me,
Mother, in this world?

The fish are safest
In deep waters.

The fisherman has cast this world
As his net.

When he sees what he wants
He grabs it by the hair.

There's no way out, so, Mind,
What will you do, bound by Death?

Ramprasad says: Call the Mother,
She can handle Death.[4]

—Ramprasad Sen

KALI—WHO IS SHE?

Kali—from *kala* which means time—is one name, one face
of the All-Pervasive Great Mother. In many Hindu scriptures and
popular legends it is told that Kali was first born from the forehead
of the goddess Durga during a battle in which the Great Mother
was called upon (by the male gods, Brahma, Vishnu, Shiva, gathered in council) to protect the earth and all its inhabitants from
the forces of evil. In waging the war, Durga had been extraordinarily successful, but the insidious ways of two demons, Canda and
Munda, catalyzed in her a rage like the world had never known.
Her forehead wrinkled as her piercing eyes targeted her prey. And
from the point of contraction in her brow, a new face and form of
the One Eternal Mother emerged—this one as loathsome and terrifying as her other forms are compellingly beautiful and radiant.

183

Ferocious Mother Kali screamed forth as a bony, sunken-breasted hag with disheveled hair, red and fiery eyes, teeth pointed and sharpened, a lolling red tongue contrasted against her black and naked torso and limbs. She was terrible because her hunger and thirst for blood was unquenchable. This Goddess was unstoppable. She carried a double-edged sword in one hand, a sword she wielded with ruthless abandon, lopping off the heads of the encroaching demons. She picked up the demons's horses, their chariots and all their instruments of destruction, devouring them in her gigantic mouth, crushing everything between her diamond-hard teeth. She drank the blood of the vanquished ones—now, not only were the demons destroyed, but all their issue in future generations. Even their blood would be denied the privilege of nourishing the plants of the earth until that blood had passed through Her body, as through an alchemical fire. All evil and violent things were rendered harmless in her. All things were transformed in her and returned to the earth, and all in *her* good time.

But Kali didn't stop in chewing up demons. She continued the rampage, threatening to devour everything on earth. That's when the gods got nervous, and sent down Shiva himself—the ever available consort to Divine Mother in many of her forms. Shiva lay himself down on the battlefield in Kali's path. She stepped on him. She felt his power under her feet. She stopped, looked down, smiled. Her work was over, at last. The balance of the primordial Feminine with the primordial Masculine had been restored.

Some say Kali is dark because she is not separate from the Ultimate Void out of which all things are born and into which all things die—the Black Hole in space. She is naked because she is ultimately pure and unashamed. She has three eyes in order to see past, present and future in one glance and to pierce through illusions throughout time. She wears a garland of fifty human heads because she is the fullness of creation, and each skull represents one of fifty sounds in the Hindu alphabet. With all sounds in her possession, she controls the Universe. Her tongue is extended because she desires blood, the life force, and because she is sexually voracious. Kali is the archetypal "anti-model" of the feminine as it has been repressed by the patriarchy. She wears a skirt of severed arms because the arms are instruments of accomplishment, and all accomplishment is subject to her power. Her hair is wild, flowing out in every direction because she herself is wild and untamed, and because each hair represents one of her children or devotees, all of whom are running wildly in different directions trying to find their way back to her.

Yet, for all the signs of terror that characterize her four-armed form, one of her left hands is raised in blessing, another is extended, welcoming whomever wishes to approach her and learn her truth.

Kali "exists" because it is necessary that illusions be shattered. Few who walk an authentic spiritual path can deny that the darkness is deep. Illusion *is* triumphing—or so it seems if we take a look at fashion magazines, shopping malls and contemporary media. The buffers that shield us against the raw confrontation with pain are so numerous and so compelling that it takes dedicated effort or large doses of benediction to keep from using them. Indeed, in this age in which the forces of self-aggrandizement seem to be winning in their intention to dominate the Mother Earth, even to rape and murder her Body, we need the Goddess of Divine Justice to show her awesome and terrible face again and again. We need her to chop off the head of illusion that we wear. We need her to chew up and swallow the abuse that our parents, in their own ignorance and pain, heaped upon, as well as the self-hatred we heap upon ourselves in our misguided attempts to subdue the Feminine.

The Goddess is One. Nothing exists apart from her, but due to the particular need and orientation of her worshipper and child, she can assume any of a thousand forms. Kali exists, therefore, not separate from all the benevolent and succoring images of Mary Immaculate, or White Tara, or Kuan Yin, or Saraswati, the creator of music and poetry and art. For the mind of the Hindu or Tibetan Buddhist there is no paradox in such dichotomies. Life and death are seen and appreciated as one.

Kali standing on Shiva. Contemporary silkscreen.

In the divine trinity of Kali, the Nature Mother; Shiva, the Absolute; and Rhadakanta, [Love], Kali is the pivot, the sovereign Mistress. She is Prakriti [substance], the Procreatrix, Nature, the Destroyer, the Creator. Nay, she is something greater and deeper still for those who have eyes to see ... She is the Universal Mother, "my Mother," as Ramakrishna would say, the All-Powerful, who reveals Herself to Her children under different aspects and Divine Incarnations, the Visible God, who leads the elect to the Invisible Reality; and if it so pleases Her, She takes away the last trace of ego from created beings and merges it in the consciousness of the Absolute, the undifferentiated God.

To the ignorant She is, to be sure, the image of destruction; but [Ramakrishna] found in Her the benign, all-loving Mother. Her neck is encircled with a garland of heads, and Her waist with a girdle of human arms, and two of Her hands hold weapons of death, and Her eyes dart a glance of fire, but strangely enough, Ramakrishna felt in her breath the soothing touch of tender love and saw in Her the Seed of Immortality. She stands on the bosom of Her Consort Shiva; is it because She is the Shakti, the Power, inseparable from the Absolute. She is surrounded by jackals and other unholy creatures, the denizens of the cremation ground. But is not the Ultimate reality above holiness and unholiness? She appears to be reeling under the spell of wine. But who would create this mad world unless under the influence of a divine drunkenness? [Is not disorder the very foundation of our seemingly ordered universe? The cosmos had evolved out of the primeval chaos.] She (Kali) is the highest symbol of all the forces of nature, the synthesis of their antinomies, the Ultimate Divine in the form of woman.[5]

187

As a woman comes to know herself without denigration or self-judgement, she finds that these forces within her that she previously shunned as being negative, or as evidence that she is out of control or even hysterical, are really the source fire for the emergence of justice and truth on the earth. It is out of her holy rage that she has both the strength and courage to wage war with any and all who threaten harm either to her own children or to any children of the world. It is out of the same holy rage that she takes the sword to her own roots which are still sunk in the mire of illusion. She says, "No!" with conviction and courage and compassion to the voices of conformity around her, especially to those who would shackle her to a pasteboard image of woman. Kali lives in every woman, and in every man. She lives in our wildness, in raw power, in deep abiding trust of the ebb and flow of the process of life. Kali is the Divine Mother—gruesome, horrific, instigator of dread. Yet at one and the same time, Kali is the Divine Mother who wants only to protect her offspring from a still greater dread— a life of absorption in phantasms.

Kali, Mistress of the Underworld, is the initiatrix of the inner transformation and the protector of all who seek refuge by not turning away from her.

> ...There's only one hope
> For Ramprasad, Mother—that in the end
> He will be safe at Your feet.[6]

Seeing Kali Everywhere

Walking along the streets in a town in India, I saw Kali's dance. That lump of flesh with two searing eyes that huddled outside the ashram gate was a woman. Her skin was whiter than mine, except for the chocolate brown palms of her hands and two brown circles around the eyes, and a scattered patch or two of dark skin on her legs. What strange disease had rendered her skin in this odd raiment? I wondered. Her condition was grotesque to observe, yet she was also compelling. Wrapped in a filthy rag of a sari, she awaited the generosity or horrified guilt of the tourists to get them to throw a rupee or two in her direction.

Walking those streets it is hard to know whom to help. The depictions of human deformity and the ravages of disease are so numerous—stumps which once were feet; bone-thin bodies, pus-soaked rags wrapped around hands or legs; an adult with a body no bigger than a two-year-old child, an enormous head and some semblance of twisted limbs—unless one were to go blindfolded one cannot escape the "freak show" which throngs every thoroughfare.

Every visitor to India must develop a strategy for dealing with such constant assault to the senses and sensibilities. For some, a roughness and condescending air of superiority triumphs as the defense mechanism of choice. For others, a daily allotment of rupees is put aside and doled out at random; for others, the *Bodhisattva* breath is the way they handle the pain: breathe in the sight, offer an internal prayer of blessing, breathe out, with a smile. The point is that Kali cannot be denied as easily on the streets of Bombay as she can be in the Scottsdale, Arizona shopping mall. She cannot be overlooked so readily in the Mott Haven section of the south Bronx in New York City where the rats are big enough to kill squirrels, and children learn to "hit the deck" daily as stray bullets fly through their church halls or their school rooms, or through the barricaded doors of their impoverished apartments, as she can be and is, in Disneyland.

But, sooner or later, death comes to Scottsdale, and death invades Disneyland. The lives we have so carefully shielded are violated by death, the great equalizer. "Cancer is the cure," says macrobiotic nutritionist and philosopher Michio Kushi, "...civilization is the disease."

Cancer *is* a great equalizer, and so is AIDS, despite all our attempts to confine it to the disreputable segments of the population—namely to homosexuals and to drug-users. AIDS, like cancer, is eating up young and old, men, women and children, of all religions and all races.

Death and birth are the two factors that we all have in common. Kali cannot be denied forever; even if she is guarded against until the last moment of life, she will insinuate herself through the cracks in the walls, she will creep in through the drainpipe and she will nestle herself in all her fierce compassion at the bedside of her dying child, coaching them into the transition with a mother's lullabies, even as she hungrily laps at their draining life force with her tongue. Divine Mother Death will ultimately have her way.

Death, as perhaps no other event, has a way of destroying illusions. For many women, the death of a fetus through miscarriage, the death of a child, the lingering death of a much-loved parent or sibling, is a unique opening into a deepened appreciation of the nature of spiritual reality. Dealing with the unavoidable details of the human body in agony, a "realness" is seen unlike any other. If the harshness of death can be embraced rather than romantically sentimentalized or defended against, death can become the greatest teacher one will ever meet.

"Death is always just waiting over your left shoulder," Carlos Castenada's teacher, Don Mateus, taught him. As chronicled in Castanada's writings of his training among the Yaqui Indians of Mexico, a warrior was one who kept death's constant presence in mind; who used that knowledge and remembrance to fuel his work and practice and service.

I've thought, lately, especially since my last trip to India, that Kali's picture should adorn the walls of every hospice in the world; that Kali's shrine should occupy a privileged place in the corner of every sick room. But, of course, that is an idle dream unless I first enshrine her in myself. Then, perhaps, she has a better chance of touching the minds and bodies and hearts of those around me. I know this is possible, and beneficial. I have met her in other women—women who embodied Death in the Service of Life.

Bhadra Kali—Her Auspicious Form

MEETING MA

I have only one path to teach
and that path is love

I use love as a razor
to scrape away the scars
left over from ego's wars
against the heart.[7]

—Ma Jaya Bhagavati

Ma Jaya Sati Bhagavati is a contemporary Western spiritual teacher. "Mother" to a wide and expanding community of devotees, Ma lives on a beautiful ashram, called Kashi, in Sebastian, Florida.

Kashi—another name for Benares, the city of death, the holy city to which devout Indians pilgrimage in their final weeks of life, hoping to die here; to be cremated in the burning *ghats* that line the Ganges river which flows through the city, and to achieve a final resting place with their ashes dissolved in these sacred waters.

The cremation grounds are a special haunt of one of Kali's seven or eight manifestations, or aspects. *Smashan* is the Hindu word for cremation ground. And *smashan* Kali is usually depicted holding a cup made from a human skull. The cup typically contains the remnants of the human brain, which Kali gulps with joy, consuming the victim's life-essence with abandon! One who practices some of the esoteric rites of left-handed Tantra will often spend the night, alone, at the burning *ghats*. To do so is to invite the most feared and fearsome elements in human understanding— the purveyors of death. It is also a means of invoking a vision or the felt presence of the Divine Mother Kali in her most gruesome and beneficial form as the Guardian of the Portal through which all her children must pass.

It is this aspect of the death-protective Kali that Ma Jaya seems to associate with most closely. Her work for more than twenty years has been to care for the dying, and particularly to minister to those with AIDS. To meet Ma Jaya is to learn something about the true nature of Kali that cannot be learned from books.

I first saw Ma Jaya Sati Bhagavati in Chicago in 1993 during the first Plenary session of the Parliament of World Religions. A massive convocation of religious leaders and their followers from all over the world, the event commemorated the 100th anniversary of the first World Parliament of 1893 which had been held in the same city. The first Parliament was memorable for many reasons, one of which was the startlingly intelligent and heartful presentation of an Indian monk named Vivekananda, the renowned and holy disciple of the preeminent sage of the day, Sri Ramakrishna.

I had been at the 1993 conference for a day and a half and was still in a strongly cynical mode—the whole event felt more like a circus or a spiritual marketplace than a place of universal sanctuary and communion, which it should have been. (Or so I judged.)

For me, seeing Ma on the stage with a panel of other religious experts was like witnessing high theater more than anything else. My first impression of her was none too positive. Another American woman decked out in a sari (there were lots of these "types" at the conference), Ma Jaya was highly distinguishable by the three pairs of gold hoop earrings that adorned her ears, a shocking mane of wild black hair, a bracelet of skulls tattooed around her ankle, her guru's name tattooed on her hand, diamond-studded eye-glasses and a shrill voice with a heavy Brooklyn accent. She was reading her poetry, about "her river, her Ganga..." and what this river meant in her life, and I was put off even further by what seemed like a self-referenced performance of the first degree. However, one theme that she kept referring to, and which the Parliament Program had attested to, was her work with the dying, primarily the AIDS population. So, the paradox of her form or manifestation, and the evident witness of her service of compassion created just the right blend of dynamic tension to set me on edge, and to keep her memory (and my first impression) rolling around in my mind.

As a brief aside here, I offer this type of paradox as an important clue to any serious seekers on the spiritual path. When one is looking for a teacher, or even just "checking out the scene," one should be alert to these dichotomies as not necessarily the indication of lack of integrity, or the presence of hypocrisy in a spiritual teacher's work. Oftentimes, in my experience, such paradoxes are actually a powerful form of teaching communication, which require the serious practitioner to chew over the pieces that aren't immediately palatable. In this mastication process I have often discovered an unexpected source of nourishment that was hidden in the food—perhaps deliberately protected from the mouths of those who, in their search for sweetness, judge everything by the first bite.

So it was that nearly a week later, as I looked through the conference program, I came across a workshop called, "Service To Your Spiritual Work," given by Ma Jaya Sati Bhagavati. The title was compelling to me, since service, and the nature of genuine service, had always been a foremost topic of my spiritual quest. (Much more about this in Chapter 8.) But I was interested even more because of Ma's long experience in caring for the dying. I was looking for some immediate help, since I was a part of the core team of women who cared for Inge, one of my teacher's German students who lived on the Arizona ashram, and who was dying a painful death of bone cancer. So I went to Ma's workshop.

Her talk was given in the Art Gallery of the Parliament, where she had a large display of some of her own paintings. I liked them—big splashing canvases with intense colors and simple lines. "The River," "The Breast," a wild depiction called "The Ancient Mother," on a background of what could be clouds or waves, a monolith stands, with two snake-like strands of thick dark hair protruding from the top and winding their way to the bottom; two wide, all-seeing eyes, a full sensuous mouth. The painting carried something of Kali's eternal nature—the repulsive and the irresistible.

Here in the gallery Ma's students and devotees had set up a couch for her, and surrounded it with flowers. Candles burned,

Ma Jaya Sati Bhagavati

and I recognized the familiar scent of my favorite incense. Despite the elaborate presentation, which might have turned me off a few days ago, I held a different attitude on this morning. I simply put my judgements of her aside, because she asked all in attendance to do exactly that, and I listened intently as she began to talk about her life and her service.

As I heard from Ma Jaya herself, and from other corroborating sources, she was born and raised in Brooklyn. Her spiritual odyssey began when, as a mother of three children, she made a trip to a Jack LaLane figure salon where she learned some rudimentary yoga techniques including one powerful yogic breath exercise which was touted as a fast way to lose weight. Practicing the breath method beyond the prescribed limit of five minutes every day, she was determined that if five minutes meant the loss of a pound or two, then hours of similar practice would have her slenderized in no time.

The results were more dramatic than anyone dreamed. Sitting on the floor of her bathroom, or in the bathtub (decidedly the only places in her house where a woman with three kids could find a little privacy), she undertook her breathing practice with a vengeance, and soon found that Christ Himself was standing in front of her. "Teach all ways, for all ways are mine," the vision said, instructing her in a path of spiritual education and service which was to characterize the rest of her life. Visions of Christ were soon augmented by sightings of several Indian holy men—including Neem Karoli Baba and Swami Nityananda.

Early on, Ma became associated with two well-known teachers of the time—Hilda Charleton and Ram Dass. A trip to India was recommended, somewhere along the line, and so this young Jewish woman from Brooklyn was launched into the world of Hindu spirituality, powered by her own unique mixture of street-wisdom, chutzpah and raw feminine courage.

More than twenty years later, Ma Jaya travels the U.S. to meet with groups of her own devotees across the country, and to address thronged rooms of HIV-positive and AIDS patients from New York to San Francisco, or to make the innumerable visits to the terminal wards and hospices where her service is most particularly directed. Her teaching is called "Kali Yoga"—the yoga of the Mother.

"The reason you burn out is because you hold back. When you give one-hundred percent you tap into an Energy that sustains you," Ma said as I listened intently, on that morning in 1994. She was speaking in whispered and raspy tones, interspersed with loud outbursts of recognition as various people entered the Hall. "When you try to hold back and protect yourself," she said, referring to how we approach most of our work, especially with the dying, "then you close down the energy flow." (I paraphrase here to the best of my recollection). At some point, the power of her words, and the evident sacrifice out of which they arose, began to have their effect on me. My own passion for service, for surrender, for annihilation into the heart of the Divine Healer and Servant of all, was being ignited. Her words hit hard. "We have no choice about who will be there at our birth. But, to be invited to be present at death is the greatest privilege," she went on. I was being slowly worn down, washed over with a wave of gratitude towards the Mother, and towards my beloved Teacher, Lee, for the enormous gift which he was affording me and our whole care-giving team by asking us to serve our dying sister, Inge.

Midway in Ma's talk, Yogi Bhajan, a prominent spiritual leader of a large group of American sikhs, entered the room with his entourage. Immediately she called for a chair to be brought to him, as she leapt off her couch, walked quickly though the crowd, and *pranamed* (bowed, touching the floor with her forehead) at his feet. I could feel the mood in the room charge up. Some people were evidently shocked by her display. But for Ma there was no problem. I had seen several large photos of her holding a dying child in her arms, or embracing a man with Karposi's Sarcoma, so I knew it made no difference to her—I knew that she was willing to bow to everyone anyway. That's when I knew that there was something here that I could definitely feed from.

I *did* access the energy of Divine Mother through Ma Jaya, and it was a deep privilege to be in her presence. Similar to what I had found in Dina Rees's company (see Chapter 4), Ma Jaya evoked the Essential Feminine in me, and in that instant I know that I was not separate from the beauty and power which I found in her.

Particularly beautiful to witness was the way certain men at this gathering seemed to flower around Ma. One gorgeous, radiant, Franciscan monk at the workshop caught my attention. I'll never forget him because the guy literally had light pouring out of his face. And I watched him as he looked at her, and it broke my heart. He was seeing Divine Mother, in the flesh, perhaps for the first time in his life. There were several priests and monks who came to her private *darshan* (Sanskrit for "the sighting of the Master") the next night, and I observed the same phenomena from them. Sure, they had Mary, Mother of Jesus, as a religious model, but I'll bet you it couldn't possibly compare in intensity with what they were seeing and feeling with the energy that was coming from Ma.

She introduced us to some of her students, several of whom had AIDS. She presented one startlingly handsome young man to the group, and then she chastised us all, saying that we could never again report that we didn't personally know somebody with full-blown AIDS. "And I want you to know," she burned these words through the space between herself and the audience, "he is *not* his disease. *He* is not AIDS, he is a human being, and so is every other person who has AIDS."

And she told many stories, about going into the hospitals, as she does every day, visiting those dying of AIDS—in Florida where her Ashram is, and in Los Angeles and San Francisco where she works among the gay communities. She described how, because of the panic about this disease, the nurses are clothed with gowns and rubber gloves and masks and hats. "Who will touch these dying people?" she asked. "What the dying most need is to be held, to be loved." So, Ma herself walks into the rooms of these dying people, and whenever it's called for, she simply gets into bed with them. Hearing her tell the story I had no doubt that she does exactly that.

Here was a woman whose life of service is a continual annihilation. Reading her newsletter, which I receive every two months or so, I get more reinforcement in my respect for Ma and her work. Her students and friends are literally dying every day—children with

AIDS who have been abandoned by their families; drug-users; homosexual couples—and Ma embraces them all, loves them fully and then releases them, over and over again, day in and day out. Their lives are enriched by her, if only for the contact of a brief moment. Like Kali, she devours them in her mouth, she strangles them in her all-embracing arms, she guides them to the abyss, and she cries to them over the edge, "Stay conscious through it all."

Meeting Ma Jaya Sati Bhagavati was a rare joy. To see such a vibrant, juicy, wild and even crazy woman who is so consumed with her love for God, and so unashamed of her devotion to her Guru, Neem Karoli Baba, and so filled with the spirit of compassionate acceptance for people of all races, all religions, all castes and outcasts, is to see another aspect of the Divine which every woman (and every man) knows or at least intuits. I heard a story second-hand, that at one of the Parliamentary sessions Ma was seated next to the monk Brother David Stendl-Rast, a contemporary mystic and writer. In her innocent enthusiasm, and for lack of anything better to say, Ma turned to the man and said: "Brother David, I love God." To which the other responded, completely unperturbed and with corresponding innocence, "Mother, thank you very much."

To see her ease with the forces of Death which are at one and the same time the forces of life, is to encounter Kali Ma's darkness and radiant light.

One poignant excerpt from Ma's writing follows. I have chosen this selection because I think it communicates the vastness of this Mother's heart, and expresses the intimacy of her relatedness to those who call upon her. In response to a question about the use of breath to relieve the fear of death, Ma wrote at length about a recent experience with a beloved devotee:

> The room is quiet and hot. I enter it slowly, almost afraid to witness what I'm about to see. I move close to the bed. I'm so quiet—so unlike me. But it's not about me; it's about Winston, whose last breaths are coming in harsh and fast.

The dim light overhead creates shadows on his handsome, ebony face. I kiss his forehead and touch his hand. I know this hand so well. This hand has taken my own when my heart was heavy from all the losses due to AIDS. His long, slender fingers are tapping against the back of my hand in time to his breath.

"Winston, my love," I whisper over the sound of the oxygen, "are you afraid?" Touching his brow with my free hand, I ask again, "Are you afraid, my friend?"

He opens his deep black eyes, and I fall into them. "No, Ma," he says as he breathes deeply through the tube in his nose. "I'm watching my breath just like you said to do. I know that Jesus is breathing with me, and when I stop He will be breathing for me. The living Christ sure enough is close, Ma. I can see Him. Ma, I can feel Him. It's going to be all right, 'cause He loves me, right, Ma?" He doesn't give me a chance to answer; he just keeps on going. "I know that He forgives me, Ma, for all I've done."

Dear God, I think, this man is the gentlest human being I've ever met. What is there to forgive?

"I'm going so deep into me with the breath, Ma, and I can see me. When I breathe out I'm breathing out into the room and then into the world. I'm breathing in and out all the love I never had, and it's making me feel so good." He looks at me. He looks into my eyes without saying a word, and I can see the breath calming down and his body relaxing. "It's going to be pretty soon, right, Ma?"

"Yes, my love," I say, holding his hand a little tighter. "Just concentrate on your breath and feel good about the journey you're going to take."

"No more pain, Ma?"

"No more pain, Winston, no more pain."

"Ma, you make me feel so free."

"Honey," I say with tears frozen in my eyes, "it's you and all those in this AIDS ward who free me."

"The breath, Ma, teach them the breath. Teach them how to focus in life on the breath so they focus on it as they die. I'm dying and I'm okay." He smiles at me and says with that familiar grin of his, "I ain't got no choice, Ma, I'm dying, so I'm going to follow my breath right up into the arms of Jesus." He closes his eyes, and before I can take another he asks, "What is that god of yours called, you know, that one with the fur that I saw a statue of on your ashram?"

"Hanuman," I reply in a voice that sounds nothing like my own. "Hanuman, the Lord of Service." I want to say more, but I see that he has closed his eyes and is drifting away. In fact, he's closed his eyes for the last time, never to open them again this life.

"I see Jesus," he whispers, never to whisper again. I watch his breath come in and out, and I am lost in this creation of God's: breath, flesh, mind, heart, and soul.

"Hey, Ma." It's Cessy, who had recently lost her husband to the virus; she is wheeling herself into Winston's room. "Teach me what you taught Winston." Cessy, my beautiful Cessy, in her thirties and confined to her wheelchair. Always looking so prim and proper.

"I'm coming, Cessy," I say as I let go of my Winston's hand.

"You know, Ma, my breath is easy to find." I laugh with her. She has a tube coming out of her throat that makes a lot of noise every time she takes a breath. "I can learn fast," she giggles. You have time, I say to myself, you have time. She smiles as if she can read my mind, and says, "If I can learn to play dominoes as good as I do, then I can learn the breath like Winston. You know, Ma, maybe there is not so much time."

I sit with this simple Haitian woman, who is always so well dressed in her pretty cotton frocks, and I begin to show her how to follow her breath as she relaxes into the moment. She takes my hand after a while and says, "Okay, enough," and she starts to laugh. "I meditated," she says, and we both smile.

Yes, you can definitely use the breath to lose the fear of death. If you can quiet the mind, the body relaxes, and you can feel the relief that the heart needs to feel by watching the breath and being in the moment. Toward the end you can feel little deaths like a death of each moment. You can get lost in its wonderment. The breath is the secret of a pleasant death and a focused life.[8]

KALI THE UGLY

There are numerous statues and paintings of Kali which, despite their grotesqueries, are compellingly attractive—they align us to something powerful and close to the bone. These faces of Divine Mother have a rare and precious purpose for women in our day. As the culture denies death, it also attempts to deny all vestiges of it—particularly aging and illness. We are all potential members of the cult of "the body beautiful" and easily susceptible to the lies which such a cult must live by.

Obsession with the fate of our physical bodies (and by fate I mean our weight, our hair color, hairstyle, hair-length, our wrinkles, our shape, our breast size, our teeth-straightness, our clothing, et-cetera) is a sickness, yet such a common sickness, so widespread, that there are many who do not even recognize that they are in-fected, since almost every other woman (and man) they know is similarly concerned.

I recognize these as harsh words, and can hear the objections of readers being shouted at me, as I have heard the voices of women in workshops I have led. "I love to adorn myself," they say. "It is woman's way to do this—to create beauty everywhere beginning with herself." I agree. I love the occasion of dressing myself too. The body is a work of art, and our clothing and adornments can be a way of celebrating that. But, let's tell the truth—preserving the body and adorning it can also become a deadly obsession. For some, these activities are all that give meaning to their lives. And for others, these obsessions are based in what I call body-hatred—a condition I have seen as clearly in women who adorn them-selves with beautiful things as in women who seem unconcerned with their physical appearance to the point of always looking a bit disheveled and unkempt. I have come to see this disease of body-hatred (or you could call it self-hatred, self-loathing, lack of self-trust, lack of self worth) as no respecter of race or class or financial status, or degree of religious dedication. The loathers of the body are to be found wearing meditation clothes and doing awesome yogic postures as well as wearing the skimpiest string bikinis, walking topless along the beaches of the Mediterranean. They are found in convents and in bordellos, in obese women, in anorexic women, and in women who fit the perfect stereotype of Miss America. They are young women, just entering their teens, and old women in their seventies or eighties. And what distin-guishes them one and all is that they do not *know*—in the core of their hearts, or their bellies, or wherever one imagines the still, silent point of absolute "center" to be in a human—that they are loved, completely and unconditionally. They may have glimpsed such a possibility at times, but they have not held to the thread of it. The screaming voices to the contrary which surround them in the prevailing culture of superficiality, have succeeded in over-powering their weak and flickering remembrance. We do not *know* that we are loved, and we do not become inflamed with the inner beauty or goodness of who we are under all our masks and acts of insecurity. Even though we might, and often do hear the words "you must love yourself" or "God loves me," we rarely allow ourselves to know these words as a living, breathing reality.

The remarkable African-American author and poet Maya Angelou is a woman who evidently knows that "God ... loves ... me." As a result, although she feels the ravages caused by the forces of racism in the world, she continually refuses to succumb to negativity within herself. Quite the opposite. The example of her life today is one of profound compassion, coupled with enormous personal courage. Maya has become a spokesperson for the resilience of the human spirit, urging young and old not to let life defeat them, but to forgive themselves and to rise up, again and again. Her many books, including, *I Know Why the Caged Bird Sings*, have inspired countless women and men with their honesty and forth-rightness, their celebration of the wonder of life.[9]

A primal recognition of God's "personal" love, or the intuition of basic goodness, has enormous healing power. It literally washes over the soul like so many waves in a benevolent flood—a baptism into the Reality, rather than the mere notion, of what is called *grace*. I have sat across the table from several women who have told me about their own moments of realization of such love, and have felt the transformative energy present within those moments.

Alisha, who was one of my young female students in a class on death and dying, spoke of the unbearable pain she suffered following the death of her grandmother. Several other losses had preceded this one, so Alisha was particularly vulnerable at this period in her life. "When grandmother died, something happened," she confided, "something that I can't really explain. I was given a taste of God's all-encompassing and all-forgiving love. It was beyond anything that I could ever imagine." Alisha appealed to me, as to her dearest friend, trying to share the effects of a seeming miracle that was as strong for her then as it had been months earlier. I found myself looking away, momentarily, in embarrassment. These things are almost too intimate to talk about sometimes. Alisha's realization was obviously changing her life. As we talked, I was impressed with the courage that seemed to be taking root within her. While I might have previously described Alisha as timid, that was swallowed up now by her enormous desire to serve others as an expression of the love she had come to know.

The amazing part of Alisha's story was her reflection that such grace seemed unearned in any usual sense. She didn't have to "be good" for God to love her. "God loves *me*" could be applied to the "me's" who were full of self-doubt and even self-loathing; full of selfishness and even unkindness. These are also the "me's" who have wrongly judged us as being at fault when really we were being victimized by others—the "me," as in the cases of millions of our sisters, who as children or young women were told that they were stupid, or incompetent, or fat, or too skinny, or too short, or too black, or too white, or irrelevant, or inarticulate, or clumsy, or bad because of some unforgivable sin which no one could name for them. Sadly, these are the "me's" who then close down the spontaneous pleasure in their fingers and toes and vaginas in favor of a guarded demeanor; who turn their humiliation and fear inwards, making themselves the victims of a still more insidious enemy, their own internalized parental voice, the voice of self-hatred. These are the "me's" who hate their bodies, their humanness, their imperfection; who can no longer revel in uniqueness, but must now conform to the warped views of others who have been similarly wounded.

It is these "me's" in every woman (and every man), that the most repulsive form of Divine Mother is committed to redeem.

Nobly she stands, even if hunched in her deformity, this Mother of Creation. She growls or stammers, yet her words are sweeter than a chorus of angels. "I am not separate from the Infinite Beauty of Divine Love," she declares by the sheer boldness of her grotesque form. "In this house of God there are 'many mansions'—there are rooms for all."

Kali teaches us about the possibility of turning our normal values and evaluations upon their heads. Jesus said it: "The least in this Kingdom (the Kingdom of 'man,') will be the greatest in the Kingdom of heaven."

Kali, our Divine Mother, can gift us with the living experience that we are loved beyond appearances. She can eat up self-hatred as she can eat up every other illusion. She can "appear" to us in the form of a sparklingly adoring infant, or in the wise and kindly eyes of a weak and dying old woman—a wizened grandmother—who nonetheless pierces us with her words: "Thank you, my child."

Not everyone who looks at a child feels that transformative energy, however. Not everyone who nurses a dying grandmother becomes convinced of such love. Only those who have allowed themselves to be softened, to be made vulnerable the way a woman is vulnerable who has just birthed a child. Exhausted, battered down by life's circumstances, suffering herself or watching a loved one suffer—these experiences prepare the soul for the glimpse, the glance, the remembrance that awakens its naturally innocent beginning. Great joy can do that awakening too! The joy of a woman who has found what was lost, or found the mate she has hungered for all her life. The joy of seeing adoration in her partner's eyes, or feeling the Universal Benevolence which the silence and awesome power of nature can instruct her with—these experiences too can soften a woman's defenses. She may, in such moments, see through these phenomena to their source. She may feel that she is loved and beloved, at the core of her being. And such a recognition, if it is strong enough, and if she is soft enough to hold it without strangling it, or without putting one face or label on it, may be the thread, the life-line she needs to slowly pull herself back to shore, and back to Life.

MOTHER MAYEE OF KANYAKUMARI, A SAINT FOR OUR TIMES

Mother Mayee of Kanyakumari first introduced herself to me in the winter of 1989 when my teacher Lee had returned from his yearly pilgrimage to India. He recounted some amazing stories about this holy madwoman and miracle-worker who lived with dogs and was purported to be well over two-hundred years old. But it was my friend Katie, who spoke to us in Chapter Four, who gave me a special gift, one day, by sharing her devotion to this relatively unknown saint and manifestation of Divine Mother.

Katie is a woman whom I deeply trust and respect. She is also a woman softened by suffering. Having been close to death several times, Katie has wisdom and insight well beyond her years.

On numerous occasions I had noticed the small but well-kept shrine in Katie's bedroom. The picture of the woman enshrined on the altar was at first shocking to look at. Indeed, I was a bit embarrassed to realize that I found the face repulsive. Although I had never mentioned my reaction to Katie, I wondered about this odd and unattractive portrait. When I interviewed her about mothering as a spiritual practice, Katie explained her love for Mother Mayee, without me having to ask.

> I always wanted to have my own personal goddess, yet this whole "Divine Mother thing" was very foreign to me. I would look at pictures of Anandamayi Ma, who was exceptionally beautiful, and I had my pictures of Mary, and my statue of Kuan Yin who is also extremely refined, gentle, feminine, sweet (not that these don't have their fierce quality as well as their gentle side). Yet, none of these Divine Mothers completely clicked with me.
>
> One day, when I was really ill, I got this image of Mother Mayee of Kanyakumari, and immediately I started crying. I could feel her holding me. Mother Mayee was the lady who sat at the river and fed all the pariah dogs, the strays. And she is

old and wrinkled, and "snaggle-toothed" and gnarly. But, that was it for me! I had found Mother, or she had found me.

There are a lot of things she reminds me of, but the most important is that true beauty comes from within. That sounds really trite, but the truth is that she is *so beautiful* to me. I am not saying this with romanticism. When I look at her I don't see her wrinkles, I see her wisdom. Even people who should know better have said, almost with disgust, "What do you have *her* picture for?" because of their attachment to the Western concept of beauty. But, for me, it is her essence that attracts. I don't even know much about her at all. I never really bothered to find out. I almost don't want to know, because sometimes that complicates the simplicity of the connections.

The first time I had a hint that I was *really* beautiful, essentially beautiful, in my daughter's eyes, I was devastated, because of my own cramp around physical beauty. She is still innocent. My daughter doesn't see my imperfections in the things I struggle with. She doesn't see my wrinkles or the bags under my eyes, in the way we adults are so obsessed with our faults.

Children are always forgiving. Like Divine Mother, it is their pleasure to forgive you your mistakes. For me, that realization was transformative. The responsibility that a mother has in honoring such absolute love and innocence in her child is no light thing. Honoring that responsibility can be an opening for one's alchemical transformation.

What little I know of Mother Mayee, biographically, I received from one of her most passionate devotees. Sadhu Rangarajan is a scholar with the heart of a *bhakta*. He lives in a

Mother Mayee of Kanyakumari

miniscule apartment in Madras, India, where he also publishes *Tattva Darshana*, a quarterly journal devoted to telling the stories of all the great saints of India. Here in the midst of his overflowing bookshelves, with piles of paper filling every square inch of space (except for the sacred space of his devotions, where a picture of the Mother is enshrined), he graciously welcomes visitors from all over the world.

Mother Mayee lived primarily in Kanyakumari, the town at the southernmost tip of India; a town named after Divine Mother herself. (*Kanya* in Sanskrit means "virgin.") She lived as a beggar among the fisherfolk of the village, and was to all intents and purposes thought to be mad. Out of their kindness, the fishermen and women gave her small jobs to do, like breaking firewood, pounding rice, drying fish. And all these labors were done with graciousness, with a smile and a laugh which came to characterize all of Mother's interactions. (Except when she was being fierce, that is.) A small handout of rice and fish were her payment. These she would carry to the seashore where she would sit and eat. Her shelter was questionable, taken wherever she found an out of the way space near some hotel or restaurant. She rarely spoke. Much of her work with people was transmitted in silence. And so passed many decades of her life, completely hidden; her greatness unknown.

One day, within sight of the Mother, a tourist van ran over a stray dog. The suffering creature lay with its intestines exposed on the road, and soon died. As the crowd gathered around the gruesome sight, the mad beggar woman with the bundle of rags approached the disemboweled animal. To the amazement of the spectators, Mother Mayee brought the dog back to life. She pushed its guts back into the wound, created a poultice of straw to cover the opening, and then laid her hand on the animal's back. Immediately the dog leapt to its feet and ran away. "That day," Professor Rangarajan wrote, "the people there realized who she was. Since then, people in Kanyakumari adore her as the Divine Mother."[10]

She loved dogs, or perhaps it was that the dogs loved her, since she was often surrounded with them—forty or fifty at a time, "always around her as her faithful guards," Rangarajan wrote. They served a useful purpose, in guarding her from attack or thievery (not that she had anything of value to steal), and it was reported that she cared for her human devotees with the same degree of loving attention that she paid to her faithful dogs, offering food to both with the same hand.

Friends who visited Mother Mayee as she lay dying in 1989 reported that the dogs kept vigil at her side throughout her long transition. One man was convinced that the dogs were actually devotees from a previous lifetime, another described the mood in her room as being that of a sacred *darshan* (usually a formal gathering around a spiritual person) in which the dogs were actually as reverential, or more, than the human attendants. A third man told me that when it was time for him to leave he was unsure of how to get back to the bus station. When he exited the Mother's house, one dog left his post and accompanied the man out onto the road, "directing" him in the appropriate direction when he came to an important crossroad.

Other miracle stories are accumulating. Dr. Lakshmikumari, a woman who had served for years as the President of Vivekananda Kendra, a nation-wide organization, was praying one day in a temple in Kanykumari when she heard a voice telling her: "Why are you standing here while I am waiting for you outside?" Leaving the temple, she immediately came upon Mother Mayee who stood in the courtyard. The Mother just looked at her and laughed. Laughter seems to have been one of her favorite occupations.

Professor Rangarajan himself, who was diagnosed with lung cancer, credits his complete cure to the Mother's direct intervention. As Rangarajan told me the story, the Mother had chewed some tobacco, spit it into his hands and told him to swallow it, which he immediately did. Faith like that is certainly its own reward. He returned home and performed a number of sacred offerings which the Mother had instructed him to do for 108 days. His health was immediately improved. This progress continued until the supposed cancer was totally disappeared.

Stories of this nature abound in India, and in relationship to any number of saints and holy people. The faith that many Indians have in their gurus and goddesses is unbelievable to us. But for me, the poignancy and importance of Mother Mayee's story is not that she performed miracles. (Experts in black magic

211

can do that too!) The point is that a low-caste beggar, and even a mad-woman, is seen and worshipped as a living manifestation of Divine Mother.

The understanding that the goddess lives in and is accessible through every female—every woman is Kali or Tara or any number of their sisters, particularly the more fierce goddesses who break convention at every turn—is common in India. While such an understanding is not always lived, the serious aspirant or tantric practitioner, at least, will meditate upon this profound truth and attempt to view humanity on this basis. (In some left-handed Tantric rituals, the *tantrika* actually seeks out the most unattractive woman in order to enshrine her as the Mother Goddess and even to make love to her.) He or she will deliberately eschew appearances, honoring the Mother of the Universe in her hundreds and even thousands of different forms. She is everyone and everything.

For me there is something irresistibly appealing about a Divine Mother who belies the normally beautiful images that we associate with the goddess. What a radical idea it would be, in this day and age, to honor a homeless beggar woman—literally a bag-lady—as a Holy One. Could we actually break through our cultural myopia enough to consider the sublime radiance of a woman who thrives on the leftovers of society, a woman whose closest companions are a team of mangy dogs? Could we hold that such a one is worthy of our respect, no less our worship?

Let us ponder this face. Let us call her name and ask her to teach us a new wisdom in relationship to physical beauty, to attachment to material possessions, to grace in the midst of the direst circumstances.

> Call her, she will hear and come. Please make yourself available to receive her grace.
> —Sadhu Rangarajan

Let us reflect that one such as she, may be the only one who can redeem the most despised elements of society, because only one who can laugh at the world's values, as Mother Mayee did, can see things as they really are. And then let us realize that, like Kali, Mother Mayee is not separate from us. That Mother Mayee lives in us, loving us in all the places that we most despise, in all the things we turn away from, in all the deformity and ugliness that we are terrified to see in ourselves.

Can we love Her? Can we embrace the Darkness? If so, we too can redeem the world.

Mother Mayee

7

THE PATH OF THE WARRIOR,
THE WAY OF POWER

The term "warrior" has a decidedly masculine connotation, and for many women engaged in spiritual life this notion of "warriorship" will be rejected as rigid or fearsome—too connected to a male dominance model which has suffocated them for too long. With that in mind, I offer the corresponding phrase "woman of power" to communicate the essence of this necessary quality, or state of being, which any serious spiritual practitioner will have to embody if she truly wants to progress in the vocation to personal integrity and selfless service or love, which is drawing her on.

Before abandoning the word "warrior" altogether, however, it may serve us to contemplate its meaning beyond our attachment to any feminine or masculine application. What are the qualities of one who goes to war, not necessarily against other human beings, but against injustice, against ignorance, against suffering? What are the qualities of the knight in the highest courtly tradition; the "peaceful warrior," if you will?

In the writings of Carlos Castenada, the warrior or "man of power" lives outside the limitations of such terms as *good* and *evil*. Not that the warrior lives without integrity; rather, his (or her) life is characterized by doing whatever is necessary, with whatever has been given. The woman warrior then, might be she who courageously stands up to the forces of injustice, or she who has the inner strength and outer know-how to amputate the hand of a child who would otherwise die. A warrior is one who does not back down in the face of death. From the ground of that fearlessness comes her effectiveness. She is one who is not afraid of her own goodness and power, and therefore is courageous in her ability to serve others, honoring the goodness and power in them.

> The first part of my life I had the attitude that life was play, and I had the need to make it more of a game. I still have that, but there's a great correlation between life is war and life is a game. You have to be ready for anything, always ready to make your next move because you never know where the next attack or the next challenge is going to come from. You just have to be ready and alert and on your toes; ready to give everything until the ultimate victory. If you manage to get a rest, fine. If you don't, that's not what it's about. This "fatigue number" has been a big struggle for me during all my years in this life. I've been very helped by Teresa of Avila who says: "I don't need rest, I need the cross." And then in a beautiful poem of hers, she writes, "If you

want me to rest I will rest for love. If you want me
to labor I will die working."
—Mother Tessa Bielecki

A warrior is characterized by vigilance built by discipline and
attention. From ancient Tibet comes the story of the scholarly
young monk, Saraha, who later became one of the most prominent
"fathers" of Buddhism. One day, while passing through a village,
the monk observed a woman sitting in front of her hut making
arrows. He watched with amazement at the discipline, which
showed up in the precision, lack of distraction, and elegance with
which she approached her task. Immediately Saraha recognized a
quality beyond the ordinary, and because he was an insightful monk,
he assumed that such attention could only indicate a person of
great spiritual achievement. He was right. Approaching her, the
monk attempted to engage her by asking some trivial question.
But the arrow-maker cut through his superficialities with her piercing words, telling him that "... the Budhha's meaning can be known
through symbols and actions, not through words and books."[1]
Saraha was so astonished by this yogini's response that he put away
his monastic robes and instead dedicated himself to her, taking
her as his guru. The yogini proceeded to pass on great wisdom to
him, and he in turn went on to carry out his destiny as one of the
great teachers of the Tantric Buddhist tradition.

Other stories in Tibetan Buddhism testify to a similar recognition of inner power in ordinary life. The great master Naropa
recognized the greatness of a female sesame-seed pounder who then
became his teacher. Another male master gazed into the eyes of a
courtesan, and in her found the guru he had longed for. In each
case, these men, because of their own innate and cultivated discipline, were primed to see through appearances, and thus to reveal
the worth of these "ordinary" women.

Those of us who wonder if our lives are making any difference in the world, would do well to remember that our power, and
therefore our impact, may be happening in "symbols and actions"
much more dynamically than in books or words. This is a hard

lesson to learn. As a book writer and publisher I am constantly fascinated and distracted by the world of the word. How easy it is to lose touch with and forget that the book of gestures, the book of attention, the book of care, the book of concentration and the book of elegance are being written all around me, day after day. The way a woman picks up a child may be the most inspiring and powerful treatise to be read.

In digging a garden, in preparing a meal, in simply walking across a room—a communication can be made more significantly than on the pages of a book. The arrow-making yogini can remind us that our daily activities, when done with awareness, can express the fullness of our personal power, our warriorship.

A warrior needs vigilance to remain calm amid chaos, or clear when confusion reigns, or unseduced in the center of temptation. Such calmness and clarity can actually mean the difference between life and death. The soldier who has to keep watch throughout the night must be able to resist the temptation to sleep or he endangers his entire company. In a similar vein, some extreme forms of Tantric practice require the yogi or yogini to meditate at night in the *smashan* or cremation grounds, considered to be one of the most fearsome places around, the places inhabited by ghosts and spirits. Inattention here can have serious consequences, especially if one is ill prepared to do battle—a battle of wills—with forces of demonic strength. Not only does the warrior yogi attempt to face such fears head on, but to confront the undeniable truth that all phenomena are illusory; that everything is transitory; that life and death are one.

In a generous and playful moment, my teacher one day confided to his students that the parallel to *smashan* practice in Western culture would be to engage self-observation and attention for an extended period in a crowded shopping mall. To watch our mind grasping, to watch the other skin-covered skeletons scurrying around in their frantic need to fill up the void of their empty lives, while we maintain a heart full of compassion for the human condition would be tantamount to a dynamic training in warriorship, especially for those who are easily distracted by the lure of possessions and by material comfort.

218

Warriorship can mean a distinct call to social or political action. The brilliant examples of women in our own times whose work for peace and justice have merited them the Nobel Prize—Mother Teresa of Calcutta and Aung Suu Kyi of Burma being two sterling examples. I am continually inspired by the courage and caring of those who practice what has been called "engaged Buddhism" today—most recently by the work of Zen Roshi Bernard Glassman, whose meditation sesshins take place on the streets of New York, where "meditators" live and practice among the homeless, the drug-users and other outcasts of the society.

I have deep admiration for Buddhist teacher and author Joanna Macy, a courageous woman who helps people to face their despair and fear as they wake up to their responsibilities for the fate of the earth. In her most recent book, *World as Lover, World as Self* she writes about the Buddhist practice of *Sarvodaya*—which means "everybody wakes up." In reflecting upon her time spent in Asia she wrote:

> In my mind I still hear the local *Sarvodaya* workers, in their village meetings and district training centers. Development is not imitating the West. Development is not high-cost industrial complexes, chemical fertilizers and mammoth hydroelectric dams. It is not selling your soul for unnecessary consumer items or schemes to get rich quick. Development is waking up—waking up our true potential as persons and as a society.[2]

The ongoing projects and calls to action which the Buddhist Peace Fellowship sponsors,[3] and the recent campaigns to Save Tibet,[4] testify to the deep commitment which many groups have for bringing their spiritual practice to the marketplace.

Activist Mirabai Bush who, as a director of the Seva Foundation, labored for years among the poor of Guatemala, today directs the Project on Contemplative Mind In Society, which works with people from all walks of life, including high-profile business executives, to reawaken them to their social and political responsibility while at the same time teaching them invaluable skills in the cultivation of the inner life.[5]

For many women of the spirit, our tasks of warriorship will be much less headlined. Yet, regardless of the dramatic scope or impact of our actions, many of us have come to recognize that if we are to transform a critical situation we must transform ourselves in the process. Otherwise we merely strengthen the collective illusion of where ultimate power resides.

Power means energy or inner force as much as it means the ability to *do*. In fact, all the women featured in this book are nourished by the power of an inner life characterized by tremendous self-honesty and dedication to truth. In this dedication they have built an inner matrix of clarity for themselves, out of which their lives of selfless service and their consistent dedication to the impossible tasks at hand have unfolded.

Such unfoldment will be the same for us. When our lives are sourced with clarity and inner strength, regardless of whether we ever do more than the raise our children with kindness, or nurse our aged parents with patience, or keep our garden with elegance, we too will be warriors of the spiritual way. We too will be women of power and grace.

THE COURAGE TO SEE

In his book, *Shambhala: The Secret Path of the Warrior*, author Chögyam Trungpa, a Tibetan Buddhist Master, wrote that the greatest test of warriorship is to look within ourselves with courage. It takes a strong inner resolve to "see" just what we are up to, and to tell the simple truth about the stuff we see that we don't like; the stuff we would rather deny as we build up some image of ourselves as spiritual beings. (A big pitfall which we must guard against diligently.)

Just as we can't use a map unless we know where we are located to begin with and what our destination is, so no progress is possible on the spiritual journey if we are unwilling to face the truth of where we are starting from—the point on which we currently stand. To keep up a practice of meditation, for example, is one surefire way to encounter, often in living color, all we would rather not see about ourselves. Indeed, it is humiliating to acknowledge that I am over fifty years old and still battling, internally at least, for freedom from Daddy's approval or disapproval. It takes courage to admit to the ugliness—that I *am* competitive, even in spiritual matters; that I begrudge my friends their spiritual "successes" or revelations, as if it meant that my own were somehow diminished. It is disturbing to uncover layer upon layer of self-obsession immediately after I have arrived at some wide-vistaed plateau of spiritual understanding. To watch the ways I subtly try to manipulate the environment and everyone around to give me the assurance, the comfort or the pleasure that I really want; well, it's not a pretty sight. For a parent to recognize that so much of her activity toward her child has been done out of a desire for her child to live out the life that she didn't have the guts to live, is devastating. For a husband or wife to *see* how little they really know of love, and how disrespectful (if not downright shaming) they have been to their partner, for twenty years or more, can be a crushing insight.

The list of such discoveries is endless, and the pain that may arise from such confrontations may seem equally endless. Yet, this is the first task for a woman of power—to take inventory of herself so that she does not foolishly enter into the battle unprepared.

We are speaking here of a courage which is every bit as great as the courage to run into a blazing building in order to rescue a sick child. In fact, the analogy is quite appropriate. Our own thoughts, and the combined projections of a lifetime, can be hotter and more terrifying to face than literal flames. The sick child in need of rescue is our own inner child—our basic innocence which has become so overcome with the toxic fumes of the prevailing culture as to render her nearly unconscious.

Human beings easily fool themselves—probably for good reason. We don't like pain, and we are willing to go to almost any extreme to avoid having to bear it. Rather than face the

221

implications of our raw fears, we construct huge systems of denial and projection, usually in the form of stories of self-deprecation and victimization, which we foolishly, but understandably, believe will somehow shield us against a greater pain. Sadly, most people would rather endure a mediocre existence of continued self-deception than face the revelation of their own hypocrisy, or greatness, since the responsibility that follows upon the recognition of our awesome *basic goodness* (to use Chögyam Trungpa's term) may be more terrifying than the prospect of exposing our dirty laundry.

The warrior senses that she can't afford the luxury of denial, in either direction. The woman of power knows that denial can lull her soul to sleep. One way she fights this sleepiness is by shedding light on those nooks and crannies of her psyche where the veils of denial are thickest. Many women do this through daily meditation or other contemplative practice, together with vigorous, but non-judgemental, self-observation. They work to keep an attitude of "empowerment"—an astute management of energy in which they honestly acknowledge what they find without condemning themselves for it; in which they take a "friendly attitude towards their thoughts" (to quote Chögyam Trungpa again), and then move on, with attention and intention to the next requirement of the task at hand.

SIMONE WEIL: WOMAN OF POWER
(1909-1943)

The short life and passionate commitment that characterized the work and writing of Simone Weil, a French philosopher, revolutionary and mystic, have been immensely instructive to me. And while there are aspects of her obsession with truth which would lead others to see her as neurotic, if not seriously unbalanced, the overall legacy which she leaves to men and women of our day is enormously rich.

It was in the writing of Simone Weil, as well as in the witness of her life, that the concept of "inner obedience" came alive for me. I understood from Simone that inner obedience had to do with a sharpened level of discrimination—one which "listens" and looks at the world as the domain of God, and then waits upon God's internal prompting to direct the next step. In practical application, Simone would not *go anywhere* or *do anything*, even to the point of not reading a particular book, except insofar as that action or non-action seemed likely to nourish her goal or strengthen her inner life. Sound easy? Actually, what I've described is probably one of the hardest assignments anyone can undertake. Literally, such a fierce intention takes a sword to thousands of legitimate distractions that crisscross through our daily lives.

Imagine the kind of inner resolve, i.e., power, required to turn attention to prayer, or to silently celebrate the beauty of nature, for instance, instead of reading the newspaper in the doctor's waiting room, or browsing a fashion catalog over lunch, or turning on the television because we suddenly feel bored. None of these activities in and of themselves is wrong. In fact, each of them can be a means of remembrance of our intention to serve God, to become women of genuine love. But the point is, each of these activities also takes time, and therefore takes energy. And that may mean less free time and less energy applied to what we say we *really* want. The hardest part of the spiritual path comes in having the strength of resolve and the consistency to actually follow through on what we glimpse as true in our moments of clarity or bliss.

Simone Weil was born in Paris in 1909 and died in England in 1943. She was Jewish by ancestry but not by practice—her parents and grandparents were agnostics, free-thinkers. The "spirituality" that dominated her childhood was revealed in the brilliant philosophy and poetics of Racine or Pascal. What replaced religious fervor, as we normally think of it, was the cultivation of a searing intellect—a hungering for the underlying truth of things, as well as a deep sensitivity to the plight of her fellow human beings. In 1914, when Simone was five years old, hearing that soldiers at the front were without sugar rations, she denied herself this privilege as well.

One of Simone Weil's early mentors, who was also a well known philosopher of the time, described her as a brilliant student, noting in her "a power of thought that was rare." In 1928, when applying for Ecole Normale, a college equivalent, she tested first among all the applicants for admission, winning over Simone de Beauvoir who was second. Her professors generally considered her eccentric, "too original," but de Beauvoir later wrote that she "envied her for having a heart that could beat right across the world."

When she graduated as a qualified teacher of philosophy in 1932 and began her teaching work, Simone Weil distinguished herself more for her revolutionary tendencies as for anything else. Her earliest writings were almost all concerned with the plight of labor, and she spent much of her time with working class people, often giving her salary to those in need.

In 1934-5 Simone left her teaching jobs to take a place in the assembly lines at a Renault factory near Paris. Here, constantly battling ill health (made more severe by her life-long refusal to cater to her bodily needs, as well as her practice of often rigorous self-mortification) she gave herself the task of experiencing the *meaning* of mechanization. What she found was that such work created dehumanization; that it was, in effect, a form of slavery. In her factory work, a circumstance of complete invisibility, as in many other conditions of hazard or pain which she willingly embraced throughout her life, Simone heightened her resolve to know the truth of existence without the buffers of privilege or education which had been her birthright. One is reminded, in the life of Siddhartha the Buddha, of the wrenching break with his protected and princely heritage that the young Siddhartha made in his quest to know the meaning of life and death. Of this type of venture Simone Weil wrote:

> I have the essential need, and I think I can say the vocation, to move among men of every class and complexion, mixing with them and sharing their life and outlook, so far that is to say as conscience allows, merging into the crowd and disap-

224

pearing among them, so that they show themselves as they are, putting off all disguises with me. It is because I long to know them so as to love them just as they are. For if I do not love them as they are, it will not be they whom I love, and my love will be unreal.[6]

Another teaching assignment followed her factory sabbatical, and then she was off to Spain in 1936 to experience the Spanish revolution first-hand. Here she intended to write, to fight, to serve in whatever way she could. The Holy Spirit which guided her life evidently had other plans, however. An accident in which she was severely burned forced Simone to leave Spain and return to the family nest in Paris. Here, her father, who was a medical doctor, and her solicitous mother attempted to nurse her back to health. It was out of this seemingly tragic experience that the mystical fire that had smoldered for so long within her heart, was unleashed.

In the spiritual autobiography which she wrote a few years before her death, Simone Weil confessed that at perhaps the age of nine, she had looked head-on to what she called "the God problem" and decided that since there was no way to prove it, or to scientifically investigate it, this issue had best be left alone. And that is precisely what she did. In 1938, however, at the age of twenty-nine, this young agnostic had a major religious experience—an awakening which changed the context of her life forever. Suffering greatly from the headaches which had plagued her since her fourteenth year (when she went through the darkest crisis of her life, propelled by a sense of absolute unworthiness), and still recovering from her trauma in Spain, Simone accompanied her parents on vacation to Portugal, where she sought the refuge of a silent retreat at a monastery in Salesmes. One day as she listened to the Gregorian chant, she experienced a level of consciousness unlike any she had known before. Focusing intently on the sounds and words of the music, she found that she was able to temporarily transcend her body—leaving it behind her "in a crumbled heap," and with it the pain that had been her constant companion.

During this same retreat Simone met a young French Catholic man who gave her copy of the poem "Love" by the renowned English metaphysical poet of the seventeenth century, George Herbert. Somehow, the vulnerability that pain created had softened Simone's heart to the degree that this poem drew her into a profound state of mystical contemplation, which she experienced as communion with the presence of Christ. As Simone later described in a letter to a friend:

> In a moment of intense physical suffering, when I was forcing myself to feel love, but without desiring to give a name to that love, I felt without being in any way prepared for it (for I had never read the mystical writers), a presence more personal, more certain, more real than that of a human being, though inaccessible both to sense and imagination, and it resembled the love that irradiates the tenderest smile of somebody one loves. Since that moment, the name of God and the name of Christ have been more and more irresistibly mingled with my thoughts.[7]

Herbert's poem is indeed worthy of contemplation. For over four hundred years it has stood as a testimony to the transcendent compassion of Divine love.

> Love bade me welcome: yet my soul drew back,
>   Guilty of lust and sin.
> But quick-eye'd Love, observing me grow slack
>   From my first entrance in,
> Drew nearer to me, sweetly questioning,
>   If I lack'd any thing.
>
> A guest, I answer'd, *worthy to be here*:
>   Love said, "You shall be he."
> I the unkind, ungrateful? Ah my dear,

226

I cannot look on thee.
Love took my hand, and smiling did reply,
"Who made the eyes but I?"

Truth Lord, but I have marr'd them: let my shame
Go where it doth deserve.
"And know you not," says Love, "who bore the blame?"
My dear, then I will serve.
"You must sit down," says Love, "and taste my meat:"
So I did sit and eat.

Simone Weil's encounter with the power of Divinity left her changed. From this point on in her life, despite her labors for the poor and forgotten—she still wrote scathingly of the injustices of her time, and still suffered from terrible loneliness and enormous physical pain—all her work was informed with a new kind of spiritual light. She was learning to pray, and being led to heights of spiritual understanding and experience which mystics throughout the ages have come to know.

In her spiritual autobiography she wrote about her time in an agricultural colony in the south of France:

> I recited the Our Father in Greek every day before work, and I repeated it very often in the vineyard...Since that time I have a practice of saying it through once each morning with absolute attention. The effect of the practice is extraordinary and surprises me every time. At times the very first words tear my thoughts from my body and transport it to a place outside space where there is neither perspective nor point of view. The infinity of the ordinary expanses of perception is replaced by an infinity to the second or sometimes the third degree. At the same time, filling every part of this infinity of infinity, there is silence, a silence which is not an absence of sound but which

is the object of a positive sensation, more positive
than that of sound....Sometimes, also, during this
recitation or at other moments, Christ is present
with me in person, but his presence is infinitely
more real, more moving, more clear than on that
first occasion when he took possession of me.[8]

Like other descriptions of the mystical experience, Simone
Weil's words should be read cautiously, appreciated as an indication of God's unique workings in one human soul, but not as any
model whereby to judge or criticize one's own inner revelation or
lack of it. Rather, the primary value of this passage is what it reveals about Simone's ability to practice. She says that she used the
Lord's prayer as a point of focus; that she held a firm intention
about her ability to remain centered in the sentiments of the prayer
rather than to have her mind drawn off into self-referenced thought.
This is what fascinates me about Simone's spiritual discipline—
how willing she is to work for what she says she wants. She wants
to pierce the cloud of unknowing that surrounds the nature of the
Divine. Well then, she sets all the faculties of her being in that
direction. And the results speak for themselves.

It is the intriguing and paradoxical blend of revolutionary,
mystic and philosopher which keeps one mesmerized by the writings of Simone Weil. She speaks to our age in ways that are unique,
calling for a new kind of saintliness. It was her firm belief and
understanding that the contemplation of the social/political scene
of one's own day could be as effective a purification of heart and
spirit as any withdrawal into a monastery or cave. To allow the
heart to be broken by the suffering of humanity was to allow for
the opening that the Divine needed in order to penetrate one's
usual, invincible defense systems. She wrote:

We are living in times that have no precedent,
and in our present situation universality, which
could formerly be implicit, has to be fully explicit.
It has to permeate our language and the whole of
our way of life.

Today it is not nearly enough merely to be a saint, but we must have the saintliness demanded by the present moment, a new saintliness, itself also without precedent.

A new type of sanctity is indeed a fresh spring, an invention. If all is kept in proportion and if the order of each thing is preserved, it is almost equivalent to a new revelation of the universe and of human destiny. It is the exposure of a large portion of truth and beauty hitherto concealed under a thick layer of dust. More genius is needed than was needed by Archimedes to invent mechanics and physics. A new saintliness is a still more marvelous invention.[9]

What she calls for is a new type of contemplative life-style. Simone Weil calls us to examine our own lives and our social/political involvement in the light of the demand to be saints. Her mystical understanding was not so much a source of comfort, but a sword that lashed out at injustice, pain and illusion. She was not afraid to remind her readers and listeners, moreover, that Christ himself suffered *malheur*—that is despair—as he hung upon the cross, weeping, looking out over the city of Jerusalem. Certainly one who experiences the calling to this type of contemplative life will need the reassurance that her despair has an eminent precedent. It is so easy to fall into the trap of thinking that we must be emotionless, unmoved by human misery if we are to exemplify the path of wisdom and surrender to God. Quite the opposite. The great lovers are not afraid to weep.

A curious stubbornness characterized the life of Simone Weil following her mystical union with Christ. One would assume that such an enormously transformative encounter would immediately send this agnostic to the feet of Christ as he is worshipped and shared in the sacrament of the Eucharist, and that she would join the Christian ranks and thereby increase the efficacy of Christ's message to the world-at-large by the power of her intelligent and passionate voice speaking on behalf of the Church. Yet, despite her great love for Christ, and even her longing to express that love through participation in the sacraments, she felt no love for the Church itself—a condition of heart which she trusted, despite the judgements of others who might (and did) interpret such resistance as the devil's ploys.

Simone trusted the rigor of honesty that had informed her life. She trusted that if God wanted her to be baptized that God would make such a demand known to her. In the meantime, she kept her thoughts focused on God, and waited upon God's good time, God's good favor. Ultimately, she concluded, "It is not my business to think about myself. My business is to think about God. It is for God to think about me." [10]

Another reason for her refusal to be baptized was her choice to remain ever an outsider (something which also cost her much personal anguish), and hence always available to men and women of every faith or religious orientation, including those who professed to be agnostics or even atheists. To receive baptism would, in her mind, have placed her in one religious camp as opposed to another; something which she never wanted to do.

As an outsider, she could never take her religious affiliation for granted. For Simone Weil that would have been the greatest travesty: to fall asleep as a Christian, to settle into the easy, "experienced" belief of the churchgoer. She reasoned that it was much better to remain as a disenfranchised and struggling seeker who must create her own path every step of the way.

Decidedly, many within formal Christianity, including her much loved confidant and spiritual director, Father Perrin, argued with her that such a hold-out was indefensible—a type of self-inflicted punishment, even a turning away from the very gift which God had offered her in the experience of Christ. And indeed their arguments are understandable. From another perspective, however, when we realize the motivation that compelled her decision, we can also stand in awe of the type of spiritual resolve that asked for Truth and then was willing to "die" for it, with a death that might entail deprivation from a source of consolation and spiritual nourishment. In a letter to Father Perrin regarding her hesitations regarding baptism she wrote:

> It seems to me that the will of God is that I should not enter the Church at present. The reason for this I have told you already and it is still true. It is because the inhibition that holds me back is no less strongly to be felt in the moments of attention, love, and prayer than at other times. And yet I was filled with a very great joy when you said the thoughts confided to you were not incompatible with allegiance to the Church, and that, in consequence, I was not outside it in spirit.
>
> I cannot help still wondering whether in these days when so large a proportion of humanity is submerged in materialism, God does not want there to be some men and women who have given themselves to him and to Christ and who yet remain outside the Church.[11]

Regardless of our opinions of her reasoning or the accuracy of her sensing, we can still admire the commitment to Truth which motivated her choices. Simone Weil was, to the very end of her short life at the age of thirty-four, a woman of immense spiritual power.

POWER OVER EVIL

As much as idealistic spiritual seekers in the Western world may seek to deny it, there are forces or agencies which do the work of "the devil," that seek to root out and destroy whatever threatens their sovereign power, or to keep control of not only the bodies but the minds and hearts of other human beings. What can be said of the activities of the Chinese Communists in Tibet, who have systematically since the early 1950s, attempted to completely undermine and destroy a culture of the highest spiritual achievement and refined elegance on the face of this earth? The cruelty of the Chinese Communists and the degradation to which they have subjected this passionate but eminently peaceful people, the Tibetans, is witnessed by the thousands of monks, nuns and laypeople they have murdered and the scores of monasteries (each containing precious and irreplaceable manuscripts and religious artifacts) that they have desecrated and looted—selling their spoils on the Black Market all over the world.

These stories are hard to hear. Especially difficult when we realize that they have been going on in our lifetime. In Communist Russia too, despite the many appearances of egalitarianism and new openness to communication, trade and commerce with the West, a slightly different but nonetheless deadly type of "evil" has been perpetrated for generations. The systematic attempt to silence the voices of artists and visionaries who speak a creed that is even slightly different from the voice of the state—this decimation of liberty, creativity and freedom of religious expression has been a source of untold personal misery for the Russian people.

Out of the horrid and dehumanizing condition of Russia's labor camps—massive prisons for thousands of nameless and faceless victims—have emerged stories of unequalled human courage and greatness. Among the most devastating have been the testimonies of Alexander Solzhenitsyn, author of *The Gulag Archipelago*, a shattering account of the Soviet Penal System from 1918 to 1956; and from the woman's perspective, the writing of Irina Rathushinskaya, a young Russian poet (born in 1954) whose confinement to the political sector of a labor camp in Barashevo for the four years from 1982 to 1986 was the subject of her stirring book, *Grey Is The Color of Hope*.

It was from Irina Ratushinskaya's account that I first heard about the *babushki*—from *babushka*, the Russian word for grandmother. The *babushski* made such an impression on my heart! I write about them here because they represent a type of power which is characteristic of true spiritual greatness; theirs was a radical and sacrificial witness, the likes of which few of us will ever be called to demonstrate.

The *babushki* were so named because of their long-term internment in the camps—most of them had spent twenty to thirty years in such conditions, others more. These heroic women were imprisoned because of their resolve to hold to the original spirit of the Christian Gospels despite the laws of a godless communistic regime. They practiced a faith that took the crucified Christ as its only authority. Consequently, they categorically refused to support any Russian state authorities, institutions or laws which attempted to undermine the dominion of their blessed Lord. Practically, these women refused to carry Soviet passports, refused to handle Russian money, and refused to work for any institution of the Soviet government. Instead, they lived like the lilies of the field, awaiting the gracious sun and benevolent rains of their heavenly Father; or in their case, the generous donations of friends and supporters of their cause, fellow lovers of their Lord, Jesus. These valiant women and men, as members of the True Orthodox Church, refused to even honor the state-sanctioned Russian Orthodox Church since it was another puppet of the Bolsheviks.

Their true freedom and power was modeled during their confinement. These women, whose hearts were the property of God, were immune to the intimidation and degradation to which their captors continually tried to subject them. Like the disciples of the early Christian Church, their willingness to accept martyrdom was a constant irritant to their accusers. The *babushki* had ultimate power over anyone who tried to harm her because no matter how the prison authorities wounded and tortured her—by depriving her of adequate clothing in sub-zero weather—by giving her only the poorest rations of often disgustingly prepared food—by subjecting her to long periods of solitary confinement—they could not touch her soul. They could hurt her body, but they could not deny her the pure happiness she found in the thinnest ray of sunshine, the tiny insect on a leaf, the ability to touch another human being with kindness and thereby to communicate her firsthand knowledge of the awesome and constant presence of God.

Such faith, such kindness and such selfless concern for others earned the *babushki* the respect and admiration of camp in-

mates. Even the guards were amazed at the invocations of blessing
and forgiveness which the *babushki* would call down upon their
captors, in startling contrast to the usual curses or invectives of
the other prisoners.

Irina wrote:

> ...the *babushki*, with endless patience, repaired ev-
> erything for everyone, any heavier work was physi-
> cally beyond them. The camp authorities tried to
> avoid placing them into the camp prison, because
> they were so frail it would have taken very little
> to kill them. But other inmates were not spared
> the camp prison and the *babushki*, their hearts
> wrung by compassion, did all they could to help
> as much as possible. In punishment cells you are
> stripped of your underwear and given a special
> smock: its low neckline rivals the most daring
> ballgown, and it has very wide, three-quarter-
> length sleeves to ensure that the wearer will freeze.
> That's what these cells are for—officially known
> as SHIZO, punishment isolation cells. Extreme
> cold is regarded as a necessary feature of the cor-
> rective process, but it never yielded the required
> results with the women in our Zone. The
> *babushki*—experienced zeks one and all—did ev-
> erything possible to beat the cold. They sewed un-
> derwear out of flannel footcloths (long strips to
> be wound around one's feet) which were issued
> for winter, and whenever possible, quilted them
> on the inside with cotton wool. Instead of bras-
> sieres, they made something akin to shortened
> vests. Everything was multilayered for maximum
> warmth. All these garments were made out of a
> multitude of scraps of cloth for large pieces of
> material were not obtainable in the camp.

So we inherited a box full of what we called the "*babushki*'s trousseau." Looking at the shirts they had made, I found them to be a veritable patchwork of all shades and textures: here a scrap of cotton, here something knitted, there a small woolen insert—all painstakingly gathered and cobbled together into a garment. The underwear they produced would hardly have merited that name elsewhere—at first glance, one was hard put to determine which part of the body it was supposed to cover. Everything was much worn, much washed, carefully darned again and again. In some cases, there were patches on patches, darns on darns. And all done with such care, such love for one's neighbor, as if for oneself! Not only were the *babushki* willing to sacrifice the shirts off their backs for others, they tried to prolong the life of every bit of clothing ad infinitum.[12]

The *babushki* were living for God—their own suffering was seen as a way to alleviate the suffering of Christ in some small way. They were women of Divine power.

Some voice in us may scoff at such obsession and dismiss it as fanaticism. Yet, as Irina noted, according to the wisdom that fired the *babushkis'* souls, "it is *we* who act unnaturally..." It is *we* who give more and more concession to the powers of evil, everyday. It is *we* who naively or foolishly assume that such powers of evil will simply go away if we don't heed them. Instead, as the *babushki* asserted, these powers insidiously work their way into our lives until they have so co-opted our worldview that we tend to see those who make a stand against them as fanatics—overzealous, reactive people, if not downright fools. Were not the same denunciations made of Gandhi and his movement of non-violence; the same made of the "fanatic" blacks who attempted to sit at segregated lunch counters only to be beaten with billyclubs by enraged police?

We should be grateful to these Russian women of power, some of whom may be our relatives. Irina sadly reported late in 1987 that some of them were still in the camps, perhaps because they refused to sign even their own release papers—a gesture which would have acknowledged the state's authority.

In our own day, we are blessed to have knowledge that living saints still exist on this earth; women of such immense commitment to God that, as Irina says, they are "ever ready to lay down their lives for the Lord."

The lives of the unnamed *babushki* may remind us to entrust them and all imprisoned women the world over to the arms of Divine Mother, as we invoke our own prayers. Perhaps we can use the guidance, the wisdom and the witness of the *babushski* to find within ourselves that same source from which their power flows.

JOAN HALIFAX—CONTEMPORARY WOMAN OF POWER

The summer I met Joan Halifax—anthropologist, former LSD researcher, author, shamanic scholar and currently a Buddhist teacher—was one of the highest and healthiest times of my life. Toronto, 1978, was the site of the conference of the International Association for Humanistic Psychology. My job was to lead the Transpersonal Psychology forum, coordinating events for author Jean Houston and other notables who were keynoting the event. Not only was my body in great shape, but my self-esteem quotient was also at an all-time peak. I was a woman fulfilled, or so I thought at the time. Jogging in the early morning through the still chill and empty streets of this cosmopolitan city, I easily made the miles from the University of Toronto to the lakeshore without breathing hard. My long hair streamed behind me highlighted by the rising sun, my florescent green running shorts were loose over my strong thighs—clearly I was a sight to behold, at six-feet-three-inches. At thirty-three years old, I delighted that I could still turn the heads of the taxi drivers, the construction workers arriving for their day's labors, and the shopowners setting out their wares. I was the goddess, proud and happy.

On the third night of this ten-day extravaganza, I danced wildly to the pounding conga beat, my full yellow-cotton skirt swirled, my hips gyrated seductively and my arms exuberantly grasped for the sky. In one moment of sheer ecstasy I leapt, hurling my body into space, uncontrolled and joyous. Landing hard, on the outside edge of my left foot, the ankle was unable to withstand the powerful impact; internally I could hear the crack. With the ankle turned completely, the rest of the body could not balance itself and the whole mighty frame collapsed—the goddess knocked unceremoniously from her pedestal. I lay in a writhing sea of pain, tears streaming, breath coming short, face red with exhilaration suddenly turned to embarrassment.

As I was carried from the room on the arms of solicitous friends, the pain grew worse, shooting in hot licks up my leg. The hospital x-ray confirmed what I already guessed. My ankle was broken, and so was I. Within a few short days, despite the sympathetic assistance of my peers, and despite my own valiant efforts to maintain business as usual as I hobbled on crutches from taxicabs to campus buildings, it was a different woman who stood inside those familiar clothes. A broken ankle had changed everything.

As I've noted to many students and friends over the years, when one part of the body is wounded, made vulnerable, the whole body-mind complex often follows suit. Floods of insecurity, which are almost always held temporarily at bay by the dikes of physical integrity, can come cascading through the tears in the wall, and soon threaten to drown us in their tumultuous whirl. Yet, what a lesson such a break can be—a meditation on the nature of impermanence, and an awakening to the shallow self-knowledge and self-appreciation that we ordinarily live with. If self-esteem can be so easily dried up by the heat of a small crisis, it must be shallow indeed. In the whole scheme of things, a broken ankle is really no big deal. Still, it was for me.

The good part of the whole emergency was the attention lavished by friends and strangers alike. Everybody I met either quietly or dramatically consoled me, or praised me for my bravery in carrying on, regardless. Which is probably, in part, why the fortuitous meeting with Joan Halifax made such a lasting impression on me.

Twenty years later I am still grateful for the quality of what this woman of power gave to me.

Our meeting was nothing extraordinary. Standing by the elevator on the ground floor of a campus building, I struggled to achieve my balance while managing a purse that bulged with papers and the necessary accessories for the day's activities. Preoccupied, I scarcely noticed the woman who had moved next to me, awaiting the same elevator. Only when she spoke and I turned my face full in her direction did I recognize Joan Halifax—I had seen her picture on the conference brochure, and on book jackets or in magazine articles over the years.

"Whaddya do?" she smiled warmly, nodding her head in the direction of my foot. As I answered her, a bit awestruck that I was here standing alone beside a woman of some notoriety, I took in the whole impression of her body. She was dressed in a fashionable, matching white top and skirt, her long hair was simply styled, a few pieces of gold jewelry at her throat and at her wrist spoke richness without being flashy.

Hers was the kind of question that any stranger might ask; a question that really doesn't expect more than the briefest acknowledgment as an answer, because the asker really doesn't care, except in the most superficial or pitying way. But her question wasn't like that. And while she too didn't expect a long, involved explanation, her question was asked from a context of caring which was palpable to me. I had been sensitized by the mechanical and empty concern of others.

So, I told her simply, "Broke my ankle, dancing."

Her response was like nothing I could have anticipated, knowing her so little. With her gaze now riveted on my face, and with kindness and a glint of playfulness in her eyes, she let out a laugh.

"Far out!" she whooped, with evident enthusiasm. Then she smiled again graciously and turned her attention to the opening elevator door. She stepped in, holding the red button down as I fumbled after her on my crutches. Then the door closed, sealing the two of us for thirty silent seconds (she had no need to speak again). Joan got off without saying goodbye, and as I navigated my way to the room where I was scheduled to speak, I noticed that I was "charged."

In the days immediately following that encounter I realized that Joan Halifax had instructed me in something significant— about illness, disaster, the superficiality of the assessments of "the sleeping world" and all that goes along with that. She herself had spent months with the Dogon people of the Sahara where she had discovered the value of taking tiny steps, learning to slow down to the rhythm of desert, sky and rock. She had also contracted hepatitis in this remote region, another means by which she was taught the fine art of slowing down. To put language to it today, I would say that Joan "told" me that the pain, or the impatience, or the inconvenience, or the sense of helplessness was a valuable training process for me—one that could help me to build an inner matrix strong enough to hold my life in an entirely different way. She reminded me of what I already knew, but so readily forgot, that by going down into darkness, (*The Fruitful Darkness: Reconnecting with the Body of the Earth* [HarperSanFrancisco, revised edition 1994] became the luscious title of a book she would write fifteen years later.) I could learn to fortify my genuine strengths. I could become a woman of power.

The reason she didn't have to speak further to me on the elevator was that she had already delivered all I needed to know in the first twenty seconds of our chance meeting. Her presence to the sheer power of life was all that was needed to communicate something worthwhile to me. She didn't need to elaborate in ways that would only have diminished the spontaneity and richness of a gift freely given.

Woman teaches by *who she is*, much more powerfully than she ever will by what she says. The "teaching" I refer to is one that requires no action or evident accomplishment to verify. The teaching that "genuine presence" communicates is available to the woman or man who is completely paralyzed and mute, as much as it is to the able-bodied and garrulous. My friend and mentor Lalitha would describe such a communication as a tangible substance which is present in the air around a powerful person, and which can be captured and inhaled (or consumed in some way) by an observant witness. In that substance, mysteries are encoded.

A woman who has used any number of means to accumulate a storehouse of such internal power-substance—whether through prayer, or through discipline and asceticism, or by the silence and focus of her life in art, or by sacrificing herself for the sake of others, or by her compassionate endurance of suffering (as Joan Halifax had done on numerous occasions) or by her association with other powerful beings or teachers (which had also been Joan's privilege)—such a woman has something which speaks by itself, with or without words. Her substance can be shared simply through a glance or a touch. Joan Halifax was such a woman.

Some who sense the aura of a powerful man or woman will not know what to do with the potentially helpful substance that he or she may be emanating. They may allow it to roll off their skin quite quickly by sensationalizing it without allowing it to penetrate, or by diminishing or defending against it. The recipient of such a potential gift may consider it "weird" to be around such power. For example, it is decidedly uncomfortable to be in the presence of someone who expresses power through silence. Our own superficial chatter becomes amplified just as it drops into dead air. But for one who has the ears to hear, or the eyes to see, or the thirsty pores to absorb it, such substance will not just be enjoyed, but will be greedily welcomed as the elixir for which the soul has longed.

In 1978, Joan Halifax had already accumulated power-substance in the underworld of suffering. She had something valuable to share with me about the nature of pain and power. Fortunately, I was temporarily wounded and needy—I was touched by what she offered and wanted more. Our brief encounter motivated me to register for the two-day workshop she gave in the post-conference.

Actually I have no recollection of *what* that workshop was called, and I remember almost nothing of what it was *about*. What I recall precisely was Joan Halifax, despite herself, reading a poem or two from Kabir, asking us to look deeply into one another's eyes (all simple tasks that required no expertise on her part and no skill on ours). What remains firmly planted in memory is that Joan honored and appreciated herself enough to exhibit no need to prove anything. Rather she seemed to do what she did because it enlivened *her*. That kind of self-assurance, while probably still immature in her, was still strong enough that I "got" this important lesson: Woman awake is her own message.

MEETING JOAN AGAIN

I visited Joan Halifax again, nearly twenty years later, when I participated in a special retreat for women that she hosted at Upaya, the Zen center she directs in Santa Fe, New Mexico. We are both in our fifties now. How interesting to gauge my own maturing into the phase of crone wisdom in the light of her dynamic and compassionate presence. Each of us had made several significant shifts in our lives during these intervening years. Hers had evidently been beneficial.

I found Joan still dressed in white, but this time, instead of the fashionable suit, she wore what my friends refer to as "yoga whites"—a loose-fitting, cotton top and three-quarter length pants. Instead of a luxurious mane of hair, which I had remembered so clearly about her, Joan gently and humbly presented her shaved head for all to wonder about or admire. She had recently undergone ordination to the priesthood as a core member of the Zen Peacemaker Order under the direction of Tetsugen Roshi Bernard Glassman, and had chosen to go "all the way" (a characteristic approach to life for Joan!)—shaved head, promise of celibacy, a commitment to lifelong service to the needs of others. Joan Halifax, in her mid-fifties, is a monk.

More than ever I found her to be woman of enormous power and charisma—a power grounded in a dedication to personal practice, and deeply rooted in the recognition of her inter-connection with all life. Since 1984, Joan has been a student of the Vietnamese peace-maker and Zen Master, Thich Nhat Hanh, and more recently has been empowered as a teacher (Dharmacarya) in his Tiep Hien Order, a world-wide movement of meditation and awareness training which engenders peace on the earth through creating peace in the lives of individuals.

As I observed Joan carefully over the few days of our time together, I saw that she drew enormous strength from silence, from the empty, expansive mind and from the earth. And because she came from within the earth, from *underneath* so to speak, her power was one of respectful and humble recognition of each creature, including each human being who ventured into her circle of awareness. Her compassion overflowed, and I found myself frequently in tears as I allowed it, like a cleansing stream, to wash me.

Each morning and afternoon we gathered in the Zendo where, sitting on our cushions under the watchful eye of the exquisite, gold painted statue of Avalokitesvara, the *Bodhisattva* of Compassion, we faced the pure white stucco walls, and focused on the movement of the breath within our bodies, especially the rise and fall of the abdomen. Nothing more—no attempts at grasping after visions, no seeking for enlightenment, and no serious faces either. "This is not meant to be a pious practice," Joan advised in one of her first *dharma* talks (instructions about practice). "That's why we always wear a little smile on the face...to remind us of that," she clarified, undermining that tendency for somberness that many of us have associated with the spiritual path. The practice of sitting in this way is just about the awareness of the in-breath followed by the awareness of the out-breath. Simply, that practice reinforces our connection to everything—since the earth herself, and the whole cosmos, in fact, is breathing too.

Joan stressed with us that the meditation she practices and teaches is not primarily focused at the heart center in the body. Rather, it is oriented to the real place of power—the belly, or "the guts" as she liked to describe it more graphically. This was an invaluable distinction to make with a group of contemporary, spiritually oriented women. What she offered in this first talk, and for the rest of the weekend, was no airy, gossamer-goddess approach to spiritual life (for which I was immensely grateful); quite the opposite. Throughout her life, Joan has worked intensely with dying people, starting in the 1960s with the LSD research she did with her former husband, Stan Grof. Today, Upaya House is the headquarters for her Being With Dying Project, a contemplative

Joan Halifax

training process for hospice workers and others who serve as witnesses in the transition of death.

"A wimpy heart is just not going to cut the mustard when it comes to dying," she quietly but firmly announced, referring both to the tremendous strength of being necessary to die well, together with our ability to courageously and compassionately serve our loved ones who are dying. So, we need to live "in" and "out of" the belly. We need to appreciate the womb as our source of power; the belly, our center.

Unknowingly I had made this trip to Santa Fe to find this power-face or power-place of the Divine Feminine within myself again. For a long time I had wanted to make a new step in my own spiritual work. Yet, I was unsure exactly what that next step would be, unsure of exactly what was needed. Then, just two weeks before I visited Joan, I received a megaton-intensity communication from my spiritual teacher. He was furious with the way I had handled a project. His words exploded inside of me and I felt my whole inner framework being dismantled. Whatever platforms of self-definition I had previously been standing on were no longer secure. His words were undoing me!

Anyone who has ever worked with a spiritual teacher knows, theoretically, that these moments of undoing are priceless—like those great shocks administered by the ancient Zen masters: Zap, and the student is enlightened. Anyone who has ever *felt* such a zap is not necessarily grateful at the time. When the shock wave comes out of the blue, as it must (mine came in a phone call at 5 a.m. when I was just about to get out of bed), it may feel more like an unfair death sentence, a massive humiliation or worse. Needless to say, I was turned upside down and inside out. Decades of unresolved pain came crashing through my self-protective defenses. "I" was crumbling, and this was the opportunity of a lifetime. I felt like hell.

Worst of all, I couldn't get a handle on how to "do" this shock-reaction *right*. I compounded and confused the issues with self-doubt and self-hatred—I denied my own maturity, forgot my ability to receive failure as a necessary part of the path. In a word, I crumbled, interiorly. I could hardly breathe, for days. I wept at unguarded moments. And I tried to hide, terrified of looking bad. Fortunately, before the shock was completely calmed by the tendency for denial, the other women in my community were available to me. Deliberately, and like skillful surgeons, they incised the wound again. Like midwives they applauded every push I made against my desire to run away and keep my pain to myself. They celebrated the vulnerability that was obvious in me as I was no longer able to keep up my facade of false strength.

By the time I arrived at the gate of Upaya House on that late summer afternoon, I was primed for my meeting with the "woman of power." I had ventured once again into the underworld. I was a different woman from the one who had made the appointment with Joan a few months prior. Consequently, my time with Joan and the other women focused on the sources of real power: honesty, vulnerability and innocence. Courage and strength were affirmed as the sisters of power, but vulnerability was honored as her mother. Together as a group we celebrated this important distinction.

I asked Joan what women needed to help them build a matrix for personal power and warriorship.

> I think it has to begin early. In my own life a lot of this came from having a relationship with an elder who was so powerful and determined—my grandmother on my father's side. She was a Southern woman, a sculptress and painter. A very enterprising, very independent person, and I think she had a tremendous influence on me. So, it's good if you have an ancestor. And if you don't have one, make one up.
>
> Another factor is suffering. There is no question that if I hadn't been through what I've been through, just on the level of my body, and also my emotional suffering ... I think that my own

physical problems and my very deep mental problems have actually been an extraordinary gift in my life. Because I was down and out—not just once, but a number of times: complete failure, completely lost, completely flattened—and I managed to pull myself up, and was a lot stronger for getting back up on my feet.

I've also been privately and publicly humiliated, and even though people are quite nice to me now that I'm older, I really went through a lot when I was younger. I had a lot of natural spunk and was ... [Joan choked up as she spoke these words, then breathed deeply and exhaled as she continued]. As a woman I was incredibly attacked for my gifts, by not only men, who were scared of me, but by my sisters who were envious of me. Obviously, I asked for it, but it was not very easy to sustain, and I had to develop friendliness inside of myself and work with forgiveness for having absorbed quite a bit of abuse; and then, of course, the amount of abuse I heaped on myself in terms of self-judgement. So, I think that the experiences of suffering—mental, physical suffering—are very consequential in the development of one's character.

It was the end of the retreat, and the hubbub in the courtyard where we sat began to increase. Women were saying their good-byes, coming over to thank Joan for her generosity and her enormous inspiration. Our interview was regularly interrupted, only to be resumed in a slightly different mood.

In a few seeming diversions from the primary question, Joan revealed pieces of herself, and invaluable clues about the path of power. She continued, elaborating upon the way in which she capitalized upon her position as a single woman as a means to explore new domains of power and knowledge.

I've said this often, that women have more room for failure than men. The lack of expectations around woman's accomplishments gives her the possibility to experience failure, which is a tremendous ground for the development of strength.

Nothing is *expected* of us, really. (In terms of a biological imperative there is, we have to stay strong for children. But some of us don't have kids, and can take risks). The social expectations of women are, "you marry and have kids," but if you *don't* conform to those social expectations, then you could have a hell of a lot of fun. And you *can* live more on the edge than men. Those men who choose a non-conventional way of life are looked at as weak or weird, and are marginalized. A woman who does that is not even marginalized, she is forgotten. And that is just incredible! Consequently, I could do the deepest, darkest, strangest things. ... You know, I choose not to talk about a lot of my life. I've lived a public life, I have a personal life, and I have a secret life. And my secret life is secret not because it's corrupt, but because it's a mystery that I guard very very deeply. My secret life is where I discover how much I don't know, and I do that by entering into situations that I can't solve.

She paused, for which I was grateful. Her last sentence had opened an internal door for me, and pointed to that degree of strength and personal power that I had intuitively recognized in Joan during my first chance meeting with her. Here was not only a risk taker, but one who deliberately kept herself in the domain of the unsolvable. How contrary this position is from the one that so many of us diligently pursue—trying to keep our lives within safe parameters; only taking on tasks that we *know* we can accomplish; decrying whatever defies logical analysis.

247

A few moments, and a few hugs to departing women later, Joan asked me to repeat my question. She was tired, and yet wanted to give me as much as she could. I rephrased it: "What are the major challenges that a woman will face who wants to explore the domain of personal power and warriorship as she walks a spiritual path?"

Women's identities have been wrapped up with the men they've been with—whether it's been a husband, a lover, a teacher, a friend, a therapist, whatever. Yet, the "individuation of woman" means, in fact, that she has to separate her identity from all the men around her. Then, when she does realign, move back into relationship with the external male, it comes as a co-equal. Her power is not derived from that relationship to the male, it is derived from her *own* strengths. Then she can have a sane relationship with a man, and pick a man (if she is "into" men) who is healthy, and a good partner for her.

Women throughout history, I think, have climbed the ladder of their spouse's or teacher's wealth, knowledge and so on, because that's where—socially, psychosocially—power has been attributed—to the male. And the shift right now is very interesting to observe in society and to anticipate over the long-term, vis à vis, how the relationship between men and women is going to change as a result of women individuating, redefining, coming into their own power separate from men, and then returning, if they choose to, to be in a co-creative relationship.

Women are change agents. The infrastructure of most spiritual traditions is vertical, very male dominated, very patriarchal. And while I think one of the incredible capacities women have is the ability to listen deeply, they also have the capacity to speak deeply.

I'm not very interested in democracy per se, because I see that often democracy falls to the lowest common denominator, which is why I have found that both *having* teachers and *being* a teacher is wonderful, because part of what I try to do, instead of relating to the lowest common denominator in the individual, is to find their highest denominator, and to go for that, unlike many therapists. And I think that, sitting in a circle with women is very interesting because it allows for both suffering *and* the greatness of the human spirit to come forth. Let's just say, it's about equality, but it's also about distinctions; it's about differentness.

Another factor [in the development of power and warriorship] has to do with the knowledge of change in a woman's body—the knowledge of the transitory nature of life: our own coming into adolescence, menstruation, and then childbirth (for those who go through childbirth), and then menopause—the aging process. We watch our own sexuality shift through time from virgin, to mother, into crone, the three aspects of the feminine. But there is one attribute of the feminine that is not really addressed very thoroughly, and that is woman as healer. And that healer can be as an artist, or herbalist, a ceremonialist or teacher, or weaver, or whatever.

Throughout the retreat it was enormously refreshing to be in a circle of women and to experience a deep, inner healing, without the need for recounting our history of pain. Joan's skillful means (*upaya* means that) had designed the weekend in such a way that we were helped to live in our bellies and to breathe deeply, while not forgetting our connection to a larger life, a life beyond the personal. That context, which she set so well, together with the benediction that flows when women are gathered together in the name of the divine Mother (and we were, as we had sung her praises frequently throughout the weekend), allowed for that healing to take place without the need for verbal expression. Another great lesson about the nature of power.

Since I haven't had kids (although I've had a lot of surrogate children), I've had a chance to redefine myself and women like me—childless women and women whose children have left the nest— watching so many of us being healers and nurturers in the culture. It is essential to allow the creative part of the feminine experience to come forth, not just in terms of bearing children and nurturing, for the sake of progeny and the continuity of the species, but for the continuity of culture through the healing arts. The healing of society, and culture, and individuals, and the role of women in that, I think, is very critical. It has to do with reconciliation of the masculine and the feminine powers.

Due to the tremendous amount of physical neglect in the lives of women, even to the point of self-abuse, we're trying to move into a place where we are not just working on our emotional development or our spiritual development, alone, or with the physical and intellectual development, but to have *all* those four elements of our nature much more balanced. Without that, women are going to be handicapped. The spiritual and physical development of women is *very* important at this time, as a matrix or access for personal work.

So, I love the diversity in our circle of women here this past weekend. I'm not Zuleikha, and Zuleikha is not Mirabai, Mirabai is not you. But each of the women could stand in whatever strength or tenderness she had, and be regarded really as equal. And I like that very much. Equal, but not the same ... a great love of diversity ... which I think women are able to see more clearly.

There is a wonderful teaching that this crazy Native American gave me years ago about the four elements in the feminine nature. In the south of the Medicine Wheel, she finds her Little Girl Shield, which is where her wound is, where her emotions are; the difficulties of her past; the crisis of sorrow. In the west of her Medicine Wheel is where her Man Shield is, and this is the shield of initiation where magic, death and change are to be found. Here she develops authority, and the experience of loss and change, and this she learns from her own body. In the north is where her Woman Shield is, which is where her mind is. And it is her ability to see very, very clearly, and this comes in the third stage of her life, where she understands what it is to be a wise woman, a mature woman and a sexual woman. And the east is where her Little Boy Shield is—her capacity for play...and that is where her spiritual life is. This capacity to take risks and to play and to go to the top of mountains or into the cave dwellings, that kind of playfulness. These are the four elements: in the south is where the water is; in the west, earth; the north, air; and the east is fire. And the call is the reconciliation, the purification by each of those elements, and the reconciliation of each of those elements into a wholeness, into a totality of bringing the emotional (her little girl shield), the physical (the man shield), the intellectual (her woman shield), and the spiritual (her little boy shield) into balance.

So when you talk about women's power it is not about falling prey to the mother complex. It is about standing in the authority of reconciliation with the masculine by going down and in—healing the suffering by touching the Little Girl shield, and then in the north, sending one's voice out in the world. Finding a true vocation. And that vocation is, of course, as a wise woman or a healer, of social, emotional, psychological suffering.

As the midday sun rose higher in the sky, our once shady spot was now blazing, and growing hotter by the minute. I had received so much more than I had anticipated. Yet, Joan still had one more stitch to make in the robe she was weaving for me.

"Winnowing," she said, gazing at the sky, and rousing me from my own reverie. "Women are specialists in detail. They have the ability to separate the seeds from the stones. They work with the small things in order to make a big meal. And, they take out that which is not useful. And it is like what sewing that robe was for me ..."

Joan had led the meditation that morning dressed in her official monks' robes, which included an intricately patterned, patchwork outer vestment known as the *kesa*. She spent the full length of the *dharma* talk telling us about the symbolism of this garment, about the many dying friends who had contributed articles of their clothing from which the patches were then made, and of the overwhelming task it was to sew this vestment for herself, rather than having it made by a professional *kesa*-maker in Japan.

> ... just like one little tiny stitch after another. Every stitch equally important. It looks like humdrum. But, in fact, to me it was the most exalted thing I've ever done, because it was completely inner, completely private.
>
> There is a line from somebody: "The soul loves detail." Why the soul has been associated with the

252

feminine is not only because of its association with the principle of communication, which I think the soul represents—the ability to go deep, down and in. They say men always deal with the big decisions, the big view, and women deal with the detail. And I think it's in the *detail* where the soul is made. It's *not* in the big decisions.

Joan winked. She smiled, and rubbed her hand sensuously across the top of her head, a gesture that she had enacted many times over the course of the weekend. The interview was over, and it was time for me to pack up for my journey across the desert, and for Joan to lie down in her hammock for a ten-minute nap before her next appointment.

That night, stopping in Gallup, New Mexico, I wrote furiously, trying to capture as much as I could that would serve me in the future. I knew I had made a step out of a prison of my own making, a step out from behind the bars of my mind, which had kept me afraid of making a mistake. Witnessing the life and teaching of a woman who was willing to live on the edge, regardless of the pain that this had created and would create for her personally, was a tremendous source of encouragement and consolation. Joan Halifax was no saint, nor would she want to be. What made her great in my eyes, however, was that she was willing to step forward into the unknown and tell the truth about what she saw and experienced there. The result, in her life, was a deeper dedication to relieving the pain of all who suffered—relieving the pain of all sentient beings.

My questions to myself had to do with whether or not I cared enough to be willing to risk as much in my life.

8

THE PATH OF SERVICE

"*Y*ou have absolutely no idea what genuine service means." These words, spoken with the deliberateness of a life or death sentence, stopped me, riveting my attention to the radio. The power and the truth in these words sent a physical pain directly to the region around my heart, took my breath away, and forced me to sit down on the spot where I stood as I heard them.

The speaker—a spiritual teacher visiting Boulder, Colorado at the time (during the late winter of 1985)—was being interviewed on a Sunday morning new-age radio program. Relaxing in my living room at the end of breakfast, I had tuned in at the urging of a long-time friend—the interviewer on the show—who knew of my passion for spiritual matters. Larry, the interviewer, and I had shared some turns in this labyrinth together, when we studied with a radical teacher in California. Both of us were weary of the hype, both of us had been badly "burned." We knew firsthand how many charlatans there were on the spiritual circuit, and Larry was convinced that Lee, his guest, was one of them. With his pointed questions, therefore, Larry was trying to discredit him.

"Your community doesn't put much emphasis on service to the broader community..." Larry began, once the formalities were over. The question he was leading to was ill-formed at best, but it did address an age-old issue, and an age-old argument about a type of isolationism common in spiritual work. Larry paused, his statement left unfinished, awaiting his guest's response.

Lee said nothing. Dead air...the capitol sin of the radio media. Silence reigned for what seemed like several minutes; it was probably more like fifteen seconds. Then, as if thunder were rolling across a vast expanse of desert, Lee's words were delivered with the solemnity of a vow: "You have absolutely no idea what genuine service really means."

Larry was evidently as unprepared for Lee's answer as I was. More dead air. My living room got very large all of a sudden. Although the rest of my family talked and laughed in the nearby kitchen, they seemed very far away. I was alone, in the silence, with this voice, and the odd sensation in my body that I was being sucked into a vortex of energy, or something. At the time there were no words for the strange experience.

I don't remember if Lee went on to explain himself, to qualify those words of power which had left me breathless and speechless. I don't remember what my friend Larry did to bring the interview to a reasonable and polite conclusion, or even how long it went on after that. Lee's indictment about service had simply cut the legs out from under Larry's assumptions.

Why were these simple words so devastating to me? After all, Lee didn't actually *say* anything about service. What was it about these words from an unknown speaker that created such a tangible pull and vibration within my body? Simply, Lee's words addressed a question of mine, not just any question, but "the" question

256

that had plagued me all my adult life; a question I had diligently asked of everyone I met who offered the slightest intimation of wisdom. If I didn't ask the question directly, I searched for the answer in their eyes. But time and again, the responses I received were superficial, at worst, untimely or unusable at best. I was more than discouraged; I was frankly in pain, bordering on hopelessness.

I wanted to know what it meant to serve, and specifically what it meant to serve God. All the nice words and lofty concepts about service, which I'd read and discussed with others hadn't satisfied my hungering soul. There was a missing piece in this puzzle I was putting together, and at times I just gave up the search, convinced that it was all just an illusion. I would never *find* what I was looking for, since I didn't know what it *was* in the first place.

Certainly, an implicit desire to serve God and to serve other people had drawn me into the convent in 1963. But the longer I lived that life, the deeper and more troubling were the questions that emerged about what it *really* meant to serve God, and whether or not the kind of work I was actually doing among the upper-middle class students at a large diocesan high school was service in the highest and truest sense of the term.

Always a gnawing dissatisfaction had accompanied my attempts at work for and with others. I had thrown myself into multiple forms of service—teaching Project Headstart for poor children in rural areas of Long Island, and later in a tiny migrant farming community in Colorado; working for years in a hospice program (if anything was real service, then working for the dying must come close); actively pursuing my commitment to pacifism in the midst of the Vietnam war, and working for social justice. But I was always discouraged. While friends and co-workers often seemed so able to settle into the heart of their service, I couldn't. "Is that all there is?" was the feeling I was more often left with. Some alignment was missing for me—an alignment which I felt helpless to bring about on my own.

By the time I heard that radio program I was primed for the appearance of my teacher—for the guidance of one who understood the intricacies of my questions, and one who had the experience, the insight and ultimately the grace to cut through this web of confusion and dissatisfaction which I had struggled with for so many years.

Lee's words woke me up, for the moment at least. With the scathing power of one who will not compromise, he had countered his interviewer's question with a challenge. There was such rawness, such directness about his answer that I sensed immediately—not by a logical sequencing of thoughts but by the intuited understanding that the body possesses—that here was one who would not let "me" get away with trite or holy rationalizations about service, or anything else anymore. Here was the voice of my own heart—a voice that had been stifled for fear of what it might reveal. That voice was answering itself.

And so it happened that I first received the teaching from this man who has since become my spiritual teacher. Over many years with him I have come to appreciate that the question about the meaning of genuine service can only really be answered when it is asked from the kind of place I was in at the time—from the bottom, from a sense of helplessness or hopelessness. As long as I had notions about service, or expectations about what I would get from service, or guilt for not serving, or shame, or an attitude of condescension, or the belief that "I" was somehow doing the work, and "I" was doing something great, then the answers I heard could only be partial answers, and ultimately unsatisfying.

Service, serving God and serving others are rife with mystery. "Who" it is that serves, what true service accomplishes for the server and for others—these are questions that might never be fully answered, but admitting them and grappling with them may transform a life.

LEARNING HOW TO SERVE

Shannon was a woman who apparently had everything in the domain of worldly success—money, great clothes, a beautiful home, a high-profile job. Working for a big company in Boston, Shannon flew all over the country, often spending weeks at a time in luxury hotels, at the company's expense. Her life was busy; so busy, in fact, that she had little time to examine it. Yet, with the impending break-up of a five-year relationship, Shannon recognized that in many domains she was still unhappy and unfulfilled.

The crash, for Shannon, came at the height of her career—many circumstances conspired at once to bring her well-planned life to a standstill. The relationship with her partner dissolved, she was passed over for a long-expected promotion; she was exhausted, physically and emotionally. It was definitely time for a change. Shannon quit her job and moved to Arizona to be closer to her mother and sister.

In the midst of her transition, and at her sister's request, Shannon attended a weekend growth seminar, an event that was designed to help participants get in touch with their deeper, unrealized potential, and to encourage them to start putting their words into action. The weekend training helped loosen the stranglehold that Shannon had on her image, and thrust her into an investigation of what she really wanted to do with her life. With an urgency that could not be denied, Shannon threw herself at the mercy of the group wisdom. She wanted some way to keep herself from going back to sleep, something that would prevent her from re-establishing her life in Arizona exactly as she had left it in Boston.

To her delight, and then her shocked amazement, the group suggested that Shannon take a short vacation to enjoy the nightlife in a hot spot of the world that she had never seen before— Calcutta, India. They challenged her to visit one of the busiest and most successful women in the world—Mother Teresa. Without thinking, the rightness of this call moved Shannon to say, "Yes."

Waking up the next morning, however, Shannon was flabbergasted by her own decision. Had she been hypnotized? To make a life-changing decision of this magnitude was far beyond anything she had dreamed of getting out of the weekend. Her hands shook as she poured herself a cup of coffee. What had she committed to?

Yet, the choice was already beginning to work its magic on her, Shannon had to admit. Despite her inner terror she felt a new-found freedom, an expanded sense that she hadn't known since her childhood when the world was still her oyster—when anything could happen. She could breathe more deeply than she had in years, she walked with a new spring in her step. Replacing her expensive Italian leather sandals with a pair of rubber beach thongs, the kind she would wear in India, Shannon began making her plans.

Actually, the group's challenge had offered her an opening—one she had been looking for over many years, but one she didn't have the courage to take. She wanted a doorway out of the life of self-obsession; she wanted a way through the gnawing dissatisfaction that had been covered over by the importance of her job, and the sheer exhaustion that accompanied it. Shannon knew she needed more than a little vacation. She bought her ticket, rearranged her life and left for India.

When I interviewed her, several months after her return, Shannon was a different woman than the one who had started on this journey a little more than a year earlier. Her face was softened—with less makeup and much less tension. Shannon was radiant. The vulnerability and generosity of her heart had been exposed by what she had seen and done, and I found her to be magnetic. I wanted to taste some of the sweet wine of God she had brought back from her few months of service in Mother Teresa's garden. So I took Shannon to lunch and over grilled cheese and veggie sandwiches she revealed something of what she learned about service.

"Mother Teresa was like a big reflecting pool," Shannon began. "But, what she reflected was an absence of the separate, individual self." Shannon tried to touch on the most essential quality first. "She and her nuns and the work they were doing were all surrounded by this aura, of sorts—it was clear they didn't have time for 'small things,' like personal complaints. There was just too much work to be done. Yet, Mother Teresa radiated a presence that was utterly compelling."

I asked her about this "presence," trying to get her to specify it in a way that was comprehensible to someone who hadn't met the aged nun.

"Actually, it wasn't a sweetness or tenderness," Shannon went on, searching for a precise description. What she tried to communicate, but found difficult to say in a few words, was that the nun's appearance and demeanor bore no resemblance to any conventionally romantic notion of holiness or goodness. Rather, what Mother Teresa had and what shone forth in her stooped body and deeply lined face, in her gnarled feet and arthritic hands, was an extreme toughness, a resiliency, a profound discipline.

> The predominant energy around the saint was an open-heartedness. Hers is a genuine love, so big it would leave you breathless, while still so personal that it felt as if her heart was touching you alone.
> She is also powerful and extremely one-pointed. She's definitely the one in command. I saw her in the Motherhouse [the place where the nuns are trained, and the base of operations], and she's like a field marshal. After all, there is just so much work to do. At the same time, however, her genuine love would show itself in the smile that would disarm you. She could look at you with such an indescribable tenderness.

As Shannon continued with her report, pausing occasionally to take a sip of water or a small bite from her sandwich, I scribbled as fast as I could to capture her words verbatim. Ten minutes into our meal we both sat back in our chairs and looked at each other, feeling the mood of divine communion which had been created between us as we talked about a subject of such significance to each of us. Although it was noon-hour, the other sounds in the bustling restaurant seemed muffled, as if we were hearing them from behind a wall of insulation. Our focus with one another had built an intimate chamber sealed off from the rest of the world, and seemed to afford us a level of invisibility that helped us dive even more deeply into the consideration.

It's like she *knows* you, and you alone, [Shannon admitted with a slight degree of embarrassment.] It's that smile. It's like she recognizes YOU. I was waiting outside an office one day—for something, I don't even remember what—when I caught a glimpse of her from the corner of my eye. She came right up to me, took my hand with a firm grip and looked piercingly, but not threateningly, into my eyes, as she asked me where I was from and what my name was. She was *completely present* to me, and the same kind of presence was available a moment later to some important bishop from Rome, or some delegation of Spanish priests, as well as some child in need of assistance.

Like many visitors before her (including Malcolm Muggeridge, the author of the bestselling book, *Something Beautiful for God*, which describes his impressions of Mother Teresa), Shannon found herself bothered by the way certain things were run. At the home for children, where Shannon worked, she wondered why the directors didn't provide any activities for the kids beyond their simple survival needs. Besides that, Shannon admitted that she was oftentimes "yelled at for doing something wrong," but that "nobody was there to show me how to do it right." "Then too, I certainly couldn't understand how Mother Teresa could support the Church's stand against abortion or birth control," she explained, noting that overpopulation seemed to be at the root of so many of India's problems.

Mother Teresa's life provoked such questioning and such wrestling with assumptions, projection and judgements. Few from the West can understand the kind of absolute obedience she lived, in relationship to the Pope and the Church. Yet, ultimately for those who were willing to hang out around her a bit longer, as Shannon was, the doubts and questions tended to be subsumed in something so much bigger—or actually something so much smaller, namely the act of selfless service to one human being enacted with so much regard that one actually saw the hand of God (in Teresa's hand) touching the face of God (in the face of the poor man or woman or child), or vice versa.

"You can't deny the kind of love which dedicates itself completely to 'the poorest of the poor.'" Shannon noted with enormous admiration. "These people who Mother Teresa works with are the people who have been completely rejected by their families and by society as well. These are the people who have nowhere to fall back to and no one to fall back on." And it is to these, the most despised and the most neglected, that the world denies its attention. As Mother Teresa reminded us again and again, a lack of material possessions is one thing, but the greater suffering is the destitution created when one is denied acknowledgment as a human being. This is the kind of destitution that destroys the soul—whether one lives in Calcutta, India, or in the South Bronx, New York.

The restaurant had quieted considerably. It was nearly two o'clock as I plunged into another line of questioning with Shannon. Most of all I wanted to know about her own inner experience— what she had found difficult, what had genuinely helped her in her own spiritual work. And what she had learned about service.

> The largest part of the struggle, especially for the new people, is that you really never get so much as a "thank you" for being there. Quite frankly, I thought of myself as giving up my life, but nobody said "thank you" for that. There was no acknowledgment by anybody for what sacrifices I was making; so I had to really work inside myself with this. But, as time went on, my need for this kind of recognition just started to evaporate. Slowly I began to see that I wasn't here because I was "helping," in any usual sense of the term. What I finally came to understand was that I was here out of my desire to know God and to be a better human. When I "got" that, everything around me was different.

Some people had more difficulty than others with this notion of doing it for God, and were not able to grasp the reality behind this statement. One of the other Westerners, an Italian woman, quite wealthy, was all excited about the fact that she had brought boxes of clothes for all the children at Shishu Bhavan where we both worked. The nuns in charge agreed that the children could get dressed up so that they could have their pictures taken (another of the Italian woman's requests). But, as soon as the photo-shoot was concluded, the children were asked to take off the new clothes, and the nuns packed the items carefully away to be taken out again for special holidays only.

This woman seemed almost dazed as she turned from one to another looking for thanks or praise. [Shannon was half-smiling as she described the rather pathetic scene.] The nuns had been very polite, but nobody was giving this woman the kind of attention for her gifts that she would have gotten in another situation. Evidently this woman was used to thanks and special treatment because of how she used her money. And here she was not getting it. I think she was really shocked. She seemed confused, actually. Somehow, I too had gotten this notion that service was being a "do-good" socialite; or when taken to the extreme, that service meant living in conditions of lack and general darkness. But my experience with Mother Teresa and the sisters in her order allowed me to see that there is strength, a silent power, and wisdom in being in service. That quality—the embodiment or manifestation of that quality of power—is what WOMAN is.

These sisters in their white saris, so involved with the disease and despair of the world, are taking in rejected humans, allowing them some dignity, some

264

comfort, some relief; by not judging them, these good women are using their own physical labor to create a safe and clean space for the poor and ne-glected. But most of all, these nuns are serving the poor and the world-at-large, by recognizing (or at least looking for) Jesus—the Divine of God—in each person. This is tremendous power, tremen-dous sacrifice and tremendous service.

We had talked for over two hours, and Shannon had already well overrun her lunch-hour time allotment. Still, as we stepped out of the empty restaurant into the blazing Arizona sun, she didn't want to leave me yet. The opportunity for sharing at such a level of honesty and prayerfulness was so rare, and so nourishing for each of us. In the middle of the sidewalk we hugged silently; then she walked me slowly to my car.

Driving home, I reflected upon the tremendous power of ser-vice that Shannon had spoken of. It was evident to me that the witness of such service, and her brief involvement in it, had changed Shannon, and I was profoundly grateful to celebrate these fruits of love.

I looked at the card that Shannon had left with me, a busi-ness card she had received from Mother Teresa. It read:

> The fruit of silence is prayer
> The fruit of prayer is love
> The fruit of love is service
> The fruit of service is peace.
> —Mother Teresa

MEETING MOTHER TERESA FOR THE VERY FIRST TIME: A MEDITATION

Since Mother Teresa's death there have been numerous books and journal articles devoted to stories about her life. It is possible that we may feel that we know her, and in many ways we probably

265

do. However, for the moment, forget everything you know about Mother Teresa of Calcutta and simply conjure up an image of her in your mind. For instance, Shannon remembers her tiny figure clothed in a white sari with a blue border, sitting on the floor, close to the back wall of the convent chapel. The old woman's legs are under her on one side and her eyes are closed. She has left her sandals at the door and like all the other Indians who fill the room, she is barefoot. Her face is set; determined, yet soft. A sea of wrinkles. Her hands and feet bear the scars of a lifetime of tireless service.

Drop any comparisons between yourself and this woman and imagine yourself approaching her as a beloved friend, or a grandmother or a wise-elder who has been through it all—been through whatever your issues are about service.

If, like mine, your question is "What really serves?" realize that Mother Teresa, your wise guardian, has grappled with that same question. If your issue has to do with finding the time or the energy to give yourself to service in the way that you genuinely desire, remember that Mother Teresa has suffered the same constraints. If you struggle with the thought of plunging into some form of service, afraid that you will not have the courage, the strength, or the stamina, allow your imagination to look upon the face of one who has dealt with those same doubts and fears. Or, if you are just plain burned out by the stress of service, fearing that you simply cannot face one more day of frustration, ingratitude and seeming failure, pour out your heart to this Mother who has been there too, for decades. Rest for a moment, knowing that your Mother knows; that she reads the desires of your heart while understanding the weaknesses of your courage and your will. She smiles at you, and like Shannon, you sense in that smile a deep acceptance and a personal love. She sees you as none other than her own Beloved, Jesus, who is suffering in and through you. Let her comfort you.

Mother Teresa

Service To Her Beloved

Mother Teresa of Calcutta wanted no biography. Yet, regardless of her wishes, the libraries are full of them. Dozens of accounts of her life, written for both children and adults, trace (and often mythologize) the story of this simple Albanian women from her birth in 1910, through her first calling into religious life, and her "second calling" when she accepted the prompting of God within her own heart to reach out to the poorest of the poor. Documentaries and nightly news broadcasts for years covered her comings and goings, up to the day of her death. Her name became a household word, synonymous with service and saintliness in our times.

"Tell the story of the poor...tell the story of the work... and the great need," she would demand of her perspective biographers. As far as the saintly nun was concerned, "she" was not important. What was newsworthy to her was the need for everyone to address the suffering of humanity, and to see the poor as human beings, not as some cause to be worked for or some program to be implemented.

What is it that moves a woman—any woman—to give up her own comfort, to literally have no life of her own, for her entire life? What drives one to work, to serve, despite the ravages of age and grueling physical pain, up until the moment of her last breath? To have no vacations, no time off, and yet still be radiantly happy? There has to be some payoff to such a life, something well beyond the smiles of gratitude of those being served, since acknowledgment is generally rare, no matter who one is. There has to be some source of constant nourishment from which this type of service flows.

Mother Teresa held her source and her payoff as no secret. Her work was not to help the poor, although that is what she was always doing; her work was to serve Her Beloved Jesus, who had first loved her. Her work was her faith—in knowing that the sick, the poor, the deformed, the destitute were the faces and forms of her Beloved, and that her God was not separate from humanity.

Your vocation is not to work for lepers.
You vocation is to belong to Jesus.[1]
—Mother Teresa addressing the nuns in her company

While her work may have looked similar to that of an ordinary social worker's, it was her intention that made it so different. Vast programs of humanitarian action often accomplish great things, make significant contributions to the cause of justice, and relieve suffering throughout the world. But, Mother Teresa and her nuns did not offer a humanitarian program. Their's was and is a vocation of service to Divinity. Who and what got served out of that overriding context was God's concern.

This may seem like a subtle distinction, and perhaps even an unnecessary one. Yet it is core to the understanding of Teresa's brand of spiritual life and service. It is a distinction based on the soul's hunger for the obliteration of the "I"—the dissolution of any separate sense of self which would keep it from complete union with the One, the All. Such a distinction—loving and serving God, rather then working for the poor and suffering—keeps one ever mindful that it isn't "I" who accomplishes anything, anyway. We are "a little pencil" in God's hands, as Mother Teresa liked to describe such things.

That distinction is also immensely freeing. It gives us the possibility of remaining somewhat un-attached to the results of our service. There is a great temptation in assuming that the success or failure of any program rests solely or even essentially, in our human hands. One of the primary causes of discouragement, and hence of burnout in service is because we see the immensity of the task, and we see how any efforts we make will only be the merest drop in the ocean of human misery. To believe that we, in our limited capacity as human individuals, are ultimately responsible for such a task, may be to encounter paralyzing inadequacy, and therefore inaction. Like so much of the world around us, the only alternative to such an enormous responsibility is to "go dead" or "go back to sleep" when faced with the challenge of really making a difference. To hold one's meager efforts as the movements of an instrument in the hands of God is to keep the urgency for vigilance, integrity and ceaseless efforts alive, while at the same time freeing us of the demand to see the results conform to some standard measure of success.

Mother Teresa and her nuns, after all, were following the example of a crucified Lord. Mother Teresa constantly encouraged her nuns and all who listened to her, that the cross of Christ was the place to address and leave all questions, doubts and fears; the place at which to discover the true understanding of one's vocation.

In the same light, Mother Teresa urged the Missionaries of Charity to a type of service characterized by "nothing to show." Despite the fact that her missionary company ministered to lepers, or provided a place to die to agonizing people, these actions barely scratched the surface of the enormous need that existed and continues to grow. The poverty of the world only multiplies or changes form. The illness of the world merely changes its name—from leprosy to AIDS. It seems there will always be a disease to be most despised, feared, and guarded against. The ministrations of charity that Mother Teresa inspired were not designed to bring about a healthy and happy society. They were not engineered to bring an end to hunger or disease on the planet. The work of the Missionaries of Charity is to love Jesus in disguise as this leper, or this AIDS patient, and to awaken us to the reality of such an immanent presence of the Divine among us.

This completely personal and non-attached approach to service sets Mother Teresa's efforts apart from many more sophisticated social service efforts. In our day, we must prove that a program is going to produce widespread and lasting results before we dare ask others to support us in it. When the statistics for success cannot be shown, the powers that be will often ridicule the whole project, joking about "pouring money down the sewer." The poor and the disempowered live in these sewers, however. Such forgotten ones are often desperate for any sign of attention. And this is exactly the cause to which Mother Teresa's life was committed. She stood, not for the institution, but for the individual.

In an age in which religious congregations of nuns and priests have modified their dress, and modernized their lifestyles and their liturgies, vocations to these up-dated communities are at an all time low throughout the world. Mother Teresa's Missionaries of Charity, however, are attracting more and more vibrant and enthusiastic people, both men and women, every year. And to what? To lives of absolute poverty, demanding service, unquestioning obedience, harsh living conditions; basically to a life of no half-measures and no compromises. For those who desire a concrete way in which to channel the burning urgency of a heart on fire with love, the life of a Missionary of Charity offers a formal structure for that expression.

Perhaps too, people are attracted to the life of total sacrifice and service because they have glimpsed the reality of God's message that only by losing your life do you have a life. Only in dying to the separate self will there be the slightest possibility for life to be experienced. A full life. A genuine life. A life unlimited in its possibilities, in its inner joy, and in its ultimate service to humanity. Our times are desperate times. And in desperate times desperate measures are called for. The life of absolute, uncompromising service is such a desperate measure.

There is another reason for such an attraction to the life that Mother Teresa offered. The presence of a living saint is such a rare commodity—in our times, perhaps in any times. A saint's life and teaching create a sort of vortex that draws like-minded and like-hearted individuals into its depths. Mother Teresa was clearly such a saint. Her personal life was consumed by God. It was clearly the power of God, or of Divine Love itself, that attracted so many men and women to her company every year, just as the apostles and disciples were magnetically drawn in love to the dusty, road-stained feet of Jesus.

We were and still are attracted to Mother Teresa because she is an emptiness—a still, clear pool (as Shannon had described her) in which we can glimpse the face of love. She looked to Jesus, her company of missionaries looked to her, and she pointed them (and all of us) to the revelation of the Divine as It exists everywhere.

One so surrendered to God, as Mother Teresa was, becomes a dispensary for the grace of God.

ETTY HILLESUM: SERVICE IN AN INTERRUPTED LIFE

All I wanted to say is this: the misery here is quite terrible and yet, late at night when the day has slunk away into the depths behind me, I often walk with a spring in my step along the barbed wire and then time and again it soars straight from my heart—I can't help it, that's just the way it is, like some elementary force—the feeling that life is glorious and magnificent, and that one day we shall be building a whole new world. Against every new outrage and every fresh horror we shall put up one more piece of love and goodness, drawing strength from within ourselves. We may suffer, but we must not succumb. [2]

These are the words of a twenty-nine-year-old Dutch woman, Etty Hillesum, written four months before her death in Auschwitz in November 1943. She wrote from the detention camp, Westerbork, where she, like thousands of Dutch Jews before her, awaited transport via railway to the concentration camps in Poland. Writing this letter and dozens more to friends and family outside, Etty chronicled not only the horrors of life around her, but more importantly the evolution of her own soul. Her letters and diaries, which were only released in English in 1983, reveal to us a woman of remarkable spiritual depth, whose prayerful dialogues with God are characterized by passion, courage and the seeds of surrender. Yet, the extraordinary honesty of her writing draws us into the life of a woman much like ourselves—a woman who loved beauty, a woman who longed for love, a woman who was troubled with doubts and fears and questions. Her words invite us to feel the pulse of life, as powerfully when she describes the tea roses on her desk in the peaceful sanctuary of her Amsterdam flat, as when she details "the tiny piercing screams of the babies" in the anguish-ridden environment of the camp.

Etty Hillesum's story of courage and service throughout her confinement in the death camps is only one of many hundreds of stories that make up the legacy of the Holocaust. What distinguishes her life and work for our purposes, is not so much that she helped those around her at the time, but rather that she enacted the discipline to write about it—with care, with an attempt at rigorous truthfulness, and with the willingness to expose her heart and soul. Etty served us by leaving us a journal of spiritual longing; of the intimate inner workings that God mysteriously undertook in preparing her for almost certain death, under the most horrifying of conditions. Her diaries testify to the dynamic power of her prayer, together with the transformational nature of the "work on self" which she was avidly pursuing under the guidance of an extraordinary man, Julius Spier. He was her teacher and lover, and in her words, "my great friend, the one who had attended at the birth of my soul."[3]

Unlike Mother Teresa, who is recognized and acknowledged throughout the world, Etty Hillesum is still virtually unknown; one among perhaps thousands of hidden saints of our own times. I first "met" Etty shortly after her letters were translated into English. My husband's sister, a hospital chaplain and a woman of dedicated service, handed me a compact book with a green cover, and enthusiastically urged me to read it.

"I know you love to learn about great women," Anne said softly, stroking the book like a long-treasured friend. "I think you'll find her spirit will speak to you. You'll want to share her life with others."

Despite my general resistance to reading what I fear will be horrifying and depressing accounts (and reading about the Holocaust is almost always devastating for me), Etty's words illuminated me, drawing me into her life and her into mine in a way that has blessed me. Speaking about her to groups of women over the years, I am always richly rewarded by their rapt attention. Whenever I enter into Etty Hillesum's inner world, I cannot help but be softened, and thereby made vulnerable to the same grace of God which embraced and carried her.

From the piecemeal accounts of her own actions, together with the reports of those who witnessed her service, Etty's life was gradually transformed into one of greater and greater selflessness and compassion. Putting aside her own ill-health (which was a constant drain on her energy reserves), she made herself available to others—comforting the sick and elderly, sitting with a crying mother who mourned the fate of her children, holding the hand of one in terror, and writing to the world. Until she was finally transported to Auschwitz (she left Westerbork on September 7, 1943 with her mother, father and brother), where she died on November 30, 1943, she chronicled life to the very best of her ability. The last piece of writing attributed to her is a weathered postcard, found and mailed by a farmer who lived near the rail lines. She had managed to throw it through an air vent in the transport car. "Mother and Father and Mischa are here..." Etty wrote, "We have left the camp singing."

Etty Hillesum did not live to see the tremendous yield which, like an abundant harvest, would be rendered from her simple service. She simply kept her diary with consistency. She looked deeply into herself and told the truth about what she found there. She set aside time for prayer, or incorporated prayer into every mundane activity, and at the same time she refused to turn her face away from the horrors of life in a Nazi camp. All the while, she attempted to root out hate and prejudice from within her own heart. She worked close to home and close to the bone, doing what was right in front of her to do; she drank deeply of the raw, compelling energy present in all things. And her work strengthened and sanctified her and many others, even in the midst of hell.

Etty Hillesum

FROM HER WRITINGS

Reading Etty's own words in the selections that follow, taken from her diaries and letters, we find a remarkable woman alive, sensitive and vibrant, between the lines. We can appreciate her skill as a writer, as well as what she reveals about her precious interior life.

About Writing and Life:

> I once thought, "I would like to feel the contours of these times with my fingertips." I was sitting at my desk with no idea what to make of life. That was because I had not yet arrived at the life in myself, was still sitting at this desk. And then I was suddenly flung into one of many flashpoints of human suffering. And there, in the faces of people, in a thousand gestures, small changes of expression, life stories, I was suddenly able to read our age—and much more than our age alone. And then it suddenly happened: I was able to feel the contours of these times with my fingertips. How is it that this stretch of heathland surrounded by barbed wire, through which so much human misery has flooded, nevertheless remains inscribed in my memory as something almost lovely? How is it that my spirit, far from being oppressed, seemed to grow lighter and brighter there? It is because I read the signs of the times and they did not seem meaningless to me. Surrounded by my writers and poets and the flowers on my desk, I loved life. And there among the barracks, full of hunted and persecuted people, I found confirmation of my love of life. Life in those draughty barracks was no other than life in this protected, peaceful room. Not for

one moment was I cut off from the life I was said to have left behind. There was simply one great, meaningful whole. Will I be able to describe all that one day? So that others can feel too how lovely and worth living and just—yes, just—life really is? Perhaps one day God will give me the few simple words I need. And bright and fervent and serious words as well. But above all simple words. How can I draw this small village of barracks between heath and sky with a few, rapid, delicate and yet powerful, strokes of the pen? And how can I let others see the many inmates, who have to be deciphered like hieroglyphs, stroke by stroke, until they finally form one great readable and comprehensible whole? One thing I now know for certain: I shall never be able to put down in writing what life itself has spelled out for me in living letters. I have read it all, with my own eyes, and felt it with many senses.[4]

On Prayer and the Inner Life:

Calling herself a "kneeler in training," Etty wrote often about her inner life, and recorded many of her dialogues with God. In these passages she speaks of several different aspects of prayer.

When I pray, I never pray for myself, always for others, or else I hold a silly, naive or deadly serious dialogue with what is deepest inside me, which for the sake of convenience I call God. Praying to God for something for yourself strikes me as being too childish for words...To pray for another's wellbeing is something I find childish as well; one should only pray that another should have enough strength to shoulder his burden. If you do that, you lend him some of your own strength.[5]

...I refresh myself from day to day at the original
source, life itself, and I rest from time to time in
prayer. And what those who say, "You live too
intensely," do not know is that one can withdraw
into prayer as into a convent cell and leave again
with renewed strength and with peace regained. I
think what weakens people most is fear of wasting their strength. If after a long and arduous process, day in day out, you manage to come to grips
with your inner sources, with God, in short, and
if only you make certain that your path to God is
unblocked—which you can do by "working on
yourself"—then you can keep renewing yourself
at these inner sources and need never again be
afraid of wasting your strength.[6]

As I walked down those overcrowded corridors
today, I suddenly felt the urge to kneel down right
there, on the stone floor, among all those people.
The only adequate gesture left to us in these times:
"kneeling down before You." Each day I learn
something new about people and realize more and
more that the only strength comes, not from others, but from within.[7]

About her inner life Etty reflected:

Thinking gets you nowhere. It may be a fine and
noble aid in academic studies, but you can't think
your way out of emotional difficulties. That takes
something altogether different. You have to make
yourself passive then, and just listen. Re-establish
contact with a slice of eternity.[8]

The Pain of the World:

> My heart is a floodgate for a never-ending tide of misery.[9]

> I believe that for every event, man has a faculty that helps him deal with it. If we were to save only our bodies, nothing more, from the camps all over the world, that would not be enough. What matters is not whether we preserve our lives at any cost, but *how* we preserve them. I sometimes think that every new situation, good or bad, can enrich us with new insights. But if we abandon the hard facts that we are forced to face, if we give them no shelter in our heads and hearts, do not allow them to settle and change into impulses through which we can grow and from which we can draw meaning, then we are not a viable generation.[10]

Etty's willingness to stay a witness to the terrors of her times, was a frequent subject of her writing.

> With all the suffering that is here, you begin to feel ashamed of taking yourself and your moods so seriously. But you must continue to take yourself seriously. You must remain your own witness marking everything that happens in the world, never shutting your eyes to reality. You must come to grips with these terrible times, and try to find answers to the many questions that they pose.[11]

Here, as in many places throughout her diaries and letters she describes in vivid detail the pain that is everywhere around her. In this next vignette she captures a poignancy and pathos in the appearance of a single woman, immortalized now because Etty cared enough to write.

You can tell that the young woman over there is used to luxury and that she must have been very beautiful. She is a recent arrival. She had gone into hiding to save her baby. Now she is here, through treachery, like so many others. Her husband is in the punishment barracks. She looks quite pitiful now. Her bleached hair has black roots with a greenish tinge. She has put on many different sets of underwear and other clothing all on top of one another—you can't carry everything by hand, after all, particularly if you have a little child to carry as well. Now she looks lumpy and ridiculous. Her face is blotchy. She stares at everyone with a veiled, tentative gaze, like some defenseless and abandoned young animal.

What will this young woman, already in a state of collapse, look like after three days in an overcrowded goods wagon with men, women, children and babies all thrown together, bags and baggage, a bucket in the middle their only convenience?

Presumably they will be sent on to another camp, and then on again from there. We are being hunted to death right through Europe...[12]

Her understanding of how people dissipated their valuable life energy was acute. In that terrible place, surrounded in misery, people were complaining and trying to figure things out. Etty wrote:

Debates, computations, laws of probability are the order of the day. I keep well out of it. All this talking takes up energy and nothing comes of it in the end. People here fritter their energy away on the thousand irksome details that grind us down every day; they lose themselves in detail and drown. That's why they get driven off course and find existence pointless. The few big things that matter in life are what we have to keep in mind; the rest can be quietly abandoned. And you find those big things anywhere, you have to keep rediscovering them in yourself so that you can be renewed. And in spite of everything you always end up with the same conviction: life is good after all, it's not God's fault that things go awry sometimes, the cause lies in ourselves. And that's what stays with me, even now, even when I'm about to be packed off to Poland with my whole family.[13]

In whatever situations we may find ourselves today, whether of external difficulty or a sense of personal limitation, or simply of boredom, we can find a resonance in the sentiments of this passionate woman. Etty Hillesum struggled with universal problems—loneliness, insecurity, friendship, family concerns, a growing sense of responsibility for others—all the issues that we face in establishing ourselves as mature and caring women in our modern world. Despite the fact that her diaries in translation have been published under the title, *An Interrupted Life*, Etty's life was whole, and her wholeness reaches out to us across the years.

SERVICE TO THE LIVING AND DYING: MEETING WITH ELISABETH KÜBLER-ROSS

Since the early '70s, in my work as an instructor in the field of death and dying, I had read the books of Elisabeth Kübler-Ross and used them as the foundation for my courses. Yet I had never met her, although I had spoken with others who had. What always struck me about their accounts was that even people who had only seen her once, and especially those who had attended one of her many workshops, thereafter referred to Elisabeth as if talking about a close friend. "So, I asked Elisabeth and she said ..." or, "When I couldn't stand the pain any longer I called Elisabeth." I remember my friend Grace whose six-year-old son Matthew had just died of leukemia, talking about her several visits to and phone conversations with Elisabeth, and I recall how it always sounded to me like the two of them were sisters who were sitting down over coffee and cigarettes to console one another over the most recent family tragedy.

The years have taught me that Grace was no more special to Elisabeth than were thousands of others, men, women, children—the rich and respectable, or the most lowly and despised of humanity, the convicts dying of AIDS in the sewers which were American's prison-hospitals only ten years ago. The planet was her patient assignment. Everyone mattered. To read one of her many books is to enter, if only briefly, into the life of one who has cared and continues to care so deeply for others that she is willing to face, day after day and year after year, a confrontation with enormous pain.

Elisabeth suffered a major stroke in 1995 which left her partially paralyzed. As I sat with her in late June of 1997 in the cool, cave-like corner of her living room in Scottsdale, Arizona—this tiny chamber that had been her prison and her monastery for the past two years—I had little trouble swallowing my awe in the presence of such greatness. She made me feel at home. She spoke to me as if she and I had always met like this. She involved herself in my life but not through intrusion, rather through a kind of honest clarity and presence that expressed itself undefended by pretense, with humor and warmth. No wonder, I thought, she has so many friends.

In one hour the phone rang seven times, and Elisabeth answered each call herself, struggling to adjust the receiver in her hands—the left one still unusable since the stroke. The calls came from everywhere—Spain, Colorado, California; from people she knew well and those whom she had never met, but who had acquired her phone number because their curiosity or their need had been rewarded. "Yes, you can come ..." she said softly and without emotion to seven different people, although she cautioned that she was hoping to be "gone" before her next birthday, which was fast approaching on July 8th. Being gone meant being dead, which she matter-of-factly awaited.

"You have made yourself so accessible to so many people," I commented, stating the obvious, after she hung up the receiver for the fifth time.

"Some of these people are still my patients. Since I cannot go out to see them then they must come here," she said. Elisabeth Kübler-Ross had dedicated her life to the service of others, and even the imminent aura of her own death was not enough to change the investment of a lifetime. I'd say she was *surrendered* to God through her surrender to others' needs, although she herself would probably revile this "s" word being applied to her as some passive, cop-out way of putting things.

Elisabeth Kübler-Ross has a built-in "phony-baloney" detector—her delightfully ornery way of saying that she doesn't suffer fools gladly. Yet in her presence, I had the impression that her compassion for humanity's pain (my pain, in this case) afforded her a wide baloney tolerance. I admit to my share of baloney, but despite her threats that she would boot such people out the door (demonstrated for me as she kicked her stroke-affected legs from the foot-rest of her recliner), she was an eminently gracious hostess to my companion and I. Nothing about Elisabeth smacks of false holiness or passivity. This degree of honesty, coupled with the personal caring of her communication is the primary and invaluable witness that Elisabeth Kübler-Ross makes, as much if not more than the example of her astounding accomplishments. Her willingness to "tell it like it is," to anyone who asks, to express her "pissed-off" attitude that she wasn't able to die when she wanted to (a state-of-affairs which many dying people go through), testified to the sacrifice which she was allowing her life to be for others. As if to make good on her own well-quoted admonition that people die generally the way they live, Elisabeth was being herself—rebellious, honest, unpretentious and available—up until the end.

In some way her attitude served to balance the romanticism that some of us still definitely hold about the dying process, and to dispel the notion that even the "guru" of death herself had some magic key to make it less, or more, than just what it is.

That Elisabeth Kübler-Ross is everywoman, everyman, wasn't lost on me. I left her with a renewed sense of the urgency to attune my own life to what really matters, and with the powerful recognition that this starts with being a "phony-baloney detector" as far as my own motives and activities are concerned.

DOWN WE GO

"No matter *who* you are, you have to go through your 'stuff,'" I remarked to my teacher, Lee, in returning from my visit to Elisabeth. For some reason, with all the other details that I had shared with him, it was that comment which had proved most interesting. He repeated it to other members of our community later that evening.

Elisabeth had told my friend and I that she had recently found a healer whose work with her over the previous two and a half weeks had caused astounding improvement in her physical abilities, and even more importantly had restored some laughter to her life, her way of saying that the whole mood of her confinement had lightened.

I knew that something extraordinary had occurred for her recently. Recent magazine interviews had revealed a woman full of anger and frustration, in sharp contrast to the extraordinary softness that greeted me. And while it is true that one tends to find what one is looking for, and also that those two states of awareness are not necessarily exclusive, I felt from her a resurgence of life that was immediate, fresh, new. It was undeniable.

Elisabeth went on to tell us that this healer, whose modesty prevented him from calling himself a spiritual healer, had been instrumental is effecting release and mobility for her on many levels. She mesmerized us with the story of how, on the night after her first treatment from the healer, she experienced herself being "dipped" into what she described as a series of vats, each of which cleansed or drew out from her one of many negative and debilitating states, like rage, like abandonment, like desperation. She smiled, and I noticed the twinkle in her eye for the first time as she described getting up the next morning with a new-found possibility—she was getting help.

Whether such help would actually result in a physical healing, Elisabeth doubted at the time. (She really *wanted* to die.) What was obvious to me, and I know was to her, was that God's inexorably fine grinding mill was obliterating some of the last traces of self, probably very old stuff that still clung to the walls of the psychic cells, or lodged itself in hidden pockets in the intestines of the emotional body. Her desire for merger in the Light, her expressed assurance that "I'm not coming back" for another lifetime, would be possible only when and if "she" were fully annihilated; when and if the steel threads of abandonment and other psychological/emotional issues, were cut, once and for all.

She had already been offered the opportunity for detachment from material things when in 1994 her house in Virginia was destroyed by fire, rendering unto dust the precious papers, letters, books and artifacts of a lifetime. Arson was suspected—since Kübler-Ross had hoped to set up a center for AIDS babies, and the township was only too happy to rid itself of the "AIDS lady"—but no arrests were ever made. Despite the initial shock and horror of such an inconceivable dispossession, she now jokes that at least she didn't have to pack!

This severing, this letting go, is generally the work of a lifetime—we call it spiritual work, i.e., the work that ultimately liberates us so that we may serve at a whole different level, unencumbered by attachments that make us less flexible tools in the hand of God. And, regardless of who we are, this Great Process of Divine Evolution *will have its way* with us, finishing off according to *its* own timing, the preparations which we have been dabbling in, or zealously pursuing, all our lives.

Elisabeth's circumstance was a further reminder of another dynamic and *dharmic* principle about suffering. Namely, that one who has given themselves away, in the sense that Kübler-Ross seems to have passionately celebrated throughout her life, may actually be gifted with the task of participation in the suffering of others. And what does that mean? Only one who is willing to venture into a reality not defined by the limitations of space or time can appreciate such a possibility, and why that could be a gift. To attempt to simplify a great mystery, let's just agree that because all things are connected, then the actions or thoughts of one affect the actions and thoughts of all. From this domain one could imagine that Elisabeth's ongoing dedication to service in the midst of her own personal hell of pain and confinement was not merely a beacon to others, strengthening them in the midst of their suffering, but at the level of the psyche or soul, her energetic intention was made available to those who had never heard of the famous Elisabeth Kübler-Ross but were dying painful, isolated deaths in need of consolation. The energy of suffering just might, in fact, be transformable into compassionate gold in some cosmic, alchemical crucible. This gold was the coin of the realm for the *Bodhisattva's* task of relieving the suffering of others.

That Elisabeth was no stranger to this dynamic process was reinforced in her autobiography where she recounted a story of one of her out-of-body experiences after which she went through a night of agony, reliving the pain and fear of all her patients who had ever died. Letting go into excruciating torment, she emerged the next day in what she described as a state of cosmic consciousness, fully attuned to her complete union with all of creation. And while such an experience of total merger was short-lived, it nonetheless served as an on-going point of reference for her in her later work, as it evidently does in her relationship to her own death.

Years ago she wrote to a child dying of cancer:

> When we have done all the work we were sent to Earth to do, we are allowed to shed our body; which imprisons our soul like a cocoon encloses the future butterfly.
>
> And when the time is right, we can let go of it and we will be free of pain, free of fears and worries—free as a very beautiful butterfly; returning home to God.[14]

We all know more about reality than we are yet fully willing or able to live. What distinguishes the great, or the woman awake,

Elisabeth Kübler-Ross

from the mediocre of spirit, is that the woman who has heard the flute of her Beloved calling her to service is willing to dance *regardless* of incomplete data, regardless of her own madness, her failings, her inconsistencies, or even her arrogant mistakes; the same accusations that have been leveled vociferously against Elisabeth Kübler-Ross. Thank God she has been so reviled. Anyone unwilling to bow to the status quo will receive the same treatment. Thank God she would risk being *anything* but a phony baloney. True service is willing to be wrong, but it is never willing to compromise its integrity.

A Closing Story

Our desire for service and our efforts to serve will not always manifest in the way we think they should. In fact, setbacks and failures may accompany our service all along the way, and are actually often signs that we are attempting something great. The story of Elisabeth's initial efforts at working with AIDS patients is a testimony to that.

Kübler-Ross's lifetime commitment to the needs of the dying took a radical and personal turn in 1984, shortly after she moved to her farm in Headwaters, Virginia. Although for years her work-shops had been open to AIDS patients, and she gave many pro-grams specifically for the victims of this dread disease, one devastatingly honest letter aimed her life of service in a new direc-tion. In this letter, the mother of a three-year-old boy painfully admitted that she could no longer look after her son, and asked, "How much would you charge to take care of him?" When similar letters began arriving, revealing to Elisabeth the tragic conditions under which hundreds of AIDS-infected children lived and died, she knew she had to take this new direction seriously.

Among the stories that these letters told, one AIDS-infected mother used the last of her strength contacting over seventy agen-cies trying to secure help for her dying, AIDS-infected child. The woman died without ever knowing whether anyone would be there to care for her infant. Another AIDS baby, abandoned in a shoebox, was placed in a hospital, but the staff failed to touch the child or attend to it sufficiently, so that at two years of age the child still could not crawl nor speak. Only with tremendous efforts did Elisabeth secure an adoptive family for the child.

Elisabeth received the inner direction that creating a hos-pice-home for children dying with AIDS would be the purpose of her new farm. News of her intention swept through the tiny com-munity and county of her residence like a brush fire in a desert wind, and so began an excruciatingly slow crucifixion that was to consume her effort and attention for years to come. The degree of ignorance, fear and hatred exemplified by the people of the county angered and saddened her. Every day brought new indignities. She was hissed and booed at when she shopped in town. Crosses were burned on the front lawn of the farm. Crank phone calls and shouted threats were mild in comparison to the bullets shot through her windows. By 1986 she was forced, at last, to give up the struggle. The county refused approval of the necessary zoning ordinances.

But, like the amazing servant that she is, Elisabeth Ross turned crisis into opportunity once again. She decided to mobilize her huge network of supporters to find adoptive parents for nearly 350 AIDS babies.

Over and over, in recounting the stories of desperation, Elisabeth would reiterate the hope and reconciliation that had concluded so many of them. In her autobiography, she closes her chapter on AIDS by saying: "I had no doubt that one day medical science would discover a cure for this horrible disease. But I hope not before AIDS cures what ails us as human beings." [15]

9

THE PATH OF ART
AND INSPIRATION

The first time I saw Janis Joplin perform I cried.

An odd reaction, certainly. I was not lamenting her loss—I only saw her on videotape long after her death. Nor was I crying for the pain and suffering of her life, which were certainly obvious and well-known.

No, these tears were not from grief or pity. I was crying because her wild wails, her sweat, and her soulful laboring as she moaned the blues tapped me into something much bigger than this individual woman's pain. When Janis sang the blues she stabbed you with the suffering of humanity, and you felt your own suffering. I wept for completely selfish reasons. With each uninhibited rendering of song after song, I felt more acutely and bitterly my own paltry courage, my own inability and unwillingness to swing out, open up, "tell it like it is" in my art and work. I wept for my smallness of heart and for the thousand daily choices to make life comfortable rather than leave it somewhat raw, clumsy, open-ended and rife with possibility.

Janis Joplin's music—regardless of the alcohol, the drugs, the flagrant sex that characterized her life (and partially because of it)—was strong enough to break through steel-girded taboos. Not that I cared to imitate her behaviors, at all. Rather, at a much deeper level, what I desperately wanted was the ability to reach down into my own body, to the interior cave in which Kundalini Shakti lived, and to ignite the fire that would send HER force up the spine and out, into the heart, the brain and the hands; into love and compassion, enlightened knowledge, art, creativity and service. The recollection of that possibility—itself a full-body experience—was the legacy Janis left me.

Every woman alive knows what I mean. She may not care for the music of Janis Joplin, but she knows that searing sensation that goes from nipples to vagina, followed by the ache—the knowledge that the "eggs" of what she is seeing or hearing in some art form or activity are waiting in her own womb for a spark, a single sperm of energy or divine grace, to fertilize them into life. And she wants that, dearly, unless she has finally given up on herself, which starts the slow process of spiritual death.

Reading or hearing good poetry read does the same awakening for me. I will never forget the first time I heard Anne Waldman, a contemporary writer and performance poet, read her own work. I was attending a writer's conference. The room was packed with about six hundred of us, avid and aspiring men and women, of all ages, sitting on the edges of our chairs, notebooks in hand, hanging on every word of the several distinguished authors who addressed us that day. Anne approached the podium with all the elegance and style that mark her for the gracious and masterful woman that she is. She warmed us with charming smiles and set us at ease with disarming words, and then she let us have it—right to the guts! She read us a piece called "To the Censorious Ones," about the arising of the Feminine from the underworld, and how it would terrify the powers that be. "I'M, COMING, UUUUUUUP..." she bellowed, with such power and abandon that the room shook (I swear the chandeliers rattled). We dropped our pens; eyes riveted now in her direction. We shook too. The people around me seemed to resonate like so many drums being pounded. [1]

There it was again, that raw Feminine nerve, that heat, that contained nuclear reaction. Here was Kali again, dancing on the bodies of the demons, her wild hair shining. Anne continued relentlessly, verse after verse, and always that same terrifying refrain: "I'm coming up...," and her whole body spoke that last word, causing a sizzling charge in my toes that raced, in her rhythm, to the top of my head.

For days after hearing Anne Waldman read I filled my journal with nothing but "rants"—long, poetic diatribes in which I allowed myself the rare and glorious permission to unleash that power that she had so shamelessly demonstrated. Herein lies the spirituality of art—that it awakens the sleeper within. That it invades, penetrates, excites and calls forth its own creation. Whether that art is as fierce or erotic as Joplin's music or Waldman's poetry or Martha Graham's dance or Camille Claudel's sculpture, or as sublime as the Gregorian chant composed by Hildegard of Bingen, there is power in art—to move the heart, to churn the gut, to illuminate the mind. Art is Divine Mother's *lila*, her play, and her Work in Creation.

THE BODY OF ART

In the summer of 1976, my husband Jere and I visited his parents in New Jersey for a week, and I was totally bored. One afternoon, as I browsed a nearby bookstore, a small paperback caught my attention. The title intrigued me: Richard Hittleman's *Yoga: 28 Day Exercise Plan* (New York: Workman, 1975). "Could a person really accomplish anything meaningful in only twenty-eight days?" I wondered. The idea of finding a way to structure time was exceedingly attractive. Engaging in something which would have measurable results, and a beginning, a middle and an end was enticing.

Standing among the musty stacks in this tiny shop, I made a commitment to myself. For twenty-eight days I would follow this book to the letter—no matter what!

A few days into the process, sitting on the floor on a worn carpet, my legs stretched out in front of me, I took a deep breath

293

and stretched as gracefully as I could, reaching down to grasp my ankles. I exhaled slowly, and felt the silence deepen around me. The air was charged. My mind was quiet. I suddenly realized that I was praying—praying with my breath, with my arms, with my legs, with my belly, my back. My whole body was moving into these various *asanas* (postures), and each posture was like a bow of devotion at the feet of the Divine. Inside and out, my body was harmonized with the movement of the Universe. God was everywhere.

Prayer had always drawn me from the time I was a child—any time spent in silence, or in attending Mass, in saying the Rosary, or in meditative reading, were among the richest times in my day. The aura that surrounded me during prayer felt like an aura of sanctity. And yet, despite my thirty years of life and my years within a convent, the realization that prayer could extend into the fingers and toes, into every cell in the body, was an idea that had remained divorced from experience. With my introduction to Yoga, that divorce was healed. I *knew* that the body could pray; that prayer was not only an activity of the heart and mind. In fact, and even more surprisingly, I learned that specific words, lofty sentiments or visualizations were not necessary to prayer. The breath alone, when done with attention, could be a prayer. The stretching of the legs was prayer. The twisting of the spine was prayer.

Certainly I had read the scriptures and heard endless sermons that exhorted me to, "Pray always." Yet, these directives were still limited to the heart-mind location of prayer. To "pray always" might mean that I would go around from task to task while silently saying *The Lord's Prayer*, perhaps. Or, that I would think about Jesus washing the feet of his disciples, as I was washing the dishes. But, the recognition that I could wordlessly "dance" prayer, or "stretch" prayer, or "move" prayer—now, that was new.

Since then I have learned other ways of prayer that different spiritual traditions have to offer. I have learned that, with practice and guidance, one can consciously transform any work into prayer. Bearing and being with children can be prayer; eating or drinking with intention can become Divine Communion; sexual intimacy has the potential for deep prayer, and even sleep can be made intentional, such that prayer is "happening" throughout the night.

Another age-old type of prayer is the creation of art. After all, art has always been connected with ritual expression and with worship of the gods. All the temples, churches, shrines, stupas, mosques ever constructed, all the great statuary and painting that fills them, and all the singing and dancing, music-making, chanting and preaching that goes on within their walls are all forms of art, designed for the purpose of invoking a universal resonance within the worshipper, as well as evoking the attention of the "heavenly powers."

The great artists have much to teach us about a type of prayer characterized by passion; by a burning desire to transform their pain, their anguish, their yearning into an enduring form that expresses their underlying recognition of the awesome grandeur of creation and their gratitude to the Creator for allowing their participation in the act of life.

By and large, however, our culture is far removed from this expression of worship through art. The filmmaker Ingmar Bergman once said that "...art lost its basic creative drive the moment it was separated from worship. It severed an umbilical cord and now lives its own sterile life, generating and degenerating itself." So much "art" today has been co-opted into advertising. A depiction of the Venus de Milo might easily provide the logo for a center for cosmetic surgery.

Few of us were raised with the appreciation that art was necessary for anything, no less for worship. In fact, we learned exactly the opposite. Certainly we were taught to copy the Easter bunny cut-out which our first grade teacher held up, or to make a potholder. But, even as an extra-curricular activity in our schools, classes in art as an expression of *interiority*, as a gateway to the soul, as a means of cultivating imagination, as a connection to the roots of human experience, as a connection to the Earth, these experiences were few and far between. As adults then, we have to relearn this connection or forge it for the first time.

In the classes I teach and in the workshops I conduct I hear a fear and a reticence expressed about the creation of art, as well as about the expression of oneself in general. "I can't write," the women say, as if to warn me that I should not expect anything of value from them. "I'm no artist," they affirm, their hands shaking as they pick up a piece of colored chalk and timidly move to the blank paper in front of them, staring into the whiteness as one stares into the void. Their responses have much less to do with their comparisons of themselves with great writers and great artists and their fear of being found wanting, and much more to do with their terror of freeing up a voice or a body that has literally been held in chains since they were children. More truthfully, what they are saying is, "I don't have the right to make my mark on the world," or "My opinion, my unique 'take' on the truth is not really worth anything," or "Nobody really cares what I do, why should I even try?" In questioning our own spontaneous expressions of joy and creativity, we reinforce the notion that we are separate from the life of God.

"God is voluptuous and delicious," said the mystic Meister Eckhart, and indeed, unless as children we are allowed to feel the voluptuousness and deliciousness of our own bodies or of nature around us, we are cut off very early and very effectively from a full participation in the celebration of the mysteries of creation.

The result of our failure to participate in the expression of our uniqueness in some form is that this potentially creative energy gets sealed off, like water in a stagnant pool. Without the movement of the current, the purifying rays of the sun, and the balance of oxygen afforded by green plants and fish, the water turns to poison. And the same thing happens in a woman's body. When her expression through poetry, through music, through dance, through pottery, through bearing and educating children, through building an environment of elegance in her home—is denied or stifled, she will use that energy to shop addictively, or eat without hunger, or she will clamp down on the movement of life within her own body, saying "no and no and no," making her inner environment a place where disease can easily find a home.

What is the source of our first suffering? It lies in
the fact that we hesitated to speak. It was born in

the moment when we accumulated silent things
within us.

—Gaston Bachelard

Women who long for God or Truth must have the courage to
enter the inner world—the courage to build an inner life. And
such a life is founded in the sensitivity and honesty to listen deeply
to what we are *really* saying to ourselves, and to what is really being "spoken" to us; the honesty and sensitivity to discern what we
are *really* feeling, deeper than our reactivity to either the wondrous or the repulsive; the courage to confront, face-to-face, what
we *really* believe and trust, beyond all the world's proscriptions.
Such a foundation builds a temple of the heart, and invites the
presence of the Divine. Such a life of spirit creates an interior fire
that purifies, and ultimately annihilates the ego, merging the soul
with the Infinite. We need art in our lives, and we need the witness of artists testifying to the process of surrender that they have
gone through in allowing the Divine to work in and through them.

Whether our expression ever reaches beyond ourselves to
the degree where others acknowledge our work as "art" will not be
the point. We each have both the necessity and an obligation to
express the unique "piece" that has been gifted to us. We must
each, in some form or another, participate in the Godly work of
creation. When we fail to work in a way that affirms this organic
generativity (which is Woman), the energy gets used for death.
It's that simple. That is why contemporary artists, like Meinrad
Craighead and others, have developed or supported programs for
women and men with cancer and other life-threatening illnesses.
Art allows people to express the pent-up emotions and the unsung
songs of a lifetime.

When my friend Inge was dying of cancer on our ashram in
Arizona, my spiritual teacher instructed her to paint, with water-
colors or fingerpaint, and to devote time to drumming each day.
Instinctively, he knew that Inge needed access to her own being
and that she needed non-linear means to release what she had
never been given permission to express as a child or a young adult.

The passion of our love for God and service to humanity will not likely show up like Mother Teresa's love and service, or Irina Tweedie's devotion and function as a spiritual teacher. Some of us will be blessed to serve by the raw honesty of the written word (the way Etty Hillesum served), others by creation of music or song that flows directly from the heart and the womb; others will serve by smearing lush paints on canvas or by smoothing the angles in stone; and others by the graceful and disciplined movements of their bodies through space. And, in so doing, we will invite each other to share the passion of our inner world, and remind one another that every gesture can be holy.

Meinrad Craighead:
Art in Praise of the Great Mother

I draw and paint from my own myth of personal origin. Each painting I make begins from some deep source where my mother and grandmother, and all my fore-mothers, still live; it is as if the line moving from pen or brush coils back to the original Matrix. Sometimes I feel like a cauldron of ripening images where memories turn into faces and emerge from my vessel. So my creative life, making out of myself, is itself an image of God the Mother and her unbroken story of emergence in our lives.[2]

Meinrad Craighead met me at her gate—a curious gate, which I later learned was designed to represent flowing water; a gate bleached light gray in the New Mexico sun. The gate rattled a slight song when I pushed it. Dangling shells, attached bits of animal bone and a bell, heralded my transit from one world to the next, as I stepped into the small, quiet sanctuary where she lives in

Meinrad Craighead

Old Albuquerque, a few minutes walk from the Rio Grande. When I remarked that I was intrigued by the gate, Meinrad smiled and asked if I had ever built one? No I hadn't, I replied, slightly thrown off by the strange question. "Everyone should build a gate at sometime in their lives," she noted, gently but enigmatically. It was the first of two suggestions that she made to me on that bright September afternoon in 1989.

Her second suggestion came as we examined her artwork—paintings of multi-layered colored ink on scratchboard—in the light-filled studio which is next to her home. Meinrad had used the image of a labyrinth, in different forms, in a number of her pieces. "Have you drawn a labyrinth?" she asked, attaching particular importance to that image. I hesitated, ashamed to say that I hadn't. In the way in which a woman educates (literally "brings forth"), Meinrad was stretching me. As kind as her questions were, they were also disturbing.

That first visit with Meinrad was disturbing in another way too. She was immensely kind, generous with her time, and amazingly present, wanting to know what my life was about, what gave joy to me. Yet, only after I left her did I realize the reason for my discomfort—I was unprepared for her. Here was a woman with such a wealth of being and experience, and yet I didn't really know how to access the treasure that was right in front of my face. My questions sounded naive, I thought, and my attitude bordered on being obsequious, since I tried to cover my ignorance and discomfort with adaptability. These were familiar feelings and habits. Living in the company of a spiritual teacher I grind my teeth continually with this same sense of being at the door of greatness without the chutzpah or the simplicity to knock. Nonetheless, I think it is important to put myself in the presence of great artists and teachers of all kinds. When I dare to step into any domain that is somewhat risky or unfamiliar, I have the possibility to learn about myself beyond my usual self-definitions, and to see a part of the world beyond the usually safe havens in which I keep myself comfortable. In the presence of greatness, moreover, we have the opportunity to witness to "I Am That." In other words, if we are simple, humble and receptive without self-deprecation, we can appreciate our own essential greatness, regardless of education, experience or accomplishments.

While I have not yet built a gate, in the years that have followed that first visit to Meinrad's realm I have begun to draw the labyrinth—venturing into a type of journal writing that explores hidden places of dark wonder, giving form to the questions, giving form to the mystery that lies at the heart of this journey through life. Labyrinth and Gate, after all, are perfect symbols of the spiritual life as a whole, as well as of particular stages. Meinrad was a good instigator.

Her book lay on the counter of a bookstore in Des Moines, Iowa in 1987—*The Mother's Songs: Images of God the Mother*, just published and throbbing with life. When I opened the cover, and encountered image after shocking or luxurious image, I remember thinking that although I had never seen or even heard of it before, I had been waiting for this book for too long. Meinrad was painting from the inside out, and those "insides," in so many of her paintings, were familiar enough to have been my own.

One picture struck me like no other. "Garden" she named it. The central image was a woman, like a tree, rising out of the center of a stone-walled garden. With her arms outstretched, her huge hands carefully pick an egg from each of two ovary-like nests. The woman's chest and belly form a generous womb in which a tiny, whited robed infant sleeps with a look of exquisite innocence. Where the woman's legs would be, there is a red cavern, like a vagina, the color of flowing blood. At the women's "feet" are more resting or sleeping figures, all female: an older woman, a middle-aged woman, a child and a young girl. Two dogs, standing at the gate, guard this threshold into her sacred precinct, this feminine enclosure. Above the garden, the sky is a tapestry of lavender, gold and teal-colored birds.

"Here is *my* body!" Someone had painted me as I knew myself and longed to be, beyond any physical evidence to the contrary. Since 1973 I had no ovaries. I had no baby. But the ovaries and the baby that Meinrad painted were mine nonetheless. I claimed this garden for my own—this fruitful, mysterious and beautiful garden was the sanctuary of the Divine Mother. Meinrad wrote in that same glorious book:

> I have never conceived, but whether or not a woman does conceive, she carries the germina-tive ocean within her, and the essential eggs. We have a spirituality, full from within. Whether we are weaving tissue in the womb or pictures in the imagination, we create out of our bodies.[3]

Meinrad paints images of God the Mother; she also writes about her, and speaks about her. She shares images from across time and culture with other men and women who wish to befriend the Divine Feminine within themselves once again. She has known this Mother intimately, unquestioningly, since her youth. On a hot summer afternoon when she was seven years old, Meinrad lay with her dog "in a cool place on the north side of my grandparents' clapboard house." While she stroked her dog, she looked into the animal's eyes and found herself traveling in a realm that was "as deep, as bewildering, as unattainable as a night sky." At the same time, she was aware of an interior movement, a sense of rushing water from a source within her. "I gazed into the dog's eyes and I listened to the sound of the water inside and I understood: 'This is God.' "[4]

"This is God," permeates all Meinrad's painting. Whether she is portraying a woman in a garden, or a Madonna with a black abyss for a belly, an all-wise and hovering owl, a gigantic tortoise with a labyrinthine design on its protective shell or a child sleeping, a sense of the sacred envelops and animates each creature. There is no point where nature stops and God starts. For Meinrad, it is all one piece.

> We are so impoverished when we divide ourselves—WE are humans, THEY are animals and IT is a tree. It is literally unreal that we don't grasp all this as part of our own bodies, and our bodies as part of this vast body.[5]

Woman's spirituality too is all one piece, not separate from nature and from woman's body. It is about milk, and blood, and fire and water, and the other substances, processes or daily events that make up our lives. The primordial act of creation is duplicated every day—in the transformations that happens in the natural cycles of things. When we take grain, grind it, bake it into bread and then share that bread in communion with one another so that bread becomes our flesh, we are participating in Creation, the Mother's work, and in a sacred ritual. When the mother breastfeeds her infant, it is clear that the substance of the Mother's body actually gives flesh to the baby. Mother's blood is what creates the milk within her, and the milk is transformed into the blood of the infant.

This understanding of natural transformation and creation saturates Meinrad's art and the prayerful way in which she conducts her life in tune with the rhythm of the seasons. Her studio, which she built herself with the help of another woman, is heated by a woodburning stove; she keeps her connection to wood and fire, the most elemental transformation. She walks daily by the Rio Grande which flows not far from her home. In the movement of this great river she hears the sound of God. She is up before dawn each day, greeting the rising sun as yet another wonder and blessing, for which her gratitude is always forthcoming. For Meinrad, ritual is organic, flowing from the same depths from which her artwork arises.

Meinrad is a woman of prayer. At thirty years of age, when she was already a well-respected artist, she entered a contemplative monastery of nuns in England, where she remained for fourteen years. She wanted prayer, "the search for God, the receiving and being in a receptive state, being an empty vessel."[6] She described beautifully the contemplative vocation and its source:

> I somehow knew that when you are filled with God, the filling of the vessel destroys the vessel— perhaps not so much a destruction as a reduction— an understanding of your self as nothing. And contemplation, the state of holding the awareness of your own nothingness, is intrinsic—it's part of the act of thanksgiving. You have been given something so powerful, of such searing, devastating beauty you are made aware of your nothingness in the face of this beauty.[7]

Meinrad Craighead has captured for me this organic connection between art and prayer, art and religion, and best of all, art and mother. I use her paintings and her heartfelt meditations to address the questions, "What is Woman?" "What is the Feminine approach to spiritual practice?" or "What is the Feminine Face of God?" in my seminars. "Here," I say, showing the participants Meinrad's compelling portrait of the Black Madonna, her belly a huge gaping blackness, "Here is what woman knows in her

Crow Mother by Meinrad Craighead

About this piece Meinrad says: "She sits enthroned in her own deepest interiority laying eggs of potential. Her wings are filled with eyes. Her sight is in her flight. This Great Mother Spirit may be understood as a manifestation of the ancient Vulture Goddess, she who eats Death and restores to Life what was dead."

own body about the mystery, the great abyss, the eternal emptiness." Or, "Here," as I hand them her painting called *Blood*, which vividly depicts two women with wings, menstruating, "Here is the truth. Our blood is holy. The body is holy. Our blood waters the earth. Our blood gives us wings of transcendence." I show them *Milk*, in which a nursing mother sits by a river of milk which has poured forth from the eternally full vessel of the Great Mother in the center of the painting, and I read them the words that Meinrad places on the facing page:

> Milk: I am born connected. I am born remembering rivers flowing from my mother's body into my body. I pray at her Fountain of Life, saturated in her milk and blood, water and honey. She passes on to me the meaning of religion because she links me to our origin in God the Mother.[8]

I most enjoy sharing her piece called *Vessel*—a large clay pot, deep enough to enter, the way in which the Pueblo Indians of the Southwest entered the *kiva*, the underground chamber used for secret ceremonies.[9] The women are fascinated. I tell them that Meinrad speaks of this piece in connection with her move to New Mexico because it was in this particular region that she found an external environment which most closely matched her own "interior landscape."

That bit of description (the "interior landscape") generally serves as a particularly compelling invitation to the women I share it with. After saying that, little more needs to be said; the women are generally itching to touch the chalks, paints, oil pastels, that I have set out for them. The suggestion to create their own inner landscape on paper, or to create some image of God the Mother, is usually enough to invoke the mood of the *kiva*. We find ourselves in a silent chamber as the women work, singly, interiorly, but very much connected in their acts of creation. As they begin I read to them from an essay Meinrad wrote in *The Feminist Mystic:*

The Mother has but one law: "Create; make as I do make." Obedience to this law is the deepest obedience and the worthiest worship of her. Make, transform one substance into another, press form into chaos, mold material into spiritual reality, fashion potential into actual, change one form of energy into another. Transmute blood into milk, clay into vessel, feeling into movement, wind into song, egg into child, fiber into cloth, stone into crystal, memory into image, body into worship.[10]

Without monastery walls, Meinrad Craighead is still a contemplative, a natural mystic. More so than ever. She is unapologetic for the passionate and radical love she has for the essence and rituals of Catholicism, without involving herself in the politics of the church. She is a gently outspoken advocate for the Feminine spirit and presence in the church, as well as for saving the Great Mother, the Earth, from the increasing devastation by a patriarchy gone wild.

Today, besides her own art and writing, Meinrad teaches the healing and liberating power of artistic expression in her creative retreats, called *Praying with Images*, for small groups of women. She invites women to "access the wisdom inside the storehouse of your memories. Let it spill out in your imagery. Let it bless and surprise you; let it teach and guide you."

Of Meinrad's work, Jungian analyst and writer Marion Woodman says: "To enter Meinrad Craighead's world is to be remembered in the cosmos of God's love. 'God lies in the details' of the earth and in the details of our bodies as her images quicken our imagination." And theologian Rosemary Radford Reuther writes:

If we are to save the earth from destruction, we must re-sacralize the earth or, to be more accurate, must rediscover its sacredness. But how can we re-sacralize that which we have profaned? Meinrad Craighead's paintings and litanies ... give us a profound glimpse of that saving sacredness.[11]

A Feather On The Breath of God—Hildegard of Bingen

Our second guide in this path of art as prayer will be a twelfth century mystic, Hildegard of Bingen, another remarkable woman who has captured the creative, political and mystic imaginations of women of our time. Hildegard's life and work has awakened a generation of women within Christianity (and now in other religious traditions) to the appreciation that Woman was not always the silent partner, in the background, throughout the dark centuries when the patriarchy ruled both the Church and the world with an iron hand. Despite the overwhelming restrictions of the times in which she lived, Hildegard of Bingen succeeded in producing a body of work—through art, writing, scholarship, science, healing, music, liturgical appreciation, education—that is awesome in its magnitude, its practicality, and its depth of theological awareness.

Hildegard lived for eighty-one years, from 1098-1179, in the verdant Rhine valley of Germany, and spent seventy-one of those years within the confines of a monastery. She was born to a wealthy family, the last of ten children, and it is believed that her father was a knight. Around the age of eight she was given, by her pious parents, as a gift in service to the holy woman, Jutta, an anchorite at the monastery of Disibodenberg. (An anchorite is one who has vowed to remain "anchored" to a church or other holy place. Once committed, the man or woman spent their entire life in a small cell adjacent to the church. The anchorite became the resident "saint" and was called upon by pilgrims and parishioners alike to serve as a source of religious inspiration and guidance.) And there, Hildegard learned the "womanly" arts of music, spinning, Biblical study, prayer and manual work.

Other young women were attracted by Jutta's holiness and a small community formed around her from 1106-1136. Together these women followed the rule of St. Benedict and lived as nuns in their own private sector of the male monastery. Nothing is reported about Hiledgard's early years, except what she later reports in letters to others, but sometime between the ages of fifteen and eighteen she determined to completely devote her life to God.

She took the habit of a Benedictine nun and in 1136, upon the occasion of Jutta's death, Hildegard (at the age of thrity-eight) was elected to take over the enormous responsibility of directing a now flourishing community of women.

In 1141, five years after assuming her role as abbess and accompanied by devastating physical illness which often left her in profound pain and even partially paralyzed, Hildegard received an inner awakening which opened the world for her. Like the baptism by fire which the disciples of Jesus received at Pentecost when they were overcome with the power of the Holy Spirit, Hildegard received an illumination of scriptures, an understanding of theological concepts beyond anything that she had formally studied, an insight into the liturgy together with a deepened knowledge of nature, of healing, of music, and many other gifts besides.

As she reports in her writings, the enlightenment was so profound that it confined her to bed for several days. Only when she forced herself to get up and began to put into form what she had been "given" did her energy and health return. In the preface to her book *Scivias* (Know The Ways) she relates:

> I heard a voice from Heaven saying, "I am the Living Light, Who illuminates the darkness. . .O human, who receives these things meant to manifest what is hidden not in the disquiet of deception but in the purity of simplicity, write, therefore, the things you see and hear." But I, though I saw and heard these things, I refused to write for a long time through doubt and bad opinion and the diversity of human words, not with stubbornness but in the exercise of humility, until, laid low by the scourge of God, I fell upon a bed of sickness; then, compelled at last by many illnesses, and by the witness of a certain noble maiden of good conduct (Rikkarda) and of that man whom I had secretly sought and found, as mentioned above (Volmar), I set my hand to the writing.[12]

Hildegard von Bingen receiving the outpouring of the Holy Spirit

Prompted by a series of powerful visions and a growing inte-rior urgency, Hildegard, with the help of her scribe and trusted ally, the priest Volmar, dictated her works and also directed the painting of the great archetypal images (known as her *Illumina-tions*) that she had witnessed with her inner sight.

Thus began her life work of creativity and service. Over the next forty-plus years, Hildegard not only tirelessly led several com-munities of nuns in the path of spiritual practice, handled the day to day details of running a monastery, wrote hundreds of letters of both encouragement and admonition (including one to Pope Eugenius III, urging him to work harder for the reform of monas-teries and churches throughout the known world), and preached all over Germany and even as far at Paris, but she composed over seventy poems and hymns for liturgical worship which she then put to music, wrote an opera and a morality play, a book on medicine, one on biology and a third on herbology, and three major theological treatises: *Scivias* (Know The Ways, in which she commented on her visions), *De Operationae Dei*, (On the Work of God), and *Liber Vitae Meritorum*, a book on ethics.

A LIFE OF DIVINE ABUNDANCE

To read Hildegard's words, in the original translations, or excerpted in the many books that are currently being written about her, is to encounter in language, a reflection of the woman's inner richness. Hildegard can speak of the varieties of plants and flowers in her monastery garden with the awesome respect of a scientist and healer, with the passion and refined vision of the artist and poet, and with the gratitude and wonder of a humble steward of the Divine Mystery. She could write about the birds and other creatures of her environment, the gemstones (she actually classified the properties of twenty-five gemstones, detailing medicinal uses and effective placement of each), and the varieties of intonation of the psalms which she and her community chanted each day. And, all this from a woman who received no more than the cursory education which was afforded the privileged women of her day. Hildegard's university was life itself—throbbing, moving, speaking in its grandeur and vast array of the incalculable magnificence of its Creator.

The scope of Hildegard's accomplishment is indeed breathtaking. Like the "greening power" of Earth, a phrase she coined and which she celebrated so easily in her poetry and song, Hildegard was a fertile and abundant woman in many domains, and her legacy to women of our times is to afford us another glimpse of the immense possibility and abundance which each woman possesses to transform her ordinary, day-to-day reality into a life of art, creativity and beauty, regardless of whether that art is ever seen or appreciated outside of the confines of her own home.

After all, at least in the beginning of her ministry, except for a few of her songs which were sent as gifts to nearby monasteries, almost all of her work was done for the benefit of those who came to the monastery for help in matter of health, or to enhance the chanting and prayer of the Mass and the Divine Office (the psalms which were sung at scheduled hours throughout the day, seven days a weeks, three-hundred sixty-five days a year) which she and her nuns embraced as their purpose in life—the constant remembrance and praise of God.

Woman, simply in being herself, is creative, full of seeds, imagination, intuition. When, like Hildegard, she is willing to lay herself open to the tending of the Divine Gardener, and to exercise the patience, courage and persistence which is called for in the cultivation of those seeds, she finds no end to the harvest that is reaped in and through her.

And it is here, in this surrender to the Force, that Hildegard's life can be so instructive to us. Her art was, in truth, an expression of her inner listening. Hildegard says that she "heard" the voice of Wisdom actually speaking to her, directing her in what to say, and in what to have written down, and in how to formulate the sequences of the chanted psalms. Hearing of her circumstances, we might be tempted to put Hildegard in a category that is alien to ourselves. Certainly such clear-cut divine inspiration might seem like a unique gift, completely outside the domains in which most of us live. Yet, I believe it is also quite possible that, despite her extraordinary visions, what Hildegard reported as a "voice" may be no more than the echo of that same resonance that lives in our hearts and souls waiting to be accessed when we are still. Once we have heard that voice for ourselves, our art merely awaits a few tools, or a minimal setting to be expressed.

We might say that her creative life grew out of a thirty-four year apprenticeship. (She did not hear the "call" to express her "art" until she was forty-three.) And, thirty-four years in one place in religious life is a long time in which to establish the kinds of roots—inner roots—which were needed to weather the storms that her garden would later be subjected to.

Choirs of Angels From the Sixth Vision of the Second Part
as described by Hildegard von Bingen.

Hildegard is honored by women today for the radical witness of her life, the enormous creative accomplishment of her hands, and the courage of her heart in confronting the official church representatives of her day. Yet, like we do with many great artists, I think we pay Hildegard a great disservice in holding her up as a model unless we constantly take those roots into account—unless we honor the type of discipline and fortitude which she would have lived and practiced for years and years prior to her "stepping forth" as the artist and the prophet which we regard her as today. Such gifts are rarely, if ever, seen in those who have no training, no grounding, in those who have not yet "paid their dues."

While we can be encouraged and inspired by our mother Hildegard, we should also afford ourselves the privilege of being annoyed by our own lack of depth in some aspects of our lives, allowing ourselves to feel the pain of our deadness and superficiality. In all the places in which we don't *burn* with intensity for expression and creation, we can look to Hildegard for guidance and help. She will show us what it takes it be a "great" artist—namely, an orientation towards, and finally a surrender into, something larger than we are. But in the process of such surrendering, only our diligent efforts in moving forward in expression and manifestation, despite the inner fears, are going to till the inner soil sufficiently to ready us for the sowing.

FROM HILDEGARD'S WORK

In a letter of response to the Abbess of another foundation, Hildegard wrote about the status of women—both married and virgins. The reason for the Abbess's letter, in the first place, was her objection that Hildegard allowed, and perhaps encouraged, the nuns in her monastery (most of whom were from families of great wealth) to bedeck themselves with jewels when they received the Holy Eucharist. In Hildegard's eyes, these virgins were the brides of Christ, and there was no problem for her in allowing them to dress for the great feast of receiving their Spouse in the sacrament. Hildegard wrote:

> The form of woman flashed and radiated in the
> primordial root ... both by being an artifact of the
> finger of God and by her own sublime beauty. Oh
> how wondrous a being you are, you who laid your
> foundations in the sun and who have conquered
> the earth![13]

In a letter describing her visions and how God was working
in her soul, Hildegard gave us the beautiful image of a feather float-
ing freely, upheld by the hand of her Creator. In some translations
this is exquisitely rendered as "a feather on the breath of God."

> God works where he wills—to the glory of his
> name, not that of earthbound man. But I am al-
> ways filled with a trembling fear, as I do not know
> for certain of any single capacity in me. Yet I
> stretch out my hands to God, so that like a feather
> which lacks all weight and strength and flies
> through the wind, I may be borne up by him.[14]

Hildegard wrote the words and music for many liturgical events.
As a part of a Mass celebrated upon the death of her dearest friend,
Rikkarda, Hildegard composed this *Responsory for a Virgin*:

> You most glorious greenness,
> You are rooted in the sun
> And out of the dazzling brightness of the clearest day
> You shine forth in a wheel
> Which no earthly excellence comprehends;
> You are encircled, embraced by the divine mysterium.
> You blush like the dawn and you burn like a flame
>   of the sun.
> You are encircled, embraced by the divine mysterium.[15]

Although as a woman of her times Hildegard was influenced
by the body-negative theology of her Church, she departs from

this negativity in many wonderful passages to praise creation. Here she writes of man and woman:

> When God created him, Adam felt a deep love within him during the sleep into which God had plunged him. And God gave a form to the image of man's love and so woman became the love of man. And the very moment woman was formed, God gave man the power of creating so that, through his love, that is, woman, he should pro-create children. When Adam beheld Eve, he was filled with all wisdom for he saw in her the mother who was to bear his children. And when Eve be-held Adam, she seemed to be looking towards Heaven, just as the soul desirous of celestial things gazes upwards, for her hopes were centered in man, that is why there must be one single love between man and woman, and no other love.[16]

Hildegard's passion for the Earth as an expression of the Divine resounds in this passage from a Hymn to the Holy Spirit:

> Out of you clouds
> Come streaming, winds
> Take wing from you, dashing
> Rain against stone;
> And ever-fresh springs
> Well from you, washing
> The evergreen globe.
>
> O teacher of those who know,
> A joy to the wise
> Is the breath of Sophia.

Praise then be yours!
You are the song of praise,
The delight of life,
A hope and a potent honor
Granting garlands of light.[17]

Matthew Fox summarized this great woman's value to us in his rich and personal treatment of Hildegard of Bingen when he wrote:

> Has there ever been a time in human history or the history of the planet when illumination, light, wisdom, was needed more than now? Can anyone be better equipped to lead us than the neglected one, St. Hildegard, who in fact defined the ultimate act of illumination as compassion?
> ... From contact with such riches we as a race might gather the splendor and trust, the beauty and imagination, to create a world worthy of ourselves and our planet and the divine splendor we carry in us and breath in all around us. This would correspond to Hildegard's deepest desires, for it was she who said: "Divinity is aimed at humanity."[18]

MIRABAI, THE POET

We turn finally to the passionate and defiant art of the poet Mirabai who lived in India from 1498 to 1573. Her ecstatic verse in praise of Krishna (The Dark One) is still treasured throughout India today. In fact, she is probably the best known poet in that country. Her poems, set to music, are sung by school children, and even occur as background tracks in contemporary films.

In these cynical times in the West, however, it is hard to tell Mirabai's story. Those who in former ages have been considered

Sophia, Divine Wisdom From the Fifth Vision of the Second Part
as described by Hildegard von Bingen

our prophets and wise women can be dismissed today under the microscope of psychological analysis. Religious fervor, obsession for truth, and uncompromising passion can easily be labeled fanaticism, or dysfunctional attempts to deal with the pressures of existence. To withdraw from society, as many great mystics, lovers and saints have done; to tear one's clothes or walk about naked; to give away one's precious possessions; to leave a job or family life to follow a calling to poverty or asceticism; to report visions or conversations with God—this is the stuff of which psychosis is made.

Ironically, our widespread psychological savvy about what's sane and what's insane, far from leading us to internal liberation, can easily become a tool for the enforcement of a more insidious conformity. When everybody can see and label the actions of everybody else, when the explanations of one's unconscious motivations are available at every newsstand, when the recommendation to therapy is the rule rather than the exception, some institutionalized version of sanity replaces magic and mystery. And when that happens, as it is already happening, we will have entered the dark ages once again.

Mirabai lived in the dark ages of a different sort. Born at the end of the fifteenth century, among a wealthy clan of princes, Mirabai's passion for the god Krishna, whom she claimed as her eternal lover, supplied her the courage to defy convention. Refusing to consummate her arranged marriage, Mira eventually succeeded in freeing herself from the prison of her caste. She spent her life wandering the hills and townships across northern India, generally alone, composing and singing the songs of freedom, passion and longing (over 5000 are credited to her) that spontaneously arose from her heart.

She was therefore considered crazy, evil or dangerous in her own times. The response of the "sleeping world" to such witnesses is the same today as it was then: Kill the messenger when you don't like the message. As was done to the prophets before her, the prevailing culture (in this case her husband's royal family) tried everything in its power to destroy what threatened its existence.

But fortunately, even with the messenger exiled or dead there is no stopping the poetry. Like the irrepressible shoots that push their way through cracks in the concrete, the messenger's poems wriggle through the bars, escaping on the wind. In our day, the efforts of Irina Ratushinskaya, the Russian poetess confined to a work camp for five years, demonstrated this irrepressible force in creation. Her poetry managed to elude the censors, the guards and the barbed wires. Smuggled hand to hand through some secret system of communication, it reached freedom and served to encourage and enlighten her countrymen and women and the world. (A small part of Irina's legacy is recounted in Chapter 7.)

Mirabai's poetry endures. Beyond the profound devotion expressed in her words, the popularity of her verses is probably due to their incitement to freedom, in radical defiance of convention. It testifies to a universal passion that will not be suppressed. Her poems are full of sensual language and penetrating longing. Mira's poetry is wet—with tears and her fiery blood. Furthermore, her art encodes a secret teaching—in the language of human love she reveals the immanent nature of her transcendent Lover, whom she calls by his many names: Govind, Lal ji, Giridhara, Hari. As she sang, Mirabai made love to Krishna. Her words have the power to awaken a similar passion in those who read them today.

> Mira is dyed deep in the love of Hari
> And all else is blocked out.
> I wear only bangles, tilak and beads:
> Beyond this, my only further ornament
> Is my virtuous life.
> No other such embellishments please me,
> Such was the wisdom
> I received from my Teacher.
> Some may revile me, others may praise me,
> But I will only sing the glories of Govind.
> Wheresoever Krishna leads,
> Thither will I follow.
> I will not steal,

I will harm no one,
How can anyone touch me?
I will not descend
From the back of an elephant
To ride upon an ass.[19]

  I first heard the story of the historical Mirabai years ago when I met a contemporary woman with the same name. And while my friend's version is somewhat generous in its historical accuracy, it captures a mood of Mira's innocence, devotion and passion more than many of the written treatments. Only Mira's poetry better expresses her life.

   Wake up, my darling flute player,
   Wake up, my darling.
   The night has passed,
   Dawn has come,
   People are opening their doors.
   You can hear the gopis churning the curds,
   Harken to the clink of their bracelets.
   Wake up, Lal ji, the dawn has come,
   Men and gods alike
   Are waiting at the door to greet Thee.
   The cowherd boys are in a frenzy,
   Everywhere there are shouts of "Jai! Jai!"
   Now the little herdsmen
   Have taken their parcels of bread and butter
   Ready to go out.
   Mira's Lord is the courtly Giridhara.
   He saves those
   Who choose Him for their refuge.[20]

  Born into a devout Brahmin family, the child Mirabai loved the practices of worship that her family kept. Like other children,

Mirabai, ecstatic poetess.

she delighted in witnessing the lighting of the *arati* lamps, watching them being waved enthusiastically before the images of the gods and goddesses which filled the shrine room or adorned the walls of the family home.

Legend has it that one day, when Mira was six, she heard a cacophony in the street—the sounds of musicians, the shouts of partygoers—and asked her mother what was happening. Mira's mother patiently explained that it was a wedding, the betrothal of husband to wife forever.

"Who is my husband?" asked the child, looking disconsolate.

Mira's mother paused for a moment, attempting to understand what her child was really asking. Leaving the room, she returned a few minutes later with a fist-sized clay figure of Lord Krishna. Handing it reverently to her daughter, Mira's mother unknowingly invoked a vow—"Your husband is Lord Krishna," she said, her own heart filled with devotion to this eternal thief of hearts.

Immediately, Mira recognized in her own heart this same mood of love which her mother had communicated. But unlike many who sense that mood and turn from it when the distractions of the world call to them, Mirabai remembered her Beloved from ages past in Vrindavan when she was a gopi and he was her playful consort. From her childhood, then, Mira dedicated her life to the Dark One, Krishna, and willingly become a slave to that love once again.

> Let me go to the house of Giridhara
> Giridhara is my true lover:
> On beholding His beauty, I long for Him much.
> As night falls I set out to see Him
> And at break of day I return.
> Day and night I sport in His company,
> I please Him in any way I can.
> Whatever He clothes me in, that I wear.
> Whatever He offers, that I eat.
> My love for Him

Is ancient and long-standing.
Without Him I could not live.
Wherever He places me, there I remain.
If He sold me into slavery,
I would acquiesce.
Mira's Lord is the courtly Giridhara,
She offers herself in sacrifice again and again.[21]

For the child Mirabai, this betrothal was the fulfillment of her life. She had no need or desire for any other. As she grew, she talked of her Beloved, and she worshipped her Lord Krishna with all the rites to which she would have been privileged, coming as she did from a devout Vaisnavite family.[22]

Mira's family, however, dismissed her devotion as the active imagination of a serious child. When she came of age, they promised her in marriage to the prince of a neighboring territory, a politically expedient move that would secure their fortunes and their lives during the turbulent times that prevailed in the empire. "Has my Lord Krishna come for me?" the child Mira asked innocently as her family began the preparations for the worldly liaison.

Mira was probably no more than fourteen years old at the time of her instatement as the princess of the region. But she had no interest in the affairs of state, or in the wealth and power associated with her position. Her one-pointed focus remained her surrender to the Divine Lord, a condition that caused extreme consternation to both sides of the family, especially since Mira refused her expected "wifely duties" to her husband, choosing instead to arrange meetings with the wise sadhus (holy men) who wandered the countryside. From them she learned of the exploits of her true husband—Giridhara Gopal, Madhava, Hari, Shyam, Krishna. To Mira, these holy names were her sustenance and security.

Sister, the sound of the flute
Has driven me crazy.
Without Hari, nothing avails.
On hearing the sounds

> I lose body-consciousness,
> My heart well caught
> In the meshes of the net.
> What vows and observances have you performed,
> O flute? Who is now at your side?
> The magic of those seven notes
> Has entrapped even Mira's Lord Himself.[23]

Legends abound about the family's attempts to straighten Mira's priorities, or to chastise her for her foolishness and stubbornness. Before and even after the death of her husband, his relatives attempted to bring her into line. When milder efforts failed, they made attacks upon her life. One story tells that her mother-in-law sent her a decorated gift basket. When Mira opened the present she was greeted with the hissing of a cobra. "Oh, beloved friend of Hari," she said, "Can you tell me where my Krishna is?" And through her tears, Mira sang a love song for her absent Lord, while the cobra began to dance.

On another occasion she was surprised to find that a bed of nails had been placed in her room. Lying down upon this platform, however, Mira went into ecstasy as the nails transformed into rose petals, a gift from her lover, Hari.

Undaunted, her husband's family attempted to murder her outright with a poisonous draught. A favorite drink was stiffly laced with arsenic and brought to the heartsick princess as a tonic. Offering the cup to Lord Krishna, as she offered all her food in an act of devotion and gratitude, Mira downed the poison as if it were the most delightful nectar. Again, she was thrown into ecstasy, drunk as if from the finest wine.

> Binding my ankles with silver
> I danced—
> people in town called me crazy.
> She'll ruin the clan,
> said my mother-in-law,
> and the prince

324

had a cup of venom delivered.
I laughed as I drank it.
Can't they see?—
body and mind aren't something to lose,
the Dark One's already seized them.
Mira's lord can lift mountains,
he is her refuge.[24]

Some say that, before his death, her husband's remorse was so great in learning of her innocence and blessedness that he finally released her from her marriage vows, leaving her free to pursue the life she most wanted, that of a free woman, sustained by the songs of her heart. In other accounts, Mira is cast out of the family fold after the deaths of her husband and his father. But in either case, she was liberated, and it was then that her legacy to history began. Mira spent the rest of her life traveling from town to town, carrying her message of annihilating love in the songs she composed and sang.

Do not mention the name of love,
O my simple-minded companion.
Strange is the path
When you offer your love.
Your body is crushed at the first step.
If you want to offer love
Be prepared to cut off your head
And sit on it.
Be like the moth,
Which circles the lamp and offers its body.
Be like the deer, which, on hearing the horn,
Offers its head to the hunter.
Be like the partridge,
Which swallows burning coals
In love of the moon.
Be like the fish,
Which yields up it life

When separated from the sea.
Be like the bee,
Entrapped in the closing petals of the lotus.
Mira's Lord is the courtly Giridhara
She says: Offer your mind
To those lotus feet.[25]

One delicious tale of her bravery and one-pointedness in later life involves a lowlife sadhu who claimed that Krishna had commanded him to make love to her. Drawing the man into a streetside crowd of worshippers who sang their songs of love to the Dark One, Mira laid a cloak upon the ground and started to remove her robe. As she looked piercingly into the sadhu's eyes, the man fell at her feet, confessed his lie, and begged to become her devotee.

FOR LOVE OF THE DARK ONE

Mira's poetry calls the reader out of complacency. Her life can touch us if we are willing to believe in love beyond reason. Mirabai shows us that a woman's soul may be frustrated with its own internal demand that any "one" or any "thing" be her ultimate fulfillment. No husband, friends, children or work will ever satisfy the woman who is not already in love with herself, that is, with the One who is her very Self. Such a woman knows that she is capable of a rare love, a love that fully embraces her partner, her family and her personal responsibilities, yet expands far beyond the limits of any singular relationship to encompass the world.

Many women (and men) today will find inspiration in Mirabai's courage in breaking with the traditional stereotypes imposed on women. She refused the expectation that she endure conventional marriage. But even more appropriate to our times, she was never put off from her goal to pursue her unique spiritual practice by the threatening actions or words of others. I know many women whose longing for spiritual life is dampened by their cynical or conservative partners or family members. Mira didn't reject such opposition, rather she transformed the energy of it. Whatever poison they attempted to feed her she turned into medicine, a nectar in fact, which only served to increase her passion, her devotion and her gratitude.

> This infamy, O my Prince,
> is delicious!
> Some revile me,
> others applaud,
> I simply follow my incomprehensible road.
> A razor-thin path
> but you meet some good people,
> a terrible path but you hear a true word.
> Turn back?
> Because the wretched stare and see nothing?
> O Mira's lord is noble and dark,
> and slanderers
> rake only themselves
> over the coals.[26]

Mira's poems are a legacy of the paradoxes of the mystical ascent. Her moods of love and bliss were intermingled with periods of great pain. While she knew beyond doubt that her Lord was completely united with her, she also experienced the all-consuming suffering of one who was separated from her lover and must seek him out everywhere, wait upon him eternally, and sometimes pine in anguish and even fear that she had lost favor with him. This mystery of love-in-separation holds a place of ultimate regard in the devotional life of the Hindu, and there are similar expressions of it in Christianity and Sufism alike. (Mira's contemporary, St. Teresa of Avila, wrote poetry filled with the same enigma.)

On one hand Mirabai could sing:

> O My dear companion,
> Now that I have seen the Lord,
> All my desires are fulfilled
> And my sufferings forgotten.

Shyam, the Ocean of Joy, Mira's Lord,
Has entered her home.[27]

And on the other hand she lamented:

O my companion,
Shyam shot an arrow
That has pierced me through.
The fire of longing
Is burning in my heart
And my whole body is in torment.
My roving mind cannot stir,
Fettered in the chains of love.
No one but myself and my Beloved
Knows the extent of my pain.
I can do nothing, my companions,
But weep copious tears.
Mira says: "My Lord, unless you come
My life cannot endure."[28]

Mira's poetry alerts us to the exquisite, fervent and even erotic
rasa that may characterize one's relationship to God. Especially if
we have been raised in body-negative religious cultures, women
today may fear this association of sexuality and spirituality. Some
will feel threatened and embarrassed when the juiciness of female-
ness begins to be awakened within their spiritual life, when sexual
feelings and images "intrude." In a recent workshop I conducted, a
young woman, very attractive and well-dressed, interrupted me
after the first hour. She was greatly disturbed by my reference to
the relationship to God in terms of a Lover, and the sexual over-
tones of this presentation. "Why, it would never occur to me," she
said, as the color in her neck began to deepen, "to think of God in
such a way. Why would anyone do that?"

For Mira, there was no separation between the heart and the
limbs. Every cell of her body longed for Krishna. She could not
compose poetry with the fire that still singes the pages of books

if she were closed off or dead as a sexual being. The whole domain of Tantra, that form of religious expression in which all elements of life are considered as sacred and used to bring one closer to the divine—this was Mira's backyard. With Mira, we can celebrate this full-bodied expression of our Love for God. We can honor ourselves and even feed this longing by reading her poetry.

> O my companion, I will install
> That lotus-like figure in my eyes.
> Now Shyam has come
> And I dare not blink.
> Murari has come to dwell in my heart,
> Every instant I enjoy His sight.
> I adorn myself to receive Shyam
> And prepare a bed for His enjoyment.
> Mira's Lord is the courtly Giridhara,
> Again and again she offers Him her all.[29]

Finally, Mira's love for Krishna drew her to Radha, Krishna's primary consort. She prayed to Radha, asking for help in how to love her Lord. There was no jealousy here, but rather the recognition that in the Lord's company all hearts have equal access.

> I offer myself in sacrifice
> To her lotus feet.
> Darling Radha stands in supplication,
> Saying, "O Krishna Murari,
> Hear my prayer."[30]

The lovers of Krishna form a community of lovers, all longing together. As the *gopis* learned after Krishna's departure, we need one another for mutual remembrance and encouragement in our devotion. We can rely upon one another for that same encouragement in the expression of our art.

AN INVITATION

Perhaps this is the time to put down the book and pick up the artifacts of creation—a drawing pad and pencils, the rake and the hoe; the clay and the water; the wool and the cotton, the pen and the paper. Perhaps it is time to begin the inner work in earnest by entering the cave of the heart with these tools of prayer; or to reinforce an ongoing practice by taking the next creative risk— like telling a deeper level of truth than we have yet allowed ourselves; giving ourselves permission to howl, like Janis Joplin and Anne Waldman; entering more courageously into the radiant darkness that Meinrad has shown us, expressing the glorious greenness that Hildegard praises or singing the longing that Mirabai lived, but in a new form—our own form. Only by "making" will we come to know the truth of Woman's way.

10

THE PATH OF THE BODY
THE PATH OF SEX

*S*exuality is part of what it means to be human. Sexual energy is synonymous with life energy, regardless of whether it is expressed genitally or not. To address the most basic questions of how sexuality and spirituality can be integrated is to touch at the heart of the human dilemma. We might as well ask, how are matter and spirit to relate? Or, what's the interplay of body and soul?

Those of us who read spiritual literature, even if we've only begun our journey of self-discovery, have probably encountered the concept of sexual tantra. If that particular term is foreign to us, we have perhaps found references to the idea that sex and sexual energy can be a most elegant and efficient doorway into spiritual ecstasy; and beyond that, a jet-propelled vehicle for bringing one to the threshold of the chamber of God. Even in the writings of some of the celibate mystics of Christianity (at least the more life-positive ones), it is clearly presented that one's sexual passion can be sublimated (made sublime, not repressed) into passion for the Divine Beloved.

The difficulty is that, despite these great claims for liberation through sex, more of us still carry in our bodies the inheritance—physical, psychological, emotional, psychic and spiritual—of at least four generations of women and men whose views on sex were clouded by fear, disconnected from an actual "body" of wisdom, and strongly influenced by the culture's perverse and rigid views. Even if we are successful in liberating our *minds* from the insanity of a sex-negative relationship to life, we will need tremendous diligence to make inroads deep into our cells, where these memories and instructions are stored. The body doesn't easily give up its rigidity—rigidity is falsely assumed to support its survival. I know this particular dilemma of the spiritual path first-hand. My own years, from age eighteen to twenty six, spent as a nun in a Catholic convent, were ripe and rich, full of great experiences and training in discipline, practice and prayer. Yet, in all that time, no education was ever offered about the interplay of my female sexuality within the lifestyle I had chosen. Here we were, dedicated, juicy and enthusiastic young women who longed for a deeper connection with the Divine, a connection that would bring full flowering to our spiritual purpose. Our training was completely lopsided and life-negative, it was completely devoid of an appreciation of the body's role in spirituality. As far as I was concerned, sexual feelings were sinful, and the random images of sexual expression that floated across my mind, uninvited, were cause for extreme concern and immediate confession.

To make matters worse, as a novice (a nun-in-training), dressed in black with a spotless white veil on my head to symbolize my purity, I was handed a small knotted whip and told by my Mother Superior that one of our community's practices was to flagellate oneself every Friday in the privacy of one's room. "Taking the discipline" as it was called, was meant to help us identify with the sufferings of Christ. But the overriding message, reinforced from years of religious indoctrination, was that the body was the source of sin and therefore must be subdued if spiritual progress was to be made.

Like so many other women, I stored my shame about my body, together with my confusion and ambivalence about sex, in my belly—specifically in my womb. No huge surprise that, less than two years after leaving the convent and getting married, at age twenty-eight, I was a candidate for a complete hysterectomy, necessitated, (I will never know whether it was necessary or not.) by a long-standing case of endometriosis which had swelled my ovaries to the size of grapefruits.

Although there are physical explanations for my condition, what I now know about energy-medicine has convinced me that this endometriosis was the result of years of sexual tension and fear localized in the area of my womb. In 1973, I too became another statistic of the "when in doubt, cut it out" approach to gynecology. My womb, which should be the seat of woman's power, was removed.

Author, teacher and former Buddhist nun, Tsultrim Allione has beautifully explained this connection between the womb and women's power:

> I really feel that the center of power and wisdom for a woman is the womb area, what I call the "triangle of power," extending above the actual pubic triangle and including the lower abdomen, or hara. I believe that women really think from their wombs; that's why they are so connected to life and to concepts of peace, rather than to war making and death. Peace and the maintenance of life are actually the "logic of the womb."
>
> I've had experiences in which I felt that I was being led by this "triangle of power" in the center of my body. All my conditioned desires to be ashamed of femaleness, to hide—which I think most women share—were gone, and I felt that I was emanating this incredible femininity and wisdom. I think women really need to find this in themselves.[1]

333

What that hysterectomy has done to me physically is relatively clear, after more than twenty years of life on synthetic hormones. What it has done emotionally, psychically and spiritually, as far as affecting the energy-body matrix, continues to reveal itself over time. How does Shakti awaken in a woman's body when she is armored in grief and fear from the waist down?[2] How does a woman with no womb relate to the necessity to become Mother to all of creation? How can one expect energy to flow smoothly throughout the body when all the major *chi*-meridians (used in acupuncture) are intersected with a massive scar from navel to pubes? These are issues that I have dealt with and continue to encounter at each new stage of sadhana.

And while I no longer blame either my doctors or my teachers in the Catholic Church—they were merely passing along the sorry legacy that they had received from their superiors—I am determined and even passionate in my desire to reclaim my body as sacred, in order to be of service to my teacher and the Work, for as long as possible.

If our involvement in the spiritual path is to profit us anything, it should profit us a transformation of body-negative/life-negative attitudes into attitudes of bodily celebration and appreciation. If our prayer is to evolve, deepen and expand, I am convinced that it must extend beyond the domains of mind and heart and allow the whole body to dance. And, if our prayer is to enter our bodies, redeeming the organs, the limbs, the skin, the glands, and reclaiming the body as the sacred vessel it is, then we have no more accurate gauge of our success in this domain than to see its effects upon our appreciation of ourselves as passionate, juicy, sensuous, full-bodied sexual beings. If we are truly becoming women of spirit, we will be loosening our rigidity, both of muscle and of attitude.

The Indian saint, Mahadeviyakka, appreciated the sacredness of her body. An ecstatic devotee of Lord Shiva, whom she referred to as her White Jasmine Lord, Mahadeviyakka stopped wearing clothing and wandered the countryside naked, singing the praise of God to all who would listen. Her poetry affirms the innate beauty of the honored body of woman.

Coins in the hand
Can be stolen,
But who can rob this body
Of its own treasure?

The last thread of clothing
Can be stripped away,
But who can peel off Emptiness,
That nakedness covering all?

Fools, while I dress
In the Jasmine Lord's morning light,
I cannot be shamed—
What would you have me hide under silk
And the glitter of jewels?[3]

      —Mahadeviyakka (12th Century)

LOVING HER HOLY BODY

At age four, my friend Annie loved her body very much. She and her mom lived in our household for nearly a year. Every day, just before noon, one of us would pick up Annie from her pre-school playgroup. Annie would typically bound from the car, run up the steps of the front porch, bang noisily through the door and announce: "I'm home," to whomever happened to be around. Then she would proceed to strip off every article of clothing she had worn so appropriately for the past three or four hours. "Ah," she'd sigh, ecstatically, "Now I can get naked again." And naked she would stay, at least during the warm months, until it was necessary to leave the house with Mom or me to shop or visit friends.

Because she had been raised consciously, unindoctrinated with shame related to her beautiful young body, Annie had no sense that anything about her was "dirty," and she therefore had no reticence about the enjoyment of her holy body. She and her other girl friends loved nothing better than to play "pregnant"—a game in which they would tie a soft toy or favorite doll over their bellies, under a loose shirt. When it came time to "give birth," the pregnant one would spread her legs and then reach up under her shirt and yank the doll out, amid the sweet cooings of the assembled friends. "Oh, what a beautiful baby you have." And then they'd have a tea party.

Sometimes the girls would surprise us, playing the game at most inauspicious times, like when an uptight relative was visiting. I often wondered if the girls deliberately planned such incidents just to see what would happen.

Annie's mother and the other women in our community had explained the processes of sex and birth and death in such a way that they were both natural and wondrous. Annie's body was wondrous to her, and she unabashedly remarked: "I love my *yoni*" (the Hindu word for vagina)—which early on she had discovered as a great source of pleasure.

Imagine for a moment how life might have been different for any of us if we too had been raised and educated with a reverence for the sacredness of our bodies? If, from birth, when mother or dad changed our diapers, they didn't wrinkle their noses at the sight or smell of our urine and feces, but had rejoiced with us and even encouraged our interest in the awesome processes of transformation that were going on within us, and in our cooperation with the earth's natural recycling—from seed to plant to food to shit to fertilizer to new plant.

Imagine how different our relationship to our own sexuality, and those of our sexual partners, might have been if we had been nursed on demand, and allowed to sleep with our parents until we were ready for a room of our own; if we bathed with Mom, and were not discouraged from touching and exploring that mysterious and good-feeling place between our legs. Suppose that our mother explained the wonder of our female anatomy in a way that communicated her reverence for her body, and that at six or seven we were even permitted to witness the actual birth of our younger

336

brother or sister, born into the family bed, as we had been?

Such life-positive education might very well result in nurturing self-confidence and self-appreciation to the degree that we would have little doubt about the interrelatedness of sexuality and spirituality. Unfortunately, women in Western culture frequently have difficulty in accepting and loving their bodies. No wonder "sacred sex" generally remains an idea, rarely penetrating us at the cellular level. No wonder we are slaves of the advertising media, so easily convinced, from our earliest years, that appearances are everything.

THE TANTRIC PATH

In 1993, at the first annual conference on Crazy Wisdom and Divine Madness, Tibetan Buddhist teacher and scholar Dr. Reginald Ray spoke about the difficulty that Westerners have in appreciating many of the concepts that are a natural foundation in the Buddhist tradition. First and foremost, he argued, those of us raised within Judaic-Christian culture are indoctrinated to believe that we are essentially flawed—sinful and needing salvation. Even if our families have long-ago decried their religious upbringing as being inadequate, the archetypes of sin versus righteousness or good versus evil still predominate as hallmarks of European-Christian civilization. The Tantric Buddhist worldview, however, arises not from a linear dichotomy but from a circle of transformation and rebirth. Its foundation is that of "basic goodness" as our birthright. (See: Chögyam Trungpa's brilliantly clear explanations in, *Shambhala: The Sacred Path of the Warrior*. New York: Bantam, 1986.) Imagine how different your life might have been if instead of fear and apprehension and comparison and inadequacy being the standards of your emotional life, there had been this appreciation of basic goodness so deeply ingrained that you would never question that you were indeed the child of God, or the embodiment of the Goddess.

To simplify a very ancient and precise science and art, tantra may be thought of as a mature spiritual practice which is characterized by the non-rejection of all things, including and especially

337

the senses. Non-rejection does not mean indulgence in everything, a common mistake of those who have a scanty understanding of this profound discipline. Tantra is unlike the moralistic religious codes most of us were raised with. Instead, it is a spiritual practice that actual embraces elements which were formally considered as sinful and unholy—the use of the senses, of sex, the use of alcohol and drugs, the use of meat, and other things. Just knowing that such a worldview exists may be sufficient to encourage us to a greater degree of self-acceptance. At best, such inkling may encourage further investigation of this vast field of study and life practice.

Author and tantric Buddhist scholar Miranda Shaw elaborated upon the theme of basic goodness in her wonderful book *Passionate Enlightenment* (Princeton University Press, 1994) when she used the life and teaching of Vajrayogini, a manifestation of the female Buddha, to describe the "divine pride" which is the distinguishing virtue of the spiritual woman.

> Vajrayogini insists that all women and female beings in the universe are her embodiments (*rupa*), or manifestations, and thus should be respected, honored, and served without exception.
>
> Respect for women was enjoined upon both men and women, although it has different implications for their respective development. For women, the relationship with Vajrayogini is one of identity. Women must discover the divine female essence within themselves. This should inspire self-respect, confidence, and the "divine pride" that is necessary to traverse the Tantric path. Divine pride, or remembering one's ultimate identity as a deity, is qualitatively different from arrogance, for it is not motivated by a sense of deficiency or compensatory self-aggrandizement. This pride is an antidote to self-doubt and discouragement and an expression of the pure Tantric view. When a woman re-

claims her divine identity, she does not need to seek outer sources of approval, for a bottomless reservoir of self-esteem emanates from the depths of her own being.

...Vajrayogini takes form so that women, seeing enlightenment in female form, will recognize their innate divinity and potential for enlightenment.[4]

The first time I read this passage, I found it so thrilling and encouraging that I wrote about it for days in my journal. Coincidentally, a few months later, my friend Nachama called to tell me that she was planning to interview Miranda Shaw for our community journal and asked if I could help her formulate appropriate questions. We both knew that we wanted to hear more about "divine pride."

Miranda's reply to our question was a message of empowerment for us as spiritual-sexual females, and a powerful revelation about how we might approach healing the illness of self-hatred that is an epidemic in female culture.

> Divine pride refers to a fundamental change that takes place on the cellular level. That's why it's related to disease, to well-being on every level. Tantric Buddhism teaches that as a woman your body is pure on every level, in every cell, in every atom. You are absolutely divine and pure. This is a very empowering message when you think about the parts of your body that you have been convinced are impure. In tantric Buddhism it is actually considered to be a transgression—the breaking of a vow—if you believe or act as if your body is impure. For example, if you don't eat enough, or become obsessed with purification, or look at certain kinds of behavior as impure, then that is actually a violation of the tantric worldview. How this plays out in practice is that you treat yourself

as if you are worthy of respect, valuable, and ultimately divine....

Not only is your own sense of worth supposed
to play itself out naturally in relationship, but they
have taken special precautions, that men and
women both know, that men have to show certain kinds of respect and honor in order to create
space for the woman to maintain that divine pride.
There are forms of ritual worship where the man
honors the woman. He offers perhaps incense and
candlelight, rubs perfume on her, honors her naked body in many ways, both externally and internally, non-sexually and sexually, and offers himself for her cultivation of bliss and emptiness. That
is a profound affirmation for the woman—to receive the man as an offering—and to receive the
act of sexuality as a gift of devotion.[5]

Divine pride is not about the posture of self-esteem. It is one
thing to put on a flowing robe, put a crystal around your neck, and
waltz through a room with your head held high. It is another thing
to have such penetrating knowledge of inherent goodness that one
radiates that recognition regardless of clothing or circumstances.
Such knowledge comes from the inside out.

Tantra remains a dangerous path. There are so many potential traps to *enhance* the ego rather than to master it, which is why
the serious practice of Tantra is never recommended without a
qualified teacher. Serious tantric practice is most often hard won
too, as is waking up, as we've discussed already.

While it is well beyond the scope of this book to suggest a
practice of Tantra, it is within our power, first of all, to recognize
and begin to tell the truth about how we don't live from the
context of self-love, how our bodies are not our own, and how
our sexuality is still being determined by the voices of others,
including the media. I suggest a "diet" for the elimination of
self-hatred—a diet that involves not the abstinence from food

but the fierce and passionate resolution to turn off the television (cold-turkey!), to burn the fashion magazines, throw away the mail order catalogs and to stay out of clothing stores, for at least one month, during which time we take a ruthlessly honest assessment of the lies that we have bought about who we are and how we are supposed to look and perform. While I doubt that many will ever attempt my method, such a "fast" is designed to help us take our power back, and to recognize that we have been duped, with our own consent, into this position of weakness and hypnotic vulnerability.

Secondly, we may wish to read further about the female deities of Tibetan Tantric Buddhism, with the recognition in mind that we are ultimately reading about ourselves—the "goddesses 'r us," so to speak. Thirdly, we can open ourselves to pursuing Tantra seriously by taking on a recognized and respected teacher, male or female, who can appropriately guide us in this vital undertaking.

DIVINE MOTHER'S SISTERS

Divine Mother, or the wisdom of the Feminine, speaks to us and instructs us in many ways, not the least of which is in the witness and words of our friends and peers. For this reason it is extremely important to cultivate friendships with women, as well as nurture opportunities for working together, particularly with women who share a spiritual aim. Whether we find wisdom in a younger woman or in a woman older than our grandmother, we should apprentice to those who exemplify wisdom, seek out their company and do everything in our power to draw from them the kind of advice, example and energy we crave. In one of our friends perhaps, we will see gentle elegance at work, even under conditions of great stress. With another, we may feel a healing energy that literally blesses all she touches. In a third woman, we may experience a joyful spontaneity which bespeaks the freedom that we deeply cherish. These are the women who will help us re-orient toward a life-positive relationship to our bodies and our sexuality. These are women to keep company with.

I consider myself an apprentice to such a woman. Lalitha came into my life shortly after I met my spiritual teacher, Lee. She gave a talk at a workshop sponsored by his community. While I actually don't remember the content of that talk, what I do recall is that she had scarcely opened her mouth when I said to myself, "This woman can teach me something." I've stayed around her ever since.

Lalitha was six years younger than I, yet her pure white hair, her sparkling blue eyes, and the power in her words communicated an ageless wisdom. She spoke with authority about conserving and managing energy for sadhana. She was well-versed in tantric practice, was highly creative in healing and the use of herbal medicine, and showed a profound understanding of children.

That was over thirteen years ago. Today her brilliance is even more enticing. Her relationship with her male partner, who is fifteen years her junior, has flowered over the years, producing a model of joyful and creative relationship which is instructive to the rest of our community. She has written two fantastic books about natural health. She currently offers workshops on sexuality and the essence of Baul practice both in the U.S. and Europe.

Accessing Lalitha's inner wisdom on the subjects that she knows well, is not always easy, however. There is a price to be paid for what the wise woman offers—and not necessarily a monetary one. Lalitha is just as likely to dismiss a merely curious questioner with a curt response. Her matter-of-fact intensity has distanced many who look to her to give them "a pill for every ill" in her capacity as healer, or to find in her some reinforcement for their own illusions of separation. Lalitha will simply not bend to neurosis. She has little choice or no choice but to call it as she sees it.

Wise women are not always easy to understand. More than simple logic must be used in apprehending their words. As will be seen in the interview which follows, Lalitha demands some effort, some reading between the lines on our part, if we are to appreciate what she talks about.

These sometimes raw and difficult aspects of Lalitha's persona and manner of presentation are like guarded gates that we have to pass through in order to reach her wisdom heart. Like the female *tantrikas* (*yoginis* or *dakinis*) that Miranda Shaw describes below, Lalitha remains a delightful, yet dangerous enigma.

The literature presents women who are physically and mentally powerful, speak the truth fearlessly, anger easily, love to argue, never back down in an argument, undergo wide mood swings, and laugh and cry easily. They are described as proud and arrogant, aggressive and domineering, fearless and intoxicated by their ferocity. They are said not only to be untamed but to revel in their untamability.[6]

For those who are ready and willing to stay in Lalitha's company, despite the fire of her eyes and her ability to wither you with a word, one who is ready to serve her and to offer her a testimony of truthworthiness (basically the knowledge that one will seriously utilize what she offers), there is so much to be gained from her dynamic and insightful presence.

LALITHA MA REMEMBERS

Lalitha's life has been marked with a series of tragedies. Her mother committed suicide when Lalitha was twenty, and it was she who cleaned her mother's blood from the walls and floor of the room. Her younger brother drowned as a young man; another brother has spent the major portion of his adolescent and adult life in prison. These experiences have earned Lalitha an attitude of fierceness and genuine broken-heartedness that serve as the foundation for her compassion.

In her mid-twenties, as an apprentice to a master healer, Lalitha began to have "remembrances" (as she calls them) of her life's destiny, coupled with the visionary instruction and teachings of Mother Mira of Pondicherry, India, who became her guide on these early steps of the path. The Mother, as Mira is known, was an accomplished musician whose ardent love for God won her a place of honor at the side of one of the most highly respected spiritual teachers of the time. She became the lifelong partner of the great Indian sage, Sri Aurobindo.

In her remembrances, Lalitha connected to the original impulse—her own union with the principle of Divine Mother, her complete identification with that One. Yet, unlike many who have gone off to establish their own teaching work as a result of such revelation, Lalitha's instructions from the Mother were to associate herself with a particular living spiritual master. Her relationship of love, enthusiastic service and devotion to him was to build the necessary matrix to sustain her own work, while serving his work. Lalitha described the revelation:

> After her death, Mother Mira would frequently appear to me and teach me. I would have conversations with her. One day I told her that I knew that I was in for a hard life and that it would be a great help to have a living master's strength and guidance. I told her I would rather bow down to someone's feet, and that it was too bad that she was not still alive. Mother agreed that there was no substitute for a living master, and that she would show me what to do.

> Also during that time I knew that I would be working with tantra, because I already had so much information that Mother had taught me about energy and sexual practices, and how men and women could work together. I had experienced a lot of these principles in my own career as a healer. But Mother told me, specifically, that it would be unsafe for me to practice tantra or teach it publicly until I had the protection of a spiritual master.
>
> The following year, some friends introduced me to a teacher they were interested in. You have to understand, by this point in my life I had been a healer for many years, and I had helped to start a successful healing center where I had seen every

kind of powerful yogi and swami, and psychic and preacher and tarot-card reader, and astrologer...men and women of power, of every race and age that you can imagine. I was not interested in meeting yet another "yogi-schmogi," as I called them. When I finally met this guy, I found him endearing and sweet, yet very clumsy—what I would call a wimp. So it was much to my surprise that Mother Mira told me that I should stick to him, no matter what, and do whatever he said.

"I know you think he's kind of klutzy and appears awkward," Mother said to me (in so many words), "but he is a pure and true master and there is no one like him. Never mind what it looks like. He is a perfect tantric master, and you'll realize the truth of all this as time goes on," which I did. Within a short period of time his "fool's garb" became transparent. He was dazzling and magnetic for me, and extraordinarily powerful in his help.

On a cool Spring morning in 1996 I interviewed Lalitha in the living room of her home. Sun poured through the huge windows that faced a mountain valley. The cactus and scrub oak outside were brilliantly contrasted by the greenness in every corner of the room in which we sat. Towering geraniums flowered red, white or pink on every window ledge. A huge fern filled one corner of the room, while a vine of philodendron wound its way up the whole length of the staircase and along the balcony to the second floor, creating a curtain of green. The healing energy of her plants was everywhere. The healing energy of her presence was even more profound.

I wanted to know about tantra and sexuality from a perspective that I was not finding in books. Lalitha has spent many years studying and practicing elements of Baul *sadhana* (spiritual practice), from the Bauls of Bengal, India, and in 1994 spent one month at a tiny Baul ashram in Bengal where her primary purpose was to

Lalitha

absorb what she could from the Baulinis, or female Bauls who lived there. In applying what she learned to Western psychology, Lalitha has many strong opinions and cautions for women who wish to pursue this path of "higher" sexuality as the way to God.

SEXUAL COMMUNION, AND BEYOND: AN INTERVIEW

I began by asking Lalitha how a woman can begin to connect, in a practical way, with sexuality as a force that will evolve into spirituality.

LALITHA: In the Baul tradition, specifically, but also in other spiritual traditions, including the Buddhist tradition, when we talk about sexuality we are not only talking about the physical act of sex. So, the woman who is celibate is not excluded from our consideration. Rather, we are talking about sexuality as a transformative process. This means that an ordinary woman can learn about the laws of energy, including sexual energy. Then by participating in these laws *on purpose*, in a conscious way, she can slowly undergo a transformation within her physical body, her subtle body, and her emotions. Everything about her, including her sexuality, will start to reflect the finely-honed attention that she is generating.

To link into these transformative elements of sexuality, which are vastly different from the common view of sexuality, requires strength and skill in many other areas first. In Baul *sadhana* I would call this "building a matrix to hold transformational substances." What I am talking about has nothing to do with skill in having sex. I've heard women say that they're "really good at sex," or that their partner can withhold ejaculation for a long time, or whatever—which is just fine at the exoteric level, and of course may feel really good. But that is not linking into a transformative mechanism. That is linking into a heightened emotional counterpart of self-gratification. This whole mood of self-gratification, that we are imbued with from birth, must be questioned if we are to pursue sex as a path of spiritual unfoldment.

REGINA: Are you speaking of surrender that must be present for any higher practice of sex?

LALITHA: Concepts like "surrender" are grossly misunderstood. Women have asked me whether "surrender," as they read about it in spiritual literature, means that they just lay down and let their partner have his (or her) way with them. When we hear these terms, which are refined spiritual principles, we automatically try to fit them into what we already know about such concepts, which really isn't much. Then we turn them into an ugly package that leaves us dissatisfied, as if something is missing in our approach to sex as a gateway to spirituality.

Well, in this case we're right—there *is* something missing. What's missing is the understanding that, in the Baul tradition, which is a tantric tradition, sexual union with a partner is about working with the balance of masculine and feminine energy within ourselves. The tantric practitioner knows that through sexual activity, the body's inherent transformative mechanism can be activated. This means moving out of self-gratification as our essential motivation, and moving toward a much broader and more profound relationship with all elements of life, which is what Tantra is. Normally, when we say, "I have a relationship with Henry," the connotation of that word "relationship" is that we are having sex with Henry. But relationship from the tantric perspective is much broader than that; it is actually all-encompassing.

REGINA: Are you saying that many of us should not even consider this higher aspect of sexuality until some other basic elements of our lives are more balanced, better handled?

LALITHA: Yes that's exactly what I'm saying. To consider the transformative mechanism of sexuality we have to be well beyond the stages of "puppy love," or attraction based solely on appearance. Well beyond the questions of, "Do you fight or not?" "Do you have enough sex or not?" These considerations should already be well on their way to being handled, if not successfully lived, before serious tantric practice is engaged. This is a process of years—long years. A great deal of honesty and patience is required in approaching this work.

To get really practical, I have a list of questions that I use in my sexuality workshop by which people can access what point in this progression of sexual/spiritual maturity they are starting from. For example, one set of questions is, "When I am out at a gathering with my sexual mate, and someone else approaches to talk to us, do I find it necessary to always be physically touching my mate?" Another is: "Do other people feel comfortable approaching us, or do they sense that they're interrupting a hot session of sexual innuendoes between us?" The point here is that many of us are so steeped in our degree of self-gratification with our partner that we negate relationship on every other level. That negation automatically closes the door on the transformative mechanism of sexuality.

To use another example, suppose a woman has the issue that many raise to me: "When I am having sex, my partner is being sexually-gratified, but I am not," or something along that line. But here again, I assert that when our attention on sexuality is focused in these areas, then we can be sure that, for the time being, we are operating from an extremely limited scope of what relationship is all about. Concern with "getting my satisfaction" or him getting "his satisfaction" is pretty much an indicator of having a closed door on transformational sexuality.

This is not to say that sexual satisfaction should be ignored! Nor am I saying that one should simply surrender to a misshapen sexual relationship under the guise of being less self-centered. But, the predominant mood of "How much am I being satisfied?" is an indicator of where the communication between the couple is. Most often, when a person says they are unsatisfied about their sexual relationship, they are also saying they are unable to talk about it with their mate, or their mate is not in agreement with them, or not able to work with them on it. In other words, the couple has no real purpose in common; no purpose that subsumes the individual issues.

Our questions and areas of discomfort as a couple can be indicators of our possibility of pursuing a common goal of sexual communion. Expressions of dissatisfaction about sex often indicate similar dissatisfaction in our relationship to life in general.

I also ask people to consider such questions as: "Do I have a quota of sexual frequency that I prefer, and which I pressure my partner to meet?" And, "If I don't get sex when I want it, do I tend to have fights with my mate? Do I tend to eat more? Does not getting enough physical sex result in side effects that are unpleasant to me?" If the answer is yes to any of these questions, that's another warning light that we are severely limiting the possibilities inherent in what I call "sexual communion."

REGINA: Can you explain what you mean by this term "sexual communion"?

LALITHA: I have coined a few terms that help to make distinctions about various stages of sexual relationship. The word "sexuality" alone might apply to the traditional, conventional activities of coupled relationship. To imply a heightened awareness of sexual possibilities, however, I use the terms "sexual communion" and "communion reciprocity." These terms imply an *exchange* of profound intimacy between people—not just sexual partners, but adults and children, adults and friends. The "exchange" is the key— a giving and receiving (not taking!) inherent in the nature of higher sexual practice. *Reciprocity* becomes the focus, as compared to issues about individual satisfaction that we often get stuck in with our conventional sexual relationships.

REGINA: How does one take the leap from conventional sexuality into sexual communion or communion reciprocity?

LALITHA: This is a good question because most couples who eventually achieve some degree of communion reciprocity, as I use the term, didn't start off with a common purpose for this. Only later, sometimes after years of experimentation with broken or unsatisfactory relationships, have they ventured into this new arena.

350

Most couples who attend my seminars start out with the basic issue of how to fix up their relational messes. Yet, these same couples voice some vague hope that something wonderful, but as yet unknown and secretly longed for, might yet come into play in their relationship. For most people, however, this "hope" is where it ends. It all remains some dream of what could be.

Nonetheless, this intuition of where we are at and where we *might go* regarding intimacy is the starting point in progressing from conventional sexuality to the consideration of transformative sexuality. The next step is establishing common purpose.

REGINA: Please say more about common purpose.

LALITHA: It is essential for a couple to have a true purpose in common regarding what they expect and where they are going with their relationship. In my seminars, couples usually start off insisting that they already have a common purpose. Very quickly, upon further questioning, the partners start arguing when they discover that neither has the same purpose as the other. Commonly, they find that they have a lot of mistaken assumptions at play. As they engage this process of determining common purpose, they undoubtedly discover that many of their privately-held desires and concerns were simply learned habits collected throughout their lives. Ideas about sexual satisfaction might stem entirely from what they learned from TV as a child. And they must see through all this before they can be available for the profound and searing intimacy involved in "communion reciprocity." Such higher purpose can subsume, and will subsume, many of our individual or privately-held concerns. This is essential to tapping into the transformative nature of sexuality.

Ideally, a true purpose for relationship would be considered before an intimate relationship was committed to, but this is rare. I'm not saying that people need to have a complete picture of their ultimate transformational destiny when they start out, but at least that they get in touch with their intuitions, and acknowledge the *possibility* for relationship as a means of transformation. We can

351

still move in the direction of some higher purpose without fully understanding its implications. We don't have to know exactly where or how we will end up, we just have to have the courage and the flexibility to work with the unexpected.

In the beginning we couldn't possibly understand the implications of genuine tantra or transformational relationship anyway. But, we can be sure that what I am talking about will not look like the "secure," conventional, convenient and predictable relationships we have been brought up to emulate.

REGINA: What you are explaining sounds like a lifelong learning process which we in the West haven't been prepared for, either by the way we have been parented, or by the spiritual-cultural milieu in which we have been raised.

LALITHA: That's true. But, transformative possibility is already locked into the body—it is a part of our cells. The problem is that we can't reach it because we don't acknowledge that it exists, first of all, and secondly because we have been raised within such narrowly-defined limits which blind us to these possibilities even once we start getting a glimpse of them.

I'll use an example with regard to children that can practically apply to us as adults. We can teach our children, physically and emotionally, even from infancy, to appreciate the endless variety of choices available to them in life. With regard to food, for instance, if I am an adult who has grown up on steak, potatoes and ice cream, and I think, "Well, I've done perfectly fine," then that is what I'll model for my kids. By narrowing their choices in the domain of food, I will be giving them a similarly limited, although unconscious view of relationships in general. Our own misguided ideas about the nature of relationship were *taught* to us in the same subtle ways.

If our children have learned that they can make choices based on a broad scope of life-positive possibilities, they will be less uptight about their sexuality in general, especially when they reach the horny stage of puberty. They will have a foundation to stand on.

Recently, I was with a group of adolescent women whose parents have been involved in spiritual life for many years. These young women have been exposed, since childhood, to the transformational principles I've been speaking about. They were talking about how to choose a sexual partner. They were saying, "I don't think Tony would be so good for you because he doesn't care about himself, and he just isn't aware of being kind and generous." I thought they were extremely mature and insightful.

Moreover, these young women have demonstrated to me, over the years, that they are able to *act* on their words. They *will* choose the young man who is kind over the aggressive, prize-winning football player, even though the more handsome or popular guy might be saying: "Com'on with me baby, and you'll be the life of the party."

In contrast, other groups of teenagers I've worked with are completely at the whim of whomever puts the most pressure on them, or offers them the most titillating sexual "food" choice. The teenage women who are growing up with familiarity in transformational principles have an internal strength that shows up in simple ways. For example, when faced with a decision of eating chocolate bars or eating a comparably sweet and enticing, but more natural treat that won't give them zits and make them feel sick, they might well choose the latter.

How many of us have this kind of strength and discrimination when we approach questions of sexuality and relationship? How many of us have even *heard* of using our bodies for transformative purposes? We have bad habits, we haven't taken care of our health, and we're so imbued with twisted psychology that to make a conscious choice is practically impossible. A lot of groundwork has to be covered before we can use sexuality as a doorway to higher spiritual work.

REGINA: Okay, we intuit such possibilities exist, and we are working to define our common purpose as a couple. What do we do next?

LALITHA: Well, a practice of rigorous self-observation is always essential. Then, meditation might help, and a better diet might help—any type of activity to strengthen our internal and external ability to pay attention with our minds, to pay attention with our emotions, to focus—that is, to *consciously* place our body's attention. Because when we start on this path, especially in the domain of sexuality and relationships, we realize that our body's attention is not focused. We see a handsome man, we get a sexual signal, immediately we think it means we want to have sex. One man told me that if he's upset he gets horny, if he's angry he gets horny, if he has a bad day at work it makes him horny. And it's the same for many women—that every little setback or signal is translated into some kind of emotional or relational need, because the body's attention is so scattered.

To read and study spiritual literature is another good way to re-gather our energies and focus them. By "studying" I mean "swamping" the mind with reading materials that build an empathy toward being more other-oriented. If we can get the mind to start humming a different tune, then the body can start humming a different tune eventually, because one patterns the other.

I don't advise trying to pick out every separate addiction and every separate bad habit and trying to work on them all separately. But a plan of study, meditation and a healthy diet can automatically take our *whole* package—our emotions, our mind, our body, our illnesses, our cravings—and slowly, steadily re-pattern them. Therefore, co-dependencies and life negative habits begin falling away. The ones that don't fall away, maybe we'll need some help, maybe we'll need therapy, or maybe we'll need to go to AA, but in general, a great majority of things will just fall away as our attention is focused.

I seriously advise everyone, at this stage (and actually all along the way), to attract good company. By that I mean, making sure our friends are people who support us in the direction we want to be going. Ideally, we would have a mate who supports us in this, and we would be making conscious use of all aspects of our life—including our reading material, and the TV that we watch, or don't watch. These influences can pollute the mind and draw it away from the direction we plan to go in. (I would actually suggest eliminating TV watching altogether!)

REGINA: Suppose a woman wants to explore her spiritual path more seriously—say she wants to meditate regularly, or to follow a spiritual teacher, for example. But she finds that the more she does this, the more threatening it becomes to her husband or partner. Or suppose she wants to explore sexuality as a more transformative mechanism, but he doesn't have a clue, so she wants to move on.

LALITHA: The fact is, at this point a lot of relationships just fall apart. A woman or a man may get a glimpse of the transformational possibility (and once you've glimpsed it you're totally hooked), and slowly, or suddenly the self-gratification that they thought they could never do without just starts dissolving. We may find ourselves becoming emptier and emptier—in the sense that we are no longer in a frenzy about food, or about sex, or about trying to find the perfect mate. Instead, we fill our day with more of the finely-honed "foods" that we are speaking about—like spiritual reading or meditation—and our mate feels more and more left out.

I don't advise throwing one's mate out, at least not right in the beginning. As a woman develops this internal and external strength, and slowly builds one-pointed attention, she actually becomes more attractive to everyone, including her partner. A woman's own spiritual practices can make her physically and subtly so radiant—as in "contagious"—that she can actually "contagion" a mate into empathy with her. By surprise, then, her husband will say: "I wasn't even interested in that meditation thing, but my wife was. So now I'll sit with her for ten minutes a day. It's not such a hard thing." Or they might say, "I was really interested in having my martinis every night, but she stopped doing it, so I went along." Over the years, I've worked with couples who have stopped drinking alcohol and are actually excited about drinking chlorophyll and pineapple juice. We can get turned on by the damnedest things! When we change where we place our attention, we can actually collect and refocus our partner's attention into the same direction.

On the other hand, the "contagion particles" which we are emanating can be so strong that they drive people away. We may find that we can't hang out with the same friends anymore, or can't stay in the same job anymore. Our mate may decide to leave us—relationships do fall apart. If we have a codependent relationship, or a violently abusive relationship, or deep-seated psychological difficulties, or addictions like alcohol, caffeine, tobacco—all these things interfere with developing empathy in transformative arenas. So, you can understand why our new ideas can be so threatening that our mate becomes even more violent, if he or she was violent to start with. The whole situation can become pretty ugly.

REGINA: What about the need for the teacher? When does that kind of input become useful?

LALITHA: If we have regrouped and refocused our energy, in the way I am describing, we have become much more finely-tuned spiritual instruments, so to speak. At this point, some women will honestly recognize that, for the time being at least, they want to focus on having a more relaxed and functional sexual life with their partner—something they haven't had before. If that is the goal, then there are many valuable awareness-building activities to engage in—through counseling, sexual seminars, books related to the subject, courses in communication and the like.

Others may feel ready to seriously consider the transformational possibilities of sexuality at a level that calls for a more radical change in their lives; something far-reaching—like "dying to oneself," as it might be called in tantric practice. These individuals really need a teacher. Just to read some books on tantric sex and start this exploration into transformative sexuality on our own is a big mistake, as far as I'm concerned. A spiritual teacher becomes crucial, because sooner or later in this process we are going to reach the dangerous edge from which we must leap into the unknown, because the transformational possibility of sexuality is a voyage into the unknown. And for a voyage into the unknown, there is great danger. A teacher is one who has walked this dangerous part of the path before, he or she can serve as a guide in that journey.

Many of us are naive because we believe we are so well intentioned. I don't think we realize the temptations to distraction that are extremely strong at this juncture, and hereafter in spiritual work, especially in this sexual/spirituality domain. There are all types of "tantric" workshops being offered that sound very enticing. We are led to believe that if we just learn these spiritual techniques and become somewhat philosophical, that we are going to reap great benefits. But what we may actually be reaping is a fancier variety of self-gratification. And the tricky part of this deal is that, to all appearances it will often look like we're getting someplace. We may feel good—after all, we've got strength; we've got a partner who can freely talk about sex, do fancy positions with us, hold back orgasms as long as they want .... It all looks wonderful, and we think we're going in the right direction. We may end up with heightened psychic senses—the ability to read emotions and even minds, pretty fluidly—but even this is all still based in developing a fancier variety of *who we still are* and have always been.

At this point if we ask who needs a teacher, we must emphatically point to ourselves. It is the catalytic spark from a true tantric master that propels the individual from the domain of who he or she has always been, into the realm of what is yet unknown. This "unknown" includes communion reciprocity—the state in which one becomes a radiant mechanism for profound intimacy, even beyond the personal affair of a couple. Such intimacy can become available, by its radiance, to anyone who wishes to access it.

Keep in mind, however, that there are a lot of good-looking teachers out there whose programs sound inviting, but they do not take us on that step into the unknown. The danger comes in that we are constantly led to think that we have "found it"—that we've actually engaged the transformative possibility of sexuality, and we then take off on tangents that will keep us distracted for the rest of our lives.

To step into this doorway of communion reciprocity through the vehicle of sexual energy, which is the unknown, we have to be willing to risk it all—our power, our psychic senses, our ability to heal, our relationship, everything. That's why most people prefer to look at the "fancier" paths—paths in which they can still look good—or simply to read *about* what is going to happen. That is not risky. But they haven't "died" to themselves at all. They are still essentially the same—no transformation!

REGINA: What you are describing is annihilation in love, as I call it. I have seen this exemplified in the lives of many extraordinary women.

LALITHA: Exactly! Annihilation in love *is* what it is all about. And let's face it, we have no idea what "dying" or "annihilation," in the way I'm speaking of it, is going to look like. For a long time we might be able to console or encourage ourselves with, "Well, it can't be *so* bad," because we know our love of God is so strong, and our desire for spiritual practice is so strong, or because we are so driven in our desires for spiritual life. But on this path to annihilation there are many distracting stages and so many convenient places to stop. It is highly useful to have a teacher who has done it first. Someone who can kick our ass through the door. And while most teachers say they can do this, I know this is not the case.

In my experience, one of the scariest things is that we even have to be willing to "lose" our spiritual master, or our love of God, or whatever we hold as our love of God. I've gone through times where even my drive to know the Divine, and my ability to rest in God has been completely wiped out, leaving no doubt that even *that* is up for grabs (even the most profound ground of our spiritual being, that we feel is there for always—that we can always lean on, that can never be taken away). In an esoteric sense, that ground can *never* be taken away. But in a human sense, the memory of that, the knowledge of that, can be wiped completely out, and we can feel that we are left with absolutely nothing. *That's annihilation!* It *could* mean that all the things we used to hold most dear, mean nothing to us, in a personal way, because there is no personal sense of self left.

For instance, what would it be like if annihilation meant that the personal and exclusive relationship that we have with our own children became identical with our relationship to "all children." What if we no longer related to the child born from our body as a separate, most beloved child? It's not that we would even agonize about it. We might remember that such thinking existed for most people, but for us it was no longer possible.

That's why this Tantric work is so difficult and dangerous, and why it requires the help of a teacher. If you don't have the proper strength built within yourself, you will break down, both physically and emotionally, when you reach a crucial stage in your *sadhana* where a leap must be taken. Sad to say, I've seen people with permanent damage—permanently damaged psyches, or physical bodies—because they were unprepared.

The auyervedic physician and tantric practitioner Robert Svoboda discussed this principle in his book *Aghora II*, about kundalini energy. He quoted his teacher, Vimalananda, to say:

> If your nervous system is strong it can endure a great deal of shakti [*life-force, or sexual energy*] before disintegrating, which is why penance [spiritual discipline or practice] is required. If you do the practices your guru sets for you and can control your tongue and your penis—
>
> [*Svoboda asks*] "Or if you are a woman?"
>
> "Or your clitoris, you can create nerves of steel. I'm sorry, but if you think you can dare to awaken Kundalini and survive while living in a body that has been weakened by dissipation you are living in a fool's paradise. How do you think Moses was able to withstand his experience with God? Only because of his long penances. Moses described a burning bush which burned but was not consumed. That bush was his own brain and nervous system, ignited by God.[7]

(Lalitha continues:)

Mother Mira used to read an epic poem about the unknown which said: "Woe to the one who when the moment comes finds himself unprepared." The "moment" meaning the moment of transformation—the moment of needing to make a leap—the moment of total annihilation.

So approach this path cautiously, intelligently. Start at the beginning, and try to tell the truth to yourself all along the way.

TESSA BIELECKI—THE PATH OF CELIBACY

To transition from Lalitha's consideration of Tantric practice to the celibate life experience of a contemporary Roman Catholic nun may seen like a broad leap. But in actuality, such a step is only difficult if one has limited the notion of sexuality to the act of physical coupling, missing the whole domain of energetic focus which the *Tantrikas* are the first to point out, and Lalitha so clearly explained.

I first saw Mother Tessa Bielecki at a talk she gave during the Buddhist-Christian dialogue that took place at Naropa Institute in Boulder, Colorado in the summer of 1988. What impresses one about Tessa is her unadorned radiance. In the floor-length brown habit of a Carmelite nun, her hair pulled away from her face and her head covered with a triangle-shaped scarf, her long brown hair falls down her back, almost to her waist—a shock to those of us raised with nuns whose veils completely covered their heads. (The question people still ask me about my time in the convent was, "Did you shave your head?" It is another indication of the fact that what is covered becomes irresistibly mysterious. Maybe there is something to be learned by contemporary women in that fact. We ogle the women in *purdah*, the Arab women clothed in largesse from head to foot, even their faces hidden from public view, and yet we also know that the sacred art of belly dancing was developed by such women for the erotic pleasure of their husbands.)

Tessa's eyes sparkle behind her oversized glasses that frame them. When she begins to speak, her voice is clear, edged with decisiveness and humor, leaving no doubt that this woman knows her task and will waste no time in doing it. I was captivated by her presence, and clearly many other people were too. The crowd that surrounded her questioned and thanked her enthusiastically, and she maintained her energetic interchange with them.

I introduce her work and words here because despite her appearance as a woman of prayer and solitude, as was pointed out in Chapter Two, I think of Tessa most of all as a brilliant example of what Woman is when she is fully alive, vibrant in her essence, and bubbling with her sexual radiance. Tessa is a rarity—a sexual attraction without seductiveness. There is no cheap thrill-seeking about her means of relating. She is open and humorous and juicy in her expressiveness. She can be tender and ecstatic as well as penetratingly cutting when she's got an incision or an emotional amputation to perform with the other monks in her community, of which she is the abbess, or with a questioner who tries to get her to support their ego-based game-plan. The fact that she is a celibate allows her some interesting and valuable insights which are both useful to those of us who wish to pursue the mystical path as married women, as well as for the many thousands of women who are no longer sexually active, celibate by circumstance but not really by choice.

The point remains that one can transform the situation in which one finds oneself into one of deepened spiritual intensity, but it takes commitment and work.

To say that Tessa's practice amounts to a kind of Christian Tantra would be stretching the limits a bit, but in truth when she speaks of her experience as a monk (she is dissatisfied with the term "nun"—her life is that of a monastic hermit, and she is proud of it), one is amazed at the liberality of her community, and the ways in which they have willingly embraced life in general as a celebration of the goodness of God. Whether it is in climbing a mountain or practicing yoga, or eating a macrobiotic diet, or engaging in the "sacrament of spaghetti" which she claims is a most worthwhile venture for raising the spirits of the community, hard physical labor from morning till night as their community builds its new foundation in Ireland, or days of solitude and contemplation in the cold winter months in Nova Scotia, Tessa's life vibrates with intensity.

In one issue of their community journal, Sister Sharon Doyle describes the celebrations of Christmas, which every year contains various elements of surprise. Once they realized the easy monotony of gift giving as a formalized ritual, they changed it, clinging to nothing, and yet embracing everything. In 1996 they were invited to leave their hermitages at midnight and to proceed to the shores of a frozen lake on the property. There, under a star-studded sky, the silence was pierced by the strains of Handel's *Messiah* booming from some hidden spot in the nearby forest. Each monk stood transfixed, allowing the glorious strains of this life-affirming music to penetrate them. At its conclusion, a bonfire was lit on the lake, and the Mass was celebrated. Then homemade beer and other food delicacies were shared by all.

No wonder Tessa's words about the vibrancy of a life fully-lived have weight. She and her community, under the inspiration of William McNamara, the Carmelite priest who was Tessa's spiritual Father, and now her co-director in the community, witness to the possibility that celibacy can be as a lifestyle which is eminently conducive to the spiritual marriage with the divine.

I interviewed Tessa in the fall of 1994 in Boulder, Colorado, where she was a speaker at the Conference on Crazy Wisdom and Divine Madness. Meeting at 7 a.m. in an unused academic office, my dear friend Debbie and I both felt as if we were meeting a long-absent friend. We shared tea with Tessa and talked about a sexual life in God.

MOTHER TESSA: I think celibacy is one of the greatest gifts, one of the greatest joys in life, but it's one of the hardest things initially. When Father William suggested to me that I had a call to celibacy I literally screamed and ran away, I was so horrified. Finally I calmed down and came back and I said, "All right. I'll do it." And in his wisdom, Father William said, "Well, why don't you just make a temporary vow for three months and then you can renew that for another three months, and then renew it for another six months." That was a great relief to me, because I felt like I had an out. I was terrified by the idea of vowing this for life all at once. That's what I mean when I have said publicly that I became a celibate gradually. But when I said that, everybody roared laughing.

I think that celibacy is one of the most marvelous, humanly congenial ways of being that exist—and talk about being underrated. I'd like to talk about the asceticism of celibacy first, because it begins as a type of asceticism and becomes mysticism. It begins as an agony and then becomes a tremendous ecstasy, which I would not trade for the world.

At first, the most obvious sacrifice is the sacrifice of genital activity, which I think is harder for men, initially. I think it's easier for women, or it used to be easier for women before so called "sexual liberation." Now I think there's a new breed of women who find the genital sacrifice more difficult. But I just turned fifty, and for women of my era, where chastity and purity were more acceptable socially, and politically correct, this was not such a hard sacrifice. The harder sacrifice for women, I think, is the giving up of one special other who is *all* for you, and you are *all* for him.

Closer to mid-life, this "special other" becomes a harder sacrifice for men. But I don't think they feel that at first ... and it varies from person to person.

The sacrifice of physical motherhood and fatherhood for me was not a sacrifice. Somehow I never felt strongly called to physical motherhood and was so fulfilled in terms of being a spiritual mother. For the true celibate, there is fecundity—a great fruitfulness; a tremendous regeneration that comes both personally and then spills over to other people.

363

REGINA: Is there a difference in the training for celibacy for men and women? How is one prepared for such a commitment?

TESSA: Speaking in terms of the training, I think it's the same for men and women, essentially, while the attitude towards what's going to be difficult is different initially. Then I think there needs to be a very radical, graphic preparation for celibacy so that we know exactly what's involved. You need to know what's going to happen to you physiologically as a result of celibacy; what's going to happen psychologically; what's going to happen emotionally.

Whether you're celibate or not, you're sexual. We like to make the distinction between genitality and sexuality, but even that's not good, because even in your sexuality if you're celibate you're very genitally aware, but not genitally active. So, it's a marvelous unity.

REGINA: When you're saying that the training involves graphic preparation, you are talking about instruction from guides speaking specifically to the younger monks and nuns, not from books?

TESSA: Oh yes, speaking specifically in order to train. When it comes to celibacy, I think, of all areas of education, books are the least helpful because you need somebody who both knows the glory of genitality and knows how hard it is to give that up, and knows how glorious it is to give that up. And the witness of a person who has done it, who is fulfilled having done it, who has no regrets having done it, who is not cold, not dried up, not bitter, not repressed; that is the strongest statement for the positive value of celibacy.

So you need happy, joyful celibates to serve as guides. And you need a great sense of humor. It needs to be out in the open. We live in a mixed community, so if you're not open and lighthearted and honest about this, it could be pretty tricky. We are rather hilarious about our celibacy. We've written a song called, "I am a happy celibate," that we sing to the tune of, "I am a happy wanderer," and we all sing it together and it's a way of diffusing the frustration sometimes. You know how the song goes—"Val da ree, val da ra," and then there's a "Ha Ha Ha Ha." [*She starts singing these words with an exuberant energy at first, then allowing them to sound cynical.*] When we're all singing that together it's just marvelous— a marvelous expression of the pain of it and the beauty of it.

People in our community are trained to see celibacy's connection with prayer and the spousal love of God. You see, traditionally there's been too much emphasis on celibacy as a means of —the expression is "apostolic efficacy." In other words, the idea that you can serve better as a celibate because you are not distracted by spouse and family. Well, that is true, but it's not going to get you through a bad night when you're all alone and you don't want to be alone. The thought that you could get up the next day and *work better* is no consolation. You have to understand celibacy in terms of the mystical graces, the mystical blessings, and then you have to pray out of that understanding. So, during a bad night like that, if I'm lying alone in bed after a very difficult day, and I don't want to be alone, and I would rather have a man's arms around me, the way I pray is: "I don't want to be alone." I'm praying to Christ: "I don't want to be alone. *You* know I don't want to be alone. You're the one who called me to this life. What are you going to do about it?" There's got to be that kind of honesty and directness about it, otherwise you can't survive it.

On a human level, celibacy involves such a sacrifice that if you don't martial all these forces in another direction you won't reach a point where you see, "Gee, this isn't really difficult at all," because of what happens as a result of it. Anybody can just decide to be celibate, but to grow into the fullness of the joy, that takes a lot of time and a lot of years and a lot of tears and a lot of loneliness. But then, the ripening of it is just so magnificent. Many, many more of us need to be speaking out on this.

Also, it's a far healthier answer to the world's over-population problem than most of the alternatives. It's a marvelous social statement, and I could go on and on. I absolutely love celibacy.

REGINA: Well that's evident about you. It's not simply a tolerance of the situation.

TESSA: Yes, oh yes. It's an embrace. Now also, another thing I love about celibacy is the freedom—that it is absolutely clear who I am and what my lifestyle is. It was hard enough in my day when you were chastely trying to find your life's mate; nowadays every minute is taken up with: "Am I going to go to bed or am I not?" I don't know how people survive it! What an absurd distraction. Whereas for me, friendship can immediately go very deep into the soul things that matter, because all that other stuff is just not part of the picture. When there is that kind of real commitment to chastity and purity, then the "sparks" also are tremendous. It's great fun, because you're very clear about what you do and what you don't do, what you say and what you don't say. There's a lot of energy there that's great fun. I enjoy it. I enjoy being a highly erotic, passionate woman. The spark is there, but it's all in the context of chastity and purity and celibacy which I think makes life much more interesting, because then you can be much more creative with it. How do you play with that? It seems like the dullest thing to me to go in one plain old direction, and just end up in bed with, well ... I mean celibacy leads to many more interesting ways of expressing love and passion than ending up in bed.

REGINA: Do you have a breathing practice or an exercise practice or anything related to the sublimation of sexual energy?

TESSA: No, it's simply organic. Christianity as a whole, compared to the religious practices of the East, is, I don't know as I want to say *weak* about specific physical practices, it's just different. Christianity is much more organic. I know that in the East, Life becomes the ultimate practice, but in the East there's much more of an emphasis on specific spiritual practices. It's simply not the Christian way, and I have trouble with Christian teachers who try to compete with the East through trying to come up with all these things. It just doesn't exist. Christ was not like that. It's totally antithetical to the free and organic way that we live. So, I don't know anything about specific practices, all this Kundalini stuff and Tantra and all. I know absolutely nothing about it, and I'm

Mother Tessa Bielecki

not even interested in it. I think it has a value, but for me the presence of sexual energy is simply the way life is. And the "practice" is simply being frank and honest with myself, and watching myself and watching others. It's not like I feel the sexual energy coming up and then I do something to cope with it. I might just go shovel the compost or laugh or do something natural.

REGINA: Your passion for your spiritual life is so clear. I wondered if you've intentionally done things to build that or if that's just always been there?

TESSA: I feel so blessed. Passion for spiritual life has always been there, and that's a gift. The way it's maintained is by love. I love Father William. I love Christ. I love the people who have come into our lives. And when I bog down, what keeps me going is the personal relatedness in love ... and a sense of duty. Again, that's another value that's in disrepute. The culture says, "If it feels good, do it, if it doesn't, don't." Or, "Be unfaithful. Pull out of relationships. Change. Do whatever you like." And I feel very medieval in that sense of duty—I feel like a knight.

The whole image of the knight is very important to me. The knight is beautiful. Out of love and beauty a knight does *what should be done*, no matter what he feels like. That value needs to be restored. It's very noble.

So when I'm not feeling the love, but in fact feeling quite unloving because I'm so frustrated by idiocy or whatever, duty sustains me. In our community, even when one doesn't feel good, we remind one another of the vow we have made of commitment. We're very open about that—we write a lot of songs, a lot of poetry, and we're constantly encouraging one another to be faithful using very chivalric language. We're very moved by that. We have each designed a coat of arms which sums up the essence of our commitment, and we very often have rituals that we've designed ourselves. We have circles where we bring out our coats of arms, sort of like the knights at the Round Table. It's very important. There are official, traditional, Christian-Catholic ways to do that, and then of course you can devise your own ceremonies and rituals, and we do a lot of that. We do it when we're bogging down in details and losing a sense of the vision. We'll say, "We need a circle."

We often do our rituals around fires, and the fire and the ritual connects us to every great celebration we've ever had. So, while we may not recreate as strong a feeling as we had four years ago, for instance, still we remember. We've written a poem, a long epic, that tells our whole story, and it begins with the words of Merlin: "Be still, be still and remember. It is the doom of men to forget." If we're not naturally remembering, then we have to bring in a ceremony and remember it there.

If you forget your vow, forget your commitment, forget what brought you alive, then you're doomed!

Those who wish to learn more about Mother Tessa and her community can write to Nada Hermitage, P.O. Box 219, Crestone, CO, 81131. See the Bibliography at the back of this book for her writings on the great saint, Teresa of Avila, with whom she strongly identifies as a guide in both her temporal and spiritual work.

11

THE PATH OF DEVOTION

For five weeks in November and December of 1995, I sat before Sri Yogi Ramsuratkumar, the elderly beggar saint of south India, affectionately known as the God-child of Tiruvannamalai, and fell under the spell of the woman seated to his right. Dressed in a white sari, her dark hair pulled back in traditional fashion to reveal her soft but determined features, Ma Devaki kept her eyes riveted on the old saint. Anticipating his every need and following his bidding unquestioningly, she was mother, servant, secretary and devotee *par excellence* to her Master. She has performed this service day in and day out for years now, and with the Yogi's blessing stands by his side as Mother of all his devotees.

Devaki is a well-educated woman. With an advanced degree in philosophy, she was senior lecturer in physics at a college in south India. Yet, despite her accomplishments and position, Devaki wanted something more—she longed to devote her life to God. In December of 1986, feeling the hunger of her soul with acute pain, she prayed for guidance at the temple of the great saint Ramana Maharshi, located at the foot of Mount Arunachala, also in Tiruvannamalai.

"Bhagawan," she implored, "I am wandering for so many years in search of a Guru; can you not show me a person like you or Bhagawan Ramakrishna to guide me to God?"[1]

Within a few days the young woman's prayers were answered. She met her Beloved in the form of one who calls himself a dirty sinner and a mad beggar, Sri Yogi Ramsuratkumar.

"What does Devaki want from this Beggar?" the elderly saint asked her with the innocence of a child.

"I want you to show me God," Devaki replied with corresponding innocence.

The Yogi laughed uproariously.

She had no doubt, however, that she had found the one to whom she had been directed. As the months and years went on, the longing of her heart began to draw her, irresistibly, to spend more time in the saint's physical presence. Then it was only a matter of time before the master drew her closer, unable to violate the "law" that required him to serve the genuine supplications of a devotee's heart.

I can't adequately describe what I saw and felt from Devaki's devotion. Today, such complete and selfless attention might be praised when it is directed to the needs of a child or the pain of the dying. But when lavished on a male guru by a female devotee (or vice versa, since some of the greatest devotees have been men, some of the greatest gurus have been women), the whole situation becomes anathema to one who equates devotion with subservience. "You mean this woman never got to develop *herself*?" "She never got to marry?" "She never got to travel, or to have the joy of independent choice?"

Yogi Ramsuratkumar and Devaki Ma

But such questions reflect an attitude so dissonant from what I saw as to make them seem pitiably naive. What I found in this woman's eyes, and in her whole posture and demeanor, was absolutely devastating—in the degree of its compassion, its power and its focus. Nor was it narrow at all. In fact, Devaki's attention on her master seemed inclusive of the whole world, which was his focus. After all, don't all the great books honestly say the same thing: that Love *is* the Ultimate Reality—the ultimate accomplishment, the final goal, to which all one's energies and activities should only and forever be directed?

I am not surprised that I meet with incredulity when I talk about Devaki. To see love and devotion embodied is actually hard to believe. While the mind can't comprehend it, the body knows the truth. Intuitive wisdom sees through the mind's objections and resonates with the place in Woman that is not separate from such Love, and in which every sacrifice, no matter how great, is transformed into a prayer of praise and service to God on behalf of her children.

I never exchanged words with Devaki, I didn't have to. For five weeks she spoke to my body and my heart every day, twice a day, as I sat at the Yogi's feet. She spoke to me about the essence of devotion, the essence of Woman, the essence of Ma.

A DANGEROUS PATH

Devotion, like Tantra, is a multi-edged sword. Following her beloved, or her belief in God's prophet or servant, a woman can end up mad, or at the foot of a cross, as did Mary Magdalen; or in prison, like the followers of Charles Manson; or starved and burned to death like the devotees of David Koresh; or with a nervous breakdown, confused and psychically burned by an inexperienced or downright malicious teacher. Fundamentalist sects can easily pervert initially pure devotion into raging fanaticism and narrow-mindedness; while charismatic leaders abound who are only too happy to prey on the innocent gullibility, or the power-hunger, of women of spirit. For example, one of my early teachers offered me a high-level position in his organization on the first day that I met him. I was too naive to recognize that I was being seduced. After two and a half years of struggling to reconcile his radical teaching with my own deeper sensitivity, I ended up in profound depression, suicidal and completely convinced that I was the source of suffering in everyone around me.

What devotion to the Divine (or ultimate Truth, or Spirit) is, where such Divinity resides, and to whom or what it should be directed—these are questions that are not easily answered. Many of us will only be able to make these distinctions by a process of trial and error. Even when one does find a teacher or path of great worth, much that masquerades as devotion is actually blind following. Furthermore, "true devotion" may be very difficult to distinguish from false devotion or even subservience, since genuine devotion is essentially a condition of the heart, and its unique qualities might not be immediately apparent in external behaviors.

These issues are vital for us to consider, however, because women by nature are devoted to life—in their children, in the protection and preservation of the earth, in their singular attachment to the well-being of the human race. Moreover, so many women today are hungering for illuminated meaning and purpose in their lives. Woman continues to want to serve, despite the fact that she has been exploited in her desire to sacrifice herself for the good of others, and even despite her own distorted co-dependencies (which I view as a necessary part of learning the discrimination needed for genuine devotion). Through it all, Woman continues steadfastly in her devotion and dedication, and even begs for more opportunities in which to show her courage, her strength, and ultimately her love.

Woman knows (at least intuitively) that only in "losing herself" as a separate entity will she find herself ultimately fulfilled in her preeminent calling—to a life lived from a broader context, in Love. Today, reports from contemporary science and sports laud the experience of being lost to self—"In the Zone" or part of the "Flow" they call it. In such cases, the separate individual is out of the way, and some other larger force or energy seems to take over and direct the movement or unfolding process. Case after case affirms that one's quality of attention, focus or concentration was so great that all minor considerations merely fell by the wayside. "There was only me, the ball and the hoop ..." says the basketball player who has just tied a court record. What more perfect analogy when applied to the kind of attention which the lover may shower upon the Beloved for a lifetime? Like the sport's player who is temporarily out of the way, the result of such one-pointed attention for the devotee of God is that the separate self-sense is dissolved in Love.

To follow a path of devotion, in the full sense that we shall consider in this chapter, will mean the annihilation of the separate individual. Her entire destiny will be fulfilled only insofar as she is lost and united with the being of her Lover. For this she will willingly lay down her own life (mind, body and emotions), her present illusion of independence and her future plans. Such annihilation or absorption, however, far from leaving the woman drained and subservient, will show up as radiance, power and passion. The "real" devotees whom I have encountered through prayer or in person have also been women of great personal magnetism and intensity, and most of them were significantly involved with the sufferings of humanity. I have seen their eyes, blazing as if with inner fire, reaching out to embrace and hold the world.

When such a devotee tells her own story, interestingly, she will often say that she herself had little or no choice in the matter—that Love Itself grasped her to Its Heart, and that she continues to live there, unable to go back to her previous life of illusion. Although her life may be full of sacrifice and even pain at times, she will speak of this opportunity to serve Her Beloved directly and all others in Her Beloved, as if it were the greatest gift.

The mystic and poet, Kabir, wrote that: "Every instant that the sun is risen, if I stand in the temple, or on a balcony, in the hot fields, or in a walled garden, my own Lord is making love with me."[2] For the devotee then, the entire Universe is literally transformed into her lover. Everything has become the Beloved, the Divine. The rocks, the trees, the smiles on the faces of children—nothing is separate from her Blessed One. She experiences the bodily comprehension that the Blessed One is never distant, although elsewhere at play in creation, dancing the Divine Play or *Lila*, in the form of all things.

The path of devotion to the Other, whether in the form of her own children, in the sick and poor, in her husband or lover, or in the person of Christ or her guru—who is ideally held as the externalized manifestation of her own deepest Divinity or truest self—has attracted Woman, forever. Within most of the world's religions—including Christianity, Buddhism and Hinduism—both the *bhakti* path and the devoted student-teacher relationship has a long and brilliant history.

Some devotees have taken on the role of children to the Great Mother or Father, others have deemed themselves warriors in defense of their Lord, others, like the gopis, as the lover or husband of the Divine. In the unique story of Mataji Krishnabai and Swami Papa Ramdas, which follows, we find the guru, Ramdas, surrendered to his devotee, Krishnabai, worshipping her as Divine

Mother. And Krishnabai, the devotee, surrendered to her guru, Ramdas, and worshipping him as Divine Mother too.

MOTHER KRISHNABAI (1903-1989)

During that same trip to India in which I fell in love with Ma Devaki, I renewed acquaintance with a remarkable women I had long admired—Mother Krishnabai of Anandashram, Kanhangad, Kerala in south India. I never actually met Krishnabai during her lifetime, although I have spoken with some who have.

Her photographs reveal a woman of humble grace. Her gentle smile invited everyone, although I know from stories that she could be as forceful as she was gentle in protecting Ramdas, her guru. Krishnabai and Ramdas were most often photographed together— Papa and Mataji, guru and devotee, one and the same.

Krishnabai blessed me, personally and tangibly, the way mothers love to bless (i.e., give to) their children. She did it through a request of the beggar saint, Yogi Ramsuratkumar, who is the spiritual son of Swami Ramdas and Mother Krishnabai. One day, as I sat in *darshan* with the Yogi, he called upon one of his Indian devotees to read aloud a piece about Krishnabai—an exceptional piece, extolling her devotion.

As soon as the reader was finished, the Yogi spoke to Ma Devaki, who sat at his right hand. Then, Devaki called my name, something which had never happened before, and asked me to read this same piece to the assembled crowd. I was shocked, but not surprised. Moments before the request, one thought had crossed my mind—a desire. I wanted to read that selection too, aloud, in praise of Krishnabai.

Audaciously, I wonder now if the Yogi put this desire in my heart to begin with, and then simply had his fun with me. After all, that is exactly the way Krishnabai would have explained such a coincidence. For her, there was *nothing*—no thought, no event, no movement of the planets—that was not the result of her guru's grace.

I stood up, faced a sea of Indian faces and read aloud the selection I had just heard—the words of the *Jnaneswari*, that classic piece about *guru-bhakti* written in the thirteenth century by Sri Jnanadev, a celebrated mystic and poet. Inwardly I thanked the Divine Beggar, Yogi Ramsuratkumar, for the privilege I had been granted, while I begged Mataji to teach a left-brained Westerner more about devotion.

> In his keen desire to serve the Guru, he [the devotee] knows neither day nor night ... He becomes as great as the sky in serving the Guru and renders all the requisite service single-handed, in time. In this respect his body runs ahead of his mind ... At times he is prepared to sacrifice his life in order to fulfill the playful wish of his Guru. He becomes lean in the service of the Guru, but is nourished by his love. He becomes the rightful recipient of the Master's command. He thinks himself respectable because of his association with the Guru's family, and noble because of his affection for his brother disciples, and rendering service to the Guru becomes his passion. He looks upon the rites and duties and stages of life and the service of the Guru as his obligatory duty.
>
> Guru for him, is the holy place, i.e., Tirtha; he is his God, his mother and father and he knows no other path leading to liberation ...[3]

HER GURU'S GRACE

To read the autobiography of Mataji Krishnabai, titled *Guru's Grace*, is to sip the essence of her, a rare and glorious flower.[4] I have frequently recommended this book as my favorite example of how to use writing as a way to re-frame or re-contextualize one's life. We are always free to tell the story of our life as if it is a tragedy in which we are the hapless victim, or to tell it in another way—as a series of wondrous challenges that we have faced in our quest for truth.

Krishnabai recorded her life from the perspective that God's hand had always been present, had directed every single aspect, and has thus determined her destiny, whether the events were catastrophic and wrought with pain, as many of them were, or ecstatic and joy-filled. Because she praised the wisdom and goodness of the Divine on every page, her autobiography is a reminder that everything can be dressed in the clothing of continuous prayer. To read her book, *Guru's Grace*, is to pray.

For Krishnabai, God was not some nebulous or distant spirit, but a tangible reality. *Ram*, the Divine, was none other than her living, breathing "Papa," the profoundly personal and affectionate title that his devotees had bestowed upon Swami Ramdas. She saw everything and everyone in and as him, and in so doing she was liberated from self-concern and merged with the Universal. Every act of her life, then, became a means to serve the entire creation.

Although Krishnabai may be said to have lost everything in surrendering to her guru and beloved, from another point of view, what really happened was quite the opposite. What she actually lost was her separation, her fear, her small vision. What she gained was Motherhood of all humankind, courage, and a vision of eternal proportions. She never lost the unique edge of feistiness and the independent spirit that had drawn her to reject a status-quo existence and to dedicate her life to a greater purpose. In fact, as is true in all cases of genuine surrender, her qualities were transformed but not obliterated. With her "faults" as gifts then, she became, in the hand of her guru, an even *more* valuable tool for the accomplishment of Divine work on earth.

The following passage, from the first two pages of her autobiography, sets the stage for the chronology of her life events. Besides Krishnabai's reference to all things as the Divine, it is expedient for women to note that, as a result of her surrender, she did not hold herself as worthless fodder, but rather as the one in whom the "magnificent glory" was made manifest. This was the same message that Mary of Nazareth delivered to her cousin Elizabeth: "My soul magnifies the Lord...because He has done great things to me."[5] The woman who knows herself to be "full of grace"—who *really* knows it, not just mentally, but in full-bodied appreciation—cannot slink around the periphery of things, beating her breast in false humility. Krishnabai's life celebrated a type of humility that stands straight. With her eyes on Papa, she entertained no distraction from the voice of self-deprecation. And so she could pray:

> O Infinite Papa! Verily I am your own embodiment. At the desire of some devotees, who are none other than yourself, you inspired me to make several attempts to dictate my life story, incorporating in it all the events from the beginning of my life, even before you revealed yourself in me. But every time, after some progress, I could not continue the work. Now again I am taking it up.
>
> O all-pervading Papa! In 1928 you awakened in me a strong urge to become one with your eternal Being, and I came to you. After passing one year in your holy company I appealed to you to initiate me with the Ram-Mantra [*Om Shri Ram Jai Ram Jai Jai Ram*, also called "Ram-Nam"]. All compassionate as you are, you gave me the most sacred Mantra. You then advised me to stop reading any kind of books, to give up the use of the rosary while repeating the Mantra and to discontinue the worship of images. Instead, you counseled me to look upon all beings and creatures in the world as Ram and to consider the service rendered to any one of them as service and worship of Ram Himself.
>
> O kindness-incarnate Papa! As I went on reciting Ram-Nam, the remembrances of my relatives came to me with added force. To get over this hurdle, you asked to take whatever thought that arose in me as Ram Himself. Whenever I thought of God as Ram I felt God was far away

from me. But when I thought of God as Papa I felt His nearness. By this practice, after some time, I realized that all my relatives are yourself, and the thoughts about them as such disappeared. Then I looked upon everybody as you alone. I got the vision to behold you as everyone and everything.

O Papa, the lover of devotees! During my spiritual discipline I reflected how, from my childhood onward, you assumed various forms to guide me on the path. I recollected how you spoke as those persons and made me also speak. Further, all the events of my life started crowding into my mind vividly one after another.

O Papa, the Divine Mother! You are omnipresent and, having become everything, you are also transcendent. You pervade within and without all that exists. You are above beginning and end. You are the sole protector of all.

O compassionate Papa! In the worlds you reside in entirety in all beings—even in the smallest particle. Likewise, you dwell in me in all your perfections. Now grant me the power to describe your magnificent glory manifest in me. [6]

HER LIFE

Krishnabai was born in September of 1903 on the day of a new moon, Mahalaya Amavasya, or "All Souls Day." Her mother gave birth in a jungle hut since she and her husband had fled to the forests to escape a plague which was sweeping through the town of Haliyal in which they lived. Like so many Indians steeped in the tradition of their religious and cultural heritage, Krishnabai's parents were highly devout practitioners and taught their children the love of the deities, particularly Dattatreya, whose temple was near to the family home. They further communicated the revered place of the guru in the hierarchy of spiritual attainment.

381

Even from the age of six, Krishnabai was already enamored of a particular swami, and honored both he and his whole lineage, according to custom.

She was married at the age of twelve years ("and three months," she adds precisely), and like the obedient Hindu wife that she was, grew to love her husband's parents and relatives, although they were previously strangers to her. From her own reports it seems to have been a happy marriage (even blissfully so, according to Ramdas who wrote about her early life in his introduction to her autobiography), and she birthed three children, one of whom did not survive. In 1923, however, her life dramatically changed. She was eighteen years old, and only seven years married, when her husband fell ill suddenly and died after a brief sickness. He was in Bombay at the time, she was away with the children visiting her family home. The news of his death overwhelmed her, but the remorse that followed because she was separated from him at the moment of his passing, devastated her. Krishnabai was inconsolable in her grief.

For a full year she barely endured the misery and torment of her life, wishing that she too could die and thus leave behind the empty and disgusting present, and an even more fearsome future. The life of a widow in India, especially of a beautiful, young widow, was not something to be coveted. Many still followed the custom of dressing in white for the remainder of their lives, shaving their heads, moving into the household of the husband's family, where they were considered to be the lowest in social status. Despite the laws against *sati*, or self-immolation on the husband's funeral pyre, there was still opprobrium attached to the death of one's husband—as if he died because one wasn't a good enough wife; or at least as if one's karma from a previous life must have been extremely negative to merit such a terrible condition as widowhood. And not the least worry for widows was the fact that they were virtually unprotected within society, and many fell prey to unscrupulous treatment—robbery and rape primarily. Add to this social situation the fact that Krishnabai desperately yearned to preserve the chastity that she had practiced for a year prior to her husband's death, one can begin to glimpse the enormous terror that hung like an ominous cloud over her circumstances.

On the day before the first anniversary of her husband's death, Krishnabai attempted to join him—she deliberately took a lethal dose of opium that she had secured over many months for this precise purpose. Such an easy exit was not in the plans for her, however. Under the influence of the drug she had a vision of another revered guru, Samarth Ramdas, who paced around at her head. She was delighted to see him, but still wished to die. About fifteen minutes later, as she still held the vision, one of her children arose from a sound sleep and called for his grandmother. The vision disappeared. The older woman quickly discovered the drugged Krishnabai on the pallet where she had laid down to die, and within moments had summoned her other son, a physician. Dr. Rama Rao, Krishnabai's brother-in-law, administered an emetic to her, and thus saved her from death.

For those who have been through a similar descent into hell and personal desolation, the fact that Krishnabai's sojourn in the underworld was so dreadful that she actually attempted suicide holds a perverse satisfaction. Our saints have not always been "saintly"—actually, the contrary is often the case. Many are the first to admit that they were and still are "great sinners" who simply turned their "sin" to good use. In Krishnabai's case, the passion that inspired suicide was the same passion that was sublimated into devoted service. Her suicide attempt was exactly the death she needed—a death of illusion that ultimately drove her to the Divine. In this respect then, the woman who attempts to follow a spiritual path may find herself valuing hardship, despite the pain involved. Even though she may offer consolation or comfort to friends in similar circumstances, she will also honor that transformation lies therein.

Krishnabai's life for the next few years was marked by a searing spiritual focus. She was introduced to four great spiritual teachers, and received initiation in several *mantras*. In place of expressing her terrible pain and loss, she took to reciting the holy names of God constantly. Still, none of the illustrious teachers captured her soul. As she would later describe it, by these events Papa "paved the way for my coming to Kasaragod." In 1928, in the strange flow of coincidences that mark intersections on the spiritual path, she was carried to her true home at last. For months she had prayed, day and night, to be shown the guru who would lead her from darkness to light. In June, her brother-in-law, Dr. Rama Rao, with whom she was living, moved the whole family to Kasaragod, the location of Ramdas' ashram.

Rama Rao was a dutiful reader of the *Jnaneswari* (the text quoted from earlier which describes the characteristics of the ideal devotee-Guru relationship). Although he himself had searched far and wide for years, it was not until he met Swami Ramdas, the guru of the ashram in Kasaragod, that he found one who embodied for him the essence of this book as no other had. When Rama told his household about this exceptional swami, Krishnabai recalled how her first feeling was one of apprehension, a sense that once she visited the holy man she might never return to her home. And, indeed, that is precisely what happened, on the level of the heart. She recounts:

> O mother Papa! As I neared your Ashram I experienced a rare and inexpressible joy, similar to what a child would feel when it was about to meet its mother after a long period of separation. ... The sublimity of your Presence was simply indescribable. The moment I saw you, the passions that were vexing me disappeared and bliss established itself in my heart. At home I was never content however long I talked about you to the people therein. I was feeling a peculiar joy in relating your talks to all I met. Your very remembrance made my hair stand on end and my joy overflow.[7]

In another segment of her story, Krishnabai admitted that her encounter with Ramdas marked the first time she had a moment of genuine laughter since the death of her husband. Papa was always smiling and laughing, bubbling with the joy of realization of God. I heard first-hand from the distinguished French spiritual teacher, Arnaud Desjardins, that during one of his meetings with Ramdas, the benevolent guru joked with some serious students: "Here we laugh the ego away."

This sense that one has "come home to rest" at last, is common in the stories of *bhakti*-devotees who find their teacher or guru. Some report a bodily ache of longing, others describe heart palpitations, or a consuming internal fire that is only quenched in gazing upon the loved one, speaking about him or her, or chanting their name. In my own case, in the winter of 1985, when a snowstorm blocked the roads I was traveling to see the unknown spiritual teacher whose words had struck me so fiercely during his radio interview, I tried to turn the car around to head for home. The sobs that wracked my body in that moment were unlike any that I had ever experienced over any physical circumstance of separation or loss before. I was inconsolable at the thought that I might not get to be with this relative stranger who had nonetheless incited my heart only a few days earlier. Braving long delays and possible accidents, I foolhardily turned back onto the treacherous road, convinced that it was better to die than to miss that meeting. (I arrived safely almost three hours later. I recognized and accepted my teacher that night.)

While such sensations and experiences are not necessary as the indication of one's alignment with a teacher or particular lineage, for those who have them they are usually so remarkably dissimilar from one's ordinary responses to meeting strangers, even people of renown, that they generally cause question and invite further investigation. That is precisely what Krishnabai did.

Over the course of two years, while living with her family and sons, Krishnabai continued to visit Papa's ashram every day, fearlessly walking two miles alone, despite the threats of robbery or attack, and the criticisms and insults of neighbors and unsympathetic relatives who found such activities by a widow to be completely inappropriate. As she later said:

Had I paid attention to those people, I would never
have been able to get absorbed in Papa's own Being. I had no time to think of anything other than
Papa...Suppose you are hurrying to the railway station to catch the train, will you take note of what
people talk on the way even if they are abusing
you? So also I was in such a hurry to merge in
Papa's Being that I had no time to care what other
people said about me. If you want to be benefited
by Papa's presence, you should not at all listen to
what others say.[8]

Ramdas wrote later of the humiliating treatment that
Krishnabai received from detractors:

It is the way that in the ordinance of God His
most beloved devotees should first be made to pass
through the fire of severe trials and ordeals before
He could clasp them to His bosom and make them
His own. Indeed blessed are those who suffer cheerfully and ungrudgingly for the sake of great Truth.[9]

When Papa left Kasaragod for a year of touring northern India, and later when her family moved back to Bombay, long separations followed, which tested Krishnabai further. Yet, despite the
excruciating pain of such physical distance from her adored guru,
Krishnabai's love actually grew stronger. Such separation is almost
always necessary for any genuine relationship of devotee and master as a test of faith, and because it serves to convince the devotee
that the Beloved lives outside of time and space, and ultimately
inhabits the heart-cave of the lover's body. When one learns to
find him or her there, she learns the most valuable lesson of all—
that there is only the One.

Finally, after many similar trials, Krishnabai left her former
life behind, including her two sons who chose to stay in their current schools, and live with their relatives, rather than to accom-

pany her to Kasaragod. Literally abandoning everything at Papa's feet, she gave her life to him, and he welcomed the gift with open arms. From there, it was only a short step to her complete liberation in him. When questioned about how Mataji achieved such eminent spiritual heights in such a short amount of time, Ramdas replied that most people are like green wood when they come to the master, but Krishnabai was dry tinder. Ramdas was only too happy to supply the match that accomplished her conflagration.

Krishnabai lived and worked for Papa alone, seeing Ram in all who approached her, until Papa's death in 1963. She continued his work until her own death in 1989.

A few of my favorite stories about this Divine Mother will hopefully serve to communicate the wisdom that she embodied, as well as the simplicity and integral surrender which characterized her life in the Divine.

Stories of Mataji

Generosity Beyond Measure

One of the earliest stories that reveals Krishnabai's generosity also reveals her childlike simplicity and complete trust in the Divine to provide whatever would be needed for her life. One day when Krishnabai was first visiting the Ashram, a poor woman, dressed in rags, approached her and begged for a sari. As Krishnabai had no other resources at the time, she unwrapped part of her own sari, which was eighteen cubits in length, and cut the woman a sizeable piece—enough to make a simple sari. When Krishnabai returned home, her sister-in-law, Sundari, noticed that she wore a very short sari and questioned her about it. Krishnabai told the tale of the poor woman, and Sundari, out of her own generosity, immediately supplied Krishnabai with another sari, of eighteen cubits.

A few weeks later the same thing occurred, this time with a different poor woman. Krishnabai could not resist giving herself away for the needs of others. This time, when Sundari saw Krishnabai with only half a sari, she again wanted to supply one.

As Krishnabai reports: "I replied that if I had a sari of that length [18 cubits] I would not be able to resist giving a piece of it to any other needy woman. Thenceforward I have been using only saris eleven cubits long."[10]

Mother of Mercy

One night, when Mataji and Papa were alone on the ashram, two drunkards entered the grounds, apparently with the intention of robbing the place. Seeing Krishnabai, one of them grabbed her by the throat as if to strangle her. Seeing this, Papa came up behind the man and pulled him away, but not before the thug had forcibly thrown Mataji to the ground. Both Papa and Mataji simply cried out "Ram" in the midst of the struggle.

Mataji was constrained to wear a neck brace for much of the rest of her life, yet she always spoke lovingly of the intruders and was never bitter toward them or her condition.

Tamer of Lions

As the Mother of Papa's students and devotees, and the host of his ashram, Krishnabai was not only an indefatigable worker, she was an eminent diplomat and the source of hospitality beyond measure. Shrewd and careful in her dealings with others, she saw her primary responsibility as the maintenance of a mood of worshipful attention throughout the master's sanctuary. This lively story testifies to her skills in this regard:

A grisly little *sadhu*, with a matted beard and ferocious eyes, hopped up and down, shook his fists with rage and screamed at an ashram woman: "You have contaminated the whole place. I cannot eat here now!"

Scooping up his entire banana-leaf plate of food, the fuming sadhu threw the bundle to the dogs, and proceeded to stomp around, prepared to leave the ashram because he had been so grossly violated.

And what had caused such a display? What had provoked this renunciate to forget himself so completely, dump his vile on an ashram woman, and then practically curse the holy place?

Among the uppity and arrogant sadhus who frequently stopped over at the Anandashram, there were always a number who complained unceasingly, no matter what the conditions. More often, they merely bickered among themselves, jockeying for territory. The accusation that one had brushed against the banana-leaf plate of another, or taken another's "seat" was enough to ignite a psychic and often a verbal warfare.

This particular *sannyasin* had refused to associate with others, altogether, claiming that the conditions of his practice did not allow him to eat the food prepared by the ashram, or to eat in the company of others—all for fear of contamination. The gracious hosts of Anandashram accommodated these demanding and often neurotic persons, regardless, if it was possible to do so. This *sadhu* had been given the necessary supplies and cooking utensils so that he could prepare his own food. Without asking, however, he had also taken a bucket from the washing area for his personal use, despite the fact that he had his own water vessel.

On the morning in question, as he sat down to his meal, one of the ashram women who was responsible for washing, approached his place and reached for the bucket which she recognized as belonging in her area, and which she needed for her work. It was at this moment that the "man of God" turned into a blathering wild man, nearly hysterical that he had been contaminated.

Needless to say, the ashram woman was upset. Immediately she ran to Krishnabai for help. By this time the whole mood on the ashram was disturbed by the *sadhu's* vociferous accusations. Papa himself heard the shouts at the other end of the courtyard.

Krishnabai wasted no time. She knew instinctively what was needed—like the good mother that she was. In the kitchen she picked out a luscious watermelon, cut it and deftly prepared delicate pieces that she arranged on a tray, together with a few ripe bananas and some juicy coconuts. Giving the tray to one of the male workers, she asked that it be brought immediately to the out-of-control man. Following at a distance, Krishnabai observed that the *sadhu* suddenly started to gain his composure when he saw this special gesture. When Krishnabai herself then approached him, offering him a pitcher of fresh warm milk, he became as docile as a housecat, honored as he was by the Mother's attention.

Krishnabai then went on to explain to the man that the woman meant no offense, but was merely trying to do her job in a responsible manner. The once fierce little demon softened his expression. He smiled, cheerfully accepting her explanation, as he finished every morsel of the food he had been offered. Thereafter, this man remarked about how "supremely gracious" Krishnabai had been. "What she gave me was the very nectar (*amrit*) ... I am most happy and grateful to her!"[11]

Ever-gracious Mother

A poor man once approached Mataji in great desperation, as he had not enough money to feed and support his wife and children. The ever-gracious Mother gifted this poor man with one of the milk-bearing cows from the ashram cowshed. In fact, because Mataji was a genuine mother, she gave her son the best cow—the one that produced the highest quantity of milk.

Overjoyed at first, the man soon became dismayed. Approaching Mataji again he declared: "But where shall I keep this cow, as I have no shed?" Whereupon Krishnabai immediately agreed to have a shed built for the cow, adjoining the man's hut.

As the man considered further, however, he wondered how he would ever feed such a cow, knowing that his own meager resources were inadequate to cover the needs of his family, let alone the insatiable appetite of a four-stomached mammal. But Mataji was again nonplussed. "I will send you hay," she said. And of course she did.

"What about oil cakes?" the man asked, to which Krishnabai replied that she would send him whatever he needed, and daily.

The man went home singing her praises, only to return grumbling a few days later. (This is the point at which many lesser souls would have told him to "shove it" and to be grateful for what he had.) But the grumble was based on the fact that the man was unable to get a fair price for his milk when he went to market to sell it.

Krishnabai had no word of recrimination whatsoever. Instead, she proposed a plan of tremendous ingenuity. "Why are you afraid?" Mataji first asked, wisely reminding this man and the rest of us that the benediction of God is unlimited, and urging us to trust in the face of such tiny wrinkles in the plan. Then, she suggested that the ashram itself would buy the milk, since they always had a great need. The man received the benediction, and did exactly as the Mother had recommended. He and his family were now satisfied and "lived happily ever after." While Mataji was supremely overjoyed that one of her children could be so completely served.[12]

I love this story. In the convoluted logic of love, therefore, the ashram actually ended up paying for the milk of one of its own cows. But such was Krishnabai's generosity. Only a love that goes beyond ordinary charity could ever have conceived of such an arrangement. In our age, where the notions of justice and fairness are touted in principle, regardless of whether they are ever practiced, people are terrified of being taken advantage of. Women especially are urged to draw reasonable and responsible boundaries in all areas of their lives. And certainly this is understandable and even essential in many cases.

At the same time, we must beware of a logic that is so airtight that it fails to take into account the possibility of all-consuming generosity. Otherwise we shall miss the experience of a love that is so all-encompassing that it sees no difference between itself and the one being served, or between the one being served and the One who serves all.

Because she knew herself as Mother to the world, Krishnabai felt no deprivation at the request of her child, her devotee. As Anandamayi Ma, another blissful Divine Mother has said: "It is

Mother Krishnabai

the mother's delight to give to her children." For Krishnabai, giving to the other was no different than giving to Papa, who was not separate from God.

Mataji's generosity melded with Papa's to create a hospital, a school, and countless work projects which supplied livelihood for many poor workers. They also offered food and clothing to all beggars and other needy people who approached their ashram. Even today, the generous spirit of Mother Krishnabai saturates the grounds of Anandashram where people are given spiritual food as well as the temporal food which they come seeking.

Mataji's Divine Economy

Krishnabai's philanthropy taxed both the incredulity of the logical mind and the resources of the ashram itself, yet her generosity never subsided. In fact, the tension created between the need to balance accounts and Mataji's overflowing unselfishness was a source of both concern, admiration and humor for Papa who occasionally joked with her about it.

Mataji used to purchase cloth from a particular shop in town. She would then freely distribute this cloth to poor devotees and sadhus. One day in 1953, one of Papa's devotees informed him that their bill at this merchant's for the past four months had amounted to two thousand rupees (an enormous sum in those days). Heaving a sigh and looking at her, Papa said to Krishnabai: "What do you say now?" But Mataji only laughed in response, inciting his own enormous playfulness. Papa was helpless to do other than laugh too; and more, to make the whole scene cause for even greater hilarity. Referring to himself, he said:

> When Ramdas heard that figure, his breath ·
> stopped. He got Kumbhaka [a type of breath
> practice in Yoga wherein the breath is retained].
> His breath went up and stopped at the sahasrara
> [the thousand petalled lotus in the cerebrum
> wherein Shiva unites with Shakti, an extremely

high state of consciousness to say the least]; he came within an ace of *nirvikalpa samadhi* [the Superconscious state wherein the Eternal Brahman is attained]. If the breath does not stop on hearing such news, when will it stop?[13]

And then he burst into laughter, rolling with it; and his face became red, and he perspired from laughing so long and so hard. Mataji was slightly disturbed and remarked that Papa was making fun of her, to which Ramdas immediately retorted: "Not at all. You are spending as you like, liberally. And no wonder. For, you are running the whole universe! But you should *get* also as you give."[14]

It was a loving response, another opportunity for the Guru to honor his most beloved devotee, speaking a truth about her role in creation. At the same time, his earthly concern for resources was given voice. Mataji, in her complete faith in God's Divine Providence and in obedience to her role, replied without hesitation, giving us another glimpse of the spirit which animated this dynamic woman: "*Getting*, you [Papa] must do. It is *your* job to get things. I can only give."[15]

Faith Unending

It may be difficult for those of us raised in the West to fathom the uncompromising faith which many Indian devotees have in the guru. Guru is revered as doctor and priest to both body and soul. As an interesting parallel, we learn from contemporary medicine that the patient's faith in her treatment and her doctor are dynamic ingredients in the effectiveness of any intervention.

Despite the fact that she honored some modern approaches to healing, Mataji's primary medicine was that of love and surrender to God. She constantly ministered to other devotees by concocting medicinals from the indigenous plants that grew on the ashram. In her mind, such plants were more than empowered substances, they were the flesh and blood of Papa, since the earth itself was his body. But by far, her favorite medicinal, which she used on innumerable occasions and with miraculous results, was *pada tirtha*: *pada* mean-ing foot, and *tirtha*, meaning holy or consecrated water.

To understand this practice and the effects of it, it is neces-sary to have a little background about the symbolism of the feet of the guru as representative of the feet of God. Quite literally, since the feet touch the earth more than any other part of the body, they establish a communication point. Energy from the body flows into the earth through the feet, and vice versa. In the case of the saint or guru, their feet transmit the blessings of the Divine onto the human plane. Whether they walk unshod, or in simple sandals, as many Indian saints have done and do, their feet remain a tangent point of Divine intervention. Whereas the face changes expression, the feet are relatively changeless, thus symbolizing the Brahman. Recall the story of Mary Magdalen who washed Christ's feet with her tears, dried them with her hair, and anointed them with pre-cious oil, as the full expression of her devotion.

In the simple *pada pooja* ceremony, the Guru's feet (or the feet of a deity) are washed with water, and then the water is col-lected and drunk by devotees, or bottled and saved for the same purposes with which Catholics might use Lourdes water, or other holy water as an artifact for consecration or protection. As far as Krishnabai was concerned, this water was incomparable medicine, since it literally contained the dust of the Guru's Feet. Moreover, anything that had touched him was sanctified, potentized.

The faith of Papa's devotees was so great that even before going to the hospital they would come to Mataji and ask for the *pada tirtha*. And on many occasions, the patient recovered so com-pletely from drinking this sacred liquid that further intervention was unnecessary. Not only humans profited from this divine elixir. When a cow suffered the throes of a painful labor, Mataji was there to ease its suffering with the *pada tirtha*, pouring the liquid into the animal's mouth.

She tells of a particularly traumatic labor that one of the cows went through in the early part of 1956. Because of some dislocated bones, an obstruction was discovered and the only rem-edy for saving the mother cow's life seemed to be to kill the calf, dismembering it within the mother's body. Those who attended the cow rushed to Mataji for the *tirtha*. Fully confidant, and wishing to strengthen their faith even more, Krishnabai asked one of the men to immediately go and wash Papa's feet and then to take the *tirtha* to the cow. Describing the situation later, Mataji said:

> Wonderfully enough, when he put his hand again to take the calf out, he found that the bone, which was causing the obstruction, slowly went in and the calf came out. Though there was great strain, both the calf and cow were saved.[16]

Her Exhortations to All

Krishnabai became an exhorter of souls—begging, demanding, joking, pleading, telling stories, whatever she could do to urge others toward surrender and service to Papa. She wanted everyone to have the absorption and complete happiness in the Divine that she had. This, after all, is Divine Mother's job—to bring her children to the ultimate banquet. She will do whatever she can, even using tricks and ploys, harsh words, if necessary.

On one intimate occasion in 1956, Mataji addressed Swami Satchidananda, who was Papa's right hand man and a dedicated monk. Her words to him reveal a blessed secret. Mataji said:

> I had better tell you when I remember. The easiest path to attain oneness with Papa is to accept him as Mother. That is the best way, especially to maintain *brahmacharya* [priestly celibacy]. You look upon Papa as Mother; that means that you look upon all as the form of Mother and yourself as a child of Her. When you have this attitude, lust will never overpower and you can remain pure like a child.[17]

The Devotee's Fire

Krishnabai was never an icon according to some worldly standard of appropriateness. Her piercing words were known to impale many a would-be helper or questioner. She could rave at the ashram workers for their shoddy attention with the same force that she would rail against the egoic ploys of Papa's followers who were only interested in his obvious attention.

Papa prized this fierceness in her, even though he admitted on many occasions that he himself had been at the effect of it in the early days. (He speaks of himself in the third person.)

> In the early days her main attack was on Ramdas, and Ramdas also was a fiery fellow....Yes, she was a terror in those days and Ramdas used to run away. But now he won't do it. He cannot sleep on thorns and stones, and in chill weather. Further, he is submissive nowadays.[18]

One day, as Mataji lamented, as she had many times, that people had not accepted nor understood Papa properly, she disclosed the essence of the guru-devotee relationship, expressing how attention to the one leads to merger with the One.

> Mind has a great power. You can gradually increase the circle of love from your mother, father, wife, children and so on to Papa who is the whole world, till you finally feel that the universe is Papa's form and that Papa is beyond that also. As you experience that you and Papa are one, you will realize that you are the entire universe.... the mental acceptance that Papa is the whole universe leads you to the experience of the formless, nameless aspect of Papa. When you come down from that experience you also know that you are the whole universe. But this experience fades

away. It takes some time before one is established
in it. When one is established in the experience
of the *nirguna* aspect which is beyond all name,
form and movement, one sees oneself as the universe. Until then, the experience comes and goes.
It requires some effort to connect the manifest and
the unmanifest aspects. It takes some time to realize that both are aspects of the same Truth and
that they co-exist.[19]

On Her Sadhana

In certain rare moments, Mataji enlightened her listeners by
specifying her own daily interior practice. Papa had instructed her
to do three things: to chant the name of God (*Ramnam*), to see all
things as himself, and to serve everyone as if she were serving him.
To hear her describe the one hundred percent-approach that she
took to everything, is to be both amazed and inspired. One must
realize, however, that Krishnabai's urgency came from holding her
sadhana as a life and death matter. Only this degree of seriousness
could have energized her to work in the way she did, and with so
much love.

> When the work was over and I was free, I used to
> keep walking in a hall or elsewhere, chanting
> Ramnam. When working, if I touched something,
> I would say, "This is Yourself, Papa. What a beau-
> tiful form you have taken! You are beyond all
> forms." So, there was no moment when I was ei-
> ther not chanting Ramnam or talking to and serv-
> ing Papa. If I saw a flower, I would take it in my
> hand and looking at it, say "O Papa! how beauti-
> ful you look in this form! What fragrance you
> emit!" So, we must be communing with Papa con-
> stantly by chanting the Name, contemplation and
> service. If, at any time, you develop some emo-

tions, do not encourage them. Pray to Papa within to take you beyond all emotions and make you merge in His Eternal Being. If you succumb to emotions, you will not progress. At another stage, you may develop some *Siddhis* [spiritual powers, like the ability to read minds, or the ability to control others]. Again, pray to Papa not to give you occult powers but only to take you to the highest. Siddhis will pull you down and take you away from the path.[20]

Krishnabai genuinely earned the name Mother. She was a Mother when she lived, and that Motherhood may still be invoked today, by any woman who comes to her as a child, a sister, or a friend in need.

Yet, together with her exalted status as Mother, Krishnabai was a devotee. She embodied this attribute of the Divine with extreme elegance and made it accessible to all who came in touch with her. Women today who wish to learn more of the mystery and the wonder of the *bhakti* path will find in Krishnabai no greater advocate and guide.

I will end by sharing a few small selections from a long poem written in praise of Krishnabai by none other than her guru, Ramdas. When we catch a glimpse of the guru bowing down at the feet of the disciple, as this poem illustrates, we are gifted with another clue to an awesome and eternal mystery.

Homage To Mother Krishnabai
O goddess of love and grace!
To whom shall I compare thee—
The incomparable!

'Tis hard to believe such purity, light, love and peace
Could hold in a frail human frame.
Thou art a flower—a star of spontaneity
Shedding beauty, love and joy
With bewildering simplicity…
Thou art forever a beacon for all struggling souls…
Thou art my guardian angel.

O Mother! With what greater word than this
Can I address thee?
Thou art the Mother of the world,
Thou dwellest in the hearts of all
Thou art the world itself—
The Divine Power, invincible, all-pervading, eternal.
Thou art the supreme Truth of truths,
Light of lights, wisdom, beauty and bliss…
All hail to thee—all hail!

To gaze on thee is to grow into thy likeness,
Thou are one with all that lives,
Thou seest no distinctions.
Thou knoweth thou art everywhere.
….Thou art the very embodiment
Of universal love and service.
Thou showeth, this is the way human life
Attains freedom and peace—immortality, God,
the highest beatitude,
Heaven or salvation, whatever you call it.
O, Omnipotent Power manifest!
What words can describe thy infinite greatness and glory?[21]
                                        —Swami Papa Ramdas

12

THE PATH OF COMMUNITY

The first time I heard the phrase "women's culture" I was captivated by it. Shortly after meeting my teacher Lee in March 1985, I traveled to his ashram in northern Arizona to meet the rest of the community that had grown up around him. I was immediately impressed with the power, the elegance and the grace of the women in this group. They laughed a lot, and heartily, which I definitely took as a good sign.

I liked these women. For one thing they were full-bodied in their spirituality. They lived with their husbands or lovers, had children, and also passionately honored the relationship to their teacher as the sacrosanct opportunity of their lives. They further intrigued me with references to "group *sadhana*" or "group enlightenment," as opposed to individual liberation or salvation. It seemed a mature consideration.

These women used the term "women's culture" to talk about something indeterminate which they were attempting to cultivate and grow, though no one could tell me *exactly* what this thing *was* that we were supposed to be cultivating. One reason, I came to find out, was that the essence of women's culture could not be expressed in words, another of those numinous realities discovered primarily through intuition. Then too, women's culture was something that one *lived*, not talked about. It was so connected to *who we were*, integral to every activity of our lives that it was like trying to get fish to talk about water. And quite frankly, the women in the community claimed to be beginners in this lifelong quest for something Real—something about the essential Feminine which they trusted would be revealed to them as they spent more time together as sisters, mothers, friends and practitioners of the way.

As years went by and I integrated into the community, I discovered a gnawing dissatisfaction among the women, myself included, that despite our intentions and the enormous help that was constantly available to us from our teacher, we were seriously missing the full potency of such a reality as "women's culture." As women raised in a twentieth-century, middle-class, TV culture, our images of who Woman was and how women could "be" together were still perversely skewed. Our competition with one another, our jealousies, our own self-hatred and self-obsession, and particularly our own acceptance of many aspects of the larger culture's mindset about women, had still kept us relatively immature and weak in this regard, in contrast to the ideal which Lee held out for us.

We found that we had so much to unlearn. Women's culture, as we fumbled in our attempts to "grow" it, was not about studying feminism and the principles and political stands of liberation. Many of us had a long history of political activism. And while we didn't reject what was of value in those domains, we often found that the militant or the reasoned approach was antithetical to the qualities that we were attempting to reinstate within our own body-minds. Like any other strategy of ego, a "position" of feminism was still a means which fostered the illusion of separation—women strong and independent, yet reveling in our separation from men; woman empowered and self-nurturing, yet still angry with and jealous of other women; women celebrating the goddess, yet still locating Her outside of themselves, despite their best intentions. We all still had a lot to learn.

Thirteen years later we still have a lot to learn. Yet, with the benediction of our teacher, our own focused practice and our on-going inquiry we have come a long way in living into this reality of women's culture. We have been slowly opening to the power and depth of the Divine Feminine as She manifests everywhere, and in one another.

THE RASA OF WOMEN IN LOVE

The hunger for women's culture is something that goes far beyond the desire to ease our loneliness by assuring that we will have a companion at dinner or the movies, a traveling partner, or a sister to share clothes and recipes with. Certainly these are all fine goals, but not the essential gift of women being together.

Nor is our bonding with women a way to find a soul-friend, a sister to confide in, to weep with, to talk over our pain, or one to hold our hands as we give birth or as we die. And here again, these friendships and even love affairs are among the greatest gifts that women can know. Gifts that only women can give to one another.

Something else, something subtler still, is the reason for and the result of women's culture. That subtlety can be expressed in Sanskrit quite easily, whereas in English the words may escape us. *Rasa* the Hindu scriptures call it, and it translates into "nectar of mood," a nebulous expression at best. "Juice" or "subtle substance," my friend and mentor Lalitha calls it. And this "juice," she says, not only waters the garden of the soul, but also flows in and through the body, causing it to radiate (to use a visual metaphor), to exude an irresistible fragrance (to use an olfactory metaphor), or to pro-duce a type of food (a bread) or a type of drink (a nectar) which will attract the attention of a hungry or thirsty entity of a higher domain—an angelic being, a goddess, a *dakini*, the Lord Krishna, Lord Jesus, or Divine Mother Herself.

403

Quite simply, women's culture is a full-scale participation in a cosmic cooking class in which the main item on the menu is Woman herself. We attempt to create of ourselves the tastiest morsel possible, through our own efforts as well as by giving ourselves over to a Master Chef, offering our own body-mind-spirit as an energetic emanation or a literal substance to feed the next highest level of creation. In being "consumed," then, the once separate individual is transformed into the "body" or substance of the "consumer." The two have become one flesh, so to speak—one nurturing the ongoing work of the other. "Interpenetrated" is a word the mystics like to use in this regard in describing how the individual soul is transformed into the very being of the Beloved. No one expresses this more elegantly than one of my favorite guides in this mystical journey of Love, Hadewijch of Antwerp (or Brabant), whom we will meet later in this chapter. Hadewijch wrote to her sister practitioners of the thirteenth century:

> Where the abyss of his wisdom is, he will teach you what he is, and with what wondrous sweetness the loved one and the Beloved dwell one in the other, and how they penetrate each other in such a way that neither of the two distinguishes himself from the other. But they abide in one another in fruition, mouth in mouth, heart in heart, body in body, and soul in soul, while one sweet divine Nature flows through them both (2 Pet. 1:4), and they are both one thing through each other, but at the same time remain two different selves—yes, and remain so forever.[1]

To ground this profound mystical consideration into our everyday experience, let us say that the purpose of women's culture is to nurture the Divine Feminine within each woman. *What* nurtures that, like mother's milk, is this *rasa*, the "nectar of mood"— the substance, subtle though it is, that is created, absorbed, drunk and eaten when women attend to one another in a way marked by conscious attention, and together attend to something higher or greater than their individual selves. When women together are willing to drop the divisions and petty jealousies of mind, and to "feel into" the essence of Woman as it is being manifest in one or more women in their company, they participate in the *rasa* of the Divine Feminine.

Examples are numberless. In the early 1980s, having just returned from my first trip to India where I had spent nearly nine months at the ashram of Bhagwan Shree Rajneesh (now referred to as Osho), I attended a workshop led by one of the women who had been in the Master's close company for over fifteen years. Ma Deva was exceptionally psychic—no sooner would a question enter my mind than she would be speaking about it. On the second day of the gathering I began to feel strong sentiments of envy coupled with anger towards another woman participant. The object of my negative attention was a younger, extremely beautiful woman whom everyone seemed to like. She possessed a quality of innocence that was both disarming and embarrassing. Her devotion to her teacher, Rajneesh, was unabashed. Whenever she spoke I found myself feeling shame at how poor my own love and commitment and faith seemed by comparison. Just as my negative feelings reached a boiling point, Ma Deva began to talk to us about the nature of life in any community surrounding a teacher or a Master. Her words are as strong to me today as they were on that crisp fall morning nearly seventeen years ago. She looked compassionately at the assembled group of women: "There is always going to be another woman who is more beautiful, more well thought of, more talented, more kindly and generous, and more devoted ... always. We each need to make our peace with that."

Her words hit me like a sudden stop at sixty miles per hour. No! I inwardly screamed. I did not want to deal with that reality. I did not want to know that for the rest of my life I would be called upon to face these same painful feelings again and again.

I made two decisions in that moment. One was to find that place within myself wherein comparison was meaningless, once and for all, and then to live from there—that is, to break through the illusion of separation. Secondly, I determined that from then on I would go *towards* the object of my jealousy, rather than retreat from her. In this decision I consciously acknowledged that by befriending the one who challenged me, I could learn to embrace the reality that this other was a part of myself which I was disowning. I could accept, love her and learn from her.

The result at the time was quite astounding. Getting to know my "competitor" literally changed everything. Of course, just like me, she turned out to be another wounded, struggling and often confused woman. But most of all, the synergistic blending of our devotion for our guru and his teaching of Love took on a life of its own. That Love became the larger context in which my jealousies and comparisons lost their meaning. Each of us was reminding the other of her inherent dignity, her great passion, her fierce hunger for truth. And together we were building something that neither of us could have done as efficiently alone.

The Beguines, that extraordinary women's culture of the Middle Ages, expressed their purpose to be that of "exhorting one another to greater holiness." Our purpose here will be the same.

THE BEGUINES

When I lived in Colorado, at all seasons of the year I would race-walk along Denver's Highline Canal—a gorgeous and merciful stretch of undeveloped land that snakes its way through the city from north to south. A thin stream of water, cattails, towering cottonwoods, wildflowers, in the spring; patches of mud and snow, bare and lonely branches in the midst of winter—the trail that bordered the canal provided a meditation on the transitory nature of existence.

In one particular spot not far from my home, the path wound through the back yard of an enormous housing development for the elderly: Windsor Gardens—eight or ten separate buildings, each six stories high. Each story had twenty identical back porches facing the canal; twenty small picture windows, curtained usually in cream or white; twenty tiny kitchen windows, most of them adorned with flower pots. And in the warm afternoons of spring and fall, these back porches were the favorite haunts of their apartment's inhabitants, who would sit there and watch the world go by. Dozens of single, elderly women in lawn chairs (the housing complex was open to both sexes, but many more women are long-term survivors than men in this culture), each alone on her own back porch. I often thought that they looked like monks emerging from their cells to get a glimpse of the sun, and I hoped that their inner lives were as happy and peace-filled as many monks I have known. But based on the looks on their faces, I doubted it.

What possibility existed for these women beyond this isolated existence, I often wondered. "You can't get too friendly with the people on your floor," one ninety-two-year-old woman told me, "or pretty soon they will be coming over to talk at all hours of the day or night."

"Do you like living alone?" I asked her.

"I always feel better when I have company," she said as she smiled bravely.

I started learning about the Beguines at about the same time that I started reflecting upon the pain of the women in Windsor Gardens. Maybe I was hoping to find an alternative future for myself and the women of my generation.

I first encountered the Beguines as I studied the mysticism of Mechtild of Magdeburg, a thirteenth century German whose ecstatic poetry leapt off the page, calling me to wake up once again:

> Woman!
>   Your soul has slept from childhood on.
> Now,
>   it is awakened
>   by the light of true love,
>   In this light,

the soul looks around her
To discover who it is
Who is showing Himself to her here.
Now,
      she sees clearly
      she recognizes for the first time
      How
           God
               is All
                    in All.[2]

Since that first meeting I have read the poetry of Mechtild and other Beguines, and often told stories about the Beguine movement. Women of our day seem encouraged by the life of spiritual sisterhood, contemplation and service which these women—their great great great great grandmothers in the Netherlands, Germany, Italy, France and Belgium—created for themselves.

History of the Movement

The Beguine movement began at the end of the twelfth century and still endures in isolated sectors of northern Europe to the present day. Marie of Oignies (1167-1213) is honored as one of several key figures in the foundation of the movement, although it was not a formal founding of sorts. Marie, like other "founders," simply attracted women who wanted to lead a life of simplicity, service and devotion. The fact that she carried the stigmata undoubtedly had something to do with her popularity, both with other pious women and with the clergy and laity as well.

The earliest Beguines were similarly pious women, many of whom were ecstatic by temperament, since the times (both ecclesiastically and politically) were calling for a return to the heart. Many of them lived initially in their own homes, and later banded together in communities, sometimes as large as small cities, for mutual support in carrying out their desire for prayer, spiritual practice (especially the recitation of the Hours of the Divine Office) and charitable work. Initially they received no official status of any kind, and probably would have been overlooked for a lot longer had it not been that their lives were so compelling that they began to attract scores, hundreds, and finally thousands of other like-minded and open-hearted women of all ages to their ranks.

Ongoing controversy continues about where the name "Beguine" actually came from. Some say from St. Begga, a seventh century duchess of the area, who was adopted as a patron saint of the Beguines. Others credit the name to a priest from Liege who lived around the year 1177. His name was Lambert Le Begue, and he proved himself to be a staunch supporter of these women. Others say that it is derived from the gray cloth that was often characteristic of their dress.

Undoubtedly, some of what we know about the Beguines is clouded by our own projections of who we want them to be—this has certainly been true for me. Some of what we know has been pieced together from random sources, which necessarily renders an incomplete picture. And, while scholarly research into this fascinating movement continues today, we can still venture a few educated guesses of our own about the whys, wherefores and practical details of their lives.

The movement seems to have originated first among women from the middle classes, many of whom probably wanted a more dynamic alternative from the dead-end of either courtly or married life, which was woman's fate in those days. They wanted a life of service and piety, but not the restrictions imposed by the vowed and male-dominated contemplative religious life within the nunneries.

The Crusades were engaging massive numbers of eligible men of the times, and one is led to imagine that the Beguines, in their own quiet ways, were forming communities of action and prayer as the feminine counterpart to the male-oriented war culture. Certainly the independence offered within Beguinages, together with opportunity for higher education, was enormously attractive to many women. The structure of Beguine life was not hierarchical, as each house was independent of the others, and made its own rules and structures.

The power to avoid traditional stereotypes, to discover their own potential and to compose and control their own institutions, however tenuous, culturally conditioned and vulnerable these attempts may have been, represent the great strength and originality of the Beguine movement.[3]

Between 1230 and 1300 in the Low Countries, almost every town had a beguinage granted to it. In and around 1250 in Nivelles, Belgium, there were reports of two thousand Beguines living in this one city alone. Between 1250 and 1350 there were one hundred houses, probably housing a thousand women, founded in the city of Köln, Germany. The movement spread from the Low Countries to northern France and then to Germany, primarily, but also made inroads into Sweden, Spain, Italy, Austria, Poland and Hungary.

The further one delves into this movement, the picture that begins to emerge is actually a colorful representation of women's culture beyond anything most of us have ever experienced or even imagined in our times. Consider living and growing up in a city of women, a city owned and operated by powerful, savvy and kind, spiritual women. Imagine having free access to the support and encouragement of one's friends and sisters at any time of day or night? What a joyful celebration must have marked such existence, insofar as jealousy and other neurotic attachments were under control, that is.

The Spirituality

Beguines who hear these words,
If life on earth
Makes you weep and complain,
Find your comfort in God:
Know that it is His will
That keeps you dwelling here below,
And the more your hearts burn with love—
As mine did, when I lived—

The more lovely to Him you will be.
It is the color that He loves best,
The color in which He is clothed.
In this you will be like Him.

And if of some of you
He requires even more,
Asks of you a payment of pain,
Praise Him more joyously still:
The great Good that awaits you
Should make your patience strong.
As a rust-covered sword soon gleams
Beneath the weight of a polishing hand,
So the soul who gives herself truly
Comes to shine with the blows of God.

And just as we plunge pure wool
In the scarlet dye again and again,
to brighten and fix the color,
God transforms and guides the soul;
Difficulty and plunging grief
Will deepen its hue and its worth.
And if for love of your Creator
You can find patience in this sorrow,
You will surely receive the highest gift—
You will walk in glory and honor
In the vision of the Savior,
Having lived and burned for Him in human flesh.[4]
       —a French Beguine, 13th century, Lille

In 1216, Jacques de Vitry obtained a papal sanction from Pope Honorius III for these women to live together and encourage one another to a good life. This interesting phrase "encourage one another" is the basis on which women of spirit have come together throughout the ages. Certainly we have come for mutual protection, for the synergistic effects of our labors, and for

411

the companionship and joy inherent in such a life, but this element of mutual encouragement, giving one another *courage* such that we may each find the pearl of great price, is the possibility that life in community affords. Women can do this for one another, if they allow their inherent goodness to express itself.

The earliest Beguines wore a simple, unadorned and even austere variety of the secular dress of the times. This eventually evolved into a gray, blue or black habit with a white veil. The manner of dress was indicative of the type of witness that these women wished to give. They were deliberately rejecting the superfluous courtly values that characterized the times, choosing instead to devote themselves to where help was desperately needed—among the sick and poor.

> In the midst of worldly people they were spiritual,
> in the midst of pleasure-seekers they were pure
> and in the midst of noise and confusion they led a
> serene, eremitical life.
> —Caesarius Heisterbach, 1180-1240 AD

> While reacting against the wealth and ostentation of secular society, the Beguines did not see poverty as an end in itself, rather they encouraged the development of the virtues of charity, humility and companionship.[5]

The Beguine spiritual commitment was not necessarily viewed as a lifelong dedication. While they promised chastity during the time in which they lived as Beguines, they were also free to leave and to pursue marriage or to enter a formal convent whenever they wished. Perhaps many of them dreamed of the return of their men-folk from the Crusades, while they focused their passion and longing on the Divine Person, Christ, who would never abandon them.

The rise of the Beguine movement in the late 1100s corresponded with an intense period of popular piety, particularly among women. The focus of such devotion was to the humanity of Christ and his passion. The"mystical marriage" was talked about in great detail—this marriage of the soul and the heavenly bridegroom. Poverty, chastity and love for the Eucharist were similarly emphasized.

The Beguines were essentially servants of God's people. Like Hadewijch, who had received a vision of God that clarified for her the inseparability of God and man in the person of Jesus, they knew that becoming fully human (the primary theme of all Hadewijch's writing) was a necessary foundation for the mystical life.

Asceticism frequently accompanied their piety, and in some cases became extreme—the idea of subduing the body and its desires was inherent in Christian religious doctrine at the time. So, despite the fact that the Beguines were considered generally quite sane, there was always this undercurrent of ecstatic (sometimes bordering on neurotic or even psychotic) expression. It is not surprising. In any body of practitioners there will always be some who have more of a mystical bent. As long as the whole group is not infected by a false mysticism, the true mystics, even if they are a bit mad, are an important ingredient in the stew.

Despite ascetical excesses by individuals, therefore, the Beguines in general were well-balanced in their approach to spiritual life. Annual visitations were made to the Beguine houses and convents by their Grand Mistresses, whose inspection was designed to determine whether the women were living such balance—neither self-indulgence nor abject poverty was prized.

In general, the Beguines as a group tended to be somewhat cool about mystical extremes. The ability to work was highly prized among them, and if some women were so enraptured by their experiences or visions that they couldn't work, they were not encouraged. If any aspect of their experiences smacked of being plagued by demons, such women were similarly not encouraged. Women reporting such phenomena might be dismissed from the group as being deranged, or accused of false holiness.

The problem was, however, that even though the more balanced women within the communities might be put off by those who exhibited extreme phenomena, many priests (their confessors) and lay people were attracted to those who expressed the more dramatic manifestations, and it was easy for cults to grow up around one or more of these women. People in those times were fascinated by the bizarre as much as we are today. Whether in the form of bliss trances, stigmata, or madness, people often view such expressions as being some sign of a special favor from God. Meanwhile, the Beguines themselves within their own houses of prayer, were urging balance and moderation which was essential to the accomplishment of their given work.

The Decline of Beguine Culture

Sentiment towards the Beguines and their way of life was always in flux. Under all sorts of pretenses, pressures subtle or great were brought to bear against both individual women and their foundations. In the early days, when many of them lived in their own homes, although they did tend to congregate around an institution, like a hospital or another monastery, they would buy houses or property closer to one another to accommodate affiliation. As time went on, however, they sought some protection for themselves in living a communal existence, and in fact in the eyes of their detractors the ones who lived alone were not viewed as favorably as those who lived in houses (usually of from ten to fifty members). The singular ones were often accused of bringing down the reputation of the rest.

Especially as the movement grew, many clerics were understandably uncomfortable with the degree of independence practiced by many of these women. Their piety was certainly drawing attention to them, even at the expense of the already established communities like the Dominican and Franciscans.

In 1311-12 a church council was held in Vienne at which the current pope, Clement V, issued a papal bull (an official proclamation) which attempted to destroy the Beguine movement. It called upon Beguines to abandon their way of life. They were to be, "... permanently forbidden and altogether excluded from the Church of God."

And on what grounds? Supposedly the Beguines were afflicted with some madness which allowed them to openly discuss the doctrine of the Holy Trinity and the Divine Essence in such a way as to lead simple people astray. The precise accusation was that they: "express[ed] opinions on matters of faith and sacraments contrary to the catholic faith." Imagine these good-hearted women, whose primary desire was to serve the poor and to cultivate their own internal lives, getting so embroiled in a theological controversy? Sounds like an example of patriarchal paranoia if ever there was one.

More likely, what was really going on was that the patriarchs were not able to control these women strongly enough, since their convents were not subject to the rules of official ecclesiastics. At the same time, the fact that the Beguines were becoming such a powerful lay movement that they threatened the authority of the ruling class would have had a hand in their denunciation.

This papal bull did have one saving clause, however. It was spelled out, to Clement's credit, that the decree was not essentially intended to forbid pious women from living as God was directing them, even if they took no official vows, provided they lived chastely, dedicating themselves to serve God in humility.

It may have been an "out" to save Clement and company from being branded throughout history, although it was not a big enough loophole that it changed the overall climate that surrounded the movement at this time. The Beguines, and their male counterparts the Beghards, were definitely on the outs. In some cities their associations were completely dissolved, and they were forced to join the existing religious orders of the time. Their property was revoked, and in some cases they were even pressured to marry.

In 1318, John XXII, who followed Clement as pope, issued a *Ratio Recta* aimed at defending the Beguines again. This was just another temporary respite from a long and troubled history which these courageous women (and men) were forced to endure. Back

415

and forth throughout the years they suffered greatly from the unpredictable religious climate.

By 1421 the tide had really turned against them. Pope Martin V actually ordered the Archbishop of Köln to "search out and destroy any small convents of persons living under the cloak of religion without a definite Rule." Germany was most vociferous in its hatred of this independent spirit. In the Low Countries and in northern France the climate was much more lenient.

The Beguines were persecuted in a variety of ways. One horror story stands out among all the rest, however. Marguerite of Porete, a Beguine mystic, was burned at the stake in Paris in the year 1310. Marguerite was accused of the heresy of the Free Spirit, a charge that was making the rounds among the Inquisitors of the day. Many women were questioned about their views on this subject, including Ida of Nivelles, a saintly women whose ideas were very similar to those of Marguerite. Ida, however, was a Cistercian nun and therefore had the protection of her entire order to back her up. Marguerite, on the other hand, being an independent Beguine, was unprotected. Her doctrine of a type of mystical love which in effect removed one from the control of the church was evidently intolerable to the powers that be, although some sources claim that her execution was not because of her views primarily, but rather because she continued to circulate her book, in disobedience to the authorities' condemnation of it.

A Future for Beguines?

Perhaps in the future, the fascination that many women feel for Beguine life and culture today will take rebirth in the creation of similar kinds of "women's houses" of prayer, or even with temporary vocations to the contemplative life. As "Rome" burns, the move to the desert becomes ever more urgent in those who want to maintain some sanity. The Beguines offer us a model of hope and a model of possibility of what women together can do.

From The Writing Of Beguine Mystics And Saints

Marguerite of Porete (died 1310)

Marguerite's condemnation is less surprising when we read some of the radical words she wrote in describing her mystical ascent.

> The soul at the highest stage of her perfection and nearest the dark night is beyond noticing the rules of the Church. She is commanded by pure love, which is a higher mistress than what we call "charitable works." She has passed so far beyond the works of virtue that she no longer knows what they are about—but yet she has assimilated them to the point where they are part of her, the Church cannot control her—the Church being understood as mainly to do with those who live in fear of the Lord, which is one of the gifts of the Holy Spirit.[6]

In this next passage, Marguerite further elaborates upon the profound freedom of the soul who, having tasted Love, rejects any offer of a separate paradise. For Marguerite as for Hadewijch and others among the Beguines, Love *was* God.

> If anyone were to ask of such free souls ... if they would wish to be in paradise, they would say no. Besides, with what would they wish it? They have no will at all, and if they were to wish for anything, that would mean severing themselves from Love ... For that one all alone is my God of whom one cannot utter a word, of whom all those in paradise cannot attain a single atom, no matter how much knowledge they have of him ... And so I say, and it is truth, that one can give me nothing, nothing that could be ... Ah what a sweet insight this is! In God's name understand it fully, for paradise is nothing other than this understanding.[7]

The fact that Marguerite never defended herself to her captors is perhaps touched upon in this closing part of her book wherein
she sings her "Farewell Song of Fine Amour":

> Thinking is no more use to me,
> nor work, nor verbal skill:
> Love draws me up so loftily
> —thinking is no more use to me.[8]

MECHTILD OF MAGDEBURG (1210-1280)

Mechtild's poetry moves! Her words are full of imagery of
dancing and leaping. In one piece she says that God had instructed
her "to leap in ordered dance," and I recall feeling my own heart
rise as I read these words. Clearly she was speaking of an interior
dance, not some kind of ego-based external form. Mechtild's life
proclaimed that only through deep silence, focus and prayer would
the soul learn to truly dance.

On Service:

> Heal the broken
>   with comforting words of God.
>   Cheer them gently
>   with earthly joys.
> Be merry
>   and laugh with the broken
> and carry their secret needs
> in the deepest silence of your heart.[9]

Of a Transformed Life:

> Are you willing to run toward emptiness
> Fleeing the self
> To Stand alone
> and Ask no one's help?

Then your soul shall be quiet,
released from its bondage to things.

And your work? Simply free other captives.
To those who dwell in a prison of mind, show the door.
Care for the sick.

Live alone, and drink gladly from the waters of sorrow.
Love's fire will be kindled only with great perseverance.
This is what it means to enter the desert.[10]

The Wound of Love:

Whoever has at any time been severely wounded
  by true love
Will never recover his health—
Unless he kisses the same mouth
Which caused his soul to become ill.[11]

A Life-positive Spirituality:

Then God praised the loving soul in which He
took delight: "You are the light of My eyes, the
lyre of My ears, the voice of My words, the purpose of My goodness, the honor of My wisdom; a
love in My life, you are a praise of My being."[12]

Her Approach to Death:

The soul spoke: "Lord, this way pleases me far more
than I deserve, but I am concerned about leaving
my body." Our Lord replied: "When that happens,
I will draw in My breath, and you will follow Me
like a magnet."[13]

BEATRICE OF NAZARETH (1220-1268)

This following description of the possession by love which the soul experiences is unequalled in its clarity and purity. Beatrice was raised by the Beguines of Zoutleeuw, where she received her education. She then went on to join a Cistercian convent and became a prioress in this foundation, at Lier, until her death.

The Power of Love:

> Sometimes it happens that love is sweetly awoken in the soul and joyfully arises and moves in the heart of itself without us doing anything at all. And then the heart is so powerfully touched by love, so keenly drawn into love and so strongly seized by love, and so utterly mastered by love and so tenderly embraced by love, that it entirely yields itself to love. And in this it experiences a great proximity to God, a spiritual radiance, a marvelous bliss, a noble freedom, an ecstatic sweetness, a great overpowering by the strength of love and her will has become love, and that she is so deeply immersed and so engulfed in the abyss of love that she herself has turned entirely into love. Then the beauty of love has bedecked her, the power of love has devoured her, the sweetness of love has submerged her, the grandeur of love has consumed her, the nobility of love has enveloped her, the purity of love has adorned her, and the sublimity of love has drawn her upward and so united herself with her that she always must be love and do nothing but the deeds of love.[14]

THE WISDOM OF HADEWIJCH OF ANTWERP

We know little of the life of Hadewijch except the few clues left behind in her letters, recorded visions and poems, which fill a handsome volume of nearly four hundred pages. What these writings reveal in the domain of richness of spirit, however, could fill a library. Her artistic command of the language, her referral to courtly imagery, her use of a poetry form (the *minnesong*, or love-song in which the knight addresses his lady love, or vice versa) which was popular at the time among the upper classes, and the interspersion of her writings with references to medieval numerology, Ptolemaic astronomy and the theory of music, among other things, all indicate that she herself was an educated woman of the upper class.[15]

It is clear that Hadewijch either founded or was mistress of a Beguine community, and because she refers to them by name in a tone of motherly affection, we know that she had a number of young women under her care whom she was encouraging in their mystical life. Despite her great affection for these women, however, she was adamant in her demands that they live this life with vigor, throwing themselves into their prayer and their work with unflagging devotion and vigilance. The letters reveal, however, that despite their initial fervor and good wishes, none of her charges met her expectations.

Scholars guess that these high standards got Hadewijch into trouble, turning some of her sister Beguines, as well as some church authorities, against her. As her wisdom and holiness increased, therefore, so did the opposition with which she met. Hadewijch was threatened with the charge of teaching "quietism"—a heresy of the times—which could have meant exile from her community, as well as imprisonment by the Inquisition. Fortunately for her, and for history, Hadewijch was exiled but not imprisoned, and the theories are that she probably lived out her later years working in one of the hospitals or leprosariums that she had supported throughout her life.

Even when she herself was unjustly accused and exiled from her post, she was quick to express to the other women in her care that this suffering at the hands of "aliens" (as she called the people who follow the ways of worldly satisfaction) was one more way of drawing her more totally to the arms of Christ, her Beloved, who was murdered by the same people who had earlier honored him.

> O sweet child, your sadness, dejection, and grief give me pain! And this I entreat you urgently, and exhort you, and counsel you, and command you as a mother commands her dear child, whom she loves for the supreme honor and sweetest dignity of Love, to cast away from you all alien grief, and to grieve for my sake as little as you can. What happens to me, whether I am wandering in the country or put in prison—however it turns out, it is the work of Love ... I well understand that you cannot easily leave off grieving over my disgrace. But be aware dear child, that this is an alien grief. Think about it yourself; if you believe with all your heart that I am loved by God, and he is doing his work in me, secretly or openly, and that he renews his old wonders in me (cf. Ecclus. 36:6), you must also be aware that these are doings of Love, and that this must lead aliens to wonder at me and abhor me. For they cannot work in the domain of Love, because they know neither her coming nor her going ...[16]

Every page of Hadewijch's work is filled with the word *Love*, and none of the references leave any doubt that she is talking either of the person of Christ, of God, of Divine Love personified, or of the experience in which the soul perceives and is perceived by the Divine. It was this subject that became her obsession. Her question: "What is love?"—synonymous with "What is God? or Who is God?"—became the form of inquiry which led to her final absorption by that Love which she thought and spoke and sung and wrote about. In the strangest of paradoxes, reflective of a much more Eastern approach to the nature of the Absolute than that of her Christian company, she wrote of Divine Love as being the highest and the lowest, the source of hate and the source of bliss. Among the many poems and letters in which she addressed the nature of love, none is more curious and more profound than her declaration that "Love is Hell":

> Hell is the seventh name
> Of this Love wherein I suffer.
> For there is nothing Love does not engulf and damn,
> And no one who falls into her
> And whom she seizes comes out again,
> Because no grace exists there.
> As Hell turns everything to ruin,
> In Love nothing else is acquired
> But disquiet and torture without pity;
> Forever to be in unrest,
> Forever assault and new persecution;
> To be wholly devoured and engulfed
> In her unfathomable essence,
> To founder unceasingly in heat and cold,
> In the deep, insurmountable darkness of Love.
> This outdoes the torments of hell.
> He who knows Love and her comings and goings
> Has experienced and can understand
> Why it is appropriate
> That Hell should be the highest name of Love.[17]

Her mysticism is distinguished by the honored place she gave to reason as a balance and counterpoint to Love. One hears in this a kind of three-centered approach (intellect, heart, will) to living: the faculty of reason is not disdained despite the enormously rich *bhakti* quality of the heart; neither is the faculty of will given a backseat to the other two. Rather, it is with clarified mind, awakened heart and determined will to action that a woman must approach and walk the spiritual path of fulfillment in Love. Hadewijch knew only too well that the extremes of either—that reason without love, would yield the cold steel dogma which created the Inquisition; and that love or passion without reason would easily degenerate from religious devotionalism to false piety, simulated madness, neurotic or even psychotic excesses—all indulgences that could easily turn the "ravished" contemplative to mundane practices of passion. Instead, she presented the women in her care with a middle path, one which was as necessary in her day as it is in ours:

> Hadewijch was ahead of her time both in the freedom with which she embraced and talked about passionate love for God, and in her understanding that passion need not be cooled or distorted by reason.[18]

Hadewijch was a unique visionary. She learned from Christ himself that despite his divine condition it was necessary that he be fully human, in order that Love be made complete. Therefore, Hadewijch championed the cause of divinity expressed through humanity and counseled her sisters and spiritual daughters to continue to serve the needs of others, despite the hardships of the journey or the attraction to hide out in the ecstasy of their mysticism.

> He who wishes to become Love performs
>   excellent works,
> For nothing can make him give way;
> He is unconquered, and equal in strength
> To the task of winning the love of Love,
> Whether he serves the sick or the well,
> The blind, the crippled or the wounded—
> He will accept this as his debt to Love.
>
> To serve strangers, to give to the poor,
> To comfort the sorrowful as best he can,
> To live in the faithful service of God's friends—
> Saints or men on earth—night and day,

With all his might, beyond possibility—
If he thinks his strength will fail,
Let him trust henceforth in reliance on Love.[19]

GUIDANCE ON THE WOMAN'S PILGRIMAGE

Hadewijch knew that those entrusted to her could, theoretically, be led interiorly by the direction of the Holy Spirit. Yet,
wise mother that she was, she saw how easily distracted and discouraged her companions were. The voice of ego could disguise
itself as the voice of the Spirit, and Hadewijch knew from long
experience in working with other women, undoubtedly because
she had studied her own mind, that it was easy to set a course that
would lead to a dead-end. The role of the Mistress of a Beguine
community was to offer certain practical guidance in making important distinctions. She did this both through example as well as
through demand.

One of the most insightful and instructive of Hadewijch's
writings as it applies to women's culture and community is a letter
in which she lays out for her sister Beguines how this path of Love
proceeds—a blueprint of how the soul is gradually prepared for
initiation. In this letter she compares the journey of the soul to a
pilgrimage up a holy mountain: She describes the preparation necessary for the trip, the ways to maximize the actual ascent and
then descent of the mountain, and finally how to incorporate what
was gained into one's everyday life upon the return.

The women of Hadewijch's day would have been well versed
in the analogy of the pilgrimage, the knight's quest or the Holy
Crusade. Interestingly, as she writes about the journey it is not a
solitary phenomenon she is referring to. Rather, she reminds us
that we will travel *with others*, and we will return *to others* to speak
the great Truth that we have found. She used this letter to present
a roadmap for the life of community—herein making a strong case
for the necessity of companionship on the Way.

"Nine points," she wrote, "are fitting for the pilgrim who has
far to travel. The first is that he ask about the way. The second is

that he choose good company ..." and so on.[20] This second requirement for pilgrimage is the one we will consider here.

Using Mother Hadewijch's analogy, if we wanted to climb any sacred mountain and get the most from the trip, we would be foolish to travel there with friends whose primary interests were in shopping at the tourist stands or eating in the restaurants that provide a spectacular view. We would be better advised to search out women or men who shared our passion for the full experience, no matter how much they were challenged by it. Furthermore, the more treacherous the mountain, the more dangerous and discouraging it would be to make an ascent alone. The mountain of spiritual liberation is a mountain full of enormous risks, and even though each woman must *ultimately* go there alone in the depth of her own heart and soul, it takes a very rare soul to go anywhere without some help from others. While certain exceptional people may have *seemed* to accomplish this without companionship, in most cases they had some connection to a broader community. Even in the strictest eremitical traditions, the monk or hermit receives a "visitation" (as it is formally called) at least once and sometimes several times a year by the teacher or the superior of the community. And this for good reason. Good company not only encourages us, because there is usually inspiration from others and a demand to uphold something which the group has determined to be a higher good (a shared purpose), but also serves as protection from physical calamity as well as the emotional and spiritual calamities created by fantasies of imagination—a disease that can beset us when we are left solely to our own devices.

Women, moreover, are generally social beings. Most of us derive a great deal of our nourishment in and through relationship—a spiritual motherhood if you will, wherein we serve those before us and after us. I serve the ones who have come before me, honoring them for their wisdom and their advanced years in the Work, and I serve the ones who have come after me, teaching and instructing them in the ways of this precious life into which we have been called.

This is why today support groups based on a variety of wounded conditions are springing up everywhere: support for the bereaved, support for the sick, support for the addicted. And for short periods of time these can be invaluable sources of consolation. What Hadewijch was suggesting in the thirteenth century was a support group for prayer, a support group for the cultivation of virtue, and a support group for building courage, strength and joy.

Hadewijch was not naive about the sacrifices that would be found in submitting oneself to a life of service within community. She herself was berated, humiliated and ultimately abandoned by her so-called friends and supporters. Yet, she knew that this life in community was necessary for the sustenance of the mood of Love, and infinitely more desirable than living with or remaining among "aliens"—those whose values were alien to the desire for spiritual integration. Despite the hardships inflicted upon her, from the very ones to whom she had dedicated her life, she continued to serve them as long as she was permitted to.

Some of us may think that to have good company means we only have sweet unions of holy exchange. But that is not the case. The second step on the spiritual journey, in joining good company, is to allow ourselves to be purified and sanctified by the searing burn that life in community affords. Even the best company is full of its idiosyncrasies, full of its foibles. Encountering such annoyances on a daily basis, or at least regularly, will give us ample opportunity in which to practice kindness, patience, generosity and compassion.

Although she doesn't list it among the nine attributes of the journey, Hadewijch called her companions to good spirit, which I interpret as the necessity for *being* good company among good company, i.e., for bringing a sense of humor to our work which will enable us to take ourselves lightly, "in a sweet spirit." Listen to how tenderly she closes her letter:

> Now I exhort you in the name of God's holy Love
> that you make your pilgrimage with beauty and
> purity, without sadness or any hindrance from

willfulness, in a sweet spirit of peace and joy. Pass through this place of exile so upright and so pure and so ardent that you may find God your Love at the end. In this may your help be God himself and his holy Love![21]

THE ROPE

Remember that you came here realizing the necessity of struggling only with yourself and thank anyone who helps you to engage in this struggle.

*—Inscription above the door of the
Study House at The Prieuré, the Fontainebleau
estate of George Gurdjieff.*

In Paris in the 1930s, a group of four woman—three independent Americans and one British—attracted the attention of an enigmatic, personally charismatic, and much sought-after teacher of a systematic means for the development of human consciousness. George Ivanovitch Gurdjieff, the Armenian-Greek who had spent his young adulthood traversing the continent of Asia in search of the occult knowledge of the great esoteric traditions; the man who had escaped the Russian Revolution with a small band of dedicated students and had established himself first in Berlin, then London, and finally in Paris, was as compelling in his late sixties as he had been in his early thirties. The "work ideas" which comprised the essential teaching of his system were already infiltrating the writer's and artist's community of the day, turning the heads of many in the intelligentsia from all other walks of life as well.

The ideas, that "man was asleep," did not know he was asleep, and would die without awakening, without ever "building the soul" that was necessary to create conscious life on earth, had captivated each of the women who would later comprise his elite group. Only when they had established the smallest toe-hold of maturity in these work principles, as a result of their association and study with Gurdjieff's designated teacher in Paris, Jane Heap, did he bring these women together, as one entity—a "Rope" as they called themselves—for purposes of maximizing their studies and their potential progress.

Author Kathryn C. Hulme, who later wrote *The Nun's Story* and based it on much of what she had learned from her beloved teacher, was a member of The Rope. In her book, *Undiscovered Country: The Search for Gurdjieff*, she describes the situation of their formation and the meaning behind it:

> In early January '36, he drew four of our company together—Miss Gordon, Solita, Wendy and myself (four of the most contrasting types one could have handpicked from all Paris in those eccentric Thirties)—and formed us into a special work group, mutually supporting. In allegory he explained: we were going on a journey under his guidance, an "inner-world journey" like a high mountain climb where we must be roped together for safety, where each must think of the others on the rope, all for one and one for all. We must, in short, help each other "as hand washes hand," each contributing to the company according to her lights, according to her means. Only faithful hard work on ourselves would get us where he wanted us to go, not our wishing.
>
> ... We knew, I believe, even from the first day what that invisible bond portended. It was a Rope up which, with the aid of a master's hand, we might be able to inch ourselves from the caves of illusory being we inhabited. Or, it was a rope from which, with sloth and lip service, we could very well hang ourselves.

> Another aspect of this Rope I discovered later. It was stronger than any bond I had ever felt before—for any man, woman or charity child who had ever crossed my zigzag path on earth ...[22]

The idea of a "work group" or small group configuration within a larger body of students or practitioners is an ancient one. One of the best-known examples we have is witnessed in the select group of disciples whom Christ designated as his apostles. They were the elite, perhaps, not in the sense that they were better than the other disciples (of which there were dozens at the time), but because they were willing and able to serve as representatives for a broader lot. From a metaphysical viewpoint, the idea was that these twelve represented the twelve tribes of Israel, and thus symbolically represented the entire nation or people. Christ would not have to work to convert thousands to his way if only he could effect transformation within these twelve. Then, energetically and magically, the twelve would serve as the microcosm which would then change the entire body of the macrocosm.

Throughout Gurdjieff's long and eclectic teaching career, he would work with many different groups in smaller and larger configurations—with his Russian upper class followers whom he would lead out of the country in the midst of the revolution; with his own family; with various influential and highly sophisticated men; with dancers and artists; with visiting dignitaries and members of the royalty. And each would have a piece of the total revelation that has come down to us today in this massive and phenomenally brilliant corpus of data known as the Gurdjieff Work.

Besides the evident and immediate value that would be offered to the members of any particular group when the teacher determined to work with them, a certain reciprocity would be established. The master would *use* the group as experimental material, observing them minutely, and thus learning more about the fascinating nature of humanity's dilemma. The master would also use the students for the accomplishment of specific tasks that were integral to his own work. The first assignment that the Rope fulfilled was to read aloud the passages of Gurdjieff's newly translated book *Beelzebub's Tales to his Grandson*, while G. scrutinized their reactions to the reading. And then there was the "idiot" value of such engagement, as G. might put it, wherein he was simply happy for the companionship, the distraction from more difficult tasks, and the entertainment which such relationship provided him. The women in the Rope were all lesbians, interestingly, and one can speculate that this group therefore held access to a type of impression "food" that G. might not be exposed to, ordinarily. The master had his own reasons for grouping them together.

.Precisely how they worked together is left to us based on hundreds of stories left in their diaries and published works. As Hulme reported, they would come together at the end of each day to piece together all that had transpired, and attempt to record, to the best of their recollection, the exact words which the master, Gurdjieff, had spoken to them. They clearly intended to preserve his teaching for their own edification as well as for posterity. Here was one very clear-cut way in which a group experienced its value— that together they remembered more and hence received more than they would ever remember or receive alone.

Secondly, when any member of the group was singled out to receive instruction about her habits or mechanical tendencies, each member of the group would receive the advantages, and would be able to apply these teachings to her own situation. Since one of the principles of the work was that each person was not singular but rather a series of multiple "I's" each vying for dominance, and each having her turn in the spotlight, such work with one was literally work with all.

I recall a specific example when my teacher was sternly criticizing one of my best women friends in the community, in her absence. I wondered whether he wanted me or another of us to pass this vital information along to the woman he was criticizing. I also wanted to know how to deal with the feelings of unfairness and anger towards him that his words had provoked in me. So I asked him, "How do we work with this?" In no uncertain terms he let me and the rest of his hearers know that the best way to profit

Kathryn Hulme, 1932. "Ready to climb the Pyramids."

from his words about our friend was to take them as if they applied to us. At this level of working with the human condition it didn't much matter whether our friend heard his words or not. What mattered was that those who *had* heard, allowed themselves to be disturbed with the force and possibility contained in this teaching communication. Only in that way would there be a bodily reso-nance, and hence an opening for more lasting change.

Kathryn tells of the way in which Gurdjieff worked with her in telling her that smoking had become her "master" and needed to become her slave. When Kathryn protested that she was not en-slaved, Gurdjieff called her bluff, and Kathryn anted up, snuffing out her cigarette in the ashtray in front of her, and abstaining from smoking for over a year. In the course of the struggle which ensued for her, both within and without, Gurdjieff gave the entire group invaluable instruction. He told them how to use the suffering that arose from this type of work on self as a means of building their inner being. He suggested that they use a statement of intention, which was similar to a form of prayer, each time the desire to smoke arose. "I wish the result of this, my suffering, be my own, for Being."

Third, such a bonded group gave one and all the opportunity to appreciate how they were their sisters' keepers, and to grasp conclusively that they were all still asleep as long as one of them was still asleep. This lesson came about for the Rope in a simple way. As was their custom, when they were to meet up with Gurdjieff for an event, one member of the group would serve as timekeeper, determined to assure that the group got to the meeting on time. On one such occasion, when they happened to be two or three minutes late, G. was evidently disturbed. Kathryn at once took responsibility. But the master dismissed her apology as worthless, letting them know that their failure was not an individual phe-nomenon, and that it merely affirmed that they all came from the same "sardine barrel" of undifferentiated humanity. The implica-tion was that if they had not yet learned to master such small in-discretions, how could they ever expect progress in a type of work which demands the utmost integrity, attention and impeccability from them. When, during this same occasion, G. complained that their lateness had resulted in the coffee being served cold, and therefore spoiled, Kathryn unwisely objected that she didn't mind it, in fact it was just like she liked it. Putting her foot in her mouth in that way became the opportunity for G. to give a profound lesson to all:

> "This is how *you* like it, Krokodeel," [his special name for Hulme] he said witheringly. "This you must not tell among many. For *you* it is good, but spoiled for another. *You must enter into the situation of another* ... see what it is and put words in your mouth to correspond with what you see."[23]

As their time with him was coming to an end, since Kathryn and her companion Wendy (also a member of The Rope) intended to return to New York in order to prepare for Mr. G.'s arrival there a few months later, G. drove them harder and harder, even for the smallest forgetfulness. ("Accustom yourself to forget nothing," he had told them.) And why was he driving them so? Because he was completely committed to their "awakening," to their breaking with "mechanicality," to destroying all illusion so that they could become the "real Man" which was the only possibility for humanity's conscious evolution.

Like the Beguines, who were called to exhort one another to holiness, the members of Gurdjieff's Rope were given a similarly gracious gift. In my own experience I have seen the possibilities for group "enlightenment" demonstrated in a women's blues band which my teacher has empowered. Like the Rope, these women are tied together for better or worse. Furthermore, the mountain of worldly success they are challenged to climb is an extremely treacherous one, which promises threatening situations around every hairpin turn. I have watched these women struggle with the issues of security, sex and power. I have heard their angry screams and threats at one another. I have also observed the awesome power of their music—all the more awesome because none are trained musicians. I have been amazed with their persistent intractability, as well as their generous service to one another. But most of all I have been touched to the point of tears at the patience of my teacher's attention to them, as well as their willingness to start over, time after time, up the rope that he has given to them. After almost four years of difficult work (holding full-time day jobs and "gigs" until three in the morning, two to three nights every week, together with several extended European tours in which they play for huge audiences), I can say that I envy them. They are being transformed by the necessity of having to consider one another, rather than just themselves. They are being transformed as they allow their individual devotion for and commitment to their teacher to subsume their petty differences with one another. Every one of them is being asked to let her ego burn at the stake so that she may be made new from the ashes.

Herein lies the essence of women's culture in the context of spiritual work. Whether it is a group of lesbians, a group of mothers, a group of musicians, a group of saleswomen, a theatre troupe, a convent of nuns—when individuals are finally willing and able to put the needs of others and the needs of the group as a whole above their own individual concerns, a model is created in humanity—a model of possibility, a model of Womanhood.

What My Sisters and I Have Learned in Over Twenty-Two Years

When women gather together with like-minded purpose, in the name of God, their spiritual teacher or master, or a female deity or representation of the Divine Mother, SHE—the Divine Feminine—takes over. Insofar as we are able to remain open and receptive to Her, women come to learn the essence of what *Woman* is by being with other women. My life in community, together with my travels as a workshop leader, have taught me that women are hungry for one another as companions in the path of love.

They readily admit to being starved for the kind of sanctuary that a regular meeting, or a day or two of retreat with other women affords them, and are usually amazed at how easily they can speak the spiritual desires and longings of their hearts in an environment where such conversation is the norm rather than the exception.

My sisters and I in community have found that we need each other's help in the serious attempt to unplug ourselves from the contemporary cultural view about who Woman is, and how she is expected to interact with men, women and children both at home and in the public forum. Some of us have deliberately taken on practices which keep us mindful of our removal from the cultural paradigm—like not using makeup, or choosing to keep our hair in a natural and simple style rather than having it fashioned. After years of having short, contemporary-styled hair, I intentionally let my hair grow, without perming it, as a means of observing my attachments to a particular "look" that I prided myself for. Even after five years I was still amazed at the insecurity that such a decision generated. These seemingly minor attachments are much more significant than many of us imagine. Without the support of my women friends (many of whom were engaging similar experiments), I would have abandoned my practice of self-observation in this area after a few months. I have learned that when any type of old programming is being challenged, we are then forced to enter a sort of emptiness in which all previous models no longer offer a platform of security. This can be a wonderful but scary place to start over from.

Such disengagement also invites us to upgrade to a more universal paradigm about the nature of human relatedness. Our women's culture has done this through using the relationship of Shiva/Shakti as the model of the play of male-female energy within each man and woman, and for insight into what Woman's role is in creation. In one outstanding passage of his book, *The Alchemy of Love and Sex*, my teacher Lee describes this dynamic interplay:

> In the essential male-female dichotomy, Shiva
> is pure knowledge, that is, Context. Shakti is

content—manifestation, form and energy. Shiva
is unmanifested allness, and Shakti is everything
else—everything sensual, alive, moving, created
... Shiva is the strong, silent type, not the warrior.
Diana, Athena, or Shakti is the warrior ... Masculine energy doesn't speak. It *is*. Feminine energy
acts: it speaks; it is alive, aggressive and powerful.
Masculine energy just radiates based on wisdom,
not based on accomplishment or beauty.[24]

Keep in mind that Lee is addressing the essential male-female
dichotomy *within each being*, calling for a greater overall balance of
these forces in the body. He goes on to explain how we do this:

A weak feminine, therefore, can be related to any
element that has difficulty acting, doing, or mani-
festing ... You strengthen the feminine, therefore,
by acting ... of course in the proper way, not just
flailing about making waves or crashing around
like a bull in a china shop ... The way you
strengthen a weak masculine is by resting in pure
knowledge—by coming to know, to discover, wisdom. If you are insecure, if you think you don't
know anything, the way to strengthen a weak
masculine is to find that place in yourself that
doesn't know and acknowledge it, embrace it.
Anytime you get this feeling that you don't understand, you immediately inquire, specifically in
relationship to that insecurity.

To strengthen the feminine is to use your energy in an optimally productive fashion, not squander it and reinforce the weaknesses. That doesn't
mean that you can't take a walk, or sit in the park
watching people, but [those activities] should be a
way of feeding one's spiritual work, one's essential
hungers, not an avoidance of one's deep being. A

> very practical way to strengthen the feminine
> through optimal activity is to never leave a project
> unfinished; another way is through conservation
> of energy in the use of speech.[25]

At one of our weekly meetings with him, Lee demonstrated this issue of the balance of masculine and feminine energies by making an example (with their permission) of two women present. He pointed out the very obvious feminine appearance of one of the women—her soft, flowing dress, her eye makeup, jewelry, styled hair. He contrasted this woman's appearance to that of the other, who was wearing loose jeans, a tee shirt, no makeup and close-cropped hair. Despite appearances, he suggested, the first woman who looked so female in fact had a weak feminine, and the other, looking so unadorned, so "unfeminine," had a weak masculine. This confusion in outer appearances was due, he stated, to the personality's attempts to compensate for the area of weakness with an outward show of the very quality missing within.

Lee suggested that once we discover which side the scale is tipped toward in our particular case, that we work to strengthen the weaker side, rather than attempt to rein in the stronger side. This consideration of the balance of our essential masculine and feminine energies is an area that our women's culture considers regularly.

As a community of women within a broader spiritual community, we have attempted to make ourselves vulnerable to the help and input of other women, not only in regard to the manifestations of our habitual and neurotic psychology (although we have often been ruthless in these domains), but in the arena of exhorting one another to the highest intentions of spiritual practice, which is what we claim to have come here for in the first place. The courage that takes has been enormous at times. At the fear of risking a precious friendship and possibly alienating a large segment of the women's culture, individuals have willingly voiced their fears for another's well-being, sometimes against a tide of denial. When Gerry, for instance, rebounding from her broken

438

marriage, immediately attracted a man whom several of her closest friends saw as a poor choice, we called a women's circle and invited Gerry to examine the potential of this relationship in terms of any long-term satisfaction and support of her spiritual life. Amid her tears and angry outbursts Gerry admitted her own fears and doubts. With the compassionate support of her friends, she agreed to take a year-long hiatus from dating. During that year she worked with other single women in the community addressing the issues of how celibacy could be an enhancement of spiritual practice.

As a group, we have agreed that we are here to birth one another into a new life, not to merely sustain a community structure, or to make death (either literal or metaphorical death) more comfortable. When Inge, a forty-five-year-old woman in our *sangha* (community of practitioners), was dying of bone cancer, her pain was often excruciating. Those of us on her care team were constantly called upon to overlook our own comforts and swallow our own pride in caring for her, allowing her to decide for herself how she was going to die. At the same time, we had to balance this spaciousness with our commitment to her as a practitioner of the Way. In the same manner that we would remind any "healthy" woman to practice, we urged Inge to examine her tenacious attachments and to drop her selfishness.

In my own *sadhana*, and in the lives of women I have known well, I find that many of us feel the enormous friction of living with or closely associating with other women to be one of the greatest difficulties as well as one of the greatest assets of our spiritual lives. Whenever we are called upon to "hang out with others"—whether these are women we share a household with, or women we work with—we get to see a lot about ourselves. Some of it will be quite embarrassing to admit. We will be thrust face-to-face with our attachments, with our pettiness, our criticalness, our jealousy, our sense of injustice—all of which is enormously valuable for our purification, nonetheless. As we actively engage in work on self, we will learn that only by putting ourselves in the middle of such situations, not by retreating to a cave (or to our own safe nuclear family), will we learn to forgive and therefore to

439

love. I remember when two women in our community needed to work together and were literally at one another's throats with jealously, competitiveness and mutual intolerance, our teacher, Lee, gave each woman a pin which he instructed them to wear at all times. The picture on the pin was of two kittens in a basket together. The basket was attached to a hot air balloon that was in flight. The message was clear: You are both in the same basket. Learn to be kind.

Every group of women will contain members who have warm, attractive personalities as well as those whose natural dispositions are sharp or tremendously eccentric. Our learned tendencies will be to exclude the latter, while spending our free time and gaining the approval of the former. Commitment to spiritual life and women's culture, however, is worth nothing if it does not include our willingness and effort to transcend personality attractions. Especially for one like myself who wants everyone to be as perfect as I think I should be, great value can be found in cultivating friendships with the "oddballs," the rebels, the women who aren't as well liked and don't fit. These women cannot only be my mentors, since they have lived and suffered in domains that are completely foreign to me, but they will also test my patience, generosity and compassion, thus revealing to me how superficial my practice of compassion may be.

As a culture of women we have attempted to bond in a way that allows us, as separate individuals (separate "cells"), to literally become one organ or series of organs in a larger body. And to what purpose? Obviously because we know that our combined strength is greater when it is aligned and focused. But, even beyond this, because we want to break through the illusion that keeps us separate from All That Is, thinking that we are isolated entities responsible for our own existence. Over years of work together we are beginning to recognize that the spiritual advancement of any one of us will enhance the awakening of us all. As the poet Kabir says: "When one flower opens, ordinarily dozens open."[26]

At this particular time in the life of our community, for instance, we are witnessing several of our sisters (and brothers) going through a type of "opening" which is both wondrous and disturbing. These openings sometimes manifest with ecstatic states of rapture, tears of longing, or even physical pain. At the same time, these women (and men) are becoming more obviously radiant in their appearance, while their ability to speak the *dharma* (the teaching) with clarity and passion is dynamically increased. As others observe these strange goings-on, some are feeling jealous and angry. Others voice their mistrust of the phenomenon. My own experience, however, is that by going forward to meet these women, by hanging out with them (despite my feelings or judgements), I have been infected, even temporarily, with their radiance and passion. As I come to appreciate our bondedness, I recognize that what they are going through is unique to their psycho-physical type, but that each women in our community is being offered her own doorway into deeper domains of surrender and devotion, if she will acknowledge it. Furthermore, if such manifestations are indicative of an advancement by one or two, that advancement merely opens the door wider for others. In the domain of the heart or soul there is no first or last.

As a women's culture we have become advocates for both mothers and children, following the lead which our teacher has taken. We view motherhood and its responsibilities as one of the most potent approaches to spiritual life. The demand for selflessness that motherhood makes, together with the profound opening of the heart in love for the child, provide a woman with a high-speed vehicle to accomplish her spiritual work aim. I once heard Lee exhorting a young mother, pregnant with her second child, to prepare to rise once again, more fully and heartfully, to the demand to surrender herself for her soon-to-be newborn child. "For the first two years *you* need to disappear," he stated forcefully. He went on to say that after those two years a mother could begin in small ways to put her own needs and preferences first, when and where appropriate. "Whew," I thought to myself, listening to him, "could I do that?" The mothers who have willingly put themselves in this fire, engaging their childraising practice twenty-four hours a day, testify that it is the hardest work they have ever done, yet the most rewarding, especially in terms of the strength of bonding it builds with the child, and the child's obvious happiness and security.

Although I have no children, Lee's demand to new mothers offers a parallel challenge for me. For women whose childraising years are over, as well as for those without children, the opportunities for service to the mothers of young children and to the children themselves are extraordinary. When the community gathers with Lee several times a week, a team of single or childless men and women take on the responsibilities for childcare so that parents can have the opportunity to spend a few hours in the teacher's company. Such advocacy is another way of moving ourselves out of self-centered existence and into a concern for the planetary culture and the future of humanity. By putting others ahead of ourselves we literally practice the fine art of compassion, the work of the *Bodhisattva* on earth.

Finally, we have learned slowly and painstakingly over the years that when we are enriched by the impression "food" which other women nurture us with, that we do not have to seek that food from our partners or husbands. The breakup of many relationships is often because women expect their male counterparts to fulfill all their needs. Personally, I have struggled mightily with these issues in relationship to my husband of twenty-five years. How to weave the fabric of a working partnership where each person is a whole, not one-half, and where the sum of two wholes is one! The possibility here is awesome and the obstacles are many. The truth must be faced—that man will never fully satisfy the need for wholeness in woman, nor will *she* fully satisfy *man*. Only ultimate Love, in the recognition of an essence of Love that goes beyond all forms, will satisfy such hungry hearts and souls.

Through her association with other women, a woman gets this kind of food that nourishes her essence. She gets it from other women, but she also learns how to feed herself from the infinite source of her own being. And it is this Divine Feminine which grants her all satisfaction.

When she joins her mate, therefore, she joins him as a full person, not as a partial person needing to be completed. When a woman in our community is having a specific problem in her relationship, she brings that problem to her own women's culture, not to her husband or partner. And he is encouraged to bring his problem to other men. The respective cultures, far from degenerating into a "isn't she a bitch" or "isn't he a monster" mentality, attempt to work with the individual to recognize his or her responsibility for mature spiritual practice, reminding one another of why they have come to spiritual life in the first place. Then, when the two partners reunite they are hopefully together in their fullness and in remembrance of their purpose, because each one has been exhorted to holiness by their peers.

As a community we are particularly blessed in having a structure in which to wake up and live the high possibility for women's culture and spiritual life. Many others do not have that immediate means. Nonetheless, I know that some aspects of women's culture are available wherever two or more women are gathered, whether in the supermarket or in the meditation hall, in the birthing chamber or at the deathbed, because wherever Woman is, there the Divine Feminine resides.

The breeze at dawn has secrets to tell you.
                    Don't go back to sleep.
You must ask for what you really want.
                    Don't go back to sleep.
People are going back and forth across the doorsill
                    where two worlds touch.
The door is round and open.
                    Don't go back to sleep.[27]
                    —Rumi

ENDNOTES

INTRODUCTION

1. Kabir. *The Kabir Book*. Versions by Robert Bly. Boston: Beacon Press, 1977, p. 25.

CHAPTER ONE—THE AWAKENING / A PATH OF ANNIHILATION

1. Kabir, *The Kabir Book*. Versions by Robert Bly. Boston: Beacon Press, 1977, p. 41.

2. Cummings, E.E. *i: six nonlectures*. Cambridge, Mass: Harvard University Press, 1953, 1981, p. 24.

3. All quotes in this section are taken from: Redington, James, D. *Vallabhacarya on the Love Games of Krsna*. New Delhi, India: Motilal Banarsidass, 1983. The text translated by Redington is from chapters 29-35 of Book Ten of the *Bhagavata Purana*.

4. Wolstein, Diana and Samuel Noah Kramer. *Inanna:Queen of Heaven and Earth*. New York: Harper and Row Publishers, 1983, p. 161.

5. Hillesum, Etty. *Letters From Westerbork*. New York: Pantheon Books, 1986, p. 247.

6. Roberts, Bernadette, quoted in: "The Experience of No Self: An Interview with Stephan Bodian." *Yoga Journal*, November/December 1986, p. 62.

7. Tweedie, Irina. *Chasm of Fire: A Woman's Experience Of Liberation Through The Teachings Of A Sufi Master*. Longmead, Shaftesbury, England: Element Books, 1979.

Tweedie, Irina. *Daughter of Fire: A Diary of a Spiritual Training with a Sufi Master*. Nevada City, Calif.: Blue Dolphin Publishing, 1986.

8. Schelling, Andrew, translation. *For Love of the Dark One: Songs of Mirabai*. Boston: Shambhala, 1993, p.69.

CHAPTER TWO—THE DESERT PATH: SILENCE, SOLITUDE, AND PRAYER

1. Duquin, Lorene Hanley. *They Called Her The Baroness: The Life of Catherine de Hueck Doherty*. New York: Alba House, 1995, p. 102.

2. Ibid., p. 226.

3. Doherty, Catherine de Hueck. *Poustinia: Christian Spirituality of the East for Western Man*. Notre Dame, Indiana: Ave Maria Press, 1975, p. 49.

4. Book catalog of Madonna House publications.

5. Doherty, p. 105.

6. Ibid., p. 21.

7. Ibid., p. 72

8. Ibid., p. 73.

9. Ibid., p. 35.

10. Cited in: Dossey, Larry, M.D. *Prayer Is Good Medicine.* (New York: HarperSanFrancisco, 1995). See: Randolph C. Byrd, "Positive Therapeutic Effects of Intercessory Prayer in a Coronary Care Unit Population," *Southern Medical Journal* 81, no. 7 (July 1988): pp. 826-29. And Daniel P. Wirth, "The Effect of Non-Contact Therapeutic Touch on the Healing Rate of Full Thickness Dermal Wounds," *Subtle Energies* 1, no. 1 (1990): 1-20; and Daniel P. Wirth, "Full Thickness Dermal Wounds Treated with Non-contact Therapeutic Touch: A Replication and Extension," *Complementary Therapies in Medicine* 1 (1993): pp. 127-32.

11. Furlong, Monica. *Contemplating Now.* Philadelphia: The Westminster Press, 1971, p. 24.

12. Doherty, Catherine de Hueck. *Soul of My Soul: Reflections from a Life of Prayer.* Notre Dame, Indiana: Ave Maria Press, 1985, pp. 7-8.

13. Ibid., p. 35.

14. Ibid., p. 82.

15. Ibid., p. 107.

16. Underhill, Evelyn. *Practical Mysticism,* Columbus, Ohio: Ariel Press, E.P Dutton, 1914, p. 38.

17. Ibid., pp. 59-60.

18. Ibid., pp. 93-94.

CHAPTER THREE—THE PATH OF WAITING / THE WAY OF SURRENDER

1. Ulanov, Ann Belford. "The God You Touch," in: *The Christ and the Bodhisattva,* Daniel S. Lopez, Jr. and Steven C. Rockefeller (editors). New York: SUNY Press, 1987, p.133.

2. Tweedie, Irina. *Chasm of Fire: A Woman's Experience Of Liberation Through The Teachings Of A Sufi Master.* Longmead, Shaftesbury, England: Element Books, p.7.

3. Ibid., p.51.

4. Ibid., p. 48.

5. Quoted in: Bancroft, Anne. *Weavers of Wisdom: Women Mystics of the Twentieth Century.* New York: Penguin, Arkana, 1989, pp. 131-132.

6. Tweedie, p. 77.

7. Ibid., p. 184.

8. Ibid., p. 186.

9. Ibid., p. 51.

10. Ibid., p. 171.

11. Ibid., pp. 151-152.

12. Ibid., p. 144.

13. Tweedie, Irina. Quoted in: Myrtle Heery, "Yoga of the Heart—An Interview with Irina Tweedie." *Yoga Journal*, May/June 1986, p. 86.

14. Tweedie, *Chasm of Fire*, p. 203.

15. Galland, China. *Longing For Darkness: Tara and the Black Madonna*. New York: Penguin, 1991, p. 275.

16. Field, Reshad. *The Last Barrier*. New York: Harper and Row, 1976, p. 90.

17. Johnson, Ann. *Miryam of Nazareth: Woman of Strength and Wisdom*. Notre Dame, Indiana: Ave Maria Press, 1984, pp. 126-127. Used with permission.

18. Rumi. *Crazy As We Are*, translations by Nevit O. Ergin. Prescott, Arizona: Hohm Press, 1992, p. 29.

19. Zuleikha performs and teaches through dance and story. Her most recent audiotape, *Heart Matters: Songs with Zuleikha and Friends* and other information about her work is available. Write: Zuleikha, P.O. Box 9139, Santa Fe, New Mexico, 87504.

20. Upton, Charles. *Doorkeeper of the Heart: Versions of Rabi'a*. Putney, Vermont: Threshold Books, 1988, p. 38. Used with permission.

21. Ibid., p. 11.

22. Ibid., p. 11.

23. Ibid., p. 46.

24. Ibid., p. 47.

25. Ibid., p. 43.

26. Farid al-Din Attar. *Tadhikirat al Awliya*. Edited by R.A. Nicholson. London, 1905, I, p. 73, cited in: Smith, Margaret. *Rabia, The Mystic*. San Francisco, Calif.: Rainbow Bridge, 1977, p. 30.

CHAPTER FOUR—THE PATH OF MOTHER

1. Woodruff, Sue. *Meditations with Mechtild of Magdeburg*. Santa Fe, New Mexico: Bear and Company, 1982, p. 109.

2. Duerk, Judith. *Circle of Stones: Woman's Journey To Herself*. San Diego, Calif.: LuraMedia, 1989, p.1.

3. Foreword to *Nimm Mein Herz: Gebete von Dina Rees*. Freiburg: Verlag Johannes Galli, 1990, pp. 9-11. (Private translation by Polly Döge.)

4. Martin, S. "A Meeting with Dina Rees." *Divine Slave Gita.* Vol. 8, No., 3, Fall 1990, p. 36.

5. Lozowick, Lee. *In The Fire.* Nevada City, Calif. and Prescott, Arizona: IDHHB and Hohm Press, 1978.

6. Rees, Dina. *Menchwerden: Gespräche mit Dina Rees* (Becoming Human: Talks with Dina Rees), Freiburg: Verlag Johannes Galli, 1990, p. 78. (Private translation by Veronique Selb.)

7. Rees, Dina. Excerpted from "Über das Gebet" in: *Nimm Mein Herz,* pp. 12-25. Used with permission. (Private translation by Polly Döge.)

8. Ibid., p. 10.

9. Ibid.. pp. 92-93.

10. Rand, Yvonne, quoted in: Boucher, Sandy. *Turning the Wheel: American Women Creating the New Buddhism.* Boston: Beacon Press, 1993. p. 153.

11. Anandamayi Ma. *Matri Darshan, A photo album about Shri Anandamayi Ma.* Westkappeln, Germany: Verlag S. Schang, 1988.

CHAPTER FIVE—THE PATH OF COMPASSION

1. Blofeld, John. *Bodhisattva of Compassion: The Mystical Tradition of Kuan Yin.* Boulder, Colorado: Shambhala, 1978, pp. 14-15.

2. Greg Campbell is a Zen monk and the former translator for the eminent Zen Master Sazaki Roshi. Greg is a poet, a writer, a beggar and a personal friend whose correspondence over the years has always been a source of profound inspiration to me. This piece is from his unpublished work.

3. Bhiksuni Laksmi, quoted in: Shaw, Miranda. *Passionate Enlightenment: Women in Tantric Buddhism.* New Jersey: Princeton University Press, 1994, p. 129.

4. Campbell, Greg. *Divine Slave Gita.* March/April 1986, Vol.6, No.2, p. 33.

5. Maezumi, Taizan, Roshi. "The Sutra of the Great Compassionate Bodhisattva," *Ten Directions.* Los Angeles: Zen Center of Los Angeles and Kuroda Institute. Vol.V, No.1, Spring 1984, p.1.

6. Willson, Martin (translator and introduction). *In Praise of Tara: Songs to the Saviouress* London: Wisdom Publications, 1986, p. 12.

7. Ibid., p. 13.

8. Ibid.

9. Ibid.

10. Galland, pp. 78-79.

11. Campbell, Greg. Unpublished work.

12. George, Christopher, S. (translator). *The Candamaharosana Tantra, Chapters 1-8: A Critical Edition and English Translation.* American Oriental Series, no. 56. New Haven: American Oriental Society, 1974, p. 32.

13. Willson, p. 17.

14. Gyatso, H.H. Tenzen, The Fourteenth Dalai Lama, "The Practices of Bodhisattvas," in: *The Christ and the Bodhisattva.* Lopez, Daniel S. Jr., and Rockefeller, Steven C. (editors). New York: SUNY Press, 1987, pp. 217-227.

15. Ibid., p. 221.

16. Ibid., p. 223.

17. Quoted in: Boucher, Sandy. *Turning the Wheel: American Women Creating the New Buddhism.* Boston: Beacon Press, 1993, p. 136.

18. Gyatso, p. 224.

19. Ibid., p. 225.

20. Chagdud Rinpoche, private teaching.

21. Gyatso, p. 225.

22. Chödrön, Pema. "News You Can Use" *Shambhala Sun*: March 1997, p. 28.

23. Shri Anandamayi Ma. *Matri Darshan.* Westerkappeln, Germany: Mangalam Verlag S. Shang, 1988.

24. Bancroft, Ann. *Weavers of Wisdom: Women Mystics of the Twentieth Century.* New York: Penguin, Arkana, 1989, p.2.

CHAPTER SIX—THE PATH OF DARKNESS

1. Aghori Vimalananda. Quoted in: Svoboda, Robert. *Aghora: At the Left Hand of God.* Albuquerque, New Mexico: Brotherhood of Life, 1986, p. 50.

2. Sen, Ramprasad. *Grace and Mercy in Her Wild Hair: Selected Poems to the Mother Goddess.* Translated by Leonard Nathan and Clinton Seely. Boulder, Colorado: Great Eastern, 1982, p. 28.

3. Roberts, Bernadette. *The Path to No-Self.* Boston: Shambhala, 1985, pp. 9-10.

4. Sen, p. 21.

5. M., *The Gospel of Sri Ramakrishna.* New York: Ramakrishna-Vivekananda Center, 1942, pp. 9-10, 12-13. Used with permission.

6. Sen, p. 24.

7. Bhagavati, Ma Jaya Sati. *Bones and Ash*, Sebastian, Florida: Jaya Press, 1995, p. 24.

8. Bhagavati, Ma Jaya Sati. "Questions & Answers," *Kashi*, Issue 2, November 1994, p. 4. Used with permission.

9. See: Angelou, Maya. *I Know Why the Caged Bird Sings*. New York: Bantam, Doubleday Dell, 1997, originally published in 1983; as well as her more recent: *Even the Stars Look Lonesome*, New York: Random House, 1997.

10. Rangarajan, Professor V. "Divine Mother Mayee of Kanyakumari." Madras: *Tattva Darshana*, Volume 4, No.1, 1987, p. 68.

CHAPTER SEVEN—THE PATH OF THE WARRIOR / THE WAY OF POWER

1. This story is well told by Miranda Shaw in her book: *Passionate Enlightenment*. Princeton, New Jersey: Princeton University Press, 1994, p. 132.

2. Macy, Joanna. *World as Lover, World as Self*. San Francisco: Parallax Press, 1991. p. 132. Also see her other books, including: *Despair and Personal Power in the Nuclear Age*. Philadelphia: New Society Publishers, 1983. Joanna is written about in: Friedman, Lenore. *Meetings with Remarkable Women*. Boston: Shambhala, 1987 and Bancroft, Anne. *Weavers of Wisdom: Women Mystics of the Twentieth Century*. New York: Penguin Arkana, 1989.

3. The Buddhist Peace Fellowship was founded in 1978 to bring a Buddhist perspective to the peace movement, and to bring the peace movement to the Buddhist community. For information contact: BPF National Office, PO Box 4650, Berkeley, Calif. 94704. Telephone: 510/655-6169. Website: www.bpf.org/bpf

4. International Campaign For Tibet, 1825 K St., NW, Suite 520, Washington, D.C., 20006. Telephone: 202/785-1515. Website: www.savetibet.org

5. See: Ram Dass and Mirabai Bush. *Compassion In Action: Setting Out on the Path of Service*. New York: Crown Publishers, 1995. Information about The Project on the Contemplative Mind in Society is available from: 38 Village Hill Road, Williamsburg, MA 01096. Telephone: 413/268-7236. Website: sfoundatio@aol.com

6. Weil, Simone. *Waiting For God* (translated by Emma Craufurd) New York: Harper Colophon Books, 1951, p. 48.

7. Weil, Simone. *The Simone Weil Reader*, "Letter to Joe Bousquet." George A. Panichas, Editor; New York: David McKay Co., 1977, p. 91.

8. Weil, *Waiting For God*, pp. 71-72

9. Ibid., pp. 98-99.

10. Ibid., pp. 50-51.

12. Ratushinskaya, Irina. *Grey Is The Color of Hope*. New York: Vintage International, 1989, pp. 54-55.

CHAPTER EIGHT—THE PATH OF SERVICE

1. Muckeridge, Malcolm. *Something Beautiful For God*. San Francisco: Harper SanFrancisco, 1986, p. 120.
2. Hillesum, Etty. *An Interrupted Life*. New York: Washington Square Books, 1985, p. 247.
3. Ibid., pp. 224-225.
4. Ibid., pp. 219-220.
5. Ibid., p. 192.
6. Ibid., p. 228.
7. Ibid., p. 197.
8. Ibid., p. 47.
9. Ibid., p. 217.
10. Hillesum, Etty. *Letters from Westerbork*. New York: Pantheon Books, 1986, pp. 30-31.
11. Hillesum, *An Interrupted Life*, p. 41.
12. Ibid., p. 266.
13. Hillesum, *Letters from Westerbork*, p. 63.
14. Kubler-Ross, Elisabeth, M.D. *The Wheel of Life: A Memoir of Living and Dying*. New York: Scribner, 1997, p. 284.
15. Ibid., p. 255.

CHAPTER NINE—THE PATH OF ART AND INSPIRATION

1. Waldman, Anne. From "To the Censorious Ones." *Kill or Cure*. New York: Penguin Books, 1994, p. 141.
2. Craighead, Meinrad. *The Mother's Songs: Images of God the Mother*. New York: Paulist Press, 1986, from the Introduction.
3. Ibid., p. 7.
4. Ibid., p. 1.
5. Craighead, Meinrad. In: Peay, Pythia. "Making the Invisible Visible," An interview in: *Common Boundary*. November/December, 1990, p. 20.
6. Bancroft, Anne. *Weavers of Wisdom: Women Mystics of the Twentieth Century*. New York: Penguin, Arkana, 1989, p. 16.
7. Ibid., pp. 16-17.
8. Craighead, *The Mother's Songs*. p. 29.

9. A modern kiva is a rectangular or circular structure with a fire pit in the center and a timbered roof; it is accessible by ladder. An opening in the floor represents the entrance to the lower world and the place through which life emerged into this world.

10. Craighead, Meinrad. "Immanent Mother." Quoted in: *The Feminist Mystic*. Mary E. Giles, editor. New York: Crossroad Publishing Co., 1982, p. 83.

11. From the brochure: "Praying with Images—Creative Retreats for Women, with Meinrad Craighead," 1998, p.2.

12. Hildegard of Bingen. *Scivias*. Trans. by Mother Columba Hart and Jane Bishop, with introduction by Barbara J. Newman; New York: Paulist Press, 1990, p. 60.

13. Dronke, Peter. *Women Writers of The Middle Ages: A Critical Study of Texts from Perpetua to Marguerite Porete*. New York and Cambridge: Cambridge University Press, 1984, p. 166.

14. Ibid., p. 168.

15. Lachman, Barbara. *The Journal of Hildegard of Bingen*. New York: Bell Tower, 1993, p. 142.

16. Brunn, Emilie Zum and Georgette Epiney-Burgard. *Women Mystics in Medieval Europe*. Translated from French by Sheila Hughes. New York: Paragon House, 1989. pp. 32–33.

17. Saint Hildegard of Bingen. *Symphonia*. Introduction, translation and commentary by Barbara Newman. Ithaca, New York: Cornell University Press, 1988, p. 151.

18. Fox, Matthew, from the Introduction to: *Illuminations of Hildegard of Bingen*. Santa Fe, New Mexico: Bear and Co., 1985, p. 20.

19. Alston, A.J. *The Devotional Poems of Mirabai*. Delhi: Motilal Banarsidass, 1980, #25, p. 43.

20. Ibid., #165, p. 102.

21. Ibid., #20, p. 41.

22. The god Vishnu in the Hindu cosmology is a member of the triumvirate of Brahma, the creator; Vishnu, the sustainer; and Shiva, the destroyer. As the sustaining, nurturing force, Vishnu takes many forms. One such form was that of the dark-skinned (blue) enchanting boy-child, warrior and king, Krishna.

23. Alston, #167, p. 103.

24. Schelling, Andrew. *For Love of the Dark One: Songs of Mirabai*. Boston, Mass: Shambhala, 1993, p. 37. Note: This superb series of translations is currently available in a revised edition from Hohm Press, Prescott, Ariz. 1-800-381-2700.

25. Alston, #191, pp. 114-115.

26. Schelling, p. 100.

27. Alston, # 144, p. 93.
28. Ibid., #155, pp. 97-98.
29. Ibid., pp. 38-39 # 15.
30. Ibid., p. 103 #171.

CHAPTER TEN—THE PATH OF THE BODY / THE PATH OF SEX

1. Allione, Tsultrim. "Women of Wisdom," *Yoga Journal*, May June 1986, pp. 28-29.
2. Shakti, in Hinduism, is the primordial female force in creation. She is the lover/consort of Shiva, the male principle.
3. Mahadeviyakka. Quoted in: Jane Hirschfield. *Women In Praise of the Sacred*. New York: HarperCollins Publishers, 1994, p. 78.
4. Shaw, Miranda. *Passionate Enlightenment: Women In Tantric Buddhism*. Princeton, New Jersey: Princeton University Press, 1994, pp. 40-41.
5. "Interview With Miranda Shaw," *Tawagoto*, Volume 10, Number 2, Spring 1997, p. 41.
6. Shaw, Miranda. "Wild, Wise, Passionate: Dakinis in America," in: *Buddhist Women On the Edge: Contemporary Perspectives from the Western Frontier*. Edited by Marianne Dresser. Berkeley, Calif.: North Atlantic Books, 1996, p. 4.
7. Svoboda, Robert. *Kundalini: Aghora II*. Albuquerque, New Mexico: Brotherhood of Life, 1993, p. 61.

CHAPTER ELEVEN—THE PATH OF DEVOTION

1. Yogini. "The Birth of an Eternal Slave." In *Yogi Ramsuratkumar Souvenir 1995*. Tirunvannamalai, India: Yogi Ramsuratkumar Trust, 1995, p. 53.
2. Kabir. *The Kabir Book*. Versions by Robert Bly. Boston: Beacon Press, 1977, p. 56.
3. Sri Jnanadev. *Jnaneswari*. Madras: Samata Books, 1954.
4. Krishnabai, Mataji. *Guru's Grace*. Fourth edition. Kanhangad, Kerala, India: Anandashram, 1989.

5. When Mary met her cousin Elizabeth, the mother of John the Baptist, Elizabeth recognized that Mary was carrying a holy child, and acknowledged her. In response, Mary proclaimed the greatness of God in accomplishing such grand things through such a humble vehicle as herself. Her words have come to be known as The Magnificat: "My soul magnifies the Lord and my spirit rejoices in God my savior because He has regarded the lowliness of His handmaid. And from henceforth, all generations will call me blessed, because He who is mighty, He whose name is holy, has wrought for me His wonders..." (Luke, 1, 46-55).

6. Krishnabai, pp. 1-2.

7. Ibid., p. 30.

8. Satchidananda, Swami. *The Gospel of Swami Ramdas*. Second Edition. Kanhangad, Kerala, India: Anandashram, 1990, p. 418.

9. Ibid., p. vi.

10. Krishnabai, p. 44.

11. Ramdas, Swami. *Krishna Bai*. Revised edition. Kanhangad, Kerala: Anandashram, Revised 1994, p. 74.

12. Ibid., pp. 76-77.

13. Satchidananda, p. 158.

14. Ibid., p. 158.

15. Ibid., p. 159.

16. Ibid., p. 476.

17. Ibid., p. 473.

18. Ibid., p. 275.

19. Ibid., p. 470.

20. Satchidananda, Swami. *Vishwamata Krishnabai* (Some Glimpses). Kanhangad, Kerala, India: Anandashram, 1991, pp. 57-58.

21. Ramdas, Ibid., p. 96.

CHAPTER TWELVE—THE PATH OF COMMUNITY

1. Hadewijch. *The Complete Work*. (Mother Columba Hart, translation and introduction), New York and Ramsey, New Jersey: Paulist Press, 1980; Letter 9, p. 66.

2. Woodruff, Sue. *Meditations With Mechtild of Magdeburg*. Santa Fe, New Mexico: Bear and Co, 1982, p. 82.

3. Bowie, Fiona. *Beguine Spirituality: Mystical Writings of Mechthild of Magdeburg, Beatrice of Nazareth, and Hadewijch of Brabant*. (Translated by Oliver Davies), New York: Crossroad, Spiritual Classics, 1990. p. 27.

4. Hirschfield, Jane. *Women in Praise of the Sacred*. New York: HarperCollins Publishers, 1994, pp. 111-112. Translation by Jane Hirshfield with Samuel Michael Halevi.

5. Bowie, p. 24.

6. Bowie, quoting from Porete, p. 152.

7. Dronke, Peter. *Women Writers of the Middle Ages*. New York and Cambridge: Cambridge University Press, 1984, p. 221.

8. Ibid., p. 227.

9. Woodruff, p. 129.

10. My own free rendering.

11. von Magdeburg, Mechtild. *Flowing Light of the Divinity* (translated by Christiane Mesch Galvani; edited and with introduction by Susan Clark), volume 72, Series B., Garland Library of Medieval Literature. New York and London: Garland Publishing, Inc. 1991, p. 40.

12. Ibid., p. 66.

13. Ibid., p. 162.

14. Bowie p. 89.

15. Hadewijch, Introduction by Hart, p. 5.

16. Hadewijch, Letter 29, p. 114.

17. Ibid., Poem 16, p. 356-7.

18. Dryer, Elizabeth. *Passionate Women: Two Medieval Mystics*. New York: Paulist Press, 1989, p. 51.

19. Hadewijch, Poems in stanzas, 8, 4-5, p. 148.

20. Ibid., Letter 15, p. 77.

21. Ibid., p. 79-80.

22. Hulme, Kathryn. *The Undiscovered Country: The Search for Gurdjieff*. New Edition. Lexington, KY: Natural Bridge Editions, 1997. (Original copyright by Kathryn Hulme, 1966) pp. 73-74.

23. Ibid., p. 115.

24. Lozowick, Lee. *The Alchemy of Love and Sex*. Prescott, AZ: Hohm Press, 1996, p. 176.

25. Ibid.

26. Kabir. *The Kabir Book*. Versions by Robert Bly. Boston: Beacon Press (A Seventies Press Book), 1977, p. 27.

27. Rumi. *Open Secret*. Versions by John Moyne and Coleman Barks. Putney, Vermont: Threshold Books, 1984, p. 7.

SELECT BIBLIOGRAPHY

Abhayananda, S. *Jnaneshvar: The Life and Works of the Celebrated Thirteenth Century Indian Mystic-Poet*. Olympia, Wash.: Atma Books, 1994.

Allione, Tsultrim. *Women of Wisdom*. New York: Arkana, 1986.

Anandamayi Ma. *Matri Darshan. A photo album about Shri Anandamayi Ma*. Westkappeln, Germany: Verlag S. Schang, 1988.

Anandamayi Ma. *Words of Sri Anandamayi Ma*. (Atmananda, Editor and compiler.) Fourth edition, Calcutta: Shree Shree Anandamayee Charitable Society, 1982.

Arunachalam, M. *Women Saints of Tamilnad*. Bombay: Bharatiya Vidya Bhavan, 1970.

Bakhtiar, Laleh. *Angels in the Making: Sufi Women of America*. Chicago: Institute of Traditional Psychoethics and Guidance, 1996.

Bancroft, Anne. *Weavers of Wisdom: Women Mystics of the Twentieth Century*. New York: Penguin, Arkana, 1989.

Beck, Charlotte Joko. *Everyday Zen*. San Francisco: HarperSanFrancisco, 1989.

Bhagavati, Ma Jaya Sati. *Bones and Ash*. Sebastian, Florida: Jaya Press, 1995.

Bhattacharyya, Bhaskar. *The Path of the Mystic Lover: Baul Songs of Passion and Intimacy*. Rochester, Vermont: Destiny Books, 1993.

Bielecki, Tessa. *Holy Daring*. Rockport, Mass.: Element, 1994. (*Also see*: Teresa of Ávila.)

_____. (Editor) *Teresa of Avila: Ecstasy and Common Sense*. Boston: Shambhala, 1996.

Blofeld, John. *Bodhisattva of Compassion: The Mystical Tradition of Kuan Yin*. Boulder, Colo.: Shambhala, 1978.

Boucher, Sandy. *Turning the Wheel: American Women Creating the New Buddhism*. Boston: Beacon Press, 1993.

Bowie, Fiona. *Beguine Spirituality: Mystical Writings of Mechthild of Megdeburg, Beatrice of Nazareth, and Hadewijch of Brabant*. (Translated by Oliver Davies.) New York: Crossroad, Spiritual Classics, 1990.

Brunn, Emilie Zum and Georgette Epiney-Burgard. *Women Mystics in Medieval Europe*. (Translated by Sheila Hughes.) New York: Paragon House, 1989.

Buck, William. *Ramayana*. New York: New American Library, 1978.

Conn, Joann Wolski (Editor). *Women's Spirituality: Resources for Christian Development*. Mahwah, New Jersey: Paulist Press, 1986.

Conway, Timothy. *Women of Power and Grace*. Santa Barbara, Calif.: The Wake Up Press, 1994.

Craighead, Meinrad. *The Mother's Songs: Images of God the Mother*. New York: Paulist Press, 1986.

Dhingra, Baldoon (Translator). *Songs of Meera: Lyrics in Ecstasy*. New Delhi, India: Orient Paperbacks, 1977.

de Hartmann, Thomas and Olga. *Our Life with Mr. Gurdjieff*. New York: Arkana, Penguin Books, 1992.

Doherty, Catherine de Hueck. *Soul of My Soul: Reflections from a Life of Prayer*. Notre Dame, Ind: Ave Maria Press, 1985.

_____. *Journey Inward*. New York: Alba House, 1984.

_____. *Not Without Parables*. Notre Dame, Ind.: Ave Maria Press, 1977.

_____. *My Heart and I*. Petersham, Mass.: St. Bede's Publications, 1987.

_____. *LUBOV: The Heart of the Beloved*. Locust Valley, N.Y.: Living Flame Press, 1985.

Dowman, Keith. *Sky Dancer: The Secret Life and Songs of the Lady Yeshe Tsogyal*. London: Routledge & Kegan Paul, 1984.

Dreyer, Elizabeth. *Passionate Women: Two Medieval Mystics—Hildegard of Bingen and Hadewijch of Antwerp*. Mahwah, New Jersey: Paulist Press, 1989.

Dresser, Marianne (Editor). *Buddhist Women on the Edge*. Berkeley: North Atlantic Books, 1996.

Dronke, Peter. *Women Writers of the Middle Ages: A Critical Study of Texts from Perpetua to Marguerite Porete*. New York and Cambridge: Cambridge University Press, 1984.

Duerk, Judith. *Circle of Stones: Woman's Journey To Herself*. San Diego, Calif.: LuraMedia, 1989.

Durham, Michael S. *Miracles of Mary: Apparitions, Legends, and Miraculous Works of the Blessed Virgin Mary*. San Francisco: HarperSanFrancisco, 1995.

Duquin, Lorene Hanley. *They Called Her the Baroness: The Life of Catherine de Hueck Doherty*. New York: Alba House, 1995.

Estes, Clarissa Pinkola. *Women Who Run With the Wolves*. New York: Ballantine Books, 1997.

Field, Joanna. *A Life of One's Own*. New York: G.P. Punam's Sons, 1981.

Field, Reshad. *The Last Barrier*. New York: Harper and Row, 1976.

Fox, Matthew. *Original Blessing*. Santa Fe: Bear & Company, 1983.

Furlong, Monica. *Visions & Longings: Medieval Women Mystics*. Boston: Shambhala, 1996.

_____. *Contemplating Now*. Philadelphia: The Westminster Press, 1971.

Galland, China. *Longing for Darkness: Tara and the Black Madonna, a Ten-Year Journey*. New York: Viking, 1990.

_____. *The Bond Between Women, A Journey to Fierce Compassion*. New York: Riverhead Books, 1998.

Ghanananda, Swami and Sir John Stewart-Wallace (Editors). *Women Saints, East and West*. Hollywood, Calif.: Vedanta Press, 1979.

Goetz, Joseph W. *Mirrors of God: Dorothy Day, Anne Morrow Lindbergh, Simone Weil, Dorothy L. Sayers, Evelyn Underhill, Mother Teresa*. Cincinnati, Ohio: St. Anthony Messenger Press, 1983.

Hadewijch. *Hadewijch, The Complete Work* (Mother Columba Hart, translation and introduction). New York and Ramsey, N.J.: Paulist Press, 1980.

Halifax, Joan. *The Fruitful Darkness: Reconnecting With the Body of the Earth*. San Francisco: HarperSanFrancisco, 1994.

Haskins, Susan. *Mary Magdalen: Myth and Metaphor*. New York: Harcourt Brace & Company, 1993.

Hildegard of Bingen. *Scivias* (Translated by Mother Columba Hart and Jane Bishop, with introduction by Barbara J. Newman). New York: Paulist Press, 1990.

_____. *Illuminations of Hildegard of Bingen* (With commentary by Matthew Fox). Santa Fe, N.M.: Bear & Co., 1985. (*Also see:* Lachman, Barbara.)

Hillesum, Etty. *Letters From Westerbork*. New York: Pantheon Books, 1986.

_____. *An Interrupted Life: The Diaries of Etty Hillesum 1941-43*. New York: Washington Square Press, 1985.

Hirschfield, Jane. *Women in Praise of the Sacred* (Translations by Jane Hirshfield with Samuel Michael Halevi). New York: HarperCollins Publishers. 1994.

Houston, Jean. *The Possible Human*. Los Angeles: J.P. Tarcher, Inc., 1982.

_____. *The Search for the Beloved: Journeys in Mythology and Sacred Psychology (Inner Workbook)*. Los Angeles: J.P. Tarcher, 1997.

____. *A Mythic Life: Learning to Live Our Greater Story*. San Francisco: HarperSanFrancisco, 1997.

Hulme, Kathryn. *The Undiscovered Country: The Search for Gurdjieff*. Revised edition. Lexington, Kentucky: Natural Bridge Editions, 1997. Original copyright, 1966, published by Little, Brown and Company.

Inayat, Taj. *The Crystal Chalice: Spiritual Themes for Women*. Lebanon Springs, NY: Sufi Order Publications, 1980.

Kabir. *The Kabir Book*. (Versions by Robert Bly). Boston: Beacon Press, (A Seventies Book), 1977.

King, Theresa (Editor). *The Spiral Path: Explorations in Women's Spirituality*. St. Paul, Minn.: Yes International Publishers, 1992.

Kinsley, David. *Tantric Visions of the Divine Feminine: The Ten Mahavidyas*. Berkeley and Los Angeles: University of California Press, 1997.

____. *Hindu Goddesses*. Berkeley and Los Angeles: University of California Press, 1988.

____. *The Goddesses' Mirror*. Albany, N.Y.: State University of New York Press, 1989.

Krishnabai, Mataji. *Guru's Grace*. Fourth edition. Kanhangad, Kerala, India: Anandashram, 1989.

Kübler-Ross, Elisabeth. *The Wheel of Life: A Memoir of Living and Dying*. New York: Scribner, 1997.

Lachman, Barbara. *The Journal of Hildegard of Bingen*. New York: Bell Tower, 1993.

Llewelyn, Robert. *All Shall Be Well: The Spirituality of Julian of Norwich for Today*. Mahwah, N.J.: Paulist Press, 1982.

____. *Prayer and Contemplation*. Oxford: SLG Press, 1985.

Lopez, Daniel S. Jr. and Steven C. Rockefeller (Editors). *The Christ and the Bodhisattva*. Albany, New York: SUNY Press, 1987.

Lozowick, Lee. *In The Fire*. Nevada City, Calif. and Prescott, Ariz.: IDHHB and Hohm Press, 1978.

_____. *The Alchemy of Love and Sex*. Prescott, Ariz.: Hohm Press, 1996.

McDaniel, June. *The Madness of the Saints: Ecstatic Religion in Bengal*. Chicago and London: University of Chicago Press, 1989.

Mechthild of Magdeburg. *The Revelations of Mechthild of Magdeburg (1210-1297) or The Flowing Light of the Godhead* (Translated by Lucy Menzies). New York & London: Longmans, Green and Co., 1953.

Mechtild von Magdeburg. *Flowing Light of the Divinity* (Translated by Christiane Mesch Galvani; edited and with introduction by Susan Clark). Volume 72, Series B., Garland Library of Medieval Literature. New York & London: Garland Publishing Inc., 1991.

Mirabai. *For Love of the Dark One: Songs of Mirabai* (Translations and introduction by Andrew Schelling). Revised edition. Prescott, Ariz.: Hohm Press, 1998.

Mirabai. *The Devotional Poetry of Mirabai* (Translations by A.J. Alston). Delhi: Motilal Banarsidass, 1980.

Mookerjee, Ajit. *Kali: The Feminine Force*. Rochester, Vt.: Destiny Books, 1988.

Moyne, John and Coleman Barks (Translators). *Open Secret: Versions of Rumi*. Putney, Vermont: Threshold Books, 1984.

M., *The Gospel of Sri Ramakrishna*. New York: Ramakrishna-Vivekananda Center, 1942.

Muckeridge, Malcolm. *Something Beautiful For God*. San Francisco: HarperSanFrancisco, 1986.

Needleman, Jacob, and Baker, George (Editors). *Gurdjieff: Essays and Reflections on the Man and His Teaching*. New York: Continuum, 1996.

Neumann, Erich. *The Great Mother* (Translated by Ralph Manheim). Princeton, N.J.: Princeton University Press, 1991.

Perera, Sylvia Brinton. *Descent to the Goddess: A Way of Initiation for Women*. Toronto: Inner City Books, 1989.

Porete, Marguerite. *The Mirror of Simple Souls*. (Translated and introduction by Ellen L. Labinsky.) New York: Paulist Press, 1993.

Ramdas, Swami. *Krishna Bai*. Revised edition. Kanhangad, Kerala, India: Anandashram, 1994.

_____. *Guru's Grace: Autobiography of Mother Krishnabai*. Fourth edition. Kanhangad, Kerala: Anandashram, 1989.

Ratushinskaya, Irina. *Grey Is The Color of Hope*. New York: Vintage International, 1989.

Redington, James, D. *Vallabhacarya on the Love Games of Krsna*. New Delhi: Motilal Banarsidass, 1983.

Rees, Dina. *Nimm Mein Herz: Gebete von Dina Rees* (Johannes Galli, Editor). Freiburg: Verlag Johannes Galli, 1990.

Rees, Dina. *Menschwerden: Gesprache mit Dina Rees* (Johannes Galli, Editor). Freiburg: Verlag Johannes Galli, 1990.

Roberts, Bernadette. *The Path to No-Self*. Boston: Shambhala, 1985.

Rumi. *Crazy As We Are* (Translations by Nevit O. Ergin). Prescott, Ariz.: Hohm Press, 1992.

Sarkar, R.M. *Bauls of Bengal*. New Delhi: Gian Publishing House, 1990.

Satchidananda, Swami. *Vishwamata Krishnabai* (Some Glimpses). Kanhangad, Kerala, India: Anandashram, 1991.

_____. *The Gospel of Swami Ramdas*. Second edition. Kanhangad, Kerala, India: Anandashram, 1990.

Sen, Ramprasad. *Grace and Mercy in Her Wild Hair: Selected Poems to the Mother Goddess*. (Translated by Leonard Nathan and Clinton Seely.) Boulder, Colo.: Great Eastern, 1982. (out of print) Contact: Hohm Press for new edition, 1-800-381-2700.

Shaw, Miranda. *Passionate Enlightenment: Women in Tantric Buddhism*. New Jersey: Princeton University Press, 1994.

Smith, Margaret. *Rabia the Mystic (A.D. 717-801) and Her Fellow Saints in Islam*. San Francisco: The Rainbow Bridge, 1977.

Sri Jnanadev. *Jnaneswari*, Madras: Samata Books, 1954.

Svoboda, Robert. *Aghora: At the Left Hand of God*. Albuquerque, N.M.: Brotherhood of Life, Inc., 1986.

_____. *Kundalini: Aghora II*. Albuquerque, N.M.: Brotherhood of Life, Inc., 1993.

_____. *The Law of Karma: Aghora III*. Albuquerque, N.M.: Brotherhood of Life, Inc., 1997.

Teresa of Avila. *The Collected Works of St. Teresa of Avila*. Volume One. (Rodriguez, Otilio and Kieran Kavanaugh, Translators.) Washington, D.C.: ICS Publications, 1976.

_____. *The Collected Works of St. Teresa of Avila*. Volume Two. (Rodriguez, Otilio and Kieran Kavanaugh, Translators.) Washington, D.C.: ICS Publications, 1980.

Teresa, Mother. *Total Surrender*. Revised edition. New York: Walker and Company, 1993.

Trungpa, Chögyam. *The Lion's Roar*. Boston and London: Shambhala, 1992.

_____. *Cutting Through Spiritual Materialism*. Boston and London: Shambhala, 1987.

_____. *Shambhala: The Path of the Sacred Warrior*. New York: Bantam, 1988.

463

Tulku, Chagdud. *Gates to Buddhist Practice*. Junction City: Padma Publishing, 1993.

Tulku, Tarthang. *Skillful Means*. Berkeley: Dharma Publishing, 1978.

Tweedie, Irina. *Chasm of Fire: A Woman's Experience Of Liberation Through The Teachings Of A Sufi Master*. Longmead, Shaftesbury, England: Element Books, 1979.

_____. *Daughter of Fire: A Diary of a Spiritual Training with a Sufi Master*. Nevada City, Calif.: Blue Dolphin Publishing, 1986.

Tworkov, Helen. *Zen in America*. New York: Kodansha, 1994.

Underhill, Evelyn. *Practical Mysticism*. Columbus, Ohio: Ariel Press, 1914.

Walker, Barbara G. *The Women's Encyclopedia of Myths and Secrets*. New York: Harper Collins, 1983.

Weil, Simone. *Waiting For God* (Translated by Emma Craufurd). New York: Harper Colophon Books, 1951.

_____. *The Simone Weil Reader* (George A. Panichas, Editor). New York: David McKay Co., 1977.

Willson, Martin (Translation and introduction). *In Praise of Tara: Songs to the Saviouress*. London: Wisdom Publications, 1986.

Wolkstein, Diane and Samuel Noah Kramer. *Inanna: Queen of Heaven and Earth*. New York: Harper and Row, 1983.

Woodruff, Sue. *Meditations with Mechtild of Magdeburg*. Santa Fe, N.M.: Bear and Co, 1982.

PHOTO AND IMAGE CREDITS

Cover: "Thirty-Three Little Girls Set Out to Hunt White Butterflies," 1958, Max Ernst. Private collection, courtesy Galerie Beyler, Basel, Switzerland.

p. 8   Ras Lila. Contemporary painting on fabric. Photo by Sylvan Incao, Prescott, Arizona.

p. 11   Inanna: Winged Goddess with her foot on the back of a lion, and a worshipper. Cylinder seal. Iraq, c. 2300 B.C.E. Courtesy of the Oriental Institute, University of Chicago.

p. 16   Inanna (same as above)

p. 23   Indian Painting 17th century. Punjab Hills, Basohli. Krishna Dancing with the Gopis (from a Gita Govinda [Song of the Cowherd] manuscript), c. 1680. Opaque watercolor and gold on paper, 19.8 cm. x 25.5 cm. actual. Credit: Courtesy of the Arthur M. Sackler Museum, Harvard University Art Museums. Anonymous Fund in memory of Henry Berg, Henry George Berg Bequest, Leslie Cheek, Jr., Louise Haskell Daly, Alpheus Hyatt, Richard Norton Memorial, and Eric Schroeder Funds and through the generosity of Albert H. Gordon and Emily Rauh Pulitzer.

p. 29   Catherine de Hueck Doherty – The Baroness. Madonna House Publications, Combermere, Ontario.

p. 37   Catherine de Hueck Doherty. Madonna House Publications, Combermere, Ontario.

p. 65   Irina Tweedie. © 1998 The Golden Sufi Center. For more information, please contact the Golden Sufi Center, P.O. Box 428, Inverness, CA 94937.

p. 81   The Pieta at the Kloster, Andechs, Germany.

p. 84   Our Lady of Guadalupe. Contemporary folk art. Photo by Sylvan Incao, Prescott, Arizona.

p. 99   Dina Rees and Greg Campbell. Courtesy of Greg Campbell.

p. 105 Dina Rees. Courtesy of Johannes Galli Verlag.

p. 135 "Wise Innocence." Contemporary bronze rendering of the Divine Mother by sculptor Kelsey Bogart. Photo by Sylvan Incao, Prescott, Arizona.

p. 123 Avalokitesvara, The *Bodhisattva* of Compassion. Private collection. Photo by M. Lodro, Prescott, Arizona.

p. 147 Green Tara. Image provided courtesy of Bob Jacobson.

p. 151 Kuan Yin. From Golden Gate Restaurant, Prescott, Arizona. Photo by Sylvan Incao, Prescott, Arizona.

p. 156   Tenzin Gyatso, His Holiness The Dalai Lama. Don Farber /
         Thubten Dharge Ling.
p. 174   Kali. Contemporary Lithograph. Courtesy of Dr. David
         Kinsley
p. 186   Kali. Contemporary silk-screen. Private collection of Sharon
         Vincent. Photo by Sylvan Incao, Prescott, Arizona.
p. 191   Bhadra Kali—Her Auspicious Form. Photo by Sylvan Incao,
         Prescott, Arizona.
p. 195   Ma Jaya Sati Bhagavati. Kashi Foundation, Sebastian, Florida.
p. 209   Mother Mayee of Kanyakumari. Source of original photo
         unknown. This copy is courtesy of Dr. Timothy Conway.
p. 213   Mother Mayee of Kanyakumari. Source of original photo
         unknown. This copy is courtesy of Dr. Timothy Conway.
p. 243   Joan Halifax, courtesy of Joan Halifax.
p. 267   Mother Teresa. Elizabeth Mangledorf, San Francisco, Calif.
p. 275   Etty Hillesum. Uitgeverij Balans, Amsterdam.
p. 289   Elisabeth Kubler-Ross. Ken Ross/Liaison International.
p. 299   Meinrad Craighead. Courtesy of Meinrad Craighead.
p. 304   "Crow Mother" by Meinrad Craighead. Courtesy of Meinrad
         Craighead.
p. 309   Hildegard of Bingen receiving the outpouring of the Holy
         Spirit. Reprinted with permission from: *Hildegard of Bingen's
         Book of Divine Works, with Letters and Songs*. Edited by
         Matthew Fox. Illustrations, based on the originals, by Angela
         Werneke. Sante Fe, New Mexico: Bear & Co., 1987,
         Frontspiece.
p. 312   Choirs of Angels. From the Sixth Vision of the Second Part.
         Hildegard von Bingen. Reprinted with permission from:
         Hildegard von Bingen's Mystical Visions. Illustrations, based on
         the originals, by Angela Werneke. Santa Fe, New Mexico:
         Bear & Co., 1986, p. 66.
p. 317   Sophia, Divine Wisdom. From the Fifth Vision of the Second
         Part, Hildegard von Bingen. Reprinted with permission from:
         Hildegard von Bingen's Mystical Visions. Illustrations, based on
         the originals, by Angela Werneke. Santa Fe, New Mexico:
         Bear & Co., 1986, p. 102.
p. 321   Mirabai. Illustration from the text: *Songs of Meera, Lyrics in
         Ecstasy*, by Baldoon Dhingra. New Delhi: Orient Paperbacks,
         1977, p. 35
p. 329   Mirabai. Same as above, p. 37.
p. 346   Lalitha. Photo by Ross Hillmoe, Prescott, Arizona.

p. 367   Mother Tessa Bielecki. Courtesy of Spiritual Life Institute, Crestone, Colorado.

p. 373   Yogi Ramsuratkumar and Devaki Ma. Souvenir of the Yogi Ramsuratkumar Ashram, Tiruvannamalai, India.

p. 392   Mother Krishnabai. Arnaud Desjardins, Hauteville, France.

p. 432   Katherine Hulme. Yale collection of American Literature, Beinecke Rare Book and Manuscript Library.

470

INDEX

A

abandonment by God 177
Absolute. *See* God
acceptance 125, 266; of ourselves 171
action 437; goddess of 146
Aghora II 359
agony 363
AIDS 189, 193, 196, 198, 200, 201, 270; children with 285, 288
Alchemy of Love and Sex 436
Allione, Tsultrim 333
Amitabha Buddha 141, 149
An Interrupted Life 281
Anandamayi Ma 101, 131, 173, 391
Anandashram 377, 389, 393
Ananga 5
ancestor 245
anchorite 307
Angelou, Maya 204, 205
anima mundi 123
annihilation (spiritual) 1, 22, 61, 170, 176, 358-60; definition 14; Inanna's path 11; of ego 152; of Irina Tweedie 19, 68; of Ma Jaya 198; of Rabi'a 87; through Kali 177; through motherhood 120, 134
apostles 430
arati 322
art 291, 292, 297, 330; as Divine Mother's play 293; as expression of prayer 295; freeing up voice and body 296
artist 295, 297, 313
Arunachala, Mount 372
asanas 294
asceticism 363
ashram 42, 140, 384, 401
attachment 127, 128
attention 217, 397; and prayer 223; conscious 354, 355, 356, 375,

405, 433; Devaki's to Yogi Ramsuratkumar 372, 373; from mother to child 128, 131; training of 51, 52, 347
Augustine, Saint 75
Aurobindo, Sri 343
Auschwitz 272, 274
Avalokita. *See* Avalokitesvara
Avalokitesvara 140-1, 143-4, 149, 154, 242. *See also* Bodhisattva of Compassion; (illus.) 139
avatar 15
awakening xxii, 2, 7, 22, 54, 154, 225, 434
awareness 218

B

babushki 232, 233, 234, 235, 236
Bachelard, Gaston 297
Baroness. *See* Doherty, Catherine
basic goodness 20, 168, 222, 337, 338
baulinis 347
Bauls of Bengal xvi; sadhana 342, 345, 347; tradition 144, 347, 348
Beatrice of Nazareth 420
beauty 137, 198, 206; inner 204; obsession with 203
Beelzebub's Tales To His Grandson 431
Begga, Saint 409
beggar 210
Beghards 415
Beguine(s) 406-9, 411-15, 420-21, 425, 434; decline of 414; forbidden by Church 415; future of 416; persecution of 416; roots of movement 410; writing of 417
Being 3, 59, 125, 433
Being with Dying Project 242
belonging 167

Beloved xvii, 22, 90-1, 100, 119, 328, 376, 386, 404, 422
Benedictine nun 308
benediction 185
Bergman, Ingmar 295
Bhagavata Purana xvii
Bhagavati, Ma Jaya Sati 192-94, 196, 198-99, 201; accessing Divine Mother through 197; artwork of 194; illus. 195; story of devotee dying 200; work with the dying 193
Bhai Sahib 63, 64, 66, 67, 69, 71
Bhajan, Yogi 197
bhakta xvii
bhakti xvi, 376, 385, 399, 423. *See also* devotion
Bielecki, Mother Tessa 47, 48, 76, 217, 360, 367, 369; as passionate celibate 366; illus. 367; interview with 363-66
birth 97, 190
Blessed Mother. *See also* Mary
blessing 234
blind following 374
bliss 340
Blofeld, John 137, 149, 150, 152, 153
Bodhichitta 162
Bodhisattva 141, 143-44, 153, 157, 159, 162, 164, 165, 286, 442; practices of 154, 157-58
Bodhisattva breath 165, 189
Bodhisattva of Compassion 142, 143, 152, 242. *See also* Avalokitesvara
Bodhisattva of Compassion: The Mystical Tradition 149
Bodhisattva vows 142
body 203, 331; as sacred 334, 336, 339; child's love of 335, 336; woman's shame of 333
body-hatred 203
body-negative 328; attitudes, transformation of 334; theology of the church 314
Bogart, Kelsey 134

bondedness 440, 441
bonding of women 403
Boucher, Sandy 120
Brahma 183
brahmacharya 396
breath 196, 200-2, 242. as prayer 294; *See also* Bodhisattva breath
broken-heartedness 343
Buddha Tara 144. *See also* Tara
Buddhism 217, 376; engaged 219
Buddhist Peace Fellowship 219
Buddhist practice 219
Buddhist tradition 337, 347
Buddhist-Christian dialogue 360
Budhha 217
Bush, Mirabai 219
Butler, Robert Olen 75

C

Caddy, Eileen 48
calling as "vocation" 76, 77, 268, 311
Campbell, Greg 99, 101, 140, 141
cancer 189
Canda 183
Carmelite nun 360
Carmelite priest 362
Castenada, Carlos 190, 216
Catholic 306, 415
celibacy 360, 362-66, 439
Chagdud Tulku Rinpoche 165
chakra, heart 43
charismatic leaders 374
charity: false 176. *See also* service
Charleton, Hilda 196
Chasm of Fire 18, 63
chastity 412, 413
child (ren) 125, 128, 129, 131, 164, 335, 352, 442; and death 107, 108; as path to God 97; as teacher 108; innocence of 132; love of body 335, 336; needs of 124; relationship to 359; unconditional love 132; with AIDS 198; withholding attention from 96; women without 250

childraising 122, 441, 442; as spiritual practice 120

China (Chinese) 155, 157, 161; Communists 231, 232

Chinnamasta 177

Chödrön, Pema 172

"Choirs of Angels": illus. of Hildegard of Bingen 312

Christ 231, 366, 376, 430. *See also* Jesus; babushki's relationship to 233; brides of 313; cross of 61, 270; for Hadewijch 422-24; for Mother Tessa 365, 368; for Simone Weil 226; longing for 412; union with 229; vision of 196, 200

Christianity 307, 327, 366, 376

church 262, 306

Circle of Stones: Woman's Journey To Herself 94

Cistercian 416, 420

Civil Rights movement 30

clarity 220, 282

Clement V 414

Cloister Walk 26

co-dependencies 354

commitment 361, 368

communication 253

communion 261; with children 126; with Christ 226

communion reciprocity 350, 351, 357, 358

community (communities) 33, 361-68, 401-2, 412, 425, 426, 435, 436, 440; of Beguines 408, 409; service within 427; surrounding a teacher 405

companionship 412, 426; on the Way 425

comparison with others 405

compassion 142, 166-7, 169, 292, 316, 427, 440; for self 158, 172; for the whole world 173; Idiot 164; of Etty Hillesum 274; of God 133; of Joan Halifax 242; of Kali 190; of Kübler-Ross

283; of Lalitha 343; of Ma Devaki 373; path of 137, 138; practice of 157, 158, 159, 160, 165; universal 170

competitiveness 402, 440

concentration 166

conscience 163

consciousness 52

Contemplating Now 42

contemplation 303, 408; and action 56

control 60, 69, 167; surrendering 181

convention 319

courage 173, 273, 412; of mothers 134

Craighead, Meinrad 297-306; author's first meeting with 300; her art and work 305; illus. 299

Crazy Wisdom and Divine Madness Conference 337

creating 136

creation 297, 302, 305, 313, 330

creativity 292

"Crow Mother", illus. by Meinrad Craighead 304

Cummings, E.E. 3

D

dakinis 143, 144, 342

Dalai Lama, the First 145

Dalai Lama, the Fourteenth 141, 142, 155, 157, 159, 161, 163, 164, 167; illus. 156

Dark Night of the Spirit 180

Dark One. *See* Krishna

darkness: author's descent into 175; embracing 213; path of 175

darshan 198, 377

Dattatreya 381

Daughter of Fire 18

Day, Dorothy 31

de Beauvoir, Simone 224

de Montfort, St. Louis Marie 83

De Operationae Dei 310

de Vitry, Jacques 411
death 106, 178, 180, 183, 218, 280, 297, 304; as teacher 22; Beguine writings on 419; domain of 176; fear of 202; Kali and 189, 190, 192; Kübler-Ross and 282, 283; Mirabai's defying of 318; physical 17, 107, 197, 286; transformation through 1, 14, 17, 109, 177; work of Joan Halifax 242, 244; work of Ma Jaya 199, 201
deities, women as 341
denial 222
depression 175, 177
desert 25, 26, 27
Desert Fathers 26
Desert Mothers 26
desire, to know God xviii
Desjardins, Arnaud 143, 385
despair 229
destitution 263
Devaki Ma 371-374, 377; illus. 373
devotee 385, 386, 394, 397, 399; as child to Great Mother 376
devotion xvi, 199, 322, 340, 374-6; a dangerous path 374; and blind following 374; Ma Devaki's 372; of Mirabai 320, 327; to spiritual teacher 371
Dharamsala, India 155
dharma 242, 441
dharma talk 252
Dharmacarya 241
disaster 239
discernment 297
disciple 399. See also devotee
discipline 51, 55, 167, 217, 261, 273, 313, 359
discrimination 110, 223
disease, repression of life energy 296
dismemberment 13, 176, 181
distractions 322
Divine 182, 316; existing everywhere 271; as Kali 187; longing for 26
Divine as Mother 95
Divine Essence 415
Divine Feminine 100, 301, 403, 405, 435, 442; power place of 244; resides in Woman 443; within each woman 404
Divine Love 422, 423
Divine Mother 97, 120, 125, 181, 202, 205, 210, 212, 341; as inspiration for mothering 96; her many forms xiv; Kuan Yin 152; Lalitha's union with 344; loved by 96; many forms of 2; power of xvi; for Mother Krishnabai 381; relationship to 83; represented in painting 301; through Ma Jaya Bhagavati 197; turned to 96
divine mysterium 314
"divine pride" 338, 339, 340
Divine Process 176
Dogon people 239
dogs 207, 210, 211
Doherty, Catherine de Heuck 26-47, 49, 50. See also poustinia; directness in communication 34; Friendship House 30, 32; her failings 31; illus. 29, 37; writings about prayer 45, writings about service 46, writings about silence 46
Doherty, Eddie 31
Dossey, Larry M.D, 41
doubt 273
drumming 297
Duerk, Judith 94
Dumuzi 13
Durga 183
dying 439. See also death; spiritually 358; to oneself 356

E

earth: as Great Mother 306; "greening power" of 310, 314; Hildegard's passion for 315

Eckhart, Meister 296
ecstasy 363
effort 166
ego 124, 125, 128, 152, 187, 192, 340, 425, 435; and laughter 385; surrender of in mothering 126
El Salvador 82
elder: relationship to 245
emotions 106, 354, 399
empowerment 222
emptiness 335, 340, 355
endometriosis 333
energy 280, 344; conservation of 438; laws of 347; sealed off 296; sexual and life 331
Enki 12
enlightened knowledge 292
envy 405
equality 249
equanimity 159, 160
Ereshkigal 13, 14, 176
Essence 71
ethics 166
Eucharist 313, 413
evil 231

F

failure 244, 246, 247
faith 104, 211, 233; in guru 394
fanaticism 374
fear 334; of creating 295
fearlessness 140, 216
female: essence 338; sexuality 332
Feminine 244; approach to spiritual practice 303; arising from the essential 198, underworld 292, wisdom of 341
feminine body: sacredness of 94
feminine energy 348, 437
feminine nature 251
feminine wisdom 155
femininity: and wisdom 333; as mood of Tavern of Ruin 87
feminism 402
Field, Reshad 83

fierceness 343
Findhorn 48
Five Sorrowful Mysteries 79
forgiveness 170, 171, 173, 234, 246
fortitude 313
Fox, Matthew 316
freedom 233, 318, 319
Freedom House 142
Friendship House. See Doherty, Catherine de Heuck
Furlong, Monica 42

G

Galland, China 82, 146
Galli, Johannes 97
Gandhi 235
Ganga 193
"Garden": painting of Meinrad Craighead 301
gate: of Meinrad Craighead 298, 299; symbol of 300
generativity 297
generosity 387, 390, 391, 427; of Krishnabai 393
gentleness 170
Germany 79, 98, 103, 307
Geshtinanna 13
Giridhara. See Krishna
giving 166
Glassman, Bernard 219, 241
God xviii, 233, 236, 277; and death 107; and nature 302; as feminine xiv, 93, 100; as Great Process 22; as Mother 124, 128; as voluptuous and delicious 296; at the center of "being" 181; attachment to form 10; babushki relationship to 235; being loved by 204-5; celebratory life in 362; children's relationship to 28; commitment to 236; creation 201; death and 109; desire for 72; directing one's life 114; embodied in form xvii; energy of 131; erotic relationship to 328;

God (cont.)

exisiting everywhere 294; finding in daily lives 129; finding in solitude 26; grace of 204; hunger for 26; in Meinrad Craighead's work 298, 301, 305, 306; instrument of 269, 270; is all 408; Kali 187; life devoted to 372; longing for 7; looking for 75; losing 358; love and surrender to as healing force 394; love for 298, 358; name of 383, 398; of fear and guilt 161; of mercy 161; Ramdas as for Krishnabai 380; relationship to, and children 130; service to 257; spousal love of 365; trust in 109; union with 60, 82, 119; waiting upon 35; withdrawal of grace 177; working with Hildegard of Bingen 314; worshipped as mother 93

God the Mother 298, 301, 305

goddess 94, 122, 146, 147, 184, 185, 211, 212, 403. See also Inanna, Kali, Tara, Kuan Yin; accessible through every female 212, 341; descent of 14

Goddess of Action 146

Goddess, Vulture 304

good company 426, 427

goodness 204, 216, 340, 412. See also basic goodness

gopas 4

gopis xvi, 4, 5, 6, 7, 9, 62, 322, 330, 376

Govind. See Krishna

grandmother 121, 124, 125

gratification: instant 59; self- 347, 349, 357

gratitude 197; of Mirabai 327

Great Mother 88, 148. See also Divine Mother; art in praise of 298

Great Process of Divine Evolution 285

"greening power": of earth 310, 314

Grey Is The Color of Hope 232

grief 334

group enlightenment 401, 434

Guadalupe, Lady of. See Lady of Guadalupe

Guest xviii

Gulag Archipelago, The 232

Gurdjieff, George 428-34

guru 211, 359, 376. See also spiritual teacher; as doorway to heart 66; as representative of feet of God 395; attachment to form 10; -bhakti 378; -devotee relationship 397; feet 395; female as teacher 217; feminine aspect of xvi; relationship to xvi; seeing everything as 377; surrendered to devotee 376, 399

Guru's Grace 378, 379

H

Hadewijch of Antwerp 404, 413, 417, 421, 423, 424, 425, 427

Halifax, Joan author's first meeting with 237; Being with Dying Project 242; illus. 243; interview with 245-53

Hamid, Sufi 83

Hanuman 201

hara 333

hardships: on the spiritual path 19

Hari. See Krishna

healer(s) 176, 249, 252, 343-44; women as 250

healing 104

healing arts 250

health 342

Heap, Jane 429

heart 192; and prayer 117; chakra 43; right attitude of 76

Heart Sutra 142

Heisterbach, Caesarius 412

help from others 426

helplessness 239

Herbert, George 226

heresy 421
hermit 26
Hildegard of Bingen 307-11, 313, 316; "Choir of Angels" illus. 312; illness and profound pain 308; illus. receiving the Holy Spirit 309; "Sophia" illus. 317; writing on man and woman 315; writing on the status of women 313-314
Hillesum, Etty 15, 272-4, 280-1; dialogues with God 277; her writing as service 273; illus. 275; on prayer and inner life 277, 278; on writing and life 276; witness to the terror of her times 279
Hindu 327
Hinduism 376
Hittleman, Richard 293
holiness, false 413
Holiness the Dalai Lama XIV. See Dalai Lama
Holocaust 273
Holy Daring 48
honesty 283, 297, 365; in relation-ship 349
hopelessness xviii
hospice 257
hospitality 36, 388
Hours of the Divine Office 408
Hulme, Kathryn 429, 431, 433, 434. See also Rope, The; illus. 432
humanity 316, 424
humiliation 246, 386
humility 380
humor 33, 427
hunger. See longing; yearning
husband: as teacher 112
hysterectomy 333, 334

I

Ida of Nivelles 416
illness 239
illumination(s) 316; of Hildegard of

Bingen 308
illusion 15, 185
impeccability 433
impermanence 143
In Praise of Tara 145, 153
In the Fire 107
Inanna 3, 11, 13-18, 176; (illus.) 11, 16
India 63, 129, 155, 196, 207, 211, 316, 318, 377, 382, 386; author's trip to 169, 188-9; of Mother Teresa 259-63,
initiation 12
inner life 297
innocence: of children 132; organic 117
Inquisition 424
inspiration 291
integrity 433
interdependence 161
interior landscape 305
interiority: art as 295
International Ass'n for Humanistic Psychology 236
intimacy 350, 357

J

japa 79
Japan 140
jealousy 402, 406, 440
Jesus xvii, 10, 55, 56, 80, 201, 206, 266, 271, 413. See also Christ; mother of 78; Mother Teresa service to 269; serving him in each person 265
Jnanadev, Sri 378
Jnaneswari 377, 384
John XXII 415
Johnson, Ann 85
Joplin, Janis 291, 292, 330
joy 128, 385
Judaic-Christian culture 337
judgement 20
Julian of Norwich xviii
Jutta 307

K

Kaaba 90
Kabir xviii, xxii, 1, 376, 440
kala 183
Kali 146, 177, 182, 206, 213, 293;
    174; and death 190-92, 199;
    author's dream of 178, 180;
    Bhadra 191; creation of 184; illus.
    174, 186, 191; Ma Jaya and 193;
    Mistress of the Underworld 188;
    poem, describing 175; smashan
    192; the Ugly 202; who is 183-89
Kali Yoga 197
Kali Yuga 110
Kanhangad 377
Kannon. *See* Bodhisattva of
    Compassion
Kanzeon Bosatsu 141. *See also*
    Bodhisattva of Compassion
Kasaragod 384, 386, 387
Kashi 192
Kennett, Jiyu Roshi 163
kenosis 34, 35
kesa 252
kindness 160, 162, 427
knight 368
knowing: usefulness of not knowing
    247
Krishna xvi, xvii, 3-9, 22, 62,
    326; illus. 8, 23, 330; Mirabai's
    Beloved 316, 318, 322, 323,
    324, 328, 329
Krishna-loka 10
Krishnabai, Mother 376-400; as
    devotee 399; "descent" of
    383; faith of 394, 396; fierceness
    with Ramdas 397; first meeting
    with Ramdas 384; generosity
    387, 391, 393; her life 381–
    386; her sadhana 398; hospitality
    388; illus. 392; liberation of
    387; passion 383; poem to
    400; stories of 387–99; suicide
    attempt 383
Kuan Shih Yin. *See* Kuan Yin

Kuan Yin 137-38, 141, 148-53;
    illus. with attendants 151
Kübler-Ross, Elisabeth 281-88; illus.
    287
kumbhaka 393
kundalini 292, 359
Kushi, Michio 189
Kwannon 141. *See also* Bodhisattva
    of Compassion
Kwong, Jokusho Roshi 143

L

labyrinth 299, 300
Lady of Guadalupe: illus. 84
Lakshmikumari, Dr. 211
Laksminkara 153
Lal ji. *See* Krishna
Lalitha xv, 61, 239, 341-58,
    403; healing presence of 345;
    illus. 346; interview on sexuality
    and transformation 348-58; meet-
    ing with spiritual teacher 345
Last Barrier, The 83
laughter 384, 394
Lazarus 55, 56
Le Begue, Lambert 409
Lentz, Robert 82
leprosy 270
lesbians 431
letting go 285
Liber Vitae Meritorum 310
liberation 387; through the guru
    378
life 118, 190, 218, 350; as
    celebratory 127, 362; as field for
    practice 366; Dina Rees on 106-
    109; Etty Hillesum on 276-77, 281;
    inner 20, 277-78, 297
life-negative: attitudes 334; habits
    354
life-positive spirituality 419
lila 376
listening 25, 77, 92, 278
loneliness: as prayer 45
longing 22, 73, 88, 122, 329,
    385, 441. *See also* hunger:

yearning; as love 67, 68;
for God 7, 26; for God as Mother
xv; in the Tavern of Ruin
87; Mirabai's for Krishna
318, 319, 328; of Beguines
412; of Irina Tweedie
67, 70, 71; of Rabi'a 91
*Longing for Darkness: Tara and the
Black Madonna* 146
Lord's prayer 227, 228
love 86, 111, 124, 319, 375, 376,
406; abundance of 9; and
devotion 373; and passion for
spiritual life 368; and prayer
45, 265; annihilating 325; as
God 417; as longing 67, 68; as
service 126; Beguine writing on
420; between man and woman
315; beyond reason 326; cannot
love two masters 69; commanded
by 417; daily life 120; Dina
Rees' 104, 106, 118; Divine
206, 226; essence of 442; failure
to 123; for Krishna 5, 6, 10,
322; for others 9, 108, 235,
263, 266; fufillment in 423; in
separation 7, 10, 62, 327; losing
self to 375; of Divine Mother
117, 213; of Krishnabai 391; of
Self 326; path of xvi, 192;
possibility of 126; power of 292,
420; Rabi'a 91; reliance on
425; seeing inability to as
transformational 121; self-
effacement 123; transcending
emotions 106; unconditional
170, 203, 205; wound of 419
love communion 111, 112
Love is Hell 423
love play. *See* Ras Lila
Lozowick, Lee 107, 142, 143, 207,
341, 401, 436; meeting with
Dina Rees 100; on service 256,
258
Lung Nü 150

M

Ma. *See* Divine Mother: specific
forms of
Macy, Joanna 219
Madonna, Black 82, 303
Madonna House 28, 32, 33, 38.
See also Doherty, Catherine de
Heuck
Madre de los Desaparecidos, (Mother
of the Disappeared) 82
Maezumi Roshi 142
Mahadeviyakka 334, 335
man: honoring woman 340
mantra(s) 43, 44, 146, 383; Ram
380; Tara 146
Marguerite of Porete 416, 417
Marie of Oignies 408
marriage 111, 112, 113
Martha and Mary 55, 56, 57
Martin V 416
Mary 85. *See also* Miryam of
Nazareth; as Black Madonna
82; as entryway into the Kingdom
of Heaven 79; as Mother of
Mercy 79; as path to God 83; as
Sorrowful Mother 80; waiting 83
Mary Magdalen 10
Mary of Nazareth. *See* Mary
masculine and feminine energies:
balance of 438; within each being
437
mate (partner, spouse) 350, 354,
355; possession of in relationship
349
Mateus, Don 190
matrix 347
McNamara, Fr. William 362, 363,
368
Mecca 90
mechanicality 434
Mechtild of Magdeburg 93, 407-8,
418
Medicine Wheel 251
mediocrity 19
meditation xix, 54, 171, 221,
222, 242, 354

mercy 388
Merton, Thomas 31, 35
"Milk": painting by Meinrad
    Craighead 305
mind 106, 183, 326, 354, 355; ne-
    cessity of surrendering 70; power
    of 397
Mirabai 22, 316, 318, 320-25, 330;
    illus. 321, 329; life story 320;
    poetry of 319, 323-24, 326;
    spiritual practice 326;
    unconventionalness 326
Miryam of Nazareth 379. See also
    Mary
Missionaries of Charity 270, 271
mistake(s) 130, 253
Mohammed 90
monastic life 26
monk 54, 241, 361
monks and nuns: intruction on
    celibacy 364
morphogenetic field 41
Mother 178, 183; all as form of
    396; dark 177; Kali as 187
mother 131, 133, 442. See also
    motherhood and mothering; as
    God 93; as healing force xiv; as
    inseparable from woman 122; as
    saints 133; becoming 103, 104;
    courage of 134; creating 136; es-
    sence of 125; God as 94; power
    of 94
Mother Earth 185. See also earth
Mother Mayee of Kanyakumari
    207, 210-213; illus. 209
Mother Mira 343-45, 360
Mother Teresa 2, 77, 259, 260-61,
    264, 265, 270; and Jesus 268-69;
    as physical representation of God
    263; calling of 268; illus. 267;
    impressions of 262; life consumed
    by God 271; meditation on 266
Mother's Songs, The: Images of God the
    Mother 300
motherhood 379, 441; spiritual 363
mothering 96, 121, 124, 126,

127, 129; as spiritual practice
    119, 130; responsibility of 132
mother's milk 305
Mt. Shasta Monastery 163
Munda 183
mystical blessings 365
mystical contemplation 226
mystical graces 365
mystical love 416
mystical marriage 413
mysticism 363, 423, 424

N

Nada Hermitage 369
Naropa 217
Naropa Institute 360
Neem Karoli Baba 196, 199
nervous system 359
Neumann, Erich 148
Nhat Hanh, Thich 241
Nimm Mein Herz 97
Ninshubur 12
nirguna 398
nirvikalpa samadhi 394
Nityananda, Swami 196
Nobel Peace Prize 157
Noble Truths (four) 20
non-violence 235
Norris, Kathleen 26
nothingness 303
nourishment 268
nun xvi, xix, 43, 47, 50, 160, 332,
    333 See also monk
Nun's Story, The 429
nurturers: women as 250

O

obedience 262, 394; inner 223
obliteration: of the "I" 269
Om Shri Ram Jai Ram Jai Jai Ram 380
Om Tare Tutare Ture Soha—Om 146
one-pointedness 326
open-heartedness 261
ordinariness 21
ordinary activities: sanctified 123

Osho. *See* Rajneesh
others: need for 435
ourselves: seeing others as 164
Ouspensky, Madame 59

P

pada pooja 395
pada tirtha 395
Padmasambhava, Guru 153
pain 176, 181, 182, 189, 201,
    221, 239, 441; confrontation
    with 282; embracing 176; of the
    world 279; transformed to prayer
    295. *See also* suffering
papal bull 414, 415
paramitas 166
parenting. *See* mothering
parents 164
Parliament of World Religions 193
passion 91, 295, 318, 319, 383,
    412; for life 216; for spiritual life
    368; Mirabai's 320, 327
Passionate Enlightenment 338
patience 61, 114, 115, 126, 161,
    166, 349, 427
patriarchs 415
patriarchy 185, 307, 415
peace 125, 241, 265, 333
Perrin, Father 230, 231
Picasso, Pablo 39
"Pieta": of Andechs, Germany 80;
    (illus.) 81
poetry of: Beguines 410-411, 418;
    Irina Ratushinskaya 319; Kabir
    xviii, xxii, 1; Hadewijch 423-24;
    Mirabai 319-20, 322-29;
    Mechtild of Magdeburg 93,
    407-08, 418-19; Rabi'a 87-8,
    90-2; Ramprasad Sen 177-78,
    182-83, 188; Rumi 86, 443
poor 263, 268
Pope 262
poustinia 27-28, 32, 35, 36,
    38-40, 43-44; of the heart 42
Poustinia Movement 27, 34
poustinik 26, 35, 36, 40

poverty 271, 413
power 198, 215, 216, 220, 231,
    233, 242, 245, 248, 249, 252;
    in art 293; woman of 239
power-hunger 374
power-substance: accumulating 240
Practical Mysticism 51
practice 142, 153, 166, 190, 359;
    of the Bodhisattva 158; Simone
    Weil's ability to 228
Prakriti 187
prayer xix, 25, 28, 43, 53, 54, 182,
    265, 273, 274, 330, 361, 365,
    379, 408, 418, 433; and
    attention 223; and waiting 61;
    as creation of art 295; awareness
    117; breath practice as 165;
    Catherine Doherty and poustinia
    32, 35, 36, 38, 45, 46; Dina Rees
    on 115-17; Etty Hillesum 227-8; in
    all activities 294; movement of
    the body as 294; power of xv, 41;
    Rabi'a on 92; stealing time for,
    47-50
Prayer is Good Medicine 41
Prayer of the Heart 43
"Praying with Images" retreats by
    Meinrad Craighead 306
presence 124, 239, 260; of
    Elisabeth Kübler-Ross 282
pride: *See* "divine" pride
Prieuré 428
prison: babushski in 234
Project on Contemplative Mind In
    Society 219
projection: psychological 222
psychological analysis 318
puja 49, 50
purpose 349, 351, 353

R

Rabi'a 87-92; life story 89
Radha 330
Rajneesh 405
Ram 379
Ram Dass 196

Ramakrishna, Sri 187, 193
Ramana Maharshi 372
Ramdas, Swami Papa 379, 384-86, 393-94, 399, 400; guru of Mother Krishnabai 377; surrendered to Krishnabai 376
Ramdas, Samarth 383
Ramnam 380, 398
Ramprasad Sen *See* Sen, Ramprasad
Ramsuratkumar, Sri Yogi 371, 372, 377, 378; illus. 373
Rand, Yvonne 119, 120
Rangarajan, Professor Sadhu 210, 211, 212
Rao, Dr. Rama 383, 384
Ras Lila 4, 6, 7, 9; image of 8
rasa 328, 403, 404; of Divine Feminine 405
Ratushinskaya, Irina 232, 234, 319
"Ratio Recta" 415
Ray, Reginald 337
reality 50, 51, 53, 54, 109, 204, 286, 373; barriers to 52; never shutting your eyes to 279
rebirth 13
receptivity 57, 303
reciprocity 350. *See also* communion reciprocity
reconciliation: of the masculine and feminine 250; with the masculine 252
Rees, Dina 17, 19, 100, 101, 102, 118; as Divine Mother 97-99; illus. 99, 105; on death 106-9; on feeding body and soul 113; on Lee Lozowick 111; on marriage and relationship 111-12; on prayer 115, 116, 117; on spiritual teachers 110; on surrender to God 114; on woman 115; prayer 104; on becoming mother 104
relationship 111, 351-52, 442-43; among all people 160; and sexuality 349; as a means of transformation 351; co-depen-

dent or violent 356; from the tantric perspective 348; honesty and patience in 349
remembering 369
"remembrances," of Lalitha 343
resistance: in prayer 55
responsibility: for others 281
"Responsory for a Virgin" 314
resurrection 109, 182
retreat, spiritual xix
Reuther, Rosemary Radford 306
Rhadakanta 187
Rikkarda 308
risk 247, 253, 300, 330, 358
ritual 303
Roberts, Bernadette 18, 181
"Rope, The" 428-34
rosary 79
Rudrananda 138
Rumi, Mevlana Jalaluddin 86-87, 443
rupa 338
Russia 232

S

Sabbath 48
sacrifice 123, 365, 375; as praise to God 373; for others 40; to humanity 271
Saddharma Pundarika Sutra 141
sadhana 71, 359, 398, 439; group 401
sadhu(s) 323, 388
sadness 124
Sai Baba, Sathya 97, 98
Sai Baba, Shirdi 114
saintliness 229
saints 236
samsara 154
sangha 439
sannyasin 389
Saqi 87
Sarada Devi 101
Saraha 217
Saraswati 185
Sarvodaya 219

sati 382
Schachter, Rabbi Zalman 125
Scivias (Know The Ways) 308, 310
"seeing" 51; within ourselves 220-21
self 375; as nothing 303; dissolution of separate sense of 269; love of and completeness in 326; no personal sense of 359
self-acceptance 124
self-awareness 180
self-centered 52, 162, 349
self-criticism 20
self-hatred 57, 158, 167, 168, 172, 203, 244, 339, 340, 402
self-honesty 170, 171
self-honoring 173
self-judgement 57, 246
self-observation 162, 222, 354, 436
self-obsession 402
self-referenced 122
self-respect 129, 338
selflessness 274
Sen, Ramprasad 178, 183, 188
separation 67, 71, 172, 403; from guru 386; illusion of 406, 440; loss of through surrender 379
service 57, 131, 190, 256, 257, 260, 265, 266, 271, 273, 274, 283, 287; and burnout 269; Beguines 408-409; genuine 255-56, 258; learning how 258; out of desire to know God 263; power in 264; selfless 182, 262; to Divinity 269; to others 30, 118, 142, 157, 163, 164, 281, 435; to your spiritual work 194; without acknowledgement 258, 263, 264
Seva Foundation 219
sex 331, 350. *See also:* sexuality; as a gateway to spirituality 348; as doorway to Chamber of God 331; transformational possibilites of 356, 357
sex-negative: relationship to life 332
sexual attraction: without seductiveness 361

sexual communion 350
sexual energy 358; presence of as a way of life 368; sublimation of 366
sexual life 356; in God 362
sexual passion 332
sexual practices 344
sexual radiance 361
sexual satisfaction 349
sexual tantra 331
sexuality 331, 336, 340, 347, 352, 355, 364; and relationships 353, 354; and spirituality 328, 331, 337; as a doorway to higher spiritual work 353; as a transformative mechanism 355; as way to God 347; workshop 349
Shakti 292, 393, 436, 437
shakti 334, 359
Shambhala: The Secret Path of the Warrior 220
Shan Ts'ai 150
Shaw, Miranda 338, 339, 342
Sheldrake, Rupert 41
Shiva 178, 183, 184, 187, 334, 393, 436, 437
Siddhartha the Buddha 224
silence xix, 25, 36, 38, 45, 46, 242, 265, 418
sisterhood 408
"skillful means" 164, 249
sleep 106, 127, 128
slowing down 44, 239
smashan 192, 218
solitude 25, 42, 361
Solzhenitsyn, Alexander 232
Something Beautiful for God 262
Sonoma Mountain Zen Center 143
Sophia 315; illus. of work of Hildegard of Bingen 317
sorrow 82, 122
sorrowing 87, 88
soul: building a 428
Spier, Julius 273
spiritual life 242
spiritual marriage 362

spiritual master. *See* spiritual teacher
spiritual path xvii
spiritual practice 337, 345, 366, 408, 438, 439, 443; feminine pole of 62
spiritual teacher 355; as embodiment of God xvii; as guide 54; author's first meeting with 258; author's negative experience 374; author's relationship to 244; community surrounding 405; dangers of 374; discrimination needed in choosing 357; giving up of 358; group work with 430; guidance in prayer 54; help of 300, 344, 345, 358; in tantric work 359; infatuation 64, 66; Irina Tweedie's meeting with 64; Krishnabai's first meeting with 385; lawful response to devotee's request 372; need for 53, 340, 356, 357; offering false hope 110; paradox of 194; patient attention 435; response to student 67; teaching lesson from 244; unscrupulous 18
spiritual tradition 54
spiritual work 285, 438
spiritual-sexual females 339
St. Paul 176
Stafford, William 15
Stendl-Rast, David 54, 199
stigmata 414
strength 277
Stuart, Maurine 120
study 354
suffering 62, 82, 146, 159, 176, 235, 252, 285, 296; as useful on spiritual path 245-46, 249, 327; cheerfully 386; for benefit of Being 433; of Christ 235; of life 17-19, 240, 291; of humanity 268, 376; removal of 141, 157, 166; spiritual 18; transformable into compassion 165, 286; usefulness of 240; without succumbing 272; witness to 279. *See also* pain

Sufis 86
Sufism 327
surrender 59, 60, 61, 69, 72, 73, 123, 313; and its relationship to sexuality 348; Elisabeth Kübler-Ross 283; in relationship to child 127; Krishnabai's to her guru 379; path of xvi; spiritual 18; to God 114
Svoboda, Robert 359

T

Tabrizi, Shams-i 86
tanka 143, 144
Tantra 116, 192, 329, 338, 340, 344; Shaktisangama 95
Tantric Buddhism 337, 339, 341; practice 153; tradition 217
Tantric master 345
Tantric practice 218, 342, 356, 359
tantrika(s) 212, 342
Tara 137-38, 143, 145-48, 153-54, 177-78; as Compassion of Lord Avalokita 145; as karma-devi 146; as Mother 146; as Mother of all Buddhas 145; as Savioress 145; feminine embodiment of compassion 138; Green 137-38, 149, illus. 147; twenty-one forms of 144; White 138, 148, 149
Tattva Darshana 210
Tavern of Ruin 86
teacher(s). *See* spiritual teachers
Tenzin Gyatso. *See* Dalai Lama
Teresa of Avila xx, 47, 50, 51, 216, 327, 369; interior castle 21
The Feminist Mystic 305
The Fruitful Darkness: Reconnecting with the Body 239
Theosophical Society 63
They Called Her Baroness. See also Doherty, Catherine de Heuck
thinking: uselessness of 278, 418
Tibet 155, 231
Tibetan Buddhist path 159
Tibetans 161, 232

Tiep Hien Order 241
tirtha 378, 396
Tiruvannamalai 371, 372
transformation 3, 60, 62, 205, 295, 337, 347, 358, 360; catalyst to 121; energy of 55; in nature 302; in the body 347, 352; in underworld 10; Kali's role in 184; possibilities of sex 349, 351, 356, 357; principles of 220, 353; spiritual 13, 18, 74; through relationship 351, 352; through service 258
transformed life 418
transition: of the spirit 176
Trungpa, Chögyam 220, 222, 337
trust xix; in God 30
truth 107, 129, 130, 182, 274, 360
Turning the Wheel: American Women Creating the New 120
Tweedie, Irina xx, 18, 19, 63, 66, 67, 71, 72; control of own money 69; death of teacher 71; illus. 65; longing for God 68, 73; meeting her spiritual teacher 64; one-pointed love 69; realization of non-duality 72

U

Ulanov, Belford Ann 61
unconscious, 13
Underhill, Evelyn 50, 51, 52
underworld 1, 11, 12, 176, 178, 181, 292, 383
Undiscovered Country: The Search for Gurdjieff 429
undoing 175
union 269; with creation 286; with God 269; with life around us 51
Universe: as lover, to devotee 376
unknown 356, 357, 358
Upaya: Zen center 241, 242, 245
upaya 249
upperworld 1, 14
urgency: in spiritual life 21, 22
Urodivi 40, 41

V

Vaikuntha 3
Vajrayogini 338, 339
vigilance 217
Vimalananda, Aghori 175, 359
Virgin Mary. *See* Mary
Vishnu 183
Vivekananda, Swami 93, 193
vocation 252. *See also:* calling
void 184
Volmar 308, 309
Vrindavan 4, 322
vulnerability 159, 171, 237

W

waiting 59-62, 73-74, 77, 86, 115; as spiritual work 76; as woman's way 60; for meaning 74; in relationship to spiritual teacher 67; in relationship to teacher 67; for Irina Tweedie 63; for Miryam of Nazareth 78, 85; for Rabi'a 87, 92
Waldman, Anne 292, 293, 330
warrior 215, 216, 217, 220, 222, 376
warriorship 219, 245, 248, 249
Watts, Alan 167
Weil, Simone 57, 222, 223, 227-29; relationship to church and Christ 230, 231; relationship to God 225; transcending the body 225; work among common man 224; writing of 223
Westerbork 272, 274
will 76
Willson, Martin 145, 153
winnowing 252
Winslow, Arizona 27, 28, 33
wisdom 145, 166, 181, 182, 311, 437; and woman 145; feminine 155; of the Feminine 341
"Wise Innocence" 134
wise women: interactions with 342

witnessing: to suffering 279
woman 95; *See also*: women, women's
culture; and devotion 373; and
service 264; as healer 249;
awake xxii, 241; being honored
by man 340; body 249; complete
in Self 326; connecting to her
own feminine 61-62; contemporary view of 436; creative force of
136, 301, 311; desire to serve 375;
Dina Rees on 115; essence of 435;
form of 314; in relationship to
the Divine 144; individuation of
248; non-conventional 247;
of power 215, 221; relationship
between man and 315; teaches by
who she is 239; unattractive
212; waiting 61; what is 303
womb 333; absence of 334; as a
source of power 244, 333
women. *See also*: woman, women's
culture; accessibility of great xx;
as guru 217; devoted to life 374;
enlightenment in female form
339; friendship with one another
341; gathered together 402-03,
442-43; Hildegard of Bingen
writing on 314; in love 403;
lives as spiritual practice 121;
non-conventional xxi; of power
236, 248; spiritual and physical
development of 250; without
children 250
women's culture 401-04, 425, 435,
438, 440, 441, 443
Woodman, Marion 306
work: Beguine's ability to 413
work group 429, 430
work ideas 428
work on self 273, 278, 439
world: as domain of God 223; seeking approval from 74
World as Lover, World as Self 219
worship of feminine principle 144,
182

writing: as spiritual practice 272-73;
to re-contextualize life 378

Y

yearning 91, 118, 119. *See also*
longing: hunger; transformed to
prayer 295
yoga 196
yoga of the Mother 197
Yoga: 28 Day Exercise Plan 293
Yogi Ramsuratkumar 170, 371-74,
377-8; illus. 373
yogini(s) 217, 342

Z

zazen 42
Zen: bringing to the West 163; story
34
Zen master(s) 120, 241, 244
Zen Peacemaker Order 241
Zuleikha 88, 250

ADDITIONAL TITLES FROM HOHM PRESS

UNTOUCHED
The Need for Genuine Affection in an Impersonal World
by Mariana Caplan   Foreword by Ashley Montagu

The vastly impersonal nature of contemporary culture, supported by massive child abuse and neglect, and reinforced by growing techno-fascination are robbing us of our humanity. The author takes issue with the trends of the day that are mostly overlooked as being "progressive" or harmless, showing how these trends are actually undermining genuine affection and love. This uncompromising and inspiring work offers positive solutions for countering the effects of the growing depersonalization of our times.

"To all of us with bodies, in an increasingly disembodied world, this book comes as a passionate reminder that: Touch is essential to health and happiness."—Joanne Macy, author of *World as Lover, World as Self*

"Mariana discusses virtually every significant human need and behavior in a language that abjures all technical terms, and speaks plainly and simply, both to the heart and the mind's consent. This is a considerable achievement." —Ashley Montagu, author of *Touching, The Human Significance of the Skin*

Paper, 384 pages, $19.95   ISBN: 0-934252-80-7

• • •

WHEN SONS AND DAUGHTERS CHOOSE ALTERNATIVE LIFESTYLES
by Mariana Caplan, M.A.

A guidebook for families in building workable relationships based on trust and mutual respect, despite the fears and concerns brought on by differences in lifestyle. Practical advice on what to do when sons and daughters (brothers, sisters, grandchildren...) join communes, go to gurus, follow rock bands around the country, marry outside their race or within their own gender, or embrace a religious belief that is alien to yours.

"Recommended for all public libraries."—*Library Journal.*

"Entering an arena too often marked by bitter and wounding conflict between worried parents and their adult children who are living in non-traditional communities or relationships, Mariana Caplan has produced a wise and thoughtful guide to possible reconciliation and healing...An excellent book."
—Alan F. Leveton, M.D.; Association of Family Therapists, past president

Paper, 264 pages, $14.95   ISBN: 0-934252-69-6

TO ORDER PLEASE SEE ACCOMPANYING ORDER FORM
OR CALL 1-800-381-2700 TO PLACE YOUR ORDER NOW.

ADDITIONAL TITLES FROM HOHM PRESS

THE ALCHEMY OF LOVE AND SEX
by Lee Lozowick
Foreword by Georg Feuerstein, Ph.D., author of *Sacred Sexuality*

Discover 70 "secrets" about love, sex and relationships. Lozowick recognizes the immense conflict and confusion surrounding love and sex, and tantric spiritual practice. Preaching neither asceticism nor hedonism, he presents a middle path— one grounded in the appreciation of simple human relatedness. Topics include: • what men want from women in sex, and what women want from men • the development of a passionate love affair with life • how to balance the essential masculine and essential feminine • the dangers and possibilities of sexual Tantra • the reality of a genuine, sacred marriage. . .and much more. The author is an American "Crazy Wisdom teacher" in the tradition of those whose enigmatic life and madcap teaching styles have affronted the polite society of their day. Lozowick is the author of 14 books in English and several in French and German translations only.
" ... attacks Western sexuality with a vengeance." —*Library Journal.*

Paper, 312 pages, $16.95   ISBN: 0-934252-58-0

• • •

THE ALCHEMY OF TRANSFORMATION
by Lee Lozowick
Foreword by Claudio Naranjo, M.D.

"I really appreciate Lee's message. The world needs to hear his God-talk. It's insightful and healing."—John White, author, and editor, *What is Enlightenment?: Exploring the Goal of the Spiritual Path.*

A concise and straightforward overview of the principles of spiritual life as developed and taught by Lee Lozowick for the past twenty years in the West. Subjects of use to seekers and serious students of any spiritual tradition include: • From self-centeredness to God-centeredness • The role of a Teacher and a practice in spiritual life • The job of the community in "self"-liberation • Longing and devotion. Lee Lozowick's spiritual tradition is that of the western Baul, related in teaching and spirit to the Bauls of Bengal, India. *The Alchemy of Transformation* presents his radical, elegant and irreverent approach to human alchemical transformation.

Paper, 192 pages, $14.95   ISBN: 0-934252-62-9

TO ORDER PLEASE SEE ACCOMPANYING ORDER FORM OR CALL 1-800-381-2700 TO PLACE YOUR ORDER NOW.

ADDITIONAL TITLES FROM HOHM PRESS

CONSCIOUS PARENTING
by Lee Lozowick

Any individual who cares for children needs to attend to the essential message of this book: that the first two years are the most crucial time in a child's education and development, and that children learn to be healthy and "whole" by living with healthy, whole adults. Offers practical guidance and help for anyone who wishes to bring greater consciousness to every aspect of childraising, including: • conception, pregnancy and birth • emotional development • language usage • role modeling: the mother's role, the father's role • the exposure to various influences • establishing workable boundaries • the choices we make on behalf of our children's education ... and much more.

Paper, 384 pages, $17.95   ISBN: 0-934252-67-X

• • •

EVERYWOMAN'S BOOK OF COMMON WISDOM
by Erica Jen, Lalitha Thomas and Regina Sara Ryan

"Forget about being self-conscious. The truth is, nobody really cares. *They* are too busy being self-conscious." So advises this postcard-sized book of bright and profound sayings for women (and their curious male friends and spouses). These sometimes provocative, often inspiring "secrets" for success in business, sex, and family life are ideal reminders—great for posting on a refrigerator door, or sending in a letter to a friend. With over 100 years of combined wisdom, poet Erica Jen of San Francisco, and Arizona authors Regina Sara Ryan (*The Wellness Workbook,* Ten Speed Press; *The Woman Awake*, Hohm Press) and Lalitha Thomas (*10 Essential Herbs,* Hohm Press) offer their unique and sometimes quirky views of life in this collection of short aphorisms about how to be happy, how to keep your man, and how to live sanely in a world gone mad.

Paper, 134 pages, $6.95   ISBN: 0-934252-52-1

TO ORDER PLEASE SEE ACCOMPANYING ORDER FORM OR CALL 1-800-381-2700 TO PLACE YOUR ORDER NOW.

ADDITIONAL TITLES FROM HOHM PRESS

FOR LOVE OF THE DARK ONE: Songs of Mirabai
Translations by Andrew Schelling

Mirabai is probably the best known poet in India today, even though she lived
400 years ago (1498-1593). Her poems of ecstatic praise to Krishna, whom she
lovingly calls "The Dark One," are set to music and sung by school children, and
frequently occur as background tracks in contemporary films.

Mira's poetry is as alive today as if was in the sixteenth century—a poetry of
freedom, of breaking with traditional stereotypes, of trusting completely in the
benediction of God. It is also some of the most exalted mystical poetry in all of
world literature, expressing her complete surrender to the Divine, her longing,
and her madness in love.

This revised edition contains the original 80 poems, a completely revised
Introduction, updated glossary, bibliography and discography, and additional
Sanskrit notations.

Paper, 128 pages, $12.00   ISBN: 0-934252-84-X

• • •

NO CHILD IN MY LIFE
by Regina Sara Ryan

"This book makes it okay to cry, and promises that by going through the fire of
loss, we will emerge more whole than before" —Peggy O'Mara, editor and
publisher, *Mothering Magazine.*

A practical resource for men or women grieving over the loss of a relationship with a child. The author recognizes that grief can be equally painful for
people who have lost children in custody settlements, or through illness or
accident, or given children for adoption, or never had a child due to infertility,
miscarriage, abortion, or for other reasons of chance or choice. In our secular era
it is sometimes difficult to remember that, in times of tragedy, the most important
issues will always be spiritual in nature—not simply medical or psychological.
This book makes that vital connection and offers step-by-step guidance through
the stories of those who have used their pain to grow into a deeper connection to
truth, life or God.

Paper, 256 pages, $12.95   ISBN: 0-913299-93-6

**TO ORDER PLEASE SEE ACCOMPANYING ORDER FORM
OR CALL 1-800-381-2700 TO PLACE YOUR ORDER NOW.**

ADDITIONAL TITLES FROM HOHM PRESS

TEN ESSENTIAL FOODS
by Lalitha Thomas

Lalitha has done for food what she did with such wit and wisdom for herbs in her best-selling *10 Essential Herbs*. This new book presents 10 ordinary, but *essential* and great-tasting foods that can: • Strengthen a weakened immune system • Rebalance brain chemistry • Fight cancer and other degenerative diseases • Help you lose weight, simply and naturally.

Carrots, broccoli, almonds, grapefruit and six other miracle foods will enhance your health when used regularly and wisely. Lalitha gives in-depth nutritional information plus flamboyant and good-humored stories about these foods, based on her years of health and nutrition counseling. Each chapter contains easy and delicious recipes, tips for feeding kids and helpful hints for managing your food dollar. A bonus section supports the use of 10 Essential Snacks.

"This book's focus is squarely on target: fruits, vegetables and whole grains—everything comes in the right natural proportions."—Charles Attwood, M.D., F.A.A.P.; author, *Dr. Attwood's Low-Fat Prescription for Kids* (Viking).

Paper, 324 pages, $16.95   ISBN: 0-934252-74-2

• • •

10 ESSENTIAL HERBS, REVISED EDITION
by Lalitha Thomas

Peppermint. . .Garlic. . .Ginger. . .Cayenne. . .Clove. . . and 5 other everyday herbs win the author's vote as the "Top 10" most versatile and effective herbal applications for hundreds of health and beauty needs. *Ten Essential Herbs* offers fascinating stories and easy, step-by-step direction for both beginners and seasoned herbalists. Learn how to use cayenne for headaches, how to make a facial scrub with ginger, how to calm motion sickness and other stomach distress with peppermint, how to make slippery-elm cough drops for sore-throat relief. Special sections in each chapter explain the application of these herbs with children and pets too. **Over 25,000 copies in print.**

Paper, 396 pages, $16.95   ISBN: 0-934252-48-3

TO ORDER PLEASE SEE ACCOMPANYING ORDER FORM OR CALL 1-800-381-2700 TO PLACE YOUR ORDER NOW.

RETAIL ORDER FORM FOR HOHM PRESS BOOKS

Name_____ Phone (_____) _____

Street Address or P.O. Box _____

City _____State _____ Zip Code _____

	QTY	TITLE	ITEM PRICE	TOTAL PRICE	
1		**THE ALCHEMY OF LOVE AND SEX**	$16.95		
2		**THE ALCHEMY OF TRANSFORMATION**	$14.95		
3		**CONSCIOUS PARENTING**	$17.95		
4		**EVERY WOMAN'S BOOK OF ...**	$6.95		
5		**FOR LOVE OF THE DARK ONE**	$12.00		
6		**NO CHILD IN MY LIFE**	$12.95		
7		**10 ESSENTIAL FOODS**	$16.95		
8		**10 ESSENTIAL HERBS**	$16.95		
9		**UNTOUCHED**	$19.95		
10		**WHEN SONS & DAUGHTERS...**	$14.95		
11		THE WOMAN AWAKE	$19.95		
		SUBTOTAL:			
		SHIPPING: (see below)			
		TOTAL:			

SURFACE SHIPPING CHARGES
1st book $4.00
Each additional item $1.00

SHIP MY ORDER

☐ Surface U.S. Mail—Priority   ☐ 2nd-Day Air (Mail + $5.00)

☐ UPS (Mail + $2.00)   ☐ Next-Day Air (Mail + $15.00)

METHOD OF PAYMENT:

☐ Check or M.O.   Payable to Hohm Press, P.O. Box 2501, Prescott, AZ 86302

☐ Call 1-800-381-2700 to place your credit card order

☐ Or call 1-520-717-1779 to fax your credit card order

☐ Information for Visa/MasterCard order only:

Card #_____ – _____ – _____ – _____ Expiration Date_____ _____

ORDER NOW!
Call 1-800-381-2700 or fax your order to 1-520-717-1779.
(Remember to include your credit card information.)

RETAIL ORDER FORM FOR HOHM PRESS BOOKS

Name_____ Phone (_____) _____

Street Address or P.O. Box _____

City _____ State _____ Zip Code _____

	QTY	TITLE	ITEM PRICE	TOTAL PRICE	
1		THE ALCHEMY OF LOVE AND SEX	$16.95		
2		THE ALCHEMY OF TRANSFORMATION	$14.95		
3		CONSCIOUS PARENTING	$17.95		
4		EVERY WOMAN'S BOOK OF ...	$6.95		
5		FOR LOVE OF THE DARK ONE	$12.00		
6		NO CHILD IN MY LIFE	$12.95		
7		10 ESSENTIAL FOODS	$16.95		
8		10 ESSENTIAL HERBS	$16.95		
9		UNTOUCHED	$19.95		
10		WHEN SONS & DAUGHTERS...	$14.95		
11		THE WOMAN AWAKE	$19.95		
			SUBTOTAL:		
			SHIPPING: (see below)		
			TOTAL:		

SURFACE SHIPPING CHARGES
1st book $4.00
Each additional item $1.00

SHIP MY ORDER

☐ Surface U.S. Mail—Priority   ☐ 2nd-Day Air (Mail + $5.00)

☐ UPS (Mail + $2.00)   ☐ Next-Day Air (Mail + $15.00)

METHOD OF PAYMENT:

☐ Check or M.O.   Payable to Hohm Press, P.O. Box 2501, Prescott, AZ 86302

☐ Call 1-800-381-2700 to place your credit card order

☐ Or call 1-520-717-1779 to fax your credit card order

☐ Information for Visa/MasterCard order only:

Card #_____ – _____ – _____ – _____ Expiration Date_____ _____

ORDER NOW!
Call 1-800-381-2700 or fax your order to 1-520-717-1779.
(Remember to include your credit card information.)

CONTACT INFORMATION

By request, Regina Sara Ryan leads several popular seminars for women, both in the U.S. and Europe. Her current offerings include: "Meetings with Remarkable Women"; "Writing Your Way Home"; and "Embracing the Dark—Kali Energy in Life and Spiritual Practice." For more information, write to her c/o: Hohm Press, P.O. Box 2501, Prescott, AZ, 86302.